Emotion In Organizations

Emotion In Organizations
second edition

edited by

Stephen Fineman

SAGE Publications
London • Thousand Oaks • New Delhi

© Stephen Fineman

First published 2000

Apart from any fair dealing for the purposes of research or
private study, or criticism or review, as permitted under the
Copyright, Designs and Patents Act, 1988, this publication
may be reproduced, stored or transmitted in any form, or by
any means, only with the prior permission in writing of the
publishers, or in the case of reprographic reproduction, in
accordance with the terms of licences issued by the
Copyright Licensing Agency. Inquiries concerning
reproduction outside those terms should be sent to the
publishers.

SAGE Publications Ltd
6 Bonhill Street
London EC2A 4PU

SAGE Publications Inc
2455 Teller Road
Thousand Oaks, California 91320

SAGE Publications India Pvt Ltd
32, M-Block Market
Greater Kailash – I
New Delhi 110 048

British Library Cataloguing in Publication data

A catalogue record for this book is
available from the British Library

ISBN 0 7619 6624 2
ISBN 0 7619 6625 0 (pbk)

Library of Congress catalog card number 00–132715

Typeset by Keystroke, Jacaranda Lodge, Wolverhampton.
Printed in Great Britain by Redwood Books, Trowbridge, Wiltshire

CONTENTS

CONTRIBUTORS

Stephen Fineman, School of Management, University of Bath, UK

Blake E. Ashforth, Department of Management, College of Business, Arizona State University

Christine Beckman, Graduate School of Management, University of California, Irvine

Gillian Bendelow, Department of Sociology, University of Warwick

Connie J. Boudens, Department of Psychology, University of Michigan

Lorna Doucet, Department of Business Administration, University of Illinois

Jane E. Dutton, School of Business Administration, University of Michigan

Peter J. Frost, Faculty of Commerce and Business Administration, University of British Columbia

Karen P. Harlos, Department of Management, University of Otago

Robert Jackall, Department of Anthropology and Sociology, Williams College

Avraham N. Kluger, School of Business Administration, Hebrew University of Jerusalem

Kathy Knopoff, Director, Pacific Consulting Group

Kathleen J. Krone, Department of Communication Studies, University of Nebraska-Lincoln

Joanne Martin, Graduate School of Business, Stanford University

Berry Mayall, Social Science Research Unit, Institute of Education, University of London

Debra E. Meyerson, Center for Work, Technology, and Organization, Stanford University

Jayne M. Morgan, Department of Communication, University of Northern Iowa

Craig C. Pinder, Faculty of Business, University of Victoria

Michael G. Pratt, Department of Business Administration, University of Illinois

Anat Rafaeli, Faculty of Industrial Engineering and Management, Technion Institute of Technology, Haifa

Lloyd E. Sandelands, Department of Psychology, University of Michigan

Marc A. Tomiuk, Department of Marketing, École des HEC, Montreal

Vincent R. Waldron, Department of Communication Studies, Arizona State University West

Varda Wasserman, School of Business Administration, The Hebrew University of Jerusalem

Annette Wilson, College of Architecture and Urban Planning, University of Michigan

Monica C. Worline, Department of Organizational Psychology, University of Michigan

ACKNOWLEDGEMENTS

Rosemary Nixon at Sage provided vital support and encouragement to make this book possible. My particular thanks to her, and also to my colleagues at Bath who have kept 'emotion' alive.

1 EMOTIONAL ARENAS REVISITED

STEPHEN FINEMAN

In the first edition of *Emotion in Organization* (1993) I characterized organizations as *emotional arenas* to capture the intense activity of lived emotion in organizational life. As emotional arenas, organizations bond and divide their members. Workaday frustrations and passions – boredom, envy, fear, love, anger, guilt, infatuation, embarrassment, nostalgia, anxiety – are deeply woven into the way roles are enacted and learned, power is exercised, trust is held, commitment formed and decisions made. Emotions are not simply excisable from these, and many other, organizational processes; they both characterize and inform them.

This, in effect, was the key message in the first edition, a theme that, at the time, was relatively muted in the study of organizations. The book developed the point in a number of different directions – emotionalizing the way meanings and order are created in organizations, the production and politics of social differences (gender, sexuality), the substance of organizational culture and change, and examining facets of emotional labour.

In looking once more into the emotional arena, what do we see? How have things developed in the intervening seven years? What might we applaud and what might we be more circumspect about? In considering these questions I do not propose a complete review of the diverse literatures on emotion and organizations – interested readers may like to refer to recent overviews in Fineman (1999), Pinder (1998) and Ashkenasy et al. (2000). In this chapter I will be partial and selective; I will also preview the chapters to come.

The expanding arena

Emotions have developed into something of a sub-discipline in the study of work and organizations. There are now emotion papers and symposia presented at major organizational and management conferences, as well as specialist web-based discussion groups. Professional associations of sociologists, both sides of the Atlantic, run forums dedicated to the study of emotions, reflecting a move towards a 'passionate sociology' (Game and Metcalf, 1996). Applied psychologists have explored the connection between emotion and motivation (George and Brief, 1996; Pinder, 1998), the consequences of affect and mood at work (Estrada et al., 1997; Weiss and Cropanzano, 1996) and emotional contagion, the 'catching' and passing-on of emotion (Doherty, 1998; Verbeke, 1997). Some aspects of this research have reached the popular management and psychological literature as *emotionalized* issues such as workplace envy, intimacy, harassment and stress. Emotional intelligence, in particular, has received considerable attention from organizational consultants and psychologists (such as Goleman, 1996; Abraham, 1999), a phenomenon I reflect upon in Chapter 6.

Aesthetics and emotion has been another area of concern. Our work lives are mediated and shaped by material objects – machines, technologies, rooms, books, walls, windows, cups, coffee machines. Indeed, some social theorists regard material objects as 'actors' in their own right in organizational relations (for example Callon, 1987; Latour, 1991). We often invest such objects or spaces with emotional qualities, reflecting our own identities and moods – 'my miserable computer', 'my happy chair', 'that cosy room', 'this depressing building', 'that wretched fax machine', 'this beautiful book', 'that ugly corridor'. Such emotional/aesthetic experiences have been examined (for example by Gagliardi, 1999; Strati, 1999), where the aesthetic captures feelings of form or flow that are experienced from the places and objects where people work. The machines, office layout, colours, geographical setting, noise, music, task activities, food are objects of sound, sight, touch or smell that trigger feelings of 'rightness', discord, warmth, harshness or alienation (see Chapter 8).

Traditional psychoanalytical perspectives on workplace emotion have been relatively eclipsed by the growth of social constructionist approaches. Organizational psychoanalysts regard the organization as a cauldron of repressed thoughts, fantasies and desires (see for example Jacques, 1995; Amado, 1995; Gabriel, 1999). Unconscious defences about anxiety, fear, envy and hate are expressed as dysfunctional organizational agendas or practices, requiring the consultant's 'treatment' – to expunge the 'demon of irrationality' (Gay, 1998: xviii). The social constructionist's line is very different. At its extreme it refutes the idea that emotions are 'in' people, ready to be studied. What matters is how our sensations, thoughts and feelings are labelled and displayed, and that has everything to do with the social and cultural contexts that provide the rules and vocabularies of emotion. Emotions, therefore, are intersubjective, a product of the way systems of meaning are created and negotiated between people (Parrott and Harré, 1996; Griffiths, 1995).

Some social constructionists focus on how social norms and 'feeling rules' shape work behaviour (Scheff, 1990; Hochschild, 1983). In this view, different work organizations will inherit the wider emotion rules of the society of which they are a part (for example on shamefulness, embarrassment, pity, kindness), but they also adapt them to create their own codes of emotion propriety – such as what is 'right' for the medical doctor, the social worker, the hamburger salesperson, accountant or police officer. Sometimes the two different sources can be in tension – what the company or profession requires of the worker is very different from customary, societal, forms of emotional behaviour. Distress at work has to be disguised, attraction suppressed, annoyance left unspoken. Conflicts are especially revealed in situations where corporate emotional indoctrination is pervasive and transnational – such as McDonald's insistence that staff in its Moscow branch should serve Big Macs with a smile, despite the wider cultural predilection to greet customers with a grimace. Or the 'smiling training' for Inuit employees of the Greenlandic Co-operative supermarket chain. The Inuit have no tradition of smiling or greeting others with a 'hi' or 'hello' (Jones, 1999).

There are social constructionists who prefer to look to the broader interrelationships between social groups (classes, occupations, elites), 'structures' which explain emotion-clusters and their effects. Shifts in the balance of power or status between interdependent social groups can generate fear or anxiety in one or more of the groups, emotions that signal that their vested interests are being threatened in some way (see Barbalet, 1995; Kemper, 1991). Resistance, rebellion and subjugation such as in worker lockouts, strikes and repressive controls can, in these terms, be traced to emotions – especially fear – arising from a loss or gain of power or control. We may view 'smile strikes' accordingly. A newspaper story tells of a Californian supermarket where unionized, female, shopworkers actively resisted being forced, under surveillance, to eye-contact customers and smile at them. They claimed it increased their exposure to sexual harassment from customers (Zeidler, 1998).

Reconciling perspectives?

Historically, emotion research has been imbued with biological and psychological determinism. It is important that organizational researchers should now give more attention to the social and relational context of emotion, and this book represents a shift in this direction. But we have moved a long way from unconscious forces at work and the organizational psychoanalyst's couch. Arguably, a full exploration of emotion in organizations that fails to take into account individuals' biographies and unconscious processes is as untenable as an account that ignores social structures and wider cultural/economic processes.

Researchers of emotion can (and do) duck these issues by claiming disciplinary allegiance (for example to psychotherapy, psychology, sociology or anthropology), or pointing to their preferred level of analysis – societal, group or individual. This, of course, is an old chestnut in social science, which is rarely dinted by exhortations to be interdisciplinary. Indeed, a recent special issue of the journal *Human Relations* attempted just such an emotion project. A call for papers which integrated psychodynamic (including psychoanalytic) theory with organization theory attracted relatively few submissions, of which even fewer were judged worthy of publication (Neumann and Hirschhorn, 1999).

One difficulty is that the psychoanalytic branch of psychodynamic theory has a language and metaphorical structure that is self-enclosed, hard to challenge or refute. There is also a clinical preoccupation with a limited range of emotions, mostly anxiety-associated. But integrating the psychological and the organizational/societal should be beyond bolting together different, staunchly defended, theoretical perspectives, a process that can often generate more epistemological heat than light. Ideally, we require theory that collapses the individual/organizational/social distinctions from the outset, and builds explanations interrelationally. To an extent the works of Giddens (1984, 1991) and Foucault (1970, 1979) do this, although they have yet to be widely exploited for emotionality. This does not preclude attempts at disciplinary eclecticism – or conversations across disciplines. For example, Gabriel (1998), a strong advocate of a psychoanalytic perspective on organizational emotions, offers a helpful critique of how Freudian frameworks need to incorporate social constructionist insights. More specifically, Long (1999) uses the psychoanalytic notion of social-defences against anxiety to explore consumerism as a societal discourse and practice. Conversely, we find some social constructionists able to engage with Freudian theory and essentialist notions of emotions – emotions we purportedly all share (Craib, 1995, 1998). There are also 'mid range' sociological theorists of emotion, such as Gibson (1997). Gibson takes it as axiomatic that the rational/hierarchical nature of organizational structures will produce certain emotions amongst its members, such as anger and fear; but, more locally, emotional meanings will be negotiated interpersonally through 'conversational' rituals, loyalties and power. Finally, John Elster's writings on emotion are worthy of mention – a grand multidisciplinary journey through social psychology, history, neuroscience, fiction and the philosophy of science (Elster, 1999).

Labouring with emotional labour

Arlie Hochschild's seminal work on emotional labour (Hochschild, 1979, 1983, 1993) rightly deserves a central place in organizational emotion theory. It has captured the attention of management and organizational scholars (see for example Morris and Feldman, 1996), and is addressed in two chapters in this book. Hochschild has shown that much work, especially face-to-face service (such as flight attendants, debt collectors, waitresses, secretaries, fast food operators) involves having to present the 'right' (that is, managerially prescribed) emotional appearance to the customer or client, and that involves real labour on the employee's part. Sometimes the employee contract includes having to 'feel good' about the customer too. Organizations can ensure that employees more or less comply by refining their personnel selection methods, inculcating required scripts and regularly monitoring performance.

For frontline workers, the 'emotional proletariat' (Macdonald and Sirianni, 1996), smiling, being 'nice', 'pleasant', 'happy', 'in control', requires acting – either 'surface' or 'deep', according to Hochschild. The emotional labour required to achieve the prescribed ends involves, at best, feigning a convincing act that can be dropped during work breaks and at the end of the day. At worst it is stressful and identity confusing: 'Who am I really?'; the disjuncture between displayed emotion and private feeling is severe. Hochschild has emphasized the psychological damage that this can cause, but other writers have been more circumspect. If we look across the studies of emotional labourers there is much to suggest that workers will often find ways of insulating themselves from the corporate scripts (see for example Wharton, 1999). Indeed, some are more than content to 'fake in good faith' in the service drama (Adelman, 1995).

Emotional labour and managing emotions are not restricted to low-skill service work. They can be found in the face-to-face work of doctors, psychiatrists, managers, teachers, nurses, police officers, professional carers, academic professors and paralegals (see for example Pierce, 1999; Brown, 1997; Leidner, 1999; Ashforth and Humphrey, 1995). Professional and organizational norms underpin what people in such roles should and should not display or feel. These are processes that define and reinforce deference patterns, worker hierarchies and power relations. Emotion work helps keep the organization organized; when emotion management fails, so can the organization. Copp (1998), for instance, shows how instructors in a sheltered workshop were expected to infuse clients with positive feelings and commitment about work, but found it impossible because of the boring, poorly paid assembly-line work offered to clients. The instructors struggled for organizational meaning and control and some experienced burnout.

Emotion work is a crucial to social regulation and, as such, it should not be left unquestioned. What degree of emotion engineering can we tolerate, even enjoy, and why? When is it a comforting part of social transactions and everyday rituals and when is it oppressive labour? Such questions will implicate structural and ideological factors. Gender expectations about workers, and the emotion traps that they can create, illustrate the point. For example, Martin describes the situation of the US policewoman:

> On the street, they must not be too emotional in responding to volatile situations; yet the woman who conforms to the emotional display rules of policing (that is, is inexpressive) is regarded [by male officers] as unfeminine. (Martin, 1999: 124)

Similar tensions could be expected in other occupational settings where someone of the 'wrong' sex occupies the job: the male nurse, male midwife, male secretary, female engineer, female firefighter, or female building construction worker. Such people are having to work with (or against) gender emotion-stereotypes in meeting the expectations of their peers, superiors and subordinates, as well as of their 'customers'. If we are concerned to democratize the workplace, how might we more effectively separate gender from 'the job'? And if emotional labour is a key, but hidden, feature, should it not be acknowledged and financially remunerated like other aspects of employee labour? (see O'Brien, 1994; Steinberg, 1999).

In search of authenticity

What happens to the true self under regimes of emotion management? The 'problem of authenticity' is a recurring theme in the writings on emotional labour, a common premise being that the true, essential, self is compromised or consumed under certain emotion-management work regimes. A typically suggested remedy is to redesign the job in ways to permit more authentic expression. For some writers authenticity is a phenomenological matter – what we happen to feel to be authentic or inauthentic in our selves in a particular setting (see Chapter 10). For others, the issue is more a positivistic one – there is a core self 'in there' which represents the authentic person, yet camouflaged by the trappings of social convention.

But there are scholars who diverge from these interpretations, suggesting that the very conception of a true self and authenticity is misconceived (see for example Fairclough, 1992; Harré and Gillett, 1994; Eriksen, 1997). We are all defined ephemerally, and illusorily, through a complex of temporally bound social discourses. The distinction between the authentic and inauthentic self is not a matter of true versus contrived, although we may experience it in this manner in our desire for ontological security, psychic roots. Both are equally real social products drawn from a cultural bundle of discourses – language, labels, ways of communication – that privilege particular meanings of self or feeling at particular points in time. Stearns (1995), for example, shows how grief in Anglo-American societies has undergone a number of discourse reformulations. Its expression was minimized before the nineteenth century, was obsessively ritualized in the Victorian era, but was regarded as distinctly vulgar and morbid in the early twentieth century.

Our emotional identities and subjectivities are constructed through exposure to discourses such as these, discourses to be found in various social practices such as jobs, professions, education, family, economic systems, literature, television, film, newspapers and advertisements. Our sense of self, in this view, is malleable and multifaceted, rather than arranged in different, hierarchical, layers of authenticity. What we think is really 'me' is always borrowed from elsewhere, even our precious utterances, such as of love:

> it is not the case that every woman and man in love magically find themselves uttering, creating and discovering afresh, for the first time, these words as the mirror or reflection of their experience, although they may well feel they are doing just that. The words instead are second-hand, already in circulation, already in there, waiting for the moment of appropriation. (Wetherall, 1996:134)

Over recent decades we have seen a growth in particular social discourses on 'authenticity', 'being real', available for popular appropriation. In Western Europe and the USA especially, 'knowing' and 'working on' one's self and feelings has permeated popular self-help rhetorics. These may be seen in books, magazine articles, videos and television programmes on 'how to': repair relationships, love, relax, lose weight, become assertive, find one's sexuality, realize one's potential, find the 'inner you', manage stress. Psychotherapeutic and counselling services have both mirrored and contributed to this ethos, supporting a popular belief that the true self is something worth striving for (Newton et al., 1995; Smith,1995; Schwalbe, 1996). One corollary of this is to make normal and acceptable emotion work and emotion management; they are necessary features of self-discovery. Consequently, some argue, the sting has been taken out of the stiffer emotional demands of the workplace; we are becoming better at managing them (see Eriksen, 1997; Wharton, 1999).

With some justification, the discourse-perspective de-romanticizes our uniqueness. But in doing so it downplays human agency. We may well appropriate ready made discourses on our emotional experiences and identities, but we also interpret and improvise. We draw upon *other* possible discourses and *negotiate* meanings, such as when we are 'lost for words'. We may probe with our loved one whether 'this is really love', 'what it means', why it is/is not requited, how it can be made to last, and so forth. Labels and discourses to express feelings will change over time because change is generated by human actors who experiment with discourses. Such change will eventually diffuse into social institutions and structures that shape and reinforce those new meanings and discourses. 'Real feelings' may not 'really' be all our own, but we are complicit in developing the illusion. We help create and reproduce the discourses of self and feeling that we then take as real.

The emotions of control

The considerable focus on the managerial control of others' emotions has obscured the flip side of the issue – *the emotions of control*.

Control is rooted in many of the formal and informal relationships within organizations – boss/subordinate, skilled-worker/unskilled-worker, old-hand/novice, male/female, inspector/inspected. It can be seen in the various ways that different people, regardless of position, try to influence each other to achieve their political ends. But as control-attempts move between actors, so will feelings and emotions – be they of anger, sympathy, confusion, irritation, warmth or admiration. These will shape, sometimes unconsciously, sometimes through performed emotions, the course and outcome of events. Emotions will *constitute*, as well as be outcomes of, the encounter. Psycho-analytic theorists have addressed some of these circumstances, such when a leader's fear of losing control can thrust him/her to the centre of the organizational stage, to be held there by followers' needs and anxieties. This is the emotional basis of charismatic leadership and its reciprocal dependencies (Kets de Vries, 1990; Bryman, 1992).

Fusing emotion with control reflects a mutuality of the rational and the emotional (see below, and Greenspan, 1997; Ashforth and Humphrey, 1995). The formal (and informal) techniques of control – such as appraisal pro-cedures, surveillance methods, performance assessments, rules of negotiation

– are organizational phenomena that are lived through feelings of being controlled or controlling others. Some of these sentiments will be historically rooted – what happened before in similar circumstances, such as concerns about trust or competence. Controller and controlled are also postured via emotion scripts, the expressive rules of the game for 'boss', 'subordinate', 'woman', 'professional', or 'specialist'. Indeed, their place in the economic/ power order will predefine how emotions such as fear, anxiety or disdain can be exploited (see Carr, 1988; Gabriel, 1998). Randall Collins's observation on implicit negotiations at work captures the point:

> I propose the mechanism is *emotional* rather than cognitive. Individuals monitor others' attitudes towards social coalitions, and hence toward the degree of support for routines, by feeling the amount of confidence and enthusiasm there is toward certain leaders and activities, or the amount of fear of being attacked by a strong coalition, or the amount of contempt for a weak one. (Collins, 1981: 994, original emphasis)

An elaboration of the emotional processes of control is offered by Fineman and Sturdy (1999), illustrated through an ethnographic exploration of specific control encounters. They used fine-grained observations of environmental inspectors (the notional controllers) enforcing environmental controls on industrial managers in face-to-face settings. The subtlety and dynamic nature of control is revealed as status and professional competence are defined and challenged between the parties. The malleability of power is noteworthy, inextricably linked to feelings of fear, humiliation, pride and achievement. What is clear from this study is how controlling is emotionally negotiated and shaped, even in situations which are not obviously 'hot' or contentious.

The emotional body

A very angry exchange with a colleague can be felt *in* and *of* the body – a tightening of the chest, dryness in the mouth, tension in the neck. Getting a much-desired promotion gives a surge of elation, which is felt as light-headedness, bouncing along, relaxation and warmth. Tedious, monotonous work is experienced as a physical sluggishness, an inability to concentrate, yawning. The fear of losing one's job is felt in the gut as a tightness or pain. Being depressed gives people a sense of dragging their bodies along, while fury can be just the opposite – an urge to hit out to relieve intense pressure. All these are important features of the phenomenology of emotion at work, reminding us that it is our corporeal being that is 'working' and 'producing' during activities we describe as emotional.

The embodiment of emotion is familiar ground for reductionist researchers who have sought to distinguish emotions in terms of the body's biochemical processes, neural pathways, postures and facial display. But they have, as yet, produced few clear-cut answers:

In sum, it appears that there is little evidence of physiological patterns which *reliably* differentiate emotions. This is particularly the case for autonomic patterns . . . There also is a serious question about the existence of 'basic' emotions. . . There is, however, strong evidence for a high degree of recognizability of a simple set of facial displays, although methodological questions have been raised regarding the assessment of agreement. (Ginsburg and Harrington, 1996: 245–6, original emphasis)

The social constructionist seeks somewhat different explanations of the body (see for example Lupton, 1998; Grosz, 1994). The important question is how people come to know and interpret their physicality and body perturbations in a particular 'emotional' way, and how they attribute emotional meanings to others' body postures and appearances. These are essentially social-cultural questions. In other words, a physical sensation, such as a churning stomach, is undoubtedly a real feeling, but it is only 'revulsion' when labelled and/or performed in a manner consistent with repulsive circumstances and behaviour. Compare, for instance, the different physical and emotional responses of a Western and an Arab diner when presented with a meal of sheep's eyes; or the reactions of a novice physician compared to a seasoned surgeon in dissecting a human cadaver. In these circumstances sight, smell and touch will produce bodily changes and neural-chemical excitations, some of which are 'known' to the actor. But they become felt emotions of disgust, pleasure, excitement or apprehension according to (a) prior learning about the type sensation as being disgusting, pleasurable and so forth, and (b) the social/cultural protocols of what emotional body-display is appropriate (such as professional, non-insulting, face-saving) in the particular circumstances. In this manner embodiment, emotion and socio-cultural processes intertwine.

To what extent do organizations interfere with and/or shape the body–emotion connection? Organizations have long attempted to control the employee's body through technology, tools and the socially engineered arrangements of work. Workstations, personal computers, production lines, types of office space, permitted work breaks, all determine what the body can do, where it can do it and for how long, These can produce certain emotional states, some anticipated, such as comfort, compliance, attentiveness; others unintended, such as job dissatisfaction, boredom, stress, anger – 'aberrations' that have long been of interest to industrial psychologists and ergonomists. Indeed, and ironically, attempts to control the body for rational, productive, ends, often give rise to further controls to offset the emotional 'dysfunctions'.

Dressing and adorning the body have also long been of interest to organizations. Uniforms and accessories (tools of the trade, badges, insignia) are required of police officers, school children, nurses, doctors, airline pilots, soldiers and executives. Rules of dress for office workers are common, such as 'Monday-to-Thursday dark suits, Friday casual'. Instructing 'the body' to smile, to be pleasant, has been vigorously pursued in 'strong culture' companies concerned with customer service (Macdonald and Sirianni, 1996).

It is often explicit, sometimes implicit, that these devices will create feelings, or an emotional aura, amongst those with whom the worker interacts – such as of fun, seriousness, coolness, warmth, caring, submissiveness, aggression or composure. The reciprocal relationship between emotion and the socialized body also means that the very donning of a prescribed uniform and its accoutrements can make one 'feel' different – partly because others treat you *as if* the expected emotional role is what you 'really are'.

A uniform can also feel 'wrong', uncomfortable, to the wearer (by touch or sight), out of tune with one's usually constructed body image. This may lead to resentful conformity or to resistance – such as 'illegally' personalizing the body by substitution or deliberate misuse (not wearing a regulation shirt, wearing a hat at the wrong angle, skewing a necktie). Realizing this, some organizations (such as traditional schools in the UK, the military) have instituted stiffer controls, while others (such as in customer services) have offered 'empowered' choices to their employees, permitting a modest deviation of dress. But for many workers, flexibility in body-presentation can conflict with the organization's compulsion for a trademarked, standardized, image, where the stereotyped frontline employee is inseparable from the product brand.

Rationality and feeling in organizations

Organizations are often presented as rational enterprises. Because human beings are able to think and act rationally to maximize their gains, organizations can capitalize on this capacity to efficiently and economically produce their goods and services:

> Successful management . . . involves the clarification of objectives, the specification of problems, and the search for and implementation of solutions. (Mullins, 1996: 57)

This is a comforting picture of the controlling, thinking, manager – able, dispassionately, to sort and prioritize information to the best of ends. The voluminous literature on cognition in organizations offers numerous thinking devices, or images, to help us understand and improve such processes – such as 'templates', 'cognitive maps', 'frames of reference', 'managerial lenses' and 'schemas'.

If we cast rationality into the emotional arena, what is revealed? Sorting priorities and making sense of events are often fraught with anxieties, self-doubt and emotional preferences; our understandings are often (always?) emotionalized. We have 'gut feelings' – what *feels* intuitively right, good, uncomfortable or uneasy. Our calculative decisions are sometimes at odds with our own, and others', intuitions. We can be emotionally swayed in our choices because of moral pressure – such as the outrage or hurt of others, or fear of reprisal. The means, ends and choices for making decisions are not always obvious – so we create them through emotionalized social processes and discourses. Cognitive theorists have generally resisted engaging with such observations – until recently. A major review of the managerial and organization cognition literatures reaches the following, cautious, conclusion:

> we have been held captive by the computer metaphor for information processing. If our research is to have strong external validity, we must consider the emotional basis of work and its relationship to the cognitive questions we have been asking. (Walsh, 1995: 307)

This is a welcome thawing of the extreme cognitivist position.

Elsewhere, I have characterized the quarrels over rationality and emotion as spilt three ways: emotions *interfere* with rationality; emotions *serve* rationality; emotions and rationality *entwine* (see Fineman, 1999). The first approach is deeply embedded in Western philosophical thought, which privileges rationality and reason. These are the highest-order mental processes, extolled by Aristotle. Emotions are an interference, 'sand in the machinery of action' (Elster, 1999: 284). Applied psychological studies indicate how the sand can damage the decision-making machine. For example, there are times when obstinate, passionate, commitment to a particular course of action becomes a fixation, regardless of the consequences (Staw and Ross, 1989; Brody and Lowe, 1995). Psychoanalytic theory is particular about the manner in which organizational members can act irrationally because of conscious and unconscious fears, anxieties, shame and guilt. These emotions can leak into organizational relationships and structures to screen the actor from an accurate reading of the situation. The removal, or better management, of these emotions, goes the argument, is the first step towards achieving (or restoring) rationality.

As servants of rationality, emotions are less problematic. The view here (see for example Mumby and Putnam; 1992; Damasio, 1994, 2000; de Sousa, 1987) is that feelings and emotions lubricate, rather than impair, rationality. They make impossible decisions possible; they help 'do' the prioritizing, resolve tie breaks, ease the dilemmas. What is important, worth thinking about, is cued by feelings – including those of the 'gut'. So let hunches, excitement, fear, unease, or comfort, be your guide.

Finally we may collapse the rational/emotional distinction. Rationality is no longer the 'master' process; nor is emotion. They both interpenetrate; they flow together in the same mould. From this perspective there is no such thing as a pure cognition; thinking and deciding is always brushed with emotion, however slight. This may be at the level of mood (gloom, excitement, tedium, anxiety) as we consider what to do, or what next. It can also be in terms of a myriad micro, thinking/feeling, adjustments as we scan alternatives, con-template possible outcomes, review interpretations, get stuck, get distracted. We may be dimly aware of these processes, or they may be unconscious. Moreover, we have different layers of thought and feeling, meta (or meta meta) processes where we contemplate, even interrogate, our (and others') feelings; have feelings about our feelings as well as feelings about our thoughts and ideas.

The blurring of rationality and emotion persuasively challenges the much canvassed cognitive appraisal school of emotion – that we firstly have a belief about something or someone ('it's dangerous', 'she likes me', 'he wants my job'), and that belief then triggers a particular emotion – fear, excitement, anger (for example, Lazarus, 1991). If beliefs and feelings are mutually constitutive, a 'pure', emotionally neutral, cognition cannot exist. Indeed, some emotional reactions, such as the joy of being deeply 'into' a task, and the pleasure/pain feelings that can attend aesthetic creation or art appreciation, defy a simple cognitive-appraisal analysis (see Elster, 1999; Vetlesen, 1994). Furthermore, cognitive appraisals in work organizations are invariably socio-emotionally contextualized. They occur in settings of hierarchical control, gender and ethnic tension, power contests, competition for scarce resources, resistance to authority, overwork, underwork, job insecurity, delayering and downsizing. Organizational cognitions are emotionally laden because they are inextricably tied to politicized organizational discourses where they take place.

The three theoretical positions suggest different ways of construing and/or unmasking rationality in organizations. Many cognitive researchers and management theorists still insist that rationality is the supreme human accomplishment, a feat achieved by 'taming' emotion (see Cacioppo and Gardner, 1999), but there is a more plausible position. What we term rationality in organizations is a remarkable facility to present – to ourselves and to others – emotionalized processes in forms that meet 'acceptable', 'rational' images of objectives and purpose. We want to believe, and we want others to believe, that we think and act rationally, so we construe the intentions and consequences of our actions as rational. We do this in social contexts that limit and shape our endeavours, and through social discourses that define norms of feeling and emotional display. For most of us, this is good enough. The public smile, the pretence of concern and the 'professional' demeanour, lubricate and reinforce social relationships. Emotional hypocrisy helps to fix a social order as well as to strain it; this is the heart of emotion work. We also accept that the expression of certain emotions is reserved for certain places: football stadiums, theatres, funerals, churches, theme parks, conferences, committee rooms, works canteens, pubs. Yet, importantly, we need to ask what *emotionally* sustains the personal and social fragmentation of emotions in these ways, and why such splits are necessary to support a much reproduced myth – which can sometimes border on tyranny – that of our powers of rationality and self-control. We also need to reflect on the occasions when our two emotion 'faces', the private and the public, are not at ease with one another; when they generate the cynicism, loss, pain, detachment, suspicion or fear that we would prefer to be without.

Phenomenal emotion – and beyond

For the student of emotion in organizations the question of how, empirically, to study emotional processes can be problematic. Should we apply traditional, quantitative research methods, or adopt qualitative techniques? Do methodology textbooks, with their language of objectivity, detachment and control, do justice to requirements of emotion research, or do we need to invent new languages and new techniques? If people find it difficult to articulate their feelings, what indirect methods are possible? How can we do justice to the often expressive richness of emotion life? Or to the fact that many people are unable to articulate what the *feeling* experiences of work are like? And what are the professional risks of 'doing it differently'?

It is not uncommon for researchers of emotion in organizations to be guided towards methods that are already familiar and accepted within their academic discipline. Thus the method and its convenience (such as questionnaire, experiment, psychological test, interview) can determine the shape of the subject, rather than the subject generating the method. Inevitably, how we study something determines the form of that 'thing', so feelings and emotions 'captured' in interviews will be texturally different from those inferred from structured questionnaires, written stories, personal diaries, observations of body movements, facial expressions or measures of adrenaline secretion. It is important, however, to have some conceptual clarity, or epistemological framing, on the nature of the organizational emotional-arena before deciding upon a form of inquiry. I have some preferences in this respect:

- Expressed emotions and private feelings do not necessarily correlate, nor are they always known to the individual.
- Emotion and feeling are often negotiative and changing, subject to interpersonal, group and political influence.
- History matters – individuals, groups and organizations have 'memories', emotional backcloths which shape the 'what' and 'how' of present feeling and emotional expression.
- Many emotional experiences will be fleeting, inchoate, even confused. We cannot always identify discrete emotions and attach them to specific objects or circumstances.
- Emotional worlds often blur the distinction between the 'public' and the 'private', 'work' and 'home'; the domains can interact.
- Situations matter – different social/organizational contexts encode different rules of feeling and emotion display.
- Wider social structures (economic, market, material) frame our emotional experiences, favouring the production and reproduction of certain feelings and emotions.

The above suggests methods that: engage with feeling and emotion in ways traditionally proscribed by codes of 'objective' social science; do so qualitatively, in a de-atomized manner; and place emotion in its wider structural and cultural contexts. Such approaches address the mobility and dynamism of the subject matter, where the researcher's emotions cannot be simply factored out. This is a tall order (see Fineman, 1993, Chapter 10; Ashkenasy et al., 2000). But there are some ways forward.

The organizational researcher as observer, interviewer, confidant or participant has, in different ways, access to how actors express and represent their feelings. A phenomenology of emotion in organizations will portray lived experiences, honouring actors' perceptions, justifications and accounts, bearing in mind that the investigator is now part of the interpretive setting. Indeed, *accounting* for what is felt by self or others is a feature of everyday discourse on emotion, a process that shapes iterative cycles of thoughts and feelings. Such situated discourses can be regarded as pivotal to 'being' and 'acting' emotionally, so are key data for the inquirer. Fine-grained accounts can track the shift and flow of emotions over a series of events or a work cycle. On some occasions emotional intensity in organizations may peak or flood, such as fear during layoffs, anxiety during mergers, or ebullience during a period of organizational success.

The socially interrelated nature of feelings and emotions means that they are exchanged amongst colleagues, clients or superiors. If people work in teams or groups these units may be taken as *affective sets* for analysis. Furthermore, the emotional arena is neither politically nor culturally neutral. Who controls the emotion scripts, feeling rules and body images? How are they resisted or negotiated? What are the gender expectations? How do economic pressures impinge on emotional outcomes? All such questions are germane to an 'engaged', critical, style of ethnographic organizational research.

Contextually rich, 'real time' emotion studies of organizational life are still relatively rare, but there are encouraging exceptions. Some are reported in this book (see also Martin et al., 1998; Tracy and Tracy, 1998). The ethnographic form has the distinct advantage of encouraging what Lofland (1976) has termed 'intimate familiarity' by the researcher – looking *onto* organizational life while being *into* or *part* of it. In emotion terms, this provides a fortuitous blend of distance and reflexive closeness. Emotion ethnographies can track events-in-context as reported by key actors. Direct, emotionalized accounts (stories, confessions, explanations, gossip) can be gathered as decisions, issues or crises unfold, and enfold different organizational members – including the ethnographer. Observations of displayed emotion at formal and informal meetings offer insights into the strategic use of emotion, gender/power scripts, varieties of emotion work and emotional labour, as well as inferences on private feelings. Material symbols of organization (office spaces, styles of written reports, notices, modes of dress) indicate, indirectly, something of the norms of emotional control, distance and status.

Studying emotion in this manner requires an agile, sensitive, researcher. It also requires the capacity to report (usually in words) imaginatively, illuminating and conceptually developing our understanding of the emotional texture of organizations. Here, perhaps, we have something to learn from the poet, novelist and dramatist who have long explored emotions 'in the round'. A social science of emotions is rendered no less systematic or rigorous by finding different voices, or expressive forms, to convey crucial experiences and meanings.

The chapters to come

This chapters in this book highlight emotions in organizations as social embedded phenomena. Understanding the experience and contexts of emotion – mainly qualitatively – is key to all chapters, and a number of the issues that I have emphasized above are addressed. Some authors focus humanistically on the detail of small, but highly significant, emotional episodes in organizations. Others take a broader, more critical, look at the organizational cultural and structural parameters of emotional forms and repertoires. In various ways, the collection gives clear voice to actors-in-context – often including the author – conceptually developing micro and meso perspectives on organizational emotion.

The book is arranged in three parts: *Emotional Textures, Appropriating and Organizing Emotion* and *Working with Emotion*. These parts are necessarily approximate as some chapters have overlapping themes.

Part I: Emotional Textures

In this first part of the book, four chapters take us into the emotional texture of organizations. In 'Narratives of Compassion in Organizations' (Chapter 2), Frost, Dutton, Worline and Wilson draw a graphic picture of the 'emotional ecology' of organizations, which facilitates or inhibits acts of compassion. Compassion is revealed as a complexly nuanced response to extreme emotional circumstances and pain in others. It is a feeling-led reaction, often spontaneous, which sits ambiguously amongst the conventional norms of emotional display within work organizations, as does the expression of personal loss and pain. If I fail in a promotion bid, or I am dealing with a death in my family, feeling very ill, dealing with a relationship break-up, feel burned out . . . what can I say at work? With whom can I share my distress and hurt? Reversing the coin, how do I know how much another person wants a compassionate response from me? Am I 'interfering'? What should I say or do? The authors of this chapter explore such issues through organizational stories and narratives at the poignant interface of the 'private' and 'public'.

In 'Feeling at Work', Sandelands and Boudens (Chapter 3) are also concerned with emotion stories, but they approach them in a more polemic manner. They argue forcefully against the traditional psychological perspective that locates feeling exclusively within the individual, a product of a moment's cognitive appraisal. This, they suggest, eviscerates feeling and also misrepresents how feeling is felt. Feeling shapes experiences and rational thought, rather than the other way round; feeling is 'how social life appears in consciousness'. They indict job satisfaction research for reducing work feeling to what it is not – a stable evaluation of an outer object on discrete scale or questionnaire items. These authors find a more convincing portrayal of work feelings in how people construct stories about their work experiences, stories that reveal not static statements of 'satisfaction' or named feelings, but where the individual's experiences of work merge with those of other people in a highly contextualized, relational, narrative. They sample a rich seam of stories of work-life documented by writers such as Terkel, Garston and Hamper.

Waldron's chapter, 'Relational Experiences and Emotion at Work' (Chapter 4), develops the relational, socially embedded, nature of work feeling and emotion – as a 'collaborative social performance'. For Waldron (like Sandelands and Boudens) it is essential to move beyond the single, individual, actor to appreciate how emotion defines the nature and experiences of work. He conceptualizes work as *constituting* emotion as well as being a distinct arena for the experience of emotion. Emotion can be regarded as a resource through which organizational relationships are shaped, as well as something shaped through interpersonal relationships. This loop of mutual influence can be seen in the way power is traded between people in performance rituals, how moral obligations are formed, and the way loyalties are fused and breached. Waldron illustrates his ideas with accounts from studies of workers in a variety of public and private organizations.

It is easy to fall into the trap of monoculturalism when theorizing on and about feeling and emotion. This is especially apparent in the case of the split between emotion and reason – which is essentially a Western construction (see Chapter 1). In Chapter 5, 'Emotion Metaphors in Management: The Chinese Experience', Krone and Morgan examine the Chinese depiction of emotion and reason as a continuous, rather than bifurcated, process; a view consistent with entwinement of thought and feeling. The authenticity of feelings, which has so exercised writers on emotional labour, is less of an issue in Chinese culture, where displaying sensitivity and responsiveness to others is regarded as a necessary part of spiritual development. Krone and Morgan add empirical flesh to their theoretical skeleton by surveying Chinese managers on the nature of pleasant or unpleasant emotional events at work, and how they have handled their feelings. The managers reveal the importance of 'restoring inner balance' and learning from emotional experiences ('use a heart to change a heart'). The authors employ 'metaphor' as a unit of analysis, scrutinizing the metaphoric language of the respondents. The typical Western view of emotions as volatile, interfering, fluids in a 'container' contrasts with the Chinese image of emotion. Emotion is neither temporary nor abnormal, but an intrinsic part of the experience of doing business. Emotion is part of a 'homeostatic' process and 'lesson', where the mind, body and emotions work together in a mutually regulatory fashion.

Part II: Appropriating and Organizing Emotion

Emotion can be organizationally appropriated by management to create an organizational ethos which, supposedly, contributes to the productive ends of the organization. Sometimes this happens by direct manipulation – such as training for emotional competence or inculcating a particular organizational culture. Other times less obviously, such as through power relationships in an organization, or the way the physical spaces in organizations (such as offices, public rooms, furniture, colour schemes) are arranged and embellished. This part of the book enters this territory.

In 'Commodifying the Emotionally Intelligent' (Chapter 6) I take a sideways look at the recent, considerable, attention to emotional intelligence. While the idea of emotional intelligence has some allure, it has now become a victim of a commodification process where it is trapped in its own rhetoric – that of a marketable package. This chapter explores the contextual, political and rhetorical reasons behind the social construction of emotional intelligence as a product – something to sell as a managerial fix, a producer of 'stars'. Emotion itself is open to politically motivated social constructions and 'emotion management' consultants are prime movers in this respect. Maybe the popularization of emotional intelligence gives us cause to celebrate – it brings emotion out of the organizational closet. But it also crudely captures and simplifies emotion. In particular: it determines a moral order of emotions where 'highly' emotionally intelligent individuals are judged as more organizationally worthy on the consultant's/psychologist's criteria than those of 'low' emotional intelligence (echoing debates on the tyranny of IQ); it creates a dependence on the emotion consultant and his/her values, questionnaires and training courses; and it misleadingly assumes that we can readily identify, sift and select 'appropriate' emotions.

What if a profit-driven organization deliberately fostered emotionality as a way of doing business? A place where organizational relationships were determined more by their expressive frankness than by the 'iron cage' of bureaucratic constraint? In 'Bounded Emotionality at the Body Shop' (Chapter 7), Martin, Knopoff and Beckman critically examine this proposition through the lens of 'bounded emotionality'. Feminist-inspired bounded emotionality suggests, amongst other things, that work-related emotions should not 'all hang out', but be expressed with sensitivity to, and recognition of, others' subjectivities. It should permit spontaneous, 'authentic', emotional behaviour, aimed at fostering a sense of community at work. The authors use a detailed, qualitative, investigation of the Body Shop to explore the extent to which the Body Shop epitomizes the ideal of bounded emotionality, and whether there is a dark side to bounded emotionality – as a covert form of control. The Body Shop is revealed to be an emotionally engineered company, regarded by its employees as liberating and communitarian. But it falls short of the ideals of bounded emotionality because of: the stresses it places on some employees; the manner in which it handles those who are uneasy about emotional intimacy; the generation of a degree of resistance and cynicism to being emotionally expressive; and the coarse manner in which it screens prospective employees.

Wasserman, Rafaeli and Kluger, in 'Aesthetic Symbols as Emotional Cues' (Chapter 8), discuss a rather different form of organizing emotion. Their interest lies in the way physical spaces are arranged or designed and how these evoke particular emotional responses from those who enter – or consider entering – them. They draw upon recent theorizing on organizational aesthetics and environmental symbols to propose that some physical designs are easily identified and labelled ('monomorphic') while others are more ambiguous ('eclectic'). These designs, in different ways, are likely to evoke emotional responses in the forms of pleasantness, arousal and power. Importantly, the manipulation of such responses through design politicizes aesthetics, a source of 'power over and control over both participants' (clients' and employees') emotions'. The authors focus their study on perceptions of different designs of restaurants, using photographs of a number of prototypical forms. Through a projective/fantasy approach, 200 people wrote stories about the restaurants, which were analysed for emotion themes – such as extreme experiences, cool emotions and sensuality. The authors reflect on the way power is suggested in the various designs and offer contrasting paradigmatic interpretations of their emotional significance.

Part III: Working with Emotion

In this part of the book contributors, with different conceptual foci, cast a critical eye over emotion and its manifestations within the structure of work relationships. There are accounts of burnout, emotional labour, emotion work, authenticity, ambivalence, morality and injustice. Various occupational groups are explored, such as nurses, doctors, service workers, police, school children and industrial managers.

In 'If Emotions Were Honoured: A Cultural Analysis' (Chapter 9), Meyerson speculates on what social science and professional practice would look like if they recognized, expressed and honoured feelings. She builds her argument from both personal experience (told in story form) and an empirical, comparative, study of burnout amongst hospital social workers. The latter describes a 'medicalized' department of social workers that sustained a 'sick', view of the burned-out social worker. He or she was someone who had lost emotional control, was professionally inadequate, a suitable case for treatment. However, a similar group of social workers in a second hospital, but part of a department concerned with rehabilitation, accepted burnout as 'OK' – normal and endemic to the occupation. It was a place where people talked openly about their feelings of being depleted, and collectively developed ways to care for one another. Burnout was not avoided, but in 'honouring' each other's feelings a cultural platform was created to move through the distress. Is there a message here for other institutions? Meyerson thinks there is. Compassion and caregiving should not be just the province of certain 'carers' but part of many different social processes and work structures. This requires a significant frame shift where expressing feelings is as valid as concealing them, where social science treats emotions as a legitimate realm of experience, where the ethic of control and emotional detachment is challenged, and where stereotypical gender attributions on emotionality are eroded. Meyerson touches on some of the barriers to such transformative aspirations.

Ashforth and Tomiuk, in 'Emotional Labour and Authenticity: Views from Service Agents' (Chapter 10), examine the finer detail of 'authenticity'. They explore the extent to which service workers – such as chefs, lawyers, librarians, social workers, funeral directors and club bouncers – construct their own authenticity in jobs that require manufactured, or role-prescribed, emotional demeanours. How do acting and authenticity interact? Can one be inauthentic in one's work role and still feel authentic to oneself? Do the display rules of a work role create conflicting senses of identity or complementary ones? What are the effects of 'emotional dissonance'? From interview data, the authors suggest two levels of authenticity – surface and deep. The former represents an alignment of private feeling and emotional display – you act as you genuinely feel. The latter is a closer coupling of one's self-identity with the expected display rules of the job, *regardless* of private feeling. This is another sort of genuineness, where being true to the role is being true to oneself – such as smiling even when you are not feeling happy. Ashforth and Tomiuk link these notions to emotional labour. They argue that surface authenticity is associated with Hochschild's 'deep acting', and surface inauthenticity with 'surface acting'.

Emotion in organizations is often spoken of, and studied, in terms of positive or negative feelings – happy or sad, excited or bored, anxious or relaxed. Pratt and Doucet, in 'Ambivalent Feelings in Organizational Relationships' (Chapter 11), suggest that such extreme states overpolarize emotional experience. Work life is more likely to be emotionally ambivalent, with mixed feelings and no clear emotional resolution. Ambivalence means that we can simultaneously hold positive and negative feelings about something or someone; be both attracted and repelled. Pratt and Doucet illustrate this by studying the experience and meanings of work amongst bank call-centre operators and doctors in a rural clinic. As these workers tell of their anxieties, fears, frustrations and aspirations, they reveal ambivalence – to their organization and/or to their colleagues, customers or supervisors. The ambivalence is sometimes targeted on the purpose or value of their work (such as having to treat patients not only as human beings but as economic units too), and sometimes on their encounters with those they serve (such as enjoying helping customers but hating their abuse). Ambivalence extends to mixed feelings about how to express emotions, such as wanting to say what you feel to a customer or co-worker but fearing the consequences of doing so. Different individual and organizational sources of ambivalence are charted, as well as different responses – such as commitment, humour, vacillation, avoidance and paralysis.

Jackall's account (Chapter 12) of the work of New York police detectives is unusual. In 'A Detective's Lot: Contours of Morality and Emotion in Police Work', we have a remarkably candid picture of police work. It shows, through a fine-tuned ethnographic eye, a melange of bureaucracy, rationality, irrationality and moral ambiguity. Rather than take emotions as a priori categories, the account permits us, as readers, to appreciate emotionalities 'where they belong', embedded in socially situated discourse. Jackall's report, therefore, can be read as a text for interpretation and inference on the emotionalities of social order. What can we see? We see the excitement, even exhilaration, of a job that involves encounters with violence, lust and aggression, but where emotional labour and emotion work are essential, and often onerous, in honing the appearance of rugged emotional distance. Mortal combat is part of the 'heart-pumping' excitement of the job, but with emotional costs that have to be kept secret. The terror and numbing effects of horrifically violent acts close avenues for intimacy and trust with friends and loved ones. We see resentments towards those 'in power' who fail to appreciate the detective's work, along with a general feeling of suspiciousness and cynicism about others' motives. Informal emotion rules shape the meaning, and moral significance, of 'criminal' events and their consequences: scorn for suicides and resentment at having to inform the next of kin; 'grim satisfaction', even mirth, at the homicide of a known robber; wrath at the shooting of an innocent victim; 'icy' rage at the murder of a baby or a brother officer. An ethos of teamwork and bonding is sustained through telling tales of the field to one another – in 'deadpan' drama or for mutual titillation. Feigning and deception become part of the everyday moral order, and duplicity an accepted way of getting things done. Deep relationships are possible with some suspects, but as sentiments to be jettisoned when the detective thinks the time is right: 'detectives violate all normal expectations of social relationships'.

It is rare for texts on organizational behaviour to consider children as organizational members, or 'employees'. We typically paint a picture of an adult world of work with adult challenges and problems. In schools, however, we have a social order formally dominated by adults but where children are central to maintaining that order. In 'How Children Manage Emotion in Schools' (Chapter 13), Bendelow and Mayall open the school gates, so to speak, to observe young children's experiences of an 'adult' organization which attempts to construct their everyday bodily and emotion lives – features normally held within the private routines of home life. Children at school, the authors argue, are not passive recipients of such endeavours; they engage in different forms of emotion work, individually and cooperatively, to adapt to, shape or simply cope with the demands. The chapter gives voice to the children as they tell of their experiences in the face of institutional demands, where they have to subordinate their bodies and sentiments to adult regimes: encounters with cramped or confusing buildings, intimidating toilet-lore, playground territories, a cognitively swamped classroom curriculum, their vulnerability when ill or injured. The children are most comfortable when they feel they are sharing control with adults. When it is felt to be imposed, compliance comes – but with a cost: boredom and/or indirect resistance. Some will enlist friends at school as 'protection' from adult demands. Bendelow and Mayall would like to see a clearer recognition of children's emotion work in the negotiation of hierarchical relationships in schools. Children should not be rendered organizationally invisible, as emotionally 'incomplete' persons.

One subtext of Bendelow and Mayall's chapter is the way school children experience and deal with perceived injustices in the face of powerful adults. The dimensions of organizational injustice – between adults – are central to Harlos and Pinder's account of 'Emotion and Injustice in the Workplace' (Chapter 14). Experiences of injustice go to the heart of socially constructed moral orders in organizations and the way power is structured and deployed. This chapter takes emotions as causes, accompaniments and consequences of injustice experiences at work. The authors interviewed men and women from a variety of professional, managerial, clerical and line positions, whose confessional candour sometimes tested one researcher's own emotional engagement. Injustice is conceptualized as predominantly *interactional* (between actors in asymmetrical power positions) or *systemic* (institution-alized in some form). Tales of intimidation, harassment, degradation and mistreatment are told, infused with fear, anger, rage, shame, guilt and cynicism. The long-term emotional legacies of injustice varied – from reported breakdowns and persistent self-doubt, to 'wounded-but-wiser'. Different emotion gender-patterns are noted, such as female bosses using less anger than male bosses, but more manipulation and criticism. Intriguingly, Harlos and Pinder find that some people become attached to their unjust employment relationships. Like Pratt and Doucet's ambivalent workers (Chapter 11), mixed feelings about injustice both repel ('it's hurtful, miserable') and attract ('there's hope, I'm resilient'). The authors conclude their chapter somewhat pessimistically, but possibly realistically: injustice and abuse are inextricably woven into the social structure of many workplaces.

Part IV: Epilogue

In Chapter 15, 'Concluding Reflections', I close the book with some brief thoughts on the present and future positioning of emotion research. Where are we stuck and what must we do?

References

Abraham, R. (1999) 'Emotional intelligence in organizations: a conceptualization', *Genetic Social and General Psychology Monographs*, 125 (2): 209–24.

Adelman, P.K. (1995) 'Emotional labor as a potential source of job stress', in S.L. Sauster and L.R. Murphy (eds), *Organizational Risk Factors for Job Stress*. Washington, DC: American Psychological Association.

Amado, G. (1995) 'Why psychoanalytic knowledge helps us understand organizations; a discussion with Elliott Jacques', *Human Relations*, 48 (4): 351–7.

Ashforth, B.E. and Humphrey, R.H. (1995) 'Emotion in the workplace – a reappraisal', *Human Relations*, 48 (2): 97–125.

Ashkenasy, N.M., Hartel, C.E.J. and Zerbe, W. (2000) *Emotions in the Workplace: Research, Theory and Practice*. Westport, CT: Quorum.

Barbalet, J.M. (1995) 'Climates of fear and socio-political change', *Journal for the Theory of Social Behaviour*, 25 (1): 15–33.

Brody, R.G. and Lowe, D.J. (1995) 'Escalation of commitment in professional tax preparers', *Psychological Reports*, 76 (1): 339–44.

Brown, R. (1997) 'Emotion in organizations: the case of English university business school academics', *Journal of Applied Behavioral Science*, 33 (2): 247–62.

Bryman, A. (1992) *Charisma and Leadership in Organizations*. London: Sage.

Cacioppo, J.T. and Gardner, W.L. (1999) 'Emotion', *Annual Review of Psychology*, 50: 191–214.

Callon, M. (1987) 'Society in the making: the study of technology as a tool for sociological analysis', in W. Bijker, T. Hughes and T. Pinch (eds), *The Social Construction of Technological Systems*. Cambridge, MA: MIT Press.

Carr, A. (1988) 'Identity, compliance and dissent in organizations: a psychoanalytic perspective', *Organization*, 5 (1): 81–99.

Collins, R. (1981) 'On the microfoundations of macrosociology', *American Journal of Sociology*, 86: 984–1014.

Copp, M. (1998) 'When emotion work is doomed to fail: ideological and structural constraints on emotion management', *Symbolic Interactionism*, 21 (3): 299–328.

Craib, I. (1995) 'Some comments on the sociology of emotions', *Sociology*, 29 (1): 151–8.

Craib, I. (1998) *Experiencing Identity*. London: Sage.

Damasio, A.R. (1994) *Descartes' Error*. New York: G. P. Putnam's Sons.

Damasio, A.R. (2000) *The Feeling of What Happens*. London: Heinemann.

de Sousa, R. (1987) *The Rationality of Emotion*. Cambridge, MA: MIT Press.

Doherty, R.W. (1998) 'Emotional contagion and social judgment', *Motivation and Emotion*, 22 (3): 187–209.

Elster, J. (1999) *Alchemies of the Mind*. Cambridge: Cambridge University Press.

Eriksen, R.J. (1997) 'Putting emotions to work (or coming to terms with a contradiction in terms)', *Social Perspectives on Emotion*, vol. 4. JAI Press. pp. 3–18.

Estrada, C.A., Isen, A.M. and Young, M.J. (1997) 'Positive affect facilitates integration of information and decreases anchoring in reasoning among physicians', *Organizational Behavior and Human Decision Processes*, 72 (1): 117–35.

Fairclough, M. (1992) *Discourse and Social Change*. Cambridge: Polity Press.

Fineman, S. (ed.) (1993) *Emotion in Organizations*. London: Sage.

Fineman, S. (1999) 'Emotion and organizing', in S. Clegg, C. Hardy and W. Nord (eds), *Studying Organizations*. London: Sage.

Fineman, S. and Sturdy, A. (1999) 'The emotions of control: a qualitative study of environmental regulation', *Human Relations*, 52 (5): 631–63.

Foucault, M. (1970) *The Order of Things*. London: Tavistock.

Foucault, M. (1979) *The History of Sexuality*. New York: Vintage Books.

Gabriel, Y. (1998) 'Psychoanalytic contributions to the study of the emotional life of organizations', *Administration and Society*, 30 (3): 291–314.

Gabriel, Y. (1999) *Organizations in Depth*. London: Sage.

Gagliardi, P. (1999) 'Exploring the aesthetic side of organizational life', in S. Clegg, C. Hardy and W. Nord (eds), *Studying Organizations*. London: Sage.

Game, A. and Metcalfe, A. (1996) *Passionate Sociology*. London: Sage.

Gay, P. (1998) *Freud: A Life for Our Time*. New York: Newton.

George, J.M and Brief, A.P. (1996) 'Motivational agenda in the workplace: the effects of feelings on focus of attention and work motivation', in B.M. Staw and L.L. Cummins (eds), *Research in Organizational Behavior*, vol. 18. Greenwich, CT: JAI Press. pp. 75–110.

Gibson, D. (1997) 'The struggle for reason: the sociology of emotions in organizations', *Social Perspective on Emotion*, vol. 4. JAI Press. pp. 211–56.

Giddens, A. (1984) *The Constitution of Society*. Cambridge: Polity Press.

Giddens, A. (1991) *Modernity and Self-Identity*. Cambridge: Polity Press.

Ginsburg, G.P. and Harrington, M.E. (1996) 'Bodily states and context in situated lines of action', in R. Harré and W.G. Parrott (eds), *The Emotions*. London: Sage.

Goleman, D. (1996) *Emotional Intelligence*. London: Bloomsbury.

Greenspan, S.I. (1997) *The Growth of the Mind*. Reading, MA: Addison Wesley.

Griffiths, M. (1995) *Feminism and the Self: The Web of Identity*. London: Routledge.

Grosz, E. (1994) *Volatile Bodies*. Bloomington: Indiana University Press.

Harré, R. and Gillett, G. (1994) *The Discursive Mind*. Thousand Oaks, CA: Sage.

Hochschild, A. (1979) 'Emotion work, feeling rules, and social structure', *American Journal of Sociology*, 39 (Dec.): 551–75.

Hochschild, A. (1983) *The Managed Heart*. Berkeley: University of California.

Hochschild, A. (1993) 'Preface', in S. Fineman (ed.), *Emotion in Organizations*. London: Sage.

Jacques, E. (1995) 'Why the psychoanalytic approach to understanding organizations is dysfunctional', *Human Relations*, 48 (4): 343–51.

Jones, L. (1999) 'Smiling lessons end service with a scowl in Greenland', *Guardian*, 23 Oct.: 21.

Kemper, T. (1991) 'An introduction to the sociology of emotions', in D. Strongman (ed.), *International Review of Studies in Emotion*, Vol. 1: Chichester: Wiley. pp. 301–49.

Kets de Vries, M. (1990) *Prisoners of Leadership*. New York: Wiley.

Latour, B. (1991) 'Technology is society made durable', in J. Law (ed.), *A Sociology of Monsters: Essays on Power, Technology and Domination*. Sociological Review Monographs. London: Routledge.

Lazarus, R. (1991) *Emotions and Adaptation*. New York: Oxford University Press.

Leidner, R. (1999). 'Emotional labor in service work', *Annals of the American Academy of Political and Social Science*, 561 (Jan.): 81–95.

Lofland, J. (1976) *Doing Social Life*. New York: Wiley.

Long, S. (1999) 'The tyranny of the customer and the cost of consumerism: an analysis using systems and psychoanalytic approaches to groups and society', *Human Relations*, 52 (6): 723–43.

Lupton, D. (1998) *The Emotional Self*. London: Sage.

Macdonald, C.L. and Sirianni, C. (1996) *Working in the Service Economy*. Philadelphia: Temple University Press.

Martin, J., Knopoff, K. and Beckman, C. (1998) 'An alternative to bureaucratic impersonality and emotional labor: bounded emotionality at the Body Shop', *Administrative Science Quarterly*, 43 (2): 429–69.

Martin, S.E. (1999) 'Police force or political service? Gender and emotional labor', *Annals of the American Academy of Political and Social Science*, 561 (Jan.) 111–26.

Morris, J.A. and Feldman, D.C. (1996) 'The dimensions, antecedents, and consequences of emotional labor', *Academy of Management Review*, 21 (4): 986–1010.

Mullins, L. (1996) *Management and Organisational Behaviour*. London: Pitman.

Mumby, D.K. and Putnam, L.L. (1992) 'The politics of emotion: a feminist reading of bounded rationality', *Academy of Management Review*, 17 (3): 465–86.

Neumann, J.E. and Hirschhorn, K. (1999) 'The challenge of integrating psychodynamic and organizational theory', *Human Relations*, 52 (6): 683–95.

Newton, T., Handy, J. and Fineman, S. (1995) *'Managing' Stress: Emotion and Power at Work*. London: Sage.

O'Brien, M. (1994) 'The managed heart revisited: health and social control', *Sociological Review*, 42 (3): 393–413.

Parrott, W.G. and Harré, R. (1996) 'Some complexities in the study of emotions.', in R. Harré and W.G. Parrott (eds), *The Emotions*. London: Sage.

Pierce, J.L. (1999) 'Emotional labor among paralegals', *The Annals of the American Academy of Political and Social Science*, 561 (Jan.): 127–42.

Pinder, C.C. (1998) *Work Motivation in Organizational Behavior*. New Jersey: Prentice Hall.

Scheff, T.J. (1990) *Microsociology: Discourse, Emotion and Social Structure*. Chicago: University of Chicago Press.

Schwalbe, M. (1996) *Unlocking the Iron Cage: The Men's Movement, Gender Politics and American Culture*. New York: Oxford University Press.

Smith, K.D. (1995) 'Social psychological perspectives on laypersons' theories of emotion', in J.A. Russell (ed.), *Everyday Conceptions of Emotion*. Dordrecht: Kluwer.

Staw, B.M. and Ross, J. (1989) 'Understanding behavior in escalating situations', *Science* October: 216–20.

Stearns, P. (1995) 'Emotion', in R. Harré and P. Stearns (eds), *Discursive Psychology in Practice*. London: Sage.

Steinberg, R. (1999) 'Emotional labor in job evaluation: redesigning compensation packages', *Annals of the American Academy of Political and Social Science*, 561 (Jan.): 143–76.

Strati, A. (1999) *Organization and Aesthetics*. London: Sage.

Tracy, S.J. and Tracy, K. (1998) 'Emotional labor at 911: a case and theoretical critique', *Journal of Applied Communication Research*, 26: 390–411.

Verbeke, W. (1997) 'Individual differences in emotional contagion of salespersons: its effects on performance and burnout', *Psychology and Marketing*, 14 (6): 617–36.

Vetlesen, A.J. (1994) *Perception, Empathy and Judgment*. University Park, Pennsylvania: Pennsylvania State University Press.

Walsh, J.P. (1995) 'Managerial and organizational cognition: notes from a trip down memory lane', *Organization Science*, 6 (3): 280–321.

Weiss, H.M. and Cropanzano, R. (1996) 'Affective events theory: a theoretical discussion of the structure, causes and consequences of affective experiences at work', *Research in Organizational Behaviour*, 18: 1–74.

Wetherall, M. (1996) 'Romantic discourse and feminist analysis: interrogating investment, power and desire', in S. Wilkinson and C. Kitzinger (eds), *Feminism and Discourse: Psychological Perspectives*. London: Sage.

Wharton, A. (1999) 'The psychosocial consequences of emotional labor', *Annals of the American Academy of Political and Social Science*, 561 (Jan.): 158–75.

Zeidler, S. (1998) 'Don't have a nice day – workers protest smile rule'. Los Angeles: Reuters, 16 Nov.

PART I
EMOTIONAL TEXTURES

---

2 NARRATIVES OF COMPASSION IN ORGANIZATIONS

PETER J. FROST, JANE E. DUTTON, MONICA C. WORLINE AND ANNETTE WILSON

As my illness progressed I was trying to keep on teaching, was trying to keep doing everything and I was keeping on, keeping on. I was on medications and increasingly ill and finally I called a friend and senior colleague on a Sunday and I said: 'You have to help me figure out how to quit doing what I am doing. I can't do another day.' And she came over and spent the afternoon with me on a Sunday, reassigning my students, figuring out all the paperwork that needed to be done and doing all of those things. (Colleen, Professor)

Organizations are sites of everyday healing and pain. Colleen's story is a story of organizational compassion, organizational response to pain. As one of our participants reminded us: 'I see lots of pain which people bring to their workplaces simply because they are human beings . . . most people actually walk in through the doors as wounded people.'

What do others do in the face of this wounding? While not often talked about, and easily missed if one is not looking for them, compassionate acts are part of the weave that keeps work communities on the mend. The giving and receiving of compassion restores a sense of humanity and connection to the experiences that people have at work (Frost, 1999). Compassion is an essential part of care-giving that is 'part of, rather than separate from, work interactions' (Kahn, 1998: 43). Pain and compassion are not separate from 'being a professional' and the 'doing of work' in organizations. They are a natural and living representation of people's humanity in the workplace.

This chapter explores some foundational assumptions in our conceptualization of compassion and its link to emotion in organizations. These foundations provide the canvas for a painting of compassion stories that reveal two important insights about compassion and organization. One insight is that people often act compassionately in the face of pain without knowing what is appropriate or how compassion should be conveyed.

Compassion involves people allowing feeling to guide action, rather than the reverse. A second insight is that organizations create an emotional ecology where care and human connection are enabled or disabled. We use these two insights to pose an invitation to further study of compassion in organizations. We close with a found poem that weaves together our study participants' words, representing what we learned in a very different way. We hope that the text and the poem together awaken recognition and interest in compassion as concept and compassion as human expression.

Foundations

We were guided in collecting these narratives of compassion by four assumptions. We assume that organizations are social systems and that people's interactions with others in the organization will comprise much of their experience of their work. The embeddedness of people's work experiences in interpersonal interactions and relationships means that the emotional tone and impact of these interactions is vital to an understanding of people's work experience (Berscheid, 1994; Brass, 1985; Dutton et al., 1999; Gersick et al., 2000; Ibarra, 1992; Ibarra and Smith-Lovin, 1997; Uzzi, 1996). Because work organizations are such important centres of people's time and energy, we assume that people in organizations seek a feeling of connection with one another, a feeling of belonging, and a feeling of being cared for and respected. Such feelings are provided in part by daily interactions that are caring (Baumeister and Leary, 1995; Kahn, 1993; Meyerson, 1998; Miller and Stiver, 1997). At the centre of our notion of compassion is the assumption that the absence or presence of caring interactions at work dramatically impact people's experience of organizations.

Our second assumption is that people are inherently emotional beings and that people experience connection and belonging through feeling (Baumeister and Leary, 1995; Miller and Stiver, 1997). As other scholars have noted, dominant discourse separates emotion from rationality and divides people in organizations from their emotional responses (Meyerson, 1998; Mumby and Putnam, 1992). Rather than separate emotion from work, we assumed that people bring emotions into their work and that emotions infiltrate the doing of work (Kahn, 1998). Sharing these emotions and responding to emotions of others is at the heart of experiences of pain and compassion in organizations.

We further assumed that people's actions and feelings are not completely determined by the organization. We attempt to understand the ways in which organizational practices bound, limit, enable and encourage the expression of pain and compassion (Shotter, 1995). We assume a world in which organizational practices provide a framework within which people experience their work (Bell and Staw, 1989).

Finally, traditional discourse in organizations often seeks to divide public from private, home from office, personal from professional (Bradbury and

Lichtenstein, 1999; Meyerson, 1998; Mumby and Putnam, 1992). We assume that these divisions are largely impossible. When we ask about acts of compassion in the workplace, we receive information about both personal and professional lives. Participants in this research described tensions that are inherent in living both a personal and an organizational life. Such tensions often limit the expression of pain in organizations. In the end, however, we cannot divide ourselves or separate pain from work (Kahn, 1998; Meyerson, 1998). Compassion is directed toward those who are suffering, regardless of whether that suffering is the result of a personal or a professional wound.

What is compassion?

We focus on a definition of compassion that centres on the connection between people. Some define compassionate acts as forms of empathy or personal support that are offered from one person to another. Psychologists who study the motivation for helping each other when in need see compassion as one of the emotions associated with empathetic concern (for example, Batson, 1991). Like empathy, compassion involves 'other-oriented feelings that are most often congruent with the perceived welfare of the other person' (Batson, 1994: 606). We assume, however, that compassion goes beyond an individual feeling of empathy and is expressed through action of some sort. In organizations, this form of caregiving often involves conveying 'an emotional presence by displaying warmth, affection and kindness' (Kahn, 1993: 546). In this sense, compassionate acts often display a form of emotional intelligence (Goleman, 1995, 1998) and are guided by a mutual concern that allows action in connection with others (Miller and Stiver, 1997).

One can also think about compassion as 'the heart's response to the sorrow' (Kornfield, 1993: 326). In compassion, a person surrenders him or herself to the pain of another by being with that person, at least for a moment. Compassion is associated with feelings that are fundamentally 'other regarding rather than self-regarding' (Solomon, 1998: 528). The Dalai Lama discusses 'genuine compassion [as] based on a clear acceptance or recognition that others, like oneself, want happiness and have the right to overcome suffering. On that basis one develops some kind of concern about the welfare of others, irrespective of one's attitude to oneself' (1981: 63). This focus outside of oneself facilitates another's feeling of being cared for, joined, seen, felt, known, and not alone (Kahn, 1993; Noddings, 1984).

Why narratives of compassion?

This chapter is built on stories that people shared about how others responded to their pain and the pain of others in their work organizations. Our empirical context involves people in university settings.[1] Thus the narratives of compassion have double meaning. As a methodology and phenomena, narratives are windows into life in organizations (Boje, 1991;

Barry and Elmes, 1997; Czarniawska, 1998; Martin et al., 1983; O'Connor, 1996; Weick and Browning, 1986). As a research setting, these narratives provide openings into the organizational worlds in which we live. Through collecting stories of how people in universities experience compassion, we have become much more attuned to universities as sites of human pain and healing. While we will use primarily the voice of 'researchers', behind this stance is an unwritten text of how all four of us as university participants – two PhD students and two faculty members – have been affected deeply by the dialogues that shaped these research observations.

For organizational researchers interested in emotion at work, compassion narratives are carriers of both the feelings of being in pain and the feelings of responding to pain as they play out during the conduct of people's work. They highlight features of emotions at work that have received scant attention. First, stories of compassion at work breathe life into deadened accounts of work feeling. As Sandelands (1998: 17) describes, 'Society [and as applied here, organization] is dissected as a cadaver, a logical structure of inert elements', extinguishing the life in the social connection that exists between people. Fineman makes a similar graphic assertion when he argues that our field is 'emotionally anorexic' (Fineman, 1993: 9). Reliance on stories as data helps to hold onto a fuller and more living account of people's feelings at work.

Organizational studies has focused on display rules and how these shape the forms of expressed feelings in organizational settings (for example, Hochschild, 1983; Rafaeli and Sutton, 1987, 1989). Compassion narratives, while evidencing some effects of these constraints, also convey feelings of care that emerge spontaneously in response to observed or known suffering. Expressed pain is often a violation of basic display rules that divide emotion from work. When these basic display rules are transgressed others often act within the space that is opened. While it does not deny the existence of toxic organizational contexts, acts of compassion are more than normative compliance to well-grooved display rules. While compassionate expression is subject to culturally bounded display rules, we found that people experienced authentic connection with each other in the context of work when pain was expressed and response was necessary.

Stories

The importance of pain

Understanding compassion in organizations means recognizing the ubiquity of pain in the workplace. Our participants helped us to see that pain in work organizations lives in many forms and emerges from many places. Their accounts of pain were vivid, honest and sometimes horrifying.

Some people described the pain of acute losses – deaths and suicides of family members and friends. For others, the losses were of connections and relationships with others as marked by divorces, separations, and ruined friendships or working relationships. Still others described the pain of career losses inflicted by demotions, rejections and tenure denials. Not all pain was brought on by significant losses. Participants also described the pain of small slights, disrespect and uncivil acts (Pearson and Porath, 1999) and being treated as invisible or unimportant. Experienced pain is part of the daily rhythm of organizational participation.

For example, faculty described working with the pain of students who had suffered traumatic events such as rape, suicide, sexual harassment, and abuse. They described acknowledging and working with this pain as a necessary part of the teaching experience. Similarly, staff members described working with the pain of students, other staff and faculty who they knew to be suffering. Students described other students' suffering in enduring the painful setbacks and degradations of being a student. Many people described the pain of being overloaded, experiencing crushing workloads, making it difficult to spend meaningful time with themselves, with partners and with families. The pain was often accentuated because people in universities described feeling so alone in much of their work.

Compassion in the face of pain – three instances

Three examples of compassion in the face of pain introduce a discussion of what we discovered about compassion through the stories we collected. Ken told us about responding compassionately to a colleague's illness over several years.

> He was a colleague in my department, in my field. We were on committees together. Then one [day] he showed up at my house distraught and at loose ends . . . He was sobbing and incoherent, so I stayed with him. And eventually I took him to the hospital for a kind of urgent clinical care. For three years or so he was not so good . . . But for some reason he glommed on to me. And every once in a while, once a month or so, I'd get a call and I would have to go wherever he was and be with him.

Lynn told of a small gesture from a student when she was overwhelmed by an illness in her family and the demands from her doctoral studies. As she described it:

> I was working on this project and trying to do my own stuff and I felt like I was going to go crazy. And there was a baby shower that was coming up . . . I didn't know how I was going to be able to do everything I had to do and get to the store to get a present . . . One of my colleagues' students called me and said she was going to the store to get a present and said, 'Can I pick up one for you?' I know that it sounds crazy but it was such a gift. It was such a small little thing, she bought a present for me. It was just wonderful. She had thought about me and done that.

Finally, acts of compassion often involved someone offering comfort in the face of the painful loss of someone loved. Ralph, a professor and former dean told the following story:

My wife and I lost three close relatives in one year, my mother and father, and her brother died of a heart attack at 37 years of age. A lot of people came to our door and chatted about relatives that had died, and so on, but one couple came to our door and wept. And I said 'Well, come on in.' So, they came in. They didn't say anything . . . And it's interesting, because at the end of the day, my wife and I would go over the day's grieving. And the couple that really served us and cared for us and showed compassion was the couple that had said nothing, but had listened and hugged and wept with us.

Visions of compassion

Compassion is one way in which people reach out to others when they are hurting. The picture of compassion seen through the stories we collected reveals a rich range of possible ways that people express and receive compassion at work – from small gestures such as buying a gift to much larger and more extensive acts such as going to a colleague's aid over a period of years.

Sometime the acts of compassion were planned and deliberate, as when someone learned about another's loss or difficulty and consciously made the effort to connect. We see this in Ralph's story of how others responded to the deaths his family suffered. We heard inspiring accounts of how people altered the rhythms of their own lives to accommodate and respond to the suffering of others. Consider the case of Abe, a graduate school dean who deliberately stepped in to help a faculty member in pain. A witness to the act told us the story:

> Jerry was a very bright academic who had a history of emotional pain that included a very unhappy and unloving childhood. He was in a faculty where he felt under-appreciated and he was regarded by most of his colleagues as a jerk. He was also a poor teacher. He would act up with the dean of the department. If the dean wanted him to write a paper or do something he was often so angry that he would put the request in his drawer and refuse to do it. One day this dean came over to him and said, 'Let's go for lunch. I want to take you out.' And he took him for lunch and he said: 'What's going on, tell me about this, what's happening?' And Jerry told him he was having all these problems, and he was just starting to work [them] out. And the dean said, 'Oh I see. Why don't you come to my place every Tuesday and Thursday evening and we will work together.' And they worked on his papers and the dean was an incredible mentor to him.

Many of the compassionate tales were of spontaneous and unplanned giving in the face of someone else's suffering. Sometimes these were the hugs, e-mails, cards or other gestures of care that people extended immediately upon learning of a colleague's suffering. On other occasions whole groups of people dropped what they were doing and responded as a collective. Angela told a heartbreaking story of her husband's death from an inheritable disease and the yearly terror of having to test her children to see if there were signs that they also harboured the disease. She described getting the dreaded phone call that indicated her son had been diagnosed as positive with the disease and having to go immediately to run a staff meeting:

> I sort of ran the meeting and they said 'we're planning for next year'. And somebody said, 'Oh Angela, you know you look a little burned out, maybe we shouldn't be talking about planning right now.' And then I said, 'Oh, it's not my job. It's not because of that,' and then I started weeping, and saying what it was, and all of a sudden, everybody in that room was offering help.

Compassionate acts can be solo or collective. In Ken's story, one colleague provides comfort and assistance to another. In Angela's story it is a group of people gathered for a meeting who spontaneously offer help. We also heard about organized efforts from groups that provided comfort in the face of experienced pain. Clare, a graduate student undergoing chemotherapy treatments for cancer, described how fellow graduate students organized a meal-cooking intervention for her and her husband. In her words:

> When I was going through treatment, shortly after I had been diagnosed with cancer, some of my fellow doctoral students volunteered to cook for my husband and me. So they would come over every two weeks with a big cooler full of prepared meals at their own expense. We decided to start paying them for the food because the gesture was just too large for us to accept. So they would just bring us ten prepared meals every couple of weeks and we would stock up our freezers and our bellies would be full.

Compassion was expressed directly and indirectly. Direct forms of compassion involved face-to-face verbal interactions or physical expressions of touch that communicated a presence and care for another. Indirect expressions of compassion were different. Sometimes people acted as buffers in attempts to alleviate the pain of another. Nathan described a boss who tried to prepare others to help a co-worker if needed:

> When Alan was breaking up with Mary he was late to work, he was making mistakes, and the boss was understanding about it. He allowed him to make more mistakes than he usually would have. He sort of let the rest of us know that we needed to keep an eye out to help him or whatever. He talked to everybody about it.

Compassion also comes in its own time. Compassionate acts were sometimes as short as the time it took to write a card or give a hug. Alternatively, expressions of compassion sometimes spanned the space of years as a person responded to repeated episodes of the same kind of pain, as in Ken's story above. Compassion often means giving time to another. As one interviewee expressed: 'To me, a compassionate work would be to make yourself available when you don't have time.' Compassionate responding involves recognizing when there is a limited opening through which people can connect. As Ken put it, 'You know these opportunities come and they slip by and you let them go and you get on with your life.' They are not moments that can be easily recovered. When someone shares that they have lost a parent or that their job is being restructured, in the words of one of our participants: 'You just have that interstitial space, that moment between the two of you where you can make a difference.'

Knowledge

One of our faculty participants, after feeling the difference others' responses made to the healing from his father's death, provided this advice:

> If you don't know what to say, say anything. If you don't know what to say, at least say something to acknowledge it happened. . . . I think even if you don't know the person well enough to do it, acknowledging it in some way is infinitely better than to not say anything. (Greg, professor)

Acting in the face of not-knowing

At the core of compassion is the idea that in some way one is moved by someone else's pain and acts to connect with the person to signal that one cares. As Josh described: compassion involves 'giving them the space to express their pain, whatever that pain might be about and to listen in a way that, you know, that is both just listening but also being active . . . in how you respond back, that is sensitive to the person. And it is more than just a passing acknowledgement that this person is in pain.' Miller and Stiver (1997) have described the kind of connection that Josh articulates as mutual empathy. They describe ways in which people connect with others and use feelings of connection to guide responses.

Often we assume that people must know before they act. However, Josh shows us that compassion is action in the face of not-knowing. The emotional connection with another provides a direction for action. Shotter (1995) describes this as 'feeling one's way forward' (p. 127) in organizations. Connection with another often demands immediate action and interplay. People rarely know when or under what circumstances compassion will be required. They do not know the facts of their co-workers' lives. Instead, people must allow room for a connection to be established and they must follow the feelings in the connection to respond in the best way they know how.

This kind of connecting seems to entail an ability to attune to the needs of the other. Being able to see or imagine another's pain implies a form of empathy or connected knowing (Belenky et al., 1986). Patricia Benner and her colleagues (1996) describe a skill of emotional attunement in highly proficient nurses that illustrates this quality. Attuned nurses have a capacity to read a situation in a patient and to grasp its emotional tone: to know when something is 'off' when it looks 'ok' on the surface, or to sense that its actually 'ok' despite appearances to the contrary. Compassionate action involves moving from not-knowing and using attunement to guide action.

We speculate that people who are skilled in compassionate responding are able to attune themselves quickly to what others are feeling, and are also able to act out of that attunement. One participant describes the feeling of attunement when his co-worker reaches out to him: 'like the times when Jenny asks me if I'm okay, I know that somebody cares about me . . . There's no rhyme or reason for when she asks me, but when she asks me I need to be asked. She knows that somehow . . . We feel the life of each other . . . And it means so much to me and I know she knows that.' In this sense, compassion involves the alignment of action with attunement. Miller and Stiver (1997) suggest that people develop larger repertoires of responses as they engage in this type of mutuality and resonance with another's feelings. Few of our participants felt that they knew how to express compassion or that they knew how to engage in compassionate action before they were called to do so. Compassion involves reaching toward another in ways that allow feeling to guide action.

When compassion fails

People's suffering is not always met with compassionate responses when it is shared in organizations. Just as there are barriers to the sharing of pain, such as fear of being seen as weak or fear of burdening others, there are also barriers to the expression of compassion in organizations. Time and timing are important barriers. When people are overloaded or overwhelmed they often feel incapable of responding compassionately. When organizations emotionally exhaust their members, people disconnect from their work and their co-workers (Kahn, 1993).

In addition to time pressure, acts of compassion are blocked when people feel unsure about what kind of expression of compassion is appropriate. Sometimes a lack of knowledge about a person or their situation creates barriers to compassionate action. As our participants told us, when people encounter pain from others whom they don't know too well, they wait for a sign that someone wants help. They worry about 'crossing a line' and getting too personal when someone may wish to keep their pain private. As Vicki explained, 'Unless they've conveyed to me that it's a problem, I don't go prying because I'm concerned they may not want to talk about it.'

People struggle with the lack of knowledge about what to do in the face of tremendous loss. Cindy asks the questions all of us face when confronting the ultimate pain of death: 'So how do we relate? How do we give them space? What do you do with the person who you are sitting across from, who knows they have only got maybe next week or maybe the next day. What do you do to relate to them?' Though we can provide no simple answers to these poignant questions, they are the questions with which all organizational members grapple. Because these questions can seem overwhelming, organizational members may be daunted by tremendous loss and compassionate responses may be hindered or lost.

Finally, not everyone is prepared to receive compassion from others, as it implies vulnerability and closeness. Some of our participants expressed not wanting compassionate attention from their colleagues. One academic gave explicit instructions that no condolences be sent on the loss of a partner. Another, whose parent had passed away, explained: 'it wasn't something I wanted to hide, but I didn't want to be getting e-mails from people I'd never known.' Sometimes too there was a sense that talking to others doesn't help, that 'There's nothing that someone can say to you to make [the pain] go away; it's just there.'

Issues of power imbalance and hierarchy may play an important role in people's reluctance to reveal their pain. Fear of unwanted repercussions on the job prevents some from opening up. An untenured professor worried about how a senior colleague would see her professionally: 'I was afraid she'd think less of me if I let her into some of the personal problems I was going through.' Internalized voices, such as 'You imagine you're handicapped in some way' or 'I don't feel as smart as I used to . . . I feel damaged and less capable . . .' reinforced the sense that revelation could hurt a career. One participant explained that it is: 'The pain of uncertainty, the pain of wondering if they're going to be used in some way, or manipulated in some way, or even, the pain of thinking the worst about yourself and your prospects within the company.'

Fear of jeopardizing one's employment future also affected those responding compassionately. When Fred took time to be with his child he would think: 'what am I doing here? It's 3 in the afternoon and I'm supposed to work on trying to get promoted, and I'm at the park for four hours on a Thursday afternoon.' Another expressed his concern: 'if I show solidarity or compassion . . . to a co-worker that is in disfavour with the . . . supervisor, then I could be looked at in a very different light professionally.' John, a supervisor, speculates that sometimes people may feel coerced to open up when they'd rather not. 'If your boss asks you a personal question . . . you may not feel like you know that person well enough to talk to them . . . It's hard, you don't want to tell the boss that it's none of her business, or that you don't feel like talking about it.' He worries about the double bind: that he now may be seen as uninterested or uncompassionate.

These fears were realized for some who experienced uncompassionate responses to their pain. One woman, who experienced severe financial hardship following a disability, states: 'I have been treated with extreme levels of condescension, contempt, and exclusion because of it.' A professor whose father had passed away recalls a colleague's impatient response to his pain: 'He said to me, "So how long do you think it will take you to get over this [death of his father]? Three weeks, maybe?" . . . and I almost said "f—— you", you know. And I just looked at him and said, "No I think it's going to take a lot longer than that."'

Organizations

Ralph, a former dean of a religious college, noted:

> I think a compassionate organization deals with the pain [of the organization].
> There will always be failure and mistakes and one of the things we look for in an
> organization is how it treats people when they make mistakes. We just made a
> huge mistake with our catalogue. One faculty member's picture and name was left
> out, a senior member of the faculty. Now that's a huge mistake when you have
> 5000 copies of the catalogue actually printed, sitting in a carton. It was a senior
> but new administrator who made the mistake. The president exercised very
> important leadership in saying that we will pay the price as a community to do
> the right thing in this and do it in such a way that there is no dishonor brought to
> anyone.

Expressed pain is an invitation to connect. Expressed compassion is a
response that affirms the human connection. While these expressions are
often exchanged between two or a few people, they are facilitated or hindered
by the organizations where people study and work.

An ecology of compassion

Organizations as behavioural settings can ease or make more difficult
people's compassion giving. Universities as organizations create cultures,
develop rules and procedures, promote leaders, and structure people's time
in ways that affect compassionate responding. At a basic level, organizations
are distinguished by shared values, beliefs and norms that place different
levels of emphasis on being caring towards others. Kahn (1998) demonstrates
patterns of organizational care that flow throughout organizational systems.
Behaviour within these systems serves either to replenish or deplete people's
emotional and caring resources (Kahn, 1993). Different cultures give rise to
different value for compassionate expressions as normal or not, valued or
not, deviant or not. Cialdini (1999), writing about dishonest practices in
organizations, finds that organizational practices spread like tumours and
beget similar practices across the organization. An organizational system that
responds with compassion time and again thus fosters compassionate seeing
and acting in its members.

Several participants had worked in different university settings and
noted the difference in compassionate responses. For example, faculty
members talked about differences in responses to tenure decisions and
the departure of organizational members at different universities. Jacques
(1993) describes an organizational culture of connection that facilitates
informational exchanges and creates a value of caring. Clearly universities
as organizations establish an emotional ecology within which their members
interact. That emotional ecology can facilitate or retard compassionate
action.

One important aspect of an emotional ecology is a working environment in which people are given permission and space to attend to their pain. Kahn (1998) describes the importance of emotional attachments that create whole social systems, with compassionate and caring relationships being developed by the collective. Meyerson (1998) describes organizations that normalize and make room for caring for people who are overloaded and experience burnout. Universities varied considerably in the degree to which they exhibited responses to their members' suffering. For example, one participant described an institution that made an apartment near a hospital available to a staff member to allow her to be near a family member in a coma. We heard stories of administrators arranging workloads and providing help for those experiencing difficulties. We heard of the importance of organizational routines such as sending flowers, notes of condolence, and other actions that represent a form of regularized caring. Actions like these help to establish a framework for compassionate action by organizational members and create a pattern of organizational care that comes out of such an emotional ecology (Kahn, 1993). The absence of these behaviours also creates patterns of organizational response that are perceived as cold or uncaring (Cialdini, 1999).

Organizational leaders and prominent organizational citizens can exemplify compassionate or uncompassionate reactions to the suffering of organizational members, and by doing so, reinforce or diminish a sense that compassionate responding is valued (Bass, 1990; Kahn, 1993). We heard several other stories of how deans' and administrators' actions were actively interpreted as signals of what the organizations cared about, and therefore the kinds of actions that would be valued (Pfeffer, 1981).

Characteristics of an ecology of compassion

Compassion can help make others in an organization feel cared for, seen, felt, known and not alone (Kahn, 1993; Noddings, 1984). In this way, compassion can be healing, even if the healing is not directed toward the initial source of pain. Because feeling and mutual empathy guides compassionate action, healing is a transformation of the connection and emotion in both the compassion giver and the recipient. Through our collection of compassion narratives we identified five characteristics of interactions within an ecology of compassion.

Compassionate responses affirm a person's existence by making the other person 'present' (Buber, 1974). Compassion requires authentic human presence with another. In 'The human moment at work', psychiatrist Edward Hallowell (1999) talks about people's need to experience moments of authentic psychological connection. He describes the human moment as having two prerequisites: 'people's physical presence and their emotional and intellectual attention' (p. 59). For the human moment to work: 'You have to set aside what you are doing, put down the memo you were reading, disengage from your laptop, abandon your day dream and focus on the person you are with' (p. 60). This skill of recognizing the need in another person is an integral part of the process of giving compassion. One of our participants explained: 'Compassion is the willingness to drop what you are engaged in, in order to attend to a person's real feelings, longings, aspirations, pain . . . to leave a task unfinished and to attune to a person is a real act of love in the organizational context.' In a similar vein, another participant told us: 'Compassion demands our patience, sensitivity, a giving over of ourselves. When people act compassionately, their world shifts to being present with another.' Conveying felt presence is a powerful message in an organizational setting, where invisibility and production are often the essence of daily experience. As Sarah Lawrence-Lightfoot (1999) claims: 'As we hurtle through our lives, such moments are altogether too rare, and the relationships in which they occur provide a reminder of what nourishes us most profoundly, perhaps even an echo or reminder of our earliest relationships. In such moments, we feel present and acknowledged' (p. 197).

Compassion giving and receiving sometimes altered the felt connection between people. In the terms of network theorists, a compassionate response in the face of pain often changes a weak tie into a strong tie (Granovetter, 1973), with a change in attendant levels of felt trust and reliance. Compassionate acts can change attachments from weak to strong, where a relationship gains greater emotional weight in someone's life (Kahn, 1998). The compassion receiver often recognized that the quality of connection between two people had been transformed. As Greg told us, 'After someone has been compassionate, they loom as an important person in my life.' Sometimes the transformation in connection was profound. Margaret described a colleague who comforted her during a painful divorce. In this case, a compassionate response dulled the pain in the short term, and created a lasting friendship in the long term. In her words: 'Wow, how did that make me feel? It made me laugh; it stopped the pain for a moment and made me laugh. It was an amazing friendship that formed through that. And again, she is not only a great friend, but a great colleague, also in academia struggling her own struggles.'

There were cases where witnessing the compassionate actions modelled a form of contact that changed the quality of connection between the whole. Anne, a faculty member in the arts, told of a student's struggle with representing her partner's suicide in a class assignment. When the student shared her creation with other class members, the professor responded in a way that affected everyone who saw it. As she described: 'We have all been touched by death, if not suicide, in some way . . . So I just talked about that . . . None of us could understand the pain she had experienced . . . And that it was incredibly valuable for all of us to have her share it with us, what it meant, and how her life would be forever affected. And that art allows us to do this.' The student's courage and openness moved the other students deeply, enabling them to share. 'They were so supportive of her and thanked her and talked about it. Some of them opened up and said things about deaths that had affected them.'

Organizational environments can be transformed by compassion. Similarly, a professor describes how a senior colleague has 'set up an environment of cooperation and collaboration . . . of mutual support', by taking compassionate action to help others: 'She is very conscious of graduate students and adjuncts, women who are struggling, who are alone . . . argu[ing] long and hard with the dean, fearlessly, on their behalf to keep them in their classes.' As a result, the participant felt that corner of her workplace was transformed from a competitive 'snake pit' to a place she felt 'comfortable and so at home'. A number of participants mentioned that they felt their units were unusually supportive: oases within a larger, hostile institution. One supervisor felt that some of his staff had transferred into his unit because of the compassionate climate, suggesting that the compassionate workplace may be a factor in both attracting and retaining staff.

An invitation to study compassion in organizations

An inquiry into compassion narratives offered our participants the possibility of sharing stories in which they were caregivers to others at work. The fact is everyone we asked had stories to tell. The roles that employees took in these stories – whether staff, faculty or students – were as validators and responders to others' suffering. The compassion stories revealed the myriad of ways that compassion is 'done' as a form of competent relational practice (Fletcher, 1999). At the same time, the stories were occasions in which people saw themselves as deeply human, emotional beings – affected by and troubled by the witnessing of another person's pain. While most people expressed doubt and discomfort about whether they were responding the 'right way', all of the storytellers expressed a form of engagement and empathy for the other (Frank, 1992).

Thus, we see in these stories the possibility of rewriting caregiving in organizational life as a daily, everyday activity in which all people participate (Kahn 1993, 1998; Meyerson, 1998). In the same way that Kolb (1992) finds that people utilize informal channels of dispute resolution in organizations, we find that compassion is practised by all organizational members. Compassion giving is not something done only by designated professionals (such as social workers, human resource practitioners or crisis counsellors), but is done by most organizational members in the everyday doing of work in organizational communities. Like Kahn (1993) we find that caregiving and compassionate action are woven into the daily interactions in organizations.

Danger and blindspots in a compassion frame

It is also important to name some of the silences and blindspots in our study account. Of course, any attempt to do so is always incomplete. First, we chose a wide brush to paint the look of compassion through the words of 22 people

I

living in academic settings. Differences and variations are brushed over in this type of account. It was often the variation or the anomalies that were most 'moving' or informative, and yet we have focused on patterned simi-larities, pushing differences into the background. This makes the compassion portrait look neater, tidier and more coherent than in fact it is. No doubt compassion varies across cultures, organizations and industries. We hope that other researchers will repaint differences that exist between individuals engaging in compassionate action in different national and organizational contexts.

Second, we have not fully explored the dynamics of power and status. Our account does not address how superior power enables people to express pain differently and, similarly, how inferior status may coerce revelation or silence, and enable or disable expression. For example, greater power in organizations is typically associated with freedom, flexibility and resources that equip people to respond compassionately. We have also not addressed the gendering of compassion giving as a partial explanation for why it is so invisible in organizations (for example, Fletcher, 1999; Jacques, 1992). There are similar silences about race, social class and other differences that could shape how compassion looks and how it feels in organizational settings.

Third, we have portrayed compassion giving implicitly as positive action. However, it is also an action that can injure the people who do it. Some of our participants noted the emotional exhaustion that can come from giving compassion without recourse to some 'protection' from the wash of pain one is dealing with. Although she loves helping, one participant reflects, 'some-times I feel I'm not respected very much for being interested . . . They sort of think of me as something to . . . empty their wastes into . . . Or they don't think about me and my feelings very much.' As Frost and Robinson note: 'Managing organizational pain that is too intense and/or too protracted can inflict great cost on the health of those who step in and try to be compassionate. The most common toll of toxic handling . . . is burnout, both psychological and professional' (1999: 100; see also Meyerson, this volume). Beyond exhaustion and burnout, the positive valuing of compassionate action offered by 'good people' masks the ambivalence and conflict that some people felt when faced with other people's pain. The possibility of acting com-passionately or not calls forth the very human dilemma of whether one wants to care for another at a particular time, in a particular place, or at a particular level of connection.

Epilogue

We have devoted this chapter to an exploration of the nature of compassion and the complex and nuanced issues that surround giving and receiving compassion in the workplace. We have discussed the notion of an ecology of compassion as a way to create the beginnings of a framework for viewing organizations in terms of how effectively they enhance or diminish the emotional and caring resources of the people who work in them. We have identified some of the limitations in our study of compassion in organizations.

We close with what we call a 'found poem', created from the words of our interview participants by Monica Worline. She writes: 'In the words of Annie Dillard, whose work inspired the idea to create a found poem, poems "seldom require explanation, but this one does. . . . I did not write a word of it. Other hands composed the poem's lines – the poem's sentences. . . . I lifted them. Sometimes I dropped extra words; I never added a word." This poem weaves the words of our participants into an original order, but captures for us the extraordinary depth and eloquence of the stories we have collected, a part of which are evidenced in this chapter.

Because You Dare to Name it

Commiseration, support, problem solving, advocacy, a feeling of
    togetherness.
I think we get worn down. Like your edges are worn.
You just don't stand out like you used to.
So, it's leaning in. It's not just a job, it's caring for people.
You can see a tension in the person's face, for one thing:

    Sometimes, you see it in their eyes
    Sometimes, in their body movements
    Sometimes, even in what they are saying.

Everybody was praying, sending condolences, sending cards, expressions,
    support;
real caring, listening, little gifts; people picking up pieces, you know, to
    help practically.

Is fear a form of pain?
Because you have to hide your true self and your true feelings;
it looks like people feeling like second class citizens;
there was a real norm in our department of modesty and always presenting
    a good face.
    Keep your skeletons at home.
    You're not supposed to have a personal life.
    You're supposed to take care of business.

The pain of uncertainty, the pain of wondering
if they're going to be used in some way, or manipulated in some way, or
    even
the pain of thinking the worst about yourself and your prospects within
    the company.
Mostly what people do is avoid you.
I understand it. Boy, I did it.
I have to catch myself from doing it again.

And so I have this memory of people who just backed away and didn't say
    anything,
thinking it was the best thing.

But I was so moved that she wanted to do that:
to go into the ugly personal slop of my life.

I think, no. I want to change this language.
I want there to be a language for saying that I have pain with dignity.

For someone on behalf of an aggrieved
or someone who is representative of the organization
to be able to say, 'I forgive you';
or 'We forgive you and we do not hold this against you.'

It changed things tremendously.

I was throwing up all over the house and she hung on to my rear end, and
    I said,
'Oh my god, this is so humiliating.'
And she said, 'Oh, fuck it, this is the bonding moment.'
That's her. Wow, how did that make me feel?
It made me laugh. It stopped the pain for a moment and made me laugh.

Well, for me, the great threshold is to do something.

And, you know, everybody put their arms around me and said,
'We want things to work out'
and everybody was offering help; it's incredible. People offering their
    services,
whether it's watch your house, take your dog, can I go to the store for
    you?
Bring you meals, cover your desk.
And you don't forget that. You do not forget that.

To actually feel what other people felt
and the ability to insist that the feeling be addressed.

She is very conscious of graduate students and adjuncts who are women
and who are struggling;
who are alone;
who are barely making it financially;
and she argues long and hard with the dean fearlessly on their behalf
to keep them in their classes.

Compassion is not in that sense a quality or a thing, it's a capacity.

I mean, we say the right things; we say that people are important,
our most important resource,
but then look at – what do people really need?
I think most people really need to feel that somewhere along the line
they're doing something valuable,
or right, or meaningful, or it's appreciated;
People work more hours than is humanly possible
and they get criticized for their mistakes
more than thanked for what they do well.

I mean, I just honestly believe that you have the moment;
An opportunity right then for something that may never come up again.
It's hard to live in the truth of that.

The story of my life is not dealing with pain;
dealing with pain is what I have to do to have my life.

So I think it's where the humanity of one person meets the humanity of
    another person.
This is a really significant thing:
If an organization can be listening and caring and compassionate.
That was what the whole miracle was. We did get to do that.
Because there is so much;
People suffer so alone and there is so much.

Acknowledgements

An earlier version of this chapter was presented at the Academy of Management National Meetings, Chicago, 8–11 August 1999. We wish to thank the colleagues whom we interviewed for the generous contributions of time and insight. Thanks to Martha Feldman, Stephen Fineman, Linda Groat, Jane Hassinger, Deb Meyerson, Beth Reed, Denise Rousseau and Amy Wrezesniewski for comments on earlier drafts. We also wish to thank the William Russell Kelly Professorship for its support of this project.

Note

1 We interviewed 22 people from three university settings, including faculty, staff
   and students. They told us stories of their own pain, of the pain they have seen in
   others, and of the ways in which they have been the givers, the receivers, and the
   observers of compassionate acts in organizations. We have given fictional names
   to our informants to provide them with anonymity and to protect their
   confidences. The people we interviewed were all people we knew and people with
   whom we had some connection. The connection to our interviewees was
   consequential in how the interviews unfolded and the kinds of stories shared. Our

interviews were often conversations – sharing what we had learned from our own life experiences about what compassion is and how it works (or does not work) in the organizations that we inhabit as places of employment and as places of study.

References

Barry. D. and Elmes, M. (1997) 'Strategy retold: toward a narrative view of strategy discourse', *Academy of Management Review*, 22 (2): 428–52.

Bass, B.M. (1990) *Bass and Stodgill's Handbook of Leadership*. New York: Free Press.

Batson, C.D. (1991) *The Altruism Question: Toward a Social-Pychological Answer*. Hillsdale, NJ: Erlbaum.

Batson, C.D. (1994) 'Why act for the public good: 4 answers', *Personality and Social Psychological Bulletin*, 20 (5): 603–10.

Baumeister, R. and Leary, M. (1995) 'The need to belong: desire for interpersonal attachments as a fundamental human motivation', *Psychological Bulletin*, 117 (3): 497–529.

Belenky, M.F., Clinchy, B.M., Goldberger, N.R. and Tarule, M. (1986) *Women's Ways of Knowing*. New York: Basic Books.

Bell, N. and Staw, B.M. (1989) 'People as sculptors vs. sculpture: the roles of personality and personal control in organizations', in M.B. Arthur, D.T. Hall and B.S. Lawrence (eds), *The Handbook of Career Theory*. Cambridge: Cambridge University Press.

Benner, P., Tanner, C. and Chesla, C. (1996) *Expertise in Nursing Practice: Caring, Clinical Judgment and Ethics*. New York: Springer Publishing Company.

Berscheid, E. (1994) 'Interpersonal relationships', *Annual Review of Psychology*, 45: 79–129.

Boje, D. (1991) 'The storytelling organization: a study of story performance in an office-supply firm', *Administrative Science Quarterly*, 36 (1): 106–26.

Bradbury, H. and Lichtenstein, B. (1999) 'Relationality in organizational research: exploring the space between'. Working paper.

Brass, D.J. (1985) 'Men's and women's networks: a study of interaction patterns and influences on organizations', *Academy of Management Journal*, 28: 327–43.

Buber, M. (1974) *I and Thou*. New York: Macmillan Publishing.

Cialdini, R. (1999) 'Of tricks and tumors: some little-recognized costs of dishonest use of effective social influence', *Psychology and Marketing*, 18 (2): 91–8.

Czarniawska, B. (1998) *A Narrative Approach to Organization Studies*. Thousand Oaks, CA: Sage.

Dalai Lama (1981) *The Power of Compassion*. London: Thorsons.

Dillard, A. (1995) *Mornings Like This: Found Poems*. New York: HarperCollins Publishers.

Dutton, J., Debebe, G. and Wrzesniewski, A. (1999) 'Being valued and devalued at work: a social valuing perspective'. Working paper, University of Michigan, Ann Arbor.

Fineman, S. (1993) *Emotions in Organizations*. London: Sage.

Fletcher, J. (1999) *Disappearing Acts: Gender, Power and Relational Practice at Work*. Cambridge, MA: MIT Press.

Frank, A.W. (1992) 'The pedagogy of suffering: moral dimensions of psychological therapy and research', *Theory and Psychology*, 2: 467–85.

Frost, P.F. (1999) 'Why compassion counts', *Journal of Management Inquiry*, 8 (2): 127–33.

Frost, P. and Robinson, S. (1999) 'The toxic handler: organizational hero and casualty', *Harvard Business Review*, July–August, 96–106.

Gersick, C., Bartunek, J.M. and Dutton, J.E. (2000) 'Learning from academia: the importance of relationships in professional life', *Academy of Management Journal*, forthcoming.

Goleman, D. (1995) *Emotional Intelligence*. New York: Bantam Books.

Goleman, D. (1998) *Working with Emotional Intelligence*. New York: Bantam Books.

Granovetter, M.S. (1973) 'The strength of weak ties', *American Journal of Sociology*, 78 (6): 1360–80.

Hallowell, E.M. (1999) 'The human moment at work', *Harvard Business Review*, Jan.–Feb., 58–66.

Hochschild, A.R. (1983) *The Managed Heart: Commercialization of Human Feeling*. Berkeley: University of California Press.

Ibarra, H. (1992) 'Homophily and differential returns: sex differences in network structure and access in an advertising firm', *Administrative Science Quarterly*, 37: 422–47.

Ibarra, H. and Smith-Lovin, L. (1997) 'New directions in social network research on gender and organizational careers', in C.L. Cooper and S. Jackson (eds), *Creating Tomorrow's Organization: A Handbook for Future Research in Organizational Behavior*. Sussex: John Wiley & Sons.

Jacques, R. (1992) 'Critique and theory building: producing knowledge from the kitchen', *Academy of Management Review*, 17 (3): 582–606.

Jacques, R. (1993) 'Untheorized dimensions of caring work: caring as structural practice and caring as a way of seeing', *Nursing Administration Quarterly*, 17 (2): 1–10.

Kahn, W.A. (1993) 'Caring for the caregivers: patterns of organizational caregiving', *Administrative Science Quarterly*, 38 (4): 539–63.

Kahn, W.A. (1998) 'Relational systems at work', in B.M. Staw and L.L. Cummings (eds), *Research in Organizational Behavior*, vol. 20. Greenwich, CT: JAI Press. pp. 39–76.

Kolb, D. (1992) 'Women's work: peacemaking in organizations', in D. Kolb and J. Bartunek (eds), *Hidden Conflict in Organizations*. Newbury Park, CA: Sage.

Kornfield, J. (1993) *A Path with Heart*. New York: Bantam Books.

Lawrence-Lightfoot, S. (1999) *Respect*. Reading, MA: Perseus Books.

Martin, J., Feldman, M.S., Hatch, M.J. and Sitkin, S.B. (1983) 'The uniqueness paradox in organizational stories', *Administrative Science Quarterly*, 28: 438–53.

Meyerson, D.E. (1998) 'Feeling stressed and burned out: a feminist reading and re-visioning of stress-based emotions within medicine and organizational science', *Organizational Science*, 8 (1): 103–18.

Miller, J.B. and Stiver, I. (1997) *The Healing Connection*. Boston, MA: Beacon Press.

Mumby, D.K. and Putnam, L.L. (1992) 'The politics of emotion: a feminist reading of bounded emotionality', *Academy of Management Review*, 17: 465–86.

Noddings, N. (1984) *Caring: A Feminine Approach to Ethics and Moral Education*. Berkeley, CA: University of California Press.

O'Connor, E.S. (1996) 'Telling decisions: the role of narrative in organizational decision making', in Z. Shapira (ed.), *Organizational Decision Making*. New York: Cambridge University Press. pp. 304–23.

Pearson, C. and Porath, C. (1999) 'Workplace incivility: the target's eye view'. Paper presented at the national Academy of Management Meetings, Chicago.

Pfeffer, J. (1981) 'Management as symbolic action: the creation and maintenance of organizational paradigms', in L.L. Cummings and Barry M. Staw (eds), *Research in Organizational Behavior*, vol. 3. Greenwich, CT: JAI Press.

Rafaeli, A. and Sutton, R. (1987) 'Expression of emotions as part of the work role', *Academy of Management Review*, 12: 23–37.

Rafaeli, A. and Sutton, R. (1989) 'The expression of emotion in organizational life', in L. Cummings and B. Staw (eds), *Research in Organizational Behavior*, vol. 11. Greenwich, CT: JAI Press. pp. 1–42.

Sandelands, L.E. (1998) *Feeling and Form in Social Life*. Lanham, MD: Rowman & Littlefield.

Shotter, J. (1995) 'The manager as practical author: a rhetorical-responsive, social constructionist approach to social organizational problems', in D. Hosking, H. Dachler and K. Gergen (eds), *Management and Organizations: Relationship Alternatives to Individualism*. Aldershot: Avebury.

Solomon, R.C. (1998) 'The moral psychology of business: care and compassion in the corporation', *Business Ethics Quarterly*, 8 (3): 515–33.

Uzzi, B. (1996) 'The sources and consequences of embeddedness for the economic performance of organizations: the network effect', *American Sociological Review*, 61: 674–98.

Weick, K.L. and Browning, L. (1986) 'Argument and narration in organizational communication', in J.G. Hunt and J.D. Blair (eds), *1986 Yearly Review of Management of the Journal of Management*, 12 (2): 243–59.

3 FEELING AT WORK

LLOYD E. SANDELANDS AND
CONNIE J. BOUDENS

It seems psychology hasn't got feeling quite right. It thinks feeling is a moment's appraisal of opportunity or threat on the way to approach or avoidance, yet we live among powerful and enduring moods that lack a clear evaluation or motive. And psychology thinks feeling is an individual affair, yet at the office water cooler, or in the tavern or therapist's office, we hear stories of feeling tangled in webs of personal and group relationships. The more psychology thinks about feeling, the more we feel it has got it wrong.

Our discomfort with the idea of feeling grows with anthropology's wagging finger of cultural bias. Most people in most times and most places do not intellectualize feeling and do not individualize feeling the way that psychology does today in the West. Watts (1961), for example, identifies feeling in the Eastern tradition of Zen Buddhism with a natural social order of mutual interdependence and oneness in which persons are not rational individuals, but instead a-rational 'beings in relation'. And Levy-Bruhl (1926), for example, describes feeling in the 'primitive' cultures of the Melanesian islands, not as an individual event born of personal experiences and judgements, but as a feature of the person's participation in the living group. The Melanesian does not think of him/herself as separate from the group (indeed he/she does not think of him/herself at all), but rather as a 'member', literally a body-part, of the group. The Melanesian feels the group's aims and activities.

This chapter is frankly philosophical – not in the pejorative sense of verbal nitpicking, but in the positive sense of conceptual husbandry. Scientific concepts have two masters. There is a requirement for empirical content. Concepts must fit experiences. And there is a requirement for theoretical system. Concepts must together make a consistent and coherent whole. We find that prevailing concepts of feeling in psychology do not satisfy both masters. In particular, these concepts put theoretical system ahead of empirical content. Powerful assumptions and propositions define feeling apart from concrete experiences. Concepts of feeling are not abstracted from experience, but imposed on it. The result is theory too open to cultural bent and not enough open to human nature. In view of the failings of current theories of feeling, we suggest new ways of thinking about feeling.

Our focus in the chapter is captured in the play on words in the title. The chapter is both a study of how feeling works *and* a study of feeling at work. To the first point, we find that psychology misunderstands and gives short shrift to feeling because it does not see how feeling works in group life. It mistakes feeling as an experience and function of an autonomous actor. We find that feeling is not primarily an individual response, but a crucial faculty of a life lived in groups. People feel their parts in the life of the group. When welcomed in a safe, vital and active group, they feel secure, vital and active themselves, and take pleasure in these feelings. When confined in a moribund or passive group, they feel deadened and passive themselves, and take no pleasure in these feelings. And when excluded from the group, they feel worst of all – cut off, isolated, alone and unhappy. Feeling is how social life appears in consciousness.

To the second point, we come to these conclusions about feeling from our studies of feeling in the workplace (see especially Sandelands, 1988; Boudens and Sandelands, 1999). Far from the psychological laboratory, which isolates people or collects them in ephemeral aggregates, the workplace enjoins people in the life of the group. Arguably, the workplace is the best place to study feeling. This is not only because as much as half of our waking life is spent at work. And it is not only because some of the most intense and varied forms of group life are found at work. Even more it is because the way work has evolved in the most industrialized nations, often in the name of 'progress', has created crises of feeling for many workers from which we can learn a great deal. Technical concerns of machinery and optimization have been put ahead of human concerns for a stable and emotionally satisfying group life (Mayo, 1945). Where the human heart is broken we learn of what it is made.

We begin the chapter by setting the stage. First, we describe the idea of work feeling in psychology today. Second, we compare this idea against feelings people report at work. We then take up the main argument of the chapter, which also comes in two parts. First, we argue that psychology misrepresents feelings at work by turning them into something they are not, rational assessments of job satisfaction. Second, we show how work feelings are more accurately and fully represented in stories about group life at work. We conclude the chapter with ideas about how research on work feelings should proceed.

Feeling in theory

Current concepts of feeling reflect a powerful tradition of Western culture that diminishes feeling in favour of reason. Beginning in the rationalism of the Greeks, Aristotle and especially Plato, continuing into the Renaissance in thinkers such as Descartes, Locke and Hume, and carrying into today's rational choice theories of Bentham, modern economics, and psychology, there has been a strong conviction that human action, unlike that of lower animals, originates in reason, and is ideally uncoloured by emotion. In all but a few domains, emotion is regarded as the enemy of reason, as something to be managed and overcome (see also Fineman, 1996). We have subordinated emotion to reason so completely and for so long that we no longer question its marginality. We build special quarters for the exercise and display of emotion, such as the concert hall, movie theatre, football field and therapist's office. Where emotions are especially intense, such as in love or grief, we confine them in ceremonies or rituals to regulate their appearance and expression.

With a focus on reason has come a focus on the individual. The individual reasons and the individual acts. Whereas emotion has traditionally been regarded as what makes people alike, reason is what distinguishes among them (Zajonc, 1998). Psychology today combines a focus on reason with a focus on the individual, to see emotion as a special form of reasoning: as valenced or 'hot' cognition. Feeling is identified with appraisal. Feelings are said to result from assessments of the *personal* significance of situations or events (Arnold, 1960; Solomon, 1976; Lazarus, 1991; Cacioppo and Gardner, 1999). Some of these assessments are made crudely and rapidly (Lazarus, 1991). Many are made unconsciously (Freud, 1920) or non-consciously (Greenwald and Banaji, 1995). All are supposed to have evolved for the benefit of the *individual* organism (Cacioppo and Gardner, 1999; Zajonc, 1998).

This Western conception of feeling is epitomized in studies of feeling at work. These studies of work psychology keep to mainstream assumptions that feeling is rational and individual. Moreover, these studies canvas work and workplaces rationally designed to keep feelings out of the way and under control. The most commonly studied feeling, by far, is rational and individual to its core – job satisfaction. According to Locke (1976: 1300), job satisfaction is 'a pleasurable or positive emotional state resulting from the appraisal of one's job or job experiences'. The most widely cited theory of job satisfaction, by far, is the Job Characteristics Theory formulated by Hackman and Oldham (1976). According to this theory, jobs that offer greater task identity and task variety, that allow for the use of varied skills, and that supply greater autonomy and knowledge of results, are judged to be more satisfying. Further, according to this theory, these relationships are most developed in persons whose needs for individual growth are most developed. Again, work feelings are reasoned judgements people make about themselves at work.

Feeling in fact

It is good to have a strong and clear idea of feeling. It is even better to have an idea of feeling that fits the facts. We want to know how well psychology's idea of feeling fits the facts of feeling at work. We want to know where is the feeling in work and what is the nature of this feeling.

We turned to three sources to find out how people feel about their work (for details, see Boudens and Sandelands, 1999). Two were studies of work today. Terkel (1972) invited 133 workers, of various ages, ethnicity and social status, and employed in a variety of occupations, to talk about their work. His book consists of edited interview transcripts and offers minimal analysis or interpretation. Garson (1975) also invited workers to talk about their work, but unlike Terkel concentrated on low-level workers from a few manufacturing concerns: among them a maker of ping-pong equipment, a fish cannery, a cosmetics factory and a car assembly plant. Her book consists of interview excerpts and summaries along with her own observation and commentary. A third source was Hamper's (1986) best-selling chronicle of his life and times working on a car assembly line. Organized in loose chronology, his book is a compendium of vivid anecdotes and tales.

Our first finding was a surprise. When asked about their jobs, people do not talk much about what they actually do. They are not closely attuned to their movements. In jobs that demand little attention, they stow their minds away in daydream. In jobs that require them to think ahead, they look past the moment to focus on goals or ends. The physical details of the job (its tasks, working conditions, movements, skills) seem to matter little to its feeling. Indeed, most jobs involve a high degree of efficient repetition. And this is as true of white collar and professional occupations as blue or pink collar occupations – heart surgery is a lot of standing on your feet and painstaking cutting, clamping and sewing. Where physical details are felt it is usually in crude terms of wear; as fatigue, tension or stress.

Also a surprise, we found that while people occasionally talk about their desire for meaningful work, this desire is not, as theories of job satisfaction would have it, born of a concern for personal growth, or 'self-actualization' (Argyris, 1957; Maslow, 1954). People are not concerned to be all they can be on the job. They are also not concerned to shed social convention to feel, think and act for themselves, as individuals. What people want for meaning is more modest and mundane. It is a connection to others. Here, for example, is one of Terkel's (1972) informants, Kitty Scanlan, an assistant professor of occupational therapy, on working with others:

> Until recently, I wasn't sure how meaningful my work was. I had doubts. A surgeon does a really beautiful job. That's meaningful to him *immediately*. But it's not the kind of sustaining thing that makes a job meaningful. It must concern the relationship you have with the people you work with. We get hung up in the competition: 'Who's responsible for saving this life?' 'Who's responsible for the change in this dying patient?' Rather than saying, 'Isn't it beautiful that we all together helped make this person's life better?' (p. 494, original emphasis)

Another informant, Steven Simony-Gindele, finds the meaning of work to be a pretence of intellectuals, who have never worked themselves but who nevertheless seek grandiosity in something higher, beyond the work itself.

> The Depression in the thirties was a unique period. People were willing to work and there wasn't work around. I think the mentality of the thirties and the mentality today is different. Now the thing is to want something *meaningful*. I despise that word. They must be willing to take whatever they find and they must

grow from that. *Fulfilling*, that's another one they stumble on. I didn't start out as president of a company with a hundred thousand subscribers. It was necessary for me to scrub toilets. I scrubbed them. Not that I liked doing it. But I didn't feel debased by it. It was better than doing nothing. Any work is better than no work. Work makes a person noble.

This is a lie about meaningful work. It comes from teachers, Ph.D.'s who've never really worked. They feel they have a special knowledge to impose upon a lower being, who goes to work when he's thirteen or fifteen and settles down and goes forwards . . . (pp. 449–50, original emphasis)

We believe Simony-Gindele's thoughts point in a useful direction. Current ideas about the meaning and feeling of work reflect values of limited generality. No doubt many academics value work that is personally challenging and that affords opportunities for personal growth. Intellectual work is solitary and growth oriented. But this is not true of all people and all work. The meaning and feeling of work may be other than or more complex than theories of job satisfaction say.

Our most important positive finding in Terkel, Garson, and Hamper is that when people talk about work, they talk primarily about other people. They talk about relationships, about the intrigues, conflicts, gossips and innuendoes of group life. They talk about their friendships and the importance of camaraderie at work. There is endless fascination in this, and endless feeling. Feeling has mostly to do with the life of the group – with its divisions and play. Contest and conflict are the engines of feeling at work. Status is a principal dynamic within and between groups. Conflicts between workers, unions and management are also important dynamics. People are pleased to be in the group on top, or at least in a group above others, and are miserable to be in the group at the bottom or beneath others. A great deal of feeling goes into the relationship between workers and management, a relationship often passionately antagonistic and full of intrigue. Workers' feeling runs hot in stories of abuse by managers or stories of union organizing and retribution. Managers' feeling runs hot in stories of worker laziness, ingratitude and subterfuge, or stories of being unjustly cast as ogres. One senses people feel most alive and most energized when there is a battle or war going on. No slight or humiliation is too small to nurse and add to the litany. Nostalgia waxes for the heady days of the wildcat strike or union revolution.

We found innumerable ties between worker's feelings and their involvement in the group. Of these, a few relate positive feelings, as in this example from Garson (1975) of a university keypunch operator speaking of her pleasure in an unspoken involvement with the operator seated next to her:

'This'll sound crazy', she said, 'but I like to keep a certain rhythm . . . sound going. I mean I'd move forward when the woman next to me was halfway through another field and then she'd move in when I was halfway through the next. So

you'd get a constant – like, bum, bum, bum, zing, bum, bum, bum, babum, zing.
You could only do that with certain jobs.'

'. . . No, no, she didn't know what I was doing. If she slowed down I'd sort of
slow down, but if she made a mistake or stopped I'd just have to go on.' (p. 155)

More common are negative feelings, in which a person is angry or hurt
by being slighted or rejected by the group. One is reminded of the troubled
attachments people feel toward parents. Hamper (1986) offers a case in point
in a story about his friend Jack.

Jack also presented me with one of my first confrontations with an enigma that
had been bothering me since I had hired in. He was so resolute in his hatred toward
General Motors that it completely baffled me as to why he hung around. He had
this persecution complex that ate at him like a bellyful of red ants. I didn't really
understand it. I was still relatively raw, but I assumed that a deal was deal. GM
paid us a tidy income and we did the shitwork. No one was holding a gun to
anyone's head. I didn't harbor any hatred toward GM. My war was with that
suffocating minute hand. With Jack, General Motors was the taproot for all that
was miserable and repellent in his life. To hear him tell it, GM was out to bury
him. He was obsessed with vengeance and anarchy . . .

Whenever I asked Jack why he just didn't quit and move on to something that
was less aggravating, he would jump all over me. 'Goddamnit, that's *precisely*
what they're banking on. That I'll weaken and bow to their endless tyranny. NO
WAY! They'll have to drag me out of here.' (pp. 49–50, original emphasis)

Rare compared to the frequency of positive and negative feelings of life
in the group are alienated or isolated feelings of being cut off from the
group. Terkel (1972) supplies a troubling example of a nurse's aide, Cathleen
Moran, whose work in a helping profession could not compensate or
overcome her aloof detachment:

I don't know any nurse's aide who likes it. You say, 'Boy, isn't that rewarding that
you're doing something for humanity?' I say, 'Don't give me that, it's a bunch of
boloney.' I feel nothin'. I like it because I can watch ball games in the afternoon.

That's why if I'm a nurse, I'd go into administrative work and I'd work in
surgery. The only thing you have to deal with in surgery is who you work with.
You don't have to deal with the patient – like sympathize with them and say, 'Gee,
we couldn't get all the cancer out', and stuff like that. I like working in ICU because
they're all half-dead, and you can give a patient good care and not have to deal
with them. I'd enjoy that. It's terrible. (p. 477)

I never thought of myself in terms of a machine – though that's what I am. I don't
have no feelings. I do, but somehow I don't have them any more. I can't explain.
Its kinda goofy. (p. 478)

Hamper (1986) provides a vivid picture of the social nature of work feeling
in the following exchange with his friend Dave. We see how feeling rests with
the life of the group: no life, no feeling.

After Dave had transferred, I occasionally visited him on his new job. I couldn't find a solitary reason to envy his relocation. All Dave did all night was shuffle back and forth poking an occasional dipstick into some half hidden hole and yawning like a hippo in the mud. His neighbors resembled the Stepford Wives at a linen sale. It was fuckin' eerie. No revelry, no pranks, no communication, no turmoil, no nothin'. No, thank you. (p. 148)

In sum, when people talk about their work and its feelings they rarely speak of what they do on the job or the meaning of the job. They talk almost exclusively about their involvement in the life of the group, including the need to limit or regulate this involvement. Feelings are not identified with evaluations of the job, even less with personal growth and development. Instead, feelings are strongly identified with a person's place and activities in the life of the group and the place of their work in the larger scheme of things. Pleasure is taken in certain involvements, pain in other involvements, and detachment or boredom in still other involvements. Work feelings vary in almost infinite degree, but always the group figures as a key element.

Upon these bare clues we come to an idea of feeling at odds with theories of job satisfaction. We come to an idea of feeling that is not embedded in job tasks or rewards, but in the life of the group at work. Feeling comes in one's relationship with others and the group. People say little about what they do on the job, but more about how they get along with others. We come to an idea of feeling tied not to static appraisals of the job but to living experiences on the job with others. Experiences of work, like experiences of relationship with others, are never constant; they change from moment to moment. This is why Hamper's and Terkel's and Garson's informants do not speak of feelings in the past tense, but always as a continuing dynamic feature of their work life.

As we are about to suggest, scientific psychology misses feelings by thinking of them too much as static appraisals rather than as ongoing experiences, and by focusing too much on individuals and not enough on groups. For missing the ongoing experience of life in the group, scientific psychology misses feelings. We find that study of feelings at work calls attention to the social dimensions of feeling, and particularly calls attention to the forms of the person's involvement in the group.

Feeling lost

Theories of job satisfaction do not work as well as they should, either to predict feelings on the job or to predict outcomes of feelings such as work motivation, performance, commitment and turnover (Brief, 1998; Côté, 1999; Wright and Doherty, 1998). It is rare to find correlation coefficients exceeding 0.30 and thus to find more than 10% of variance in outcomes explained by job satisfaction.

The empirical deficiencies of job satisfaction theories begin with the concept of job satisfaction itself. This concept is a poor map of work feeling for two reasons. First, job satisfaction and work feeling are different kinds of psychic states. Job satisfaction is what philosophers call an intention. It is an inner state, of evaluation, that refers to an outer object, the job. The person stands apart from the job as its judge. Thus, Hackman and Oldham (1976) describe job satisfaction as an individual evaluation of objective job characteristics. Work feeling, however, is not an intention. It is an inner state that refers to no outer object. Work feeling is *of* work, not *about* work. The person is, in an entirely non-mystical sense, one with the work. James (1890) describes feeling as an appearance of bodily activity in consciousness. Bruner (1962) describes feeling as a play of impulses at the fringe of awareness. And echoing these views, Sandelands (1988) describes work feeling as an aspect of doing on the job. 'Feeling and doing are coexistent, coterminous, and coordinate. Feeling merges with doing and is experienced as a quality of its form' (p. 439). Although feelings may be subsequently attributed to specific entities (such as jobs), or to characteristics thereof (such as job characteristics), such attributions come only after the fact, upon further thinking. This difference of intentionality between job satisfaction and feeling implies that the former is more logical and reasonable than the latter. Job satisfaction is supposed to be stable and internally consistent. One cannot both think well and think poorly of one's job. A job is good or bad, hard or easy, boring or exciting. Indeed it is this very consistency that allows researchers to construct reliable questionnaires to measure job satisfaction. Work feeling, however, is not stable or internally consistent. Just as we can feel both love and hate in relations with significant others, we can feel both love and hate in our work, even at the same time.

Second, and related, job satisfaction is a poor map of work feeling because the two belong to different things. Job satisfaction is a property of the individual; it is a judgement he/she makes about his/her job. Work feeling is a property of the group; it is an awareness of its living form. As noted earlier, in Terkel, Garson, and Hamper we find that feelings always involve the group. This is not the surprise it seems. The group turns out to be a central figure even in theories of job satisfaction that are supposed to be about individuals. To wit, a close look at the job characteristics said to decide feelings by Hackman and Oldham (1976) finds they are not about a person working on a job alone, but about a person immersed in the life of a group. *Autonomy* is not simply about the person's ability to decide actions for him/herself. Even more it is about the person's responsibility in the group, a responsibility that fixes his/her place in the group and directs his/her attentions and energies in the life of the group. Likewise *task identity* and *task significance* are more than personal vanities. They indicate one's place in the social scheme, as central or peripheral, valued or not, needed for a reason. To have a job that relates obviously and importantly to the work of the group is to be firmly put in the life of the group. And finally, *feedback* is not only about the self-satisfaction and esteem of accomplishment. It is also about being noticed and recognized by the group, perhaps for doing something of value to the group. Hackman and Oldham confuse group life and feeling with individual experience and judgements of job satisfaction. Their confusion notwithstanding, feelings belong to the group, not to the individual.

Thus, theories of job satisfaction misread work feeling as a personal judgement about an objective job. Job satisfaction is no feeling. Whereas job satisfaction is an intention, work feeling is not. Whereas job satisfaction is of the mind, work feeling is of the body. Whereas job satisfaction is personal, work feeling is social. And whereas job satisfaction is static, work feeling moves. As we might expect, the mistake in the idea of job satisfaction is clearest where work feeling is clearest – as for example in instances of play, art, flow, transcendence and peak experience. Here ideas of job satisfaction based on judgements of objective job characteristics become awkward, heavy, even ugly. According to writers such as Koch (1956), Bruner (1962), Buber (1958) and Sandelands and Buckner (1989), to explain such poignant feelings there is no use in objective appraisals. In these instances, the person merges with the group, the person merges with the job, and feeling comes not by evaluation or thinking, but directly and unmediated through the body (it is 'bodied forth', in Buber's terms). In these instances, the person becomes one with the work and one with the group, as this report by Hamper (1986) illustrates:

> After about four months down on the Rivet Line, I had truly perfected the mental and physical strain of the pin-up job. The blisters of the hand and the mind had hardened over, leaving me the absolute master of the puppet show. I developed shortcuts at every turn. I became so proficient at twirlin' my rivet gun to and fro that the damn thing felt as comfortable as a third arm. I mashed my duties into pitiful redundancy.

> The truth was loose: I was the son of a son of a bitch, an ancestral prodigy born to clobber my way through loathsome dung heaps of idiot labor. My genes were cocked and loaded. I was a meteor, a gunslinger, a switchblade boomerang hurled from the pecker driblets of my forefathers' untainted jalopy seed. I was Al Kaline peggin' home a beebee from the right field corner. I was Picasso applyin' the final masterstroke to his frenzied *Guernica*. I was Wilson Pickett stompin' up the stairway of the Midnight Hour. I was one blazin' tomahawk of m-fuggin' eel snot. Graceful and indomitable. Methodical and brain-dead. The quintessential shoprat. The Rivethead. (p. 94)

We could ask Ben Hamper to tell us about the objective characteristics of his job (about its skill variety, identity, significance, autonomy and feedback), but this would bring us no closer to understanding his feelings than asking him the time of day. His feelings have nothing to do with the objective job.

Whitehead (1937) observed that ideas relate to experiences in different ways. Properly scientific ideas are abstracted from experiences. They distil the essence of experiences. Improperly scientific ideas are put over on experience, like a wool cap. They do not follow experience, but abduct experience to their own ends. We believe psychology puts ideas of feeling such as job satisfaction ahead of experiences of feeling. And we believe psychology, as a result, does not see feeling as it is. Feeling takes the shape of the theoretical mould into which it has been poured. Work feelings are fitted to the concept of job satisfaction, rather than the other way around. Work feelings have not had a chance to make themselves known.

Feeling found

We need new concepts to represent feelings: concepts true to experiences, not imposed on them by theory. The irony of this need is that the problem of putting feelings to words is met and mastered all the time in daily life, by everyone *except* scientists who demand that language be used literally and denotatively. The key to conveying feeling appears to be indirection. In the three works we examined, people rarely speak directly of their feelings at work. They speak instead about significant events and especially about relationships at work. When people do name a feeling at work – 'I am happy in my job' or 'I feel like a robot at the plant' or more commonly 'I find work stressful' – they rarely go on to describe or explain the feeling. It is as if stating a feeling leads nowhere and leaves nothing more to say. More typically, when people name a feeling at work, they follow it up with a story about an event at work that exemplifies the feeling. Indeed, a common pattern is to name a feeling either just before or just after telling a story about the job, as if to preview or summarize the feeling of the story. A case in point is this excerpt from one of Terkel's informants, a piano tuner named Eugene Russell. The excerpt begins and ends with a stated feeling sandwiched around a story:

> I have a mood of triumph. I was sitting one day tuning a piano in a hotel ballroom. There was a symposium of computer manufacturers. One of these men came up and tapped me on the shoulder. 'Someday we're going to get your job.' I laughed. 'By the time you isolate an infinite number of harmonics, you're going to use up a couple of billion dollars' worth of equipment to get down to the basic fundamental that I work with my ear.' He said, 'You know something? You're right. We'll never touch your job.' The cost of computerized tuning would be absolutely prohibitive. I felt pretty good at that moment. (pp. 322–3)

If people do not often name their feelings and almost never describe them, how do they get them across? And how do readers of Terkel, Garson, and Hamper come away with a clear sense of the feeling of work? When we ask where is feeling in people's accounts of work, we find it not in statements of feeling, but in stories about work. We found stories everywhere in the accounts of work we studied, 399 in all. Terkel's book is a compendium of life stories in which we find many shorter stories. Garson's interviews and Hamper's chronicle likewise comprise and consist of stories. These books succeed because their stories succeed. Their stories invite readers into the workplace, to see and feel what workers see and feel. Many of the stories are moving, some deeply so.

Narratives are ubiquitous in daily life. Theodore Sarbin conducts an informal ongoing survey of the way people talk about their emotions. He asks them to give him an illustration of a particular emotion; almost always they tell a story (Sarbin, 1989). Narratives organize experiences into coherent wholes (Polkinghorne, 1988). This tells us not only that stories are pervasive, but that they are a primary means of making sense of experience, and a common and well-accepted way of communicating that experience to others.

Given the prominence of stories as expressions of feeling in everyday life, it is no surprise that stories are an important means and method in psychotherapy, where they are used to elicit and convey emotion that cannot be brought out and expressed in any other way (Siegelman, 1990). It is a surprise, however, that for all the attention given them in clinical psychology, stories are ignored in other research disciplines of psychology focused on feeling, where they are thought too subjective and too idiosyncratic to lead to general understandings. This is a mistake.

Narratives have long been a staple in the study of human experience in the humanities. Lately, encouraged by the postmodern turn of the humanities away from scientific claims of objective truth, and by the multicultural turn of the humanities toward unique perspectives and personal truths, a number of behavioural and social scientists have embraced narratives as a means for discovering and validating the experiences of the disenfranchised (for example, Polkinghorne, 1988). We too urge the use of narratives in the human sciences, but not for these reasons. We believe, instead, that narratives can be used to discover universal human truths about the feelings and forms of human life. Campbell (1973), following Jung, showed that people of widely disparate cultures independently invented many of the same stories or myths. Stories, which can be repeated in folk tales, written down in scriptures, or limned on the walls of caves or pyramid burial chambers, are objects that represent universal human feelings and forms of life. By studying these objects we come to understand and know these feelings and forms. By studying these objects a science of feeling at work becomes possible.

How do stories work?

Where is the feeling in a story? Music is an apt comparison. In both instances, feeling is of the whole, is immanent in the whole (Langer, 1953; Davies, 1997). We feel the movements and dynamics – the life – of the whole. The psychological key to the success of music and narrative alike is empathy. Empathy is a perceptual capacity – probably our first and oldest perceptual capacity – to feel with others. Empathy is the ability to discern in the whole of a performance – be it a piece of music, or a story or a simple emotional outburst – the feeling that went into its making and informed its every part. Through empathy, the listener forges a connection to the performer that is more direct and fully developed than any that could be denoted in words.

We looked at stories of work to ask how they convey feelings. We found they do this the way all stories do, by epitomizing the felt forms of group life. This is effected by the story device of plot – a device like melody in music. Plots are not inert listings of events in sequence (first A happened, then B, then C), but rich patterns of play, opposition, conflict, cause and effect (Goodman, 1954). Plot is a Gestalt representation of group life. It links characters, actions, and events in a unified whole. And it is this unified whole that is felt. Aristotle described plot as 'unified action'. He found plot to be an abstract whole made of a stage-setting *beginning* which identifies characters and their intents, an action-developing and tension-articulating *middle* which brings characters into richer and more intense interaction, and a climactic, tension-resolving *end* which brings or reclaims a more stable order among the characters. Unlike the skeleton to which it is often and inaptly compared, plot is not an inert structure but a vital process, a living form. It is more organism than mechanism. By means of plot, stories convey living form in a way that invites a reader or listener to participate in it and to share its feelings. Thus, we come to an understanding of stories reached years ago by Goodman (1954):

> Then we can see the plausibility of looking for the importance of the experience in the internal structure of the presented work. When we are absorbed, the motions, proportions, and conflicts presented are the motions, proportions, and conflicts of our experiencing bodies (at rest, in isolation). And these motions, conflicts, and resolutions of experiencing *are* the various feelings, attitudes, and concerns that are important for us. Thus it is plausible to say, as we shall, 'Fear *is* such-and-such a sequence in the complex plot', or 'The characteristic attitude of Catullus *is* the Phalaecean rhythm'. (original emphasis)

Elsewhere, one of us, following Langer (1967), described art broadly as the objectification of feeling by living forms (see Sandelands and Buckner, 1989; Sandelands, 1998). Stories are a kind of art; a kind of living form that objectifies feeling. Stories share with other arts four basic features of form: boundaries, dynamic tensions, growth (movement), and possibility. *Boundaries* distinguish a story from other elements in the flow of communication. Boundaries allow a listener to appreciate the story openly, for what it is, an emotional communique. The story's *dynamic tensions* capture the listener's interest and draw him or her into the story by eliciting curiosity about what will happen next and especially about whether everything will turn out all right. *Growth* is that element of a story which projects a pathway for tensions to be elaborated and eventually released. Growth is a significant element of the story because it affirms life in the dimension of time. All living things change over time and most change in ways that indicate a cumulative development. Finally, *possibility* appears in the most artistic stories as a hint or indication that while a reconciliation of the story's immediate tensions may have been reached, there are questions and unresolved issues to ponder. The best stories invite the listener to return, to ask for more. These four elements conspire in the story to establish a semblance of life and feeling. All living things, all things that feel and are felt, are bounded in time and space, are animated by forces in constructive tension, are growing, and are full of unrealized possibility. These principal elements of life and feeling are the generic elements of art – art being our 'language' of life and feeling. Art is the most general name we have for objects or events found or made to represent life and feeling (Sandelands and Buckner, 1989; Sandelands, 1998).

By representing feeling at work, stories serve two important functions in the workplace. One is to collect and communicate the life and feeling of work. With stories people can grab hold of feelings that would be otherwise inexpressible and unmemorable. For better and worse, stories reinforce and amplify feelings at work. A second and probably more important function of stories is to define the group for those inside and outside the group. By virtue of who is included in them and who they are told to, stories are almost always, implicitly, about an 'us' and a 'them'. Stories are thus a powerful way that people learn about who they are and who they like and dislike. Certainly, a profound pleasure in many stories told at work, in the army, in church, among one's peers, especially those told in secret, is the sense of belonging they inspire.

We can illustrate the workings and functions of stories in representing the forms and feelings of work life with a story from Terkel (1972) by Diane Wilson, a process clerk in a social service bureaucracy, who recounts a morning with a boss, Mr Roberts:

> One day I'd gotten a call to go to his office and do some typing. He's given me all this handwritten script. I don't know to this day what all that stuff was. I asked him, 'Why was I picked for this job?' He said his secretary was out and he needs this done by noon. I said, 'I'm no longer a clerk-typist and you yourself said for me to get it out of my mind. Are you trying to get me confused? Anyway, I can't read this stuff.' He tells me he'll read it. I said, 'Okay, I'll write it out as you read it.'
>
> There's his hand going all over the script, busy. He doesn't know what he's reading', I could tell. I know why he's doing it. He just wants to see me busy.
>
> So we finished the first long sheet. He wants to continue. I said, 'No, I can only do one sheet at a time. I'll go over and type this up.' So what I did, I would type a paragraph and wait five or ten minutes. I made sure I made all the mistakes I could. It's amazing, when you want to make mistakes, you really can't. So I just put Ko-rect type paper over this yellow sheet. I fixed it up real pretty. I wouldn't stay on the margins. He told me himself I was no longer a clerk-typist.
>
> I took him back this first sheet and, of course, I had left out a line or two. I told him it made me nervous to have this typed by a certain time, and I didn't have time to proofread it, 'but I'm ready for you to read the other sheet to me'. He started to proofread. I deliberately misspelled some words. Oh, I did it up beautifully. (Laughs.) He got the dictionary out and he looked up the words for me. I took it back and crossed out the words and squeezed the new ones in there. He started on the next sheet. I did the same thing all over again. There were four sheets. He proofread them all. Oh, he looked so serious! All this time he's spendin' just to keep me busy, see? Well, I didn't finish it by noon.
>
> I'm just gonna see what he does if I don't finish it on time. Oh, it was imperative!

I knew the world's not gonna change that quickly. It was nice outside. If it gets to be a problem, I'll go home. It's a beautiful day, the heck with it. So twelve-thirty comes and the work just looks awful. (Laughs.) I typed on all the lines, I continued it anywhere. One of the girls comes over, she says, 'You're goin' off the line.' I said, 'Oh be quiet. I know what I'm doin'. (Laughs.) Just go away.' (Laughs.) I put the four sheets together. I never saw anything as horrible in my life. (Laughs.)

I decided I'd write him a note. 'Dear Mr. Roberts: You've been so much help. You proofread, you look up words for your secretary. It must be marvelous working for you. I hope this has met with your approval. Please call on me again.' I never heard from him. (A long laugh.) (pp. 350–1)

This story objectifies feeling in two ways. First, it depicts feelings of persons and groups. We see Wilson's vindictiveness punish Roberts and play ambivalently against accepted norms of responsible work. We see Roberts's cowing submission to Wilson and imagine his ambivalence in patronizing someone who manipulates him. And we see group feelings, as the disenfranchised enjoy revenge on the powerful, and as the powerful grapple with the exasperation and fear of failing to understand and control workers. Second, and more important theoretically, this story symbolizes the feeling of group life. This is the artistic function of the story. We see the excitement of a well-told story that builds to a climax and is then resolved with the question of what will happen and whose wishes will prevail. Here we do not feel the actions of either person alone – their separate movements on the job have little intrinsic meaning. Rather, we feel the actions of both persons as they together exemplify the life of the larger group. This story is not only or even primarily about the individuals Wilson and Roberts (it could be about anybody); it is a story about a living group riven by conflicts of status, dignity, work values and will.

Regarding this second more important function of the story, we can note how the artistic elements of living form represent feeling. Plot *boundaries* are marked by a clear beginning and end. The story begins, as if a fable, with a variant of 'Once upon a time' – in this case, 'One day I'd gotten a call'. The story ends, again as if a fable, with a variant of 'And they lived happily ever after' – in this case, 'I never heard from him again'. With these markers the listener recognizes the story as a bounded event, as an episode told to communicate feeling. Plot *tension* is established early in the story with the revelation that Wilson is no longer a clerk typist and resents being asked to perform in that capacity. With the tension of opposition established, the listener is drawn into the story, curious to know how it will turn out, and with what effects. The plot thickens and *grows* as this tension is elaborated in the middle of the story. The listener learns of the many obstacles Wilson has thrown Roberts's way and of the shoddy work she returns for his troubles to help her. The listener learns also of the impending deadline that promises to bring that conflict to a head. With this growth of tension the listener is drawn further into the story and further into its feelings. And finally, while the plot draws to a close with Wilson's snide note and departure from the scene, it leaves the listener to mull *possibilities* in wonder about what will become of the principals.

We can also look at this story to see how it functions in the workplace. A clear function of the story is to capture and hold onto the feelings of work. As noted, feelings of resentment, vindictive hostility, pride, self-satisfaction, ambivalence, patronizing submission, exasperation, frustration and excitement are conveyed by its basic elements of plot. For old-timers in the group, the story confirms familiar feelings. The story literally 're-minds' them of these feelings. For newcomers to the group, the story is a map of the workplace. Hearing the story, even for the first time, a newcomer learns what it feels like to work there. A related and perhaps more important function of the story – for old-timers and newcomers alike – is to make the group real (Sandelands, 1998). The story establishes the life of the group. It shows that the group is bounded in space and time, that the group is animated by tensions, that the group's tensions grow and develop through time, and that the group holds interest by reconciling tensions while leaving room for unresolved possibilities. By making the group real, the story answers the most basic human need to belong. By establishing the life of the group, the story brings interest and even a kind of joy to members who live in and through it.

For the note-taking and catalogue-making social scientist, this story articulates the structure and dynamics of the group. It shows how the group is divided into parts – in this case between management and staff – and how parts play with and upon one another to create social order. By defining the structure and process of the group, the story identifies key actors and locates them in time, space and relation. Thanks to Wilson's story, her troubled workplace is made a little more real and a little more comprehensible in the mind's eye. No doubt other stories would tell us more and help complete the picture.

We found a great many stories in Terkel, Garson, and Hamper that speak of the feelings and forms of work life. All of these stories could be analysed according to their artistic properties of living form and according to their functions in the workplace. Many of the better-told stories are moving and impossible to forget. They are poetry to cherish because they do their tellers and listeners the most good. To live among good stories is to really live.

Finally, we note that stories have a unique epistemological significance. They can tell a truth about feeling even while they tell many lies about fact. This is because a story states facts but exemplifies feelings. A story has to be put together a certain way, in light of a certain feeling, in order to be a story. A person tells a story about work and, accurate or not about details, we know the feeling. The emotional truth of a story is evident. This is a crucial point for scientists whose concern is with the truth. Stories supply truths about feeling at work, even when they are fables or myths.

Feeling's future

Fineman (1993) describes work organizations aptly as richly textured social dramas, 'emotional arenas'. We have argued that stories offer a unique and indispensable opportunity to study feeling at work. Stories are objects (scientists can collect them, analyse them, talk about them). Stories are general (people in all cultures and all places tell stories). And stories are indicative (they exemplify the feelings and forms of work). It remains, finally, to say a few words about how social scientists can use stories to study feeling at work.

The considerable scientific value of stories comes in their mapping of the feelings and forms of social life. This mapping suggests two courses for science to take. First, research is needed to explore how stories can be used to discover the feelings and forms of work. What kinds of stories are told about work? What do these stories tell us about the forms and feelings of work? And how do the forms and feelings of work map onto one another? Carlo Gozzi proposed that there are only 36 kinds of stories and only 36 kinds of emotions to go with these stories (see Polti, 1921). Rudyard Kipling said there were 69 kinds of stories and, presumably, 69 kinds of feelings in reading them (see Tobias, 1993). To answer such questions, we must collect as many stories about work as we can with the aim to establish their kinds and the aim to establish how they map feelings of work onto forms of work. To this end, the editor and several contributors to the present volume look at stories to chart the feelings and forms of organized life. We join these efforts in work that focuses on formal elements of story – particularly of setting, character and plot – that we believe represent formal elements of work life and feeling (see Boudens and Sandelands, 1999).

Second, research is needed to explore how feelings of work are used in creating, telling and enjoying stories about work. As noted earlier, psychotherapy shows that one way people come to terms with their feelings is by telling stories about their lives. By telling stories that capture their feelings people learn that they can change their feelings by changing their stories – that is, by altering the plot lines of their lives. We agree with Fineman (1993) to suppose that people at work use stories in the same way to come to terms with feelings and, in some cases, to change their feelings. To address this issue, we should ask people to create, tell and interpret stories at work. Then, by looking at the forms of stories, and by looking at the steps taken to create, tell and interpret stories, we can again see how feelings at work map onto the forms of work.

Stories are an appealing focus for research on work because they reveal its profoundly social and restlessly vital feeling. For too long researchers have studied feeling at work with measures of job satisfaction that mistake feeling for an intellectual judgement about an individual job. We have been at pains in this chapter to argue that feeling is not a judgement and is not about an individual job. Feeling at work is a non-intentional awareness of the life of the group. Feeling at work is symbolized figuratively in art forms such as stories. By offering an image of feeling faithful to its logical form and social nature, stories offer an objective basis for a science of feeling at work.

References

Argyris, C. (1957) *Personality in Organization*. New York: Harper & Brothers.

Arnold, M.B. (1960) *Emotion and Personality*. New York: Columbia University.

Boudens, C.J. and Sandelands, L.E. (1999) 'The narrative psychology of work'. Working paper, University of Michigan, Fall.

Brief, A.P. (1998) *Attitudes in and around Organizations*. Thousand Oaks, CA: Sage.

Bruner, J. (1962) *Essays for the Left Hand*. Cambridge, MA: Harvard.

Buber, M. (1958) *I and Thou*. New York: Charles Scribner's Sons.

Cacioppo, J.T. and Gardner, W.L. (1999) 'Emotion', *Annual Review of Psychology*, 50: 191–214.

Campbell, J. (1973) *The Mythic Image*. Princeton, NJ: Princeton.

Côté, S. (1999) 'Affect and performance in organizational settings', *Current Directions in Psychological Science*, 8: 65–8.

Davies, S. (1997) 'Contra the hypothetical persona in music', in M. Hjort and S. Laver (eds), *Emotion and the Arts*. New York: Oxford University Press. pp. 95–109.

Fineman, S. (1993) 'Organizations as emotional arenas', in S. Fineman (ed.), *Emotion in Organizations*. London: Sage. pp. 9–35.

Fineman, S. (1996) 'Emotion and organizing', in S.R. Clegg, C. Hardy and W.R. Nord (eds), *Handbook of Organization Studies*. London: Sage. pp. 543–64.

Freud, S. (1920) *A General Introduction to Psychoanalysis*. New York: Liveright.

Garson, B. (1975) *All the Livelong Day: The Meaning and Demeaning of Routine Work*. Garden City, NY: Doubleday.

Goodman, P. (1954) *The Structure of Literature*. Chicago: University of Chicago.

Greenwald, A. and Banaji, M.R. (1995) 'Implicit social cognition: attitudes, self-esteem, and stereotypes', *Psychological Review*, 102 (1): 4–27.

Hackman, J.R. and Oldham, G.R. (1976) 'Motivation through the design of work: test of a theory', *Organizational Behavior and Human Decision Processes*, 16: 250–79.

Hamper, B. (1986) *Rivethead: Tales from the Assembly Line*. New York: Warner Books.

James, W. (1890) *The Principles of Psychology*. New York: Holt.

Koch, S. (1956) 'Behavior as intrinsically "regulated": work notes towards a pre-theory of phenomena called "motivational"', in M.R. Jones (ed.), *Nebraska Symposium on Motivation*. Lincoln: University of Nebraska Press.

Langer, S.K. (1953) *Feeling and Form*. New York: Charles Scribner's Sons.

Langer, S.K. (1967) *Mind: An Essay on Human Feeling*, Vol. 1. Baltimore: Johns Hopkins University Press.

Lazarus, R. (1991) *Emotions and Adaptation*. New York: Oxford University Press.

Levy-Bruhl, L. (1926) *How Natives Think*. Princeton, NJ: Princeton University Press.

Locke, E.A. (1976) 'The nature and causes of job satisfaction', in M. Dunnette (ed.), *Handbook of Industrial and Organizational Psychology*. Chicago: Rand McNally.

Maslow, A.H. (1954) *Motivation and Personality*. New York: Harper & Brothers.

Mayo, E. (1945) *The Social Problems of an Industrial Civilization*. Boston: Harvard University Press.

Polkinghorne, D. (1988) *Narrative Knowing and the Human Sciences*. Albany, NY: State University of New York.

Polti, G. (1921) *The Thirty-Six Dramatic Situations*, trans. by L. Ray. Franklin, OH: James Knapp Reeve.

Sandelands, L.E. (1988) 'The concept of work feeling', *Journal for the Theory of Social Behavior*, 18 (4): 437–57.

Sandelands, L.E. (1998) *Feeling and Form in Social Life*. Lanham, MD: Rowman & Littlefield.

Sandelands, L.E. and Buckner, G.C. (1989) 'Of art and work: aesthetic experience and the concept of job satisfaction', in B.M. Staw and L.L. Cummings (eds), *Research in Organizational Behavior*, Vol. 11. Greenwich, CT: JAI Press.

Sarbin, T.R. (1989) 'Emotions as narrative emplotments', in M.J. Packer and R.B. Addison (eds), *Entering the Circle: Hermeneutic Investigation in Psychology*. Albany, NY: SUNY Press. pp. 185–201.

Siegelman, E.Y. (1990) *Metaphor and Meaning in Psychotherapy*. New York: Guilford Press.

Solomon, R. (1976) *The Passions*. Garden City, NY: Doubleday.

Terkel, S. (1972) *Working*. New York: The New Press.

Tobias, R. (1993) *Twenty Master Plots*. Cincinnati: Writer's Digest.

Watts, A. (1961) *Psychotherapy East and West*. New York: Random House.

Whitehead, A.N. (1937) *Adventures of Ideas*. New York: Macmillan.

Wright, T.A. and Doherty, E.M. (1998) 'Organizational behavior "rediscovers" the role of emotional well-being', *Journal of Organizational Behavior*, 19: 481–5.

Zajonc, R.B. (1998) 'Emotions', in D.T. Gilbert, S.T. Fiske and G. Lindzey (eds), *Handbook of Social Psychology*, Vol. 1, 4th edn. Boston: McGraw-Hill.

4 RELATIONAL EXPERIENCES AND EMOTION AT WORK

VINCENT R. WALDRON

I was falsely accused by a co-worker I had known for ten years of stealing from the family business. I had always turned to this co-worker for advice. Trust between us was shattered. I did not know what to say to him. I felt sorry for him, but hatred was my main emotion. I had this instinct to kill him for what he did to our business and our family. I will always remember the dejected look on my father's face.

Nearly 10 years of analysing hundreds of accounts like the one above convinces me that work relationships are more emotionally complicated than might be presumed from our academic literature. Not all of these accounts so clearly illustrate the interplay of work and personal allegiances. Not all (but more than one might expect) describe murderous intent. But, when asked, most working people easily recollect intense emotional experiences that punctuated their careers and reverberated across their relationship networks. Yet, in our haste to measure and quantify, we researchers have sometimes sanitized the emotional messiness of working life (Waldron, 1994). The restricted vocabulary of operationalized variables and standardized surveys seems particularly ill-suited for representing the passions that erupt forcefully, if only intermittently, to define and redefine relationships among co-workers.

Fortunately, we can draw from a variety of sources in developing a more nuanced appreciation of the emotional side of work relations. In contrast to most organizational cultures, Western popular culture embraces the role of emotion in relationships, celebrates it, sometimes wallows in it. With relentless prodding by radio psychologists, romance novelists, celebrity tabloid headlines, and daily soap operas, most of us can engage in an imaginative discourse about the myriad intersections of emotional and relational experience. The emotional tension of potential romance, the ecstasy of falling in love, the jealousy of relational competition, the anguish of relationship decay, the bitterness of divorce, the emotional tranquility of long-term partnership, the emotional numbing associated with long-term relational neglect are familiar themes. These are the obsession of modern magazines and certain Shakespearian dramas, of countless popular songs and more than a few operas, of religious texts produced thousands of years in the past and self-help books with a six-month shelf-life. Just by listening to the buzz of popular media we assimilate the language of 'emotional blackmail', 'love addiction', 'fear of commitment', and a hundred other terms that link emotions and personal relationships. It turns out that, in the accounts of working people, the language of work relationships is not that different.

Against this backdrop, the general reader can be forgiven for finding what researchers have had to say (until fairly recently) about organizational relationships to be, well, comparatively dull. For example, from management textbooks, one can learn that properly conducted supervisory relationships can be 'satisfying' and that that affect is a resource that can be 'exchanged' as part of the social contract between employee and employer (Day and Crain, 1992). And we know that the 'management' and 'regulation' of emotion is an essential part of customer service work. In the last decade, researchers have provided much richer accounts of the emotional fabric of organizational life (Fineman, 1993) and the emotional labour associated with the performance of work like customer service (for example, Wharton, 1993), policing (Stenross and Kleinman, 1989) and patient care (for example, Maynard, 1992). But the consuming emotional labour that is intrinsic to 'doing' work relationships has received too little attention, despite the fact that managing relationships with other 'team members' has become a substantial, if not the central, feature of the work of many employees (Waldron, 1999).

My purpose in this chapter is to illustrate just how important and varied emotional experience is in work relationships. I hope to stimulate researchers and general readers to ask different kinds of questions, to broaden the vocabulary of emotion at work. I do so in part by sharing accounts given to me by workers in a variety of public and private US organizations: production workers at a factory in the rural south; probation workers in the criminal justice system; clerks at a large payment processing centre in the southwest; members of a politically embattled government agency; attorneys and judges who negotiate plea bargains in criminal court.[1] For me, these accounts provide a window through which the most meaningful of work processes can be observed: the construction and destruction of human relationships.

Reframing emotion as a relational phenomenon

Emotional experience has been examined as an individual, cultural or political phenomenon in the organizational literature. All of these dimensions influence this chapter, but my primary interest is in exploring how organizational emotion is *relational*, a term I intend to have several meanings. First, organizational relationships constitute a unique context for emotional experience. Because work relationships have certain characteristics which can make them partially distinct from personal relationships, we experience emotions differently. Second, emotion can be a resource through which organizational relationships are created, interpreted and altered. Third, the interdependent nature of work roles creates the need in some organizations for collective emotional performances. Here emotion is relational in the sense that certain kinds of affect are experienced primarily because employees learn to work as partners in its production.

Work relationships as a unique context for emotional experience

The sources of organizational emotion at work are many. Catastrophic organizational events, like layoffs or plant closures are an obvious source of extreme emotion. It can be a reaction to bad news about one's performance, as when a worker's request for a raise is rejected (Wagoner and Waldron, 1999). But, in most accounts provided by employees, the dynamics of organizational relationships are among the most frequently cited sources of intense emotion. This point was illustrated in a study of probation officers and prison guards in the United States (Waldron and Krone, 1991). Organization members toiled daily at psychologically challenging, relatively low paid jobs. Their clients, convicted and potentially violent criminals often described as manipulative, were a frequent source of emotional stress. Yet, we found that these workers on the front lines of the justice system expected emotional abuse from clients and developed psychological defences against it. In contrast, it was their relations with co-workers and supervisors that caused them to experience deep, and in most cases negative, emotion.

One promising new recruit who had caught the eye of her supervisor because of her performance found work with the prisoners to be less stressful than dealing with a suspicious colleague, who:

> wrongly assumed that I was trying to make him look bad in front of our supervisor. He covertly tried to take revenge [by spreading rumours] but refused to talk about it. The emotional tension became so electric that I was emotionally drained just preparing for work each day. I felt traumatized and when he refused to cease his game playing, I swore at him, which only made the situation worse.

In my studies of organizations since that time, I have confirmed that it is nature of work relationships, not the nature of the task itself, that creates the highest potential for intense emotional experience, including emotional abuse. There are several features of work relationships that seem to explain this phenomenon.

Balancing public and private   As in personal liaisons, work relationships are governed by informal rules and expectations. Partners expect, for example, to be listened to, to be respected, to be taken seriously, to have the opportunity to correct relational injustices when they occur. The experiences of emotional tranquility and relational satisfaction are constructed in part from a history of conformity with these informal agreements. In intimate relations, agreements are negotiated and violated mostly in private.

In contrast, private and public dimensions of work relationships are in constant tension. Relationship violations often occur in public view, with limited options for recourse. Even when we manage to develop private arrangements, as when a leader privately shares 'inside information' with a trusted member, the bulk of their communication occurs in the open, subject to the expectations and scrutiny of peers. At work, relationship violations can be humiliatingly public. For example, if the member reveals the leaders' secrets, they may be quickly communicated down the hallways through gossip, discussed quietly in meetings, broadcast to the whole department through e-mails.

The public/private tension in work relationships can have the effect of intensifying emotional reactions. Consider the account provided by Helen, a first-rung manager at a government agency. Helen thought she 'had the ear' of the director, who frequently asked for her advice in their private talks. At a staff meeting in which the director described plans for the coming fiscal year, Helen recognized what she thought was a flaw in budget projections. Confident that her success in private conversations with the boss gave her credibility, Helen expressed her reservations in the staff meeting. She described being 'floored', 'hurt', and 'shocked' when the director reacted defensively with a derisive snort and dismissive rejection of her logic.

The emotional tyranny associated with public humiliation of the weak by the powerful is a common theme in the narratives I have collected from employees. An employee at a large bank reported an experience very similar to Helen's. He described his feelings:

> I was angry – felt humiliated and betrayed. [I] felt like I had been stabbed in the back, with no way to defend myself or explain my position. [Because of the audience] . . . I probably would not have confronted the senior management person in this meeting even if time permitted. . . . He forever damaged my credibility. I never trusted him again.

The emotional reaction seems most profound when the power differential between leader and member is pronounced, when the audience includes one's peers, when the violator's public behaviour conflicts with previously displayed private behaviour, and when the victim believes she or he is acting in the best interests of the organization (as opposed to self-interest). In the world of emotion work, public disqualification of this type is equivalent to the 'roundhouse punch' delivered by a heavyweight boxer.

In immediate response to this most public breach of the work relationship, a member faces a series of questions that define the nature of emotional labour she or he must perform in the situation and during its aftermath. Should the intense feeling of public humiliation be masked behind a self-deprecating smile? Should the frustration of not being taken seriously be voiced or subverted? Helen wondered if she should provide additional evidence to support her position or would that just create the impression of 'defensiveness'.

Emotional labour extends well beyond the original event. Justifiably afraid to confront more powerful individuals, employees sometimes engage in a long period of private 'stewing' over the injustice of the public violation.

A desire for revenge may build over time. I continue to be shocked by the number of workers who describe wanting to inflict physical harm in these situations. Due to a highly publicized series of violent acts initiated by US mail carriers against co-workers and supervisors, the grim term 'going postal' has evolved to describe workplace violence. But I have found tales of vengeance in factories, corporate offices and the hallways of government buildings. Ray, a long-time office worker for a state government agency, described his reaction to an incident in which a senior co-worker made him look foolish while talking to a client:

> In the past nine years I have been repeatedly verbally harassed in public by [senior co-worker]. I think of myself as a professional person who is pretty much in control of his emotions except when he pushes my buttons. I felt anger, frustration, helplessness. I wanted to kill . . . to choke the SOB.

The urge toward violence is typically associated with long periods of perceived humiliation combined with limited options for redressing the situation. In some cases, the urge for violence is turned inward. Ann, a probation officer, represents an extreme and disturbing example.

> My co-workers harassed me because they did not want to work with a woman. They criticized and demeaned me [in front of clients and peers], anything to make me feel bad. This went on for 18 months. I should have told them to get off my back and filed a grievance. I felt humiliated and angry. I wanted to strike out and hurt them; instead I attempted suicide.

Actual violence against self or other is of course the exception. These narratives represent a certain kind of emotional fantasy, through which emotional experiences are replayed, violent intentions are expressed in a harmless way, and the emotional force of the event is vented. Escaping into fantasy may be a primary means by which workers endure otherwise intolerable situations and prevent themselves from reacting violently. The need for fantasy may be produced by systems that provide members with limited options for non-violent resolution of relational conflicts.

Distributed emotion: relational networks and emotional 'buzzing'   The interdependent and 'nested' nature of work relationships makes certain that the emotional implications of a relational event will be distributed and magnified. Accounts of the event and the emotion they produce will ripple across relational connections that are activated and reactivated through the buzz of daily interaction. Returning to the case of Helen, emotion work continues after the ill-fated staff meeting. Public humiliation lingers in a hundred conversations as members of the original audience re-encounter one another and negotiate the meaning of the original event.

Helen (and her peers) must decide what to do or say about the event. Will she confront the boss in private after the meeting or simply 'let it go'. Will she admit to sympathetic co-workers her 'true feelings' about the unpleasant episode or will she deny its importance? Will Helen manufacture an upbeat emotional response in a display of emotional bravado? Will her peers offer their sympathies for the public humiliation or perhaps 'spare her feelings' by simply ignoring it in her presence? Will some co-workers, jealous of her private relationship with the boss, share their delight in her come-uppance? If she 'got emotional' in the meeting, will she feel the need to defend her response, to avoid being labelled 'unprofessional'? Will Helen feel the sting of unfair gender stereotypes or the burden of trying to counter them? In this way, emotion in work relationships is not confined to 'events'. It is a lingering residue, a buzz, sometimes a contagion, that spreads through an organization in a chain of interaction until it finally fades from public view.

Employees sometimes describe fear in terms that highlight the importance of relationship networks in magnifying emotional experience. Typically the fear stems from a rumour: a supervisor is angry, an employee is slated to be let go, a co-worker has made an accusation. As time passes and the rumour circulates, fear grows until some workers experience dread, panic, and emotional paralysis. 'Ray', a caseworker for the state, switched positions with a co-worker. Later he heard through the rumour mill that the co-worker had accused him of mishandling his case load (he was later exonerated). As time passed and rumours flew, Ray:

> experienced fear and panic, first for being wrongfully accused and second for [possibly] being terminated from my chosen career. As time passed, I felt strong anger [at the co-worker] and hurt. I wanted to lash out violently, both verbally and physically, but felt it would only contribute to what would have been a no-win situation.

Conflicting allegiances: loyalty and betrayal   A common theme in the most bitter emotional accounts involves conflicting allegiances. In some accounts, the complexities of managing romantic and professional allegiances come to the foreground. In one case, a staff member forwarded an e-mail to a manager with whom she was having an affair, appending an erotic description of their previous night's encounter. Her lover failed to see the attachment and inadvertently forwarded it to his supervisor. Employees who saw the e-mail shared it with local newspapers. In a subsequent newspaper story, the agency director chastised the employees for using the agency's public communication system for conducting their private affairs. E-mail was to be used for the conduct of professional relationships only. In addition to having their affair exposed in the most embarrassing way possible, both employees were demoted.

More frequently, extreme emotion arises from a perception that personal loyalties have been betrayed in favour of allegiance to the organization. Particularly in oppressive work environments, low-power employees draw strength from their peer relationships. Informal allegiances may form the basis for resistance to injustice, abuse of power, and mindless bureaucracy. This seemed to be the case among employees at the 'Department of

Regulation' (DOR), which regulates business transactions in a politically conservative western state within the United States. The agency operates with resistance from business interests and considerable apathy from the general public. It is the subject of anti-government criticism from conservative politicians who have threatened to 're-engineer' and 'streamline' the agency (which they have) or replace it with private contractors (which they have not). Organization members receive relatively low salaries compared to private industry counterparts. The agency leadership changes frequently as a function of the election cycle and the whims of the elected administration.

At DOR, underpaid and embattled workers report high levels of camaraderie and a collective sense of 'sticking up for' one another. Camaraderie is, interestingly, a kind of 'group emotion' fostered through rituals that emphasize common identity and interdependence. At the DOR, members (but not management) fostered camaraderie by baking a cake and holding a birthday celebration for every one of the agency's 90 employees. They gathered in lunch-time 'bitch sessions' where they complained bitterly about politically appointed, technically incompetent managers. At the agency, a certain degree of treachery and disloyalty is expected from management. In interviews, employees express disgust, futility and even hostility at a system that makes them pawns in a continuing political tug-of-war. Typical was this reaction by a clerk who believed she would be promoted after two years of exemplary work, only to see the job awarded to a politically connected individual with no experience.

> When I found the job was given to someone else I was very upset. Depression and jealousy set in. I hated this gentleman and didn't even know him. Why should someone with no experience get the job I had strived for? We stayed enemies until I left.

Solidarity among the rank and file combined with a certain jaded pessimism about the future is the emotional antidote to these feelings of frustration with the system. It is not surprising, then, that betrayal by co-workers is among the most emotionally devastating work experiences. Accounts of relational betrayal are typically related using language that is both colourful and bitter. In many cases, the account describes a peer who 'sold out to' management. The disloyal peer is characterized as 'sucking up' to management, a 'brown-noser', a 'backstabber', as in this account:

> I thought I used to have a very good relationship (with a senior co-worker). He would always stay after work and talk to me. Later, I found out from some other officers that he was backstabbing me the whole time and belittling me. I believe he was jealous of my 'clout' because I had a lot of friends in other departments. He would tell others I was probably [sleeping with] men in those departments. I was very angry.

In other cases, betrayal involves the unauthorized sharing of secrets. Co-workers who become friends share confidences, but the realities of the workplace make secrets hard to keep. Keeping the secret becomes difficult when confronted by a powerful manager, or the secret involves a violation of work rules, or the secret interferes with one's work performance. For example, employees at DOR knew that one of their peers was occasionally using a state car for personal trips. He asked them not to tell. But, keeping the secret made it difficult for accurate records of vehicle use to be compiled; employees had to offer ambiguous answers to a supervisor investigating the whereabouts of the car; the jobs of innocent employees were eventually put at risk. The outcome was an emotional round of accusation and resentment. In this case, both the rule breaker and those asked to cover for him felt betrayed.

In another example, an employee 'counted on' a peer to recommend him for promotion despite a mediocre performance record. He expected his peers to 'stand up' for him. Loyalty was more important than task performance. However, the peer could not in good conscience recommend the promotion. It would be unfair to harder working employees and a blow to his credibility with management. Again, both parties experienced high levels of resentment.

Finally, many accounts of betrayal describe situations where co-workers feel 'used' by peers, particularly when they fail to 'share the credit'. A co-leader of a state educational programme described her reactions when her co-worker failed to share the spotlight when interviewed by the local media about the programme's success.

> My emotional reaction was disbelief that this co-worker could continue to lie (to the media) . . . about our 'shared project'. Our relationship is strained to say the least. I find this to be an extremely emotional experience which causes me doubt, weariness, and physical stress. [Now] I do not trust her and do not share information she can use.

Relational morality: emotional rights and obligations at work   As suggested in the discussion of betrayal above, emotion at work is linked closely to issues of relational justice and fairness (see Bies, 1987; Trevino, 1992; Harlos and Pinder, this volume). Close proximity, forced interdependence, and potential vulnerability to abuses of power encourage workers to develop an unwritten code of relational ethics to supplement formal work rules. Workers frequently get emotional about violations of unspoken relational obligations and values. A worker who has been criticized too harshly by a supervisor complained: 'He/she had *no right* to treat me that way.' Statements like this one comment directly on ethically appropriate modes of emotional expression that *ought* to be followed. They are also offered as explanation for feelings of intense anger or humiliation.

Emotion functions to define the boundaries between formal and informal rights. The formal supervisory guidelines at organizations like Parts Inc. (a manufacturing facility in the rural American south) specify that supervisors have the right to correct employee mistakes. But the worker's emotional reaction determines when the supervisor has violated informal norms of interaction. The intense emotional reaction of an employee on the plant floor makes other workers aware that a relational injustice may have occurred and it can quickly create a spreading tide of emotional hostility. Of course, co-workers must determine that the emotional response is 'justified'. In other words, it has to be interpreted as an appropriate response to a violation of the prevailing moral order. At Parts Inc., emotional expressions of this type are often redressed by an apology from the supervisor. In this way, employee emotion signals violations of the moral order and reasserts it.

On the plant floor, emotional obligations extend to relationships between the sexes. In sharing her perspective on sexual harassment, Susan, a 33-year veteran who spent years on production lines, reveals her perspective on the kinds of emotional labour she expects from women exposed to the sexual banter of male co-workers.

> It's kind of depressing to see women who come in on the defensive and shouldn't be. A lot of time you use joking to lighten up the atmosphere. Here everybody's worked together so long it's more like a family and nobody takes it serious. (Excerpted from Waldron et al., 1993: p. 248)

However, when a male co-worker 'crossed the line' by accusing her of sleeping her way to a promotion, she favoured a more direct enforcement of relational ethics:

> I took my fist and cold-cocked that little sucker, and said [to him] 'file a grievance'. I have never had another comment, to my face, about what I have done. (Waldron et al., 1993: 249)

The moral tinge of emotional experience is obvious in the accounts workers provide: a colleague had 'no right to be angry' about a perceived insult; a worker felt 'guilty' for embarrassing a colleague; a moody employee has 'no respect for the rights of others' who have to put up with her emotional outbursts; co-workers who laughed at the misfortunes of their peers were 'morally bankrupt' . Employees may express dissatisfaction with their tasks or their formal roles, but they seem to get intensely emotional about violations of relational morality.

Guilt is powerfully linked to relational ethics, particularly for employees with the responsibility to make decisions that have profound effects on others. A supervisor at a large construction company described transferring a worker, who also happened to be a close friend, to a more dangerous job.

> A phone call from one of my foreman told me that he [the transferred employee] had taken a serious fall that ultimately lead to his death. I experienced a feeling of guilt and responsibility for making the transfer that very morning. I was at his wedding and the christening of his two children. Much confusion and fear . . . a sense of loss that I still experience to this day, 12 years after the fact. Even though it was an accident, the bureaucracy had to put the blame on someone which ultimately was me.

Emotion as a resource for constructing work relationships

Thus far, work relationships have been considered as a context for emotional experiences. But emotion is not merely a reaction to relational circumstances; it is also a resource that allows relationships to be defined, maintained, and in some cases abused.

Work relationships are defined along such dimensions as liking, respect, openness, formality and trust. But these relational qualities are enacted in part through the language of emotion and the tactical uses of communication to create emotional experiences (Waldron, 1994).

Using the language of emotion

Emotional language is sometimes celebratory and at other times degrading in its characterization of relational bonds. For example, at the Credit Corp. (a large bank), a team leader described being so 'excited by' and 'proud of' the 'emotional synergy' created by the members of his team. This 'heartfelt' description presumably signals a relational connectedness exceeding that required by any organizational contract. In describing their teamwork, members frequently indicated that it was about 'more than work'; it was 'personal'. Getting members to take work personally (that is, getting emotionally involved) is one reason organizations move to team-based systems of control. Barker's (1993) ethnography of manufacturing teams illustrates how the concertive control practised by team members involves a level of emotional manipulation that exceeds that practised in traditional control structures. The language of emotion is central to concertive control. At Credit Corp., team members described a peer who was struggling with personal problems that interfered with her work in emotional terms. She was 'emotionally needy', 'pouty' and 'high maintenance', and her frequent tears were 'unprofessional'.

Emotion tactics

Organization members manage work relationships with communication tactics designed to manipulate emotion (Waldron, 1999). Flattery is used frequently to create feelings of pride in others and (perhaps) increased liking for the flatterer (Wayne et al., 1995). Workers show the proper amount of enthusiasm if they want to be 'part of the team'. Praise, particularly when it is applied in a judicious and timely manner by a powerful leader, can create feelings of elation, gratitude and respect. After a lengthy period of hard work and overtime in her job in a tax preparation office, Mary had such an experience:

> After being drained and exhausted from putting all I had in[to the job] during the busy season, my supervisor called me into her office and told me I did an outstanding job. This meeting revived my emotions. It exhilarated me. It boosted

my ego and made me very happy with myself. [Since that day] I feel we respect each other and we relate on a personal level.

Veiled threats (and more blatant ones) are used by supervisors to create fear or anxiety in workers and remind them who is in charge. Employees who recall receiving threats at work often view them as definitive moments, particularly with regard to relational respect. A veteran probation worker recalled being threatened with his job as part of this emotional incident:

> The supervisor made me write a recommendation to have a parolee returned to prison (against my judgment). No respect for all of the time and effort I had spent with my client. I was crying and upset. [The supervisor] had lack of respect for me.

In contrast, the expression of sympathy or emotional support may discourage workers from abandoning work relationships. One stressed office worker considered quitting her job when she was unfairly overworked by a supervisor. She described 'profound emotional relief' when co-workers expressed their sympathy and support. She persevered until the supervisor was transferred. A new employee struggling with the emotional stress of her job described 'joy', 'closeness' and 'feeling like part of a fraternity' when peers expressed their willingness to help.

Intentional embarrassment has long been viewed by researchers as a social leveller and relational weapon (Goffman, 1952). At work, practical jokes, snide comments, or public revelations are used to embarrass others and sometimes to 'put them in their place'. This term illustrates how persons assert or reassert relational power through emotional manipulation (Sharkey, 1997). Indeed, manipulating the internal experience of a co-worker without their consent ('getting under their skin', 'getting their goat') is a potent, if sometimes fleeting, power tactic. However, the elicitation of genuine emotion can define relationships in more positive ways. For example, humour can be used to tap genuine emotions (delight, glee, joy) that for some employees are experienced primarily as fabrications (for example, in the performance of customer service). Humour can release emotional tension and smooth relational conflict (Morreal, 1991). The relational value of genuine emotional experiences is highlighted when co-workers choose to 'let down their hair', 'lay it on the line' and 'clear the air' . These phrases suggest that workers intend to abandon the emotional façade that defines formal work relationships. By doing so they signal a certain degree of relational trust and acceptance.

The suppression of anger is a tactic frequently used to minimize damage to the relationship with a supervisor. In fact, what may be most important about angry events in the workplace is not what is said, but what is withheld. Insults, protests and justifications are among the messages that employees choose not to deliver in such situations (Waldron and Krone, 1991), largely because they fear the consequences. Protests are the types of messages that question the relational status quo and signal that something is amiss. Justifications help the parties make sense of the underlying reasons for emotional encounters. Suppression of this information may lead to rigidity in work relationships, misinterpretation of emotional events, and perhaps to more emotionally explosive encounters in the future. Of course, it may also prevent relationship deterioration. Interestingly, Waldron and Krone found that incidents in which employees suppressed negative emotion yielded more negative and long-lasting relational effects than those in which emotions were expressed.

The tactics of emotional suppression are less commonly reported with positive emotions, but they remain an important tool in managing work relationships. For example, a state employee's delight at receiving an employee award was modulated to avoid inflaming the envy of co-workers.

> I was thrilled to receive it. And I wanted to skip and shout because of all of my hard work was finally being recognized. But I knew there were others who wanted it too and actually deserved it. Some were looking for me to be boasting and gloating and maybe they were jealous. I still had to work with them every day. I tried to be like 'no big deal' until I got home.

Based on the accounts of employees, the appropriate use of emotion tactics appears to be an integral part of working together. Fear. Enthusiasm. Pride. Sympathy. Anger. Delight. Envy. These and other emotions must be detected, manufactured, elicited and controlled as ordinary working relationships are enacted. Yet, to some extent organizational theory glosses the complex and subtle emotional character of work interactions. Looking more closely at these emotions would likely lead researchers to theory refinements. Just as importantly, leaders and members who are more attuned to the emotional consequences of their actions might be better prepared to participate in ethical and humane relationships.

Emotion as collective performance

A further way in which emotion is *relational* involves situations in which employees collaborate to produce emotion in themselves or others. In some professions, 'task interdependence' involves a kind of emotional partnership in which the emotion will not be experienced unless everyone works together to create it. This can be a highly visible process, as when American football players gather before a match to get 'psyched up'. This is a collective effort to emotionalize the game. Individuals can get psyched up on their own, but it is generally considered essential to team chemistry for all to participate. Winning teams must be collectively 'charged up' , 'fired up', 'emotionally pumped'. Researchers have documented other kinds of interdependence in emotional performances. Detectives and police officers work together to produce fear (and compliance) in crime suspects (Stenross and Kleinman,

1989). Doctors and nurses learn to 'co-implicate' patients when they offer diagnostic information (Maynard, 1992). By encouraging patients to describe their worse case scenario, they lessen the emotional blow experienced by the patient when bad news is delivered.

I have observed numerous instances of a kind of collective emotion work described long ago by Goffman (1952) as 'cooling the mark'. Using a con game metaphor, Goffman (1952) explains the interaction between the parties:

> The potential sucker [the 'mark'] is first spotted and one member of the working team . . . arranges to make social contact with him. The confidence of the mark is won, and he is given an opportunity to invest money in a gambling venture which is understood to have been fixed in his favor. The venture, of course, is fixed, but not in his favor. The mark is permitted to win some money and then persuaded to invest more. There is an 'accident' or 'mistake' and the mark loses the total investment. The operators then depart in a ceremony called the blow off or sting. The mark is expected to go on his way, a little wiser and a lot poorer. (p. 451)

Embarrassment and the possibly negative consequences of being associated with a shady venture often discourage the mark from protesting loudly about his/her misfortune. Occasionally, however, marks will express loudly their displeasure, or, using Goffman's (1952) term, 'squawk'. For the operators, this kind of emotional display can result in unwanted publicity, which in turn is 'bad for business'. For this reason one of the operators (the 'cooler') typically stays behind after the blow off to convince the mark to accept quietly his/her fate. This final stage of the con, part persuasion and part emotion management, is the 'cooling out' process.

Goffman's analysis came to mind as I observed the relationships that developed between attorneys and judges in a criminal court in the United States (Waldron and Catchings, 1996).[2] In the US justice system, weak cases are (theoretically) eliminated from the judicial system by a series of checks and balances. The result is that, despite the supposedly adversarial relationship between prosecutor and defence attorneys, they often engage in a kind of cooperative emotion work with the objective of convincing defendants to plead guilty (usually to a lesser charge) rather than risk going to trial. (For a detailed discussion of the plea bargain process see, Neurbauer, 1984.) The plea hearing is where the attorneys cooperate to make this sometimes dubious 'deal' look acceptable to the 'mark', who in the court I observed is typically a poorly educated, impoverished young male. In doing so, they use several varieties of collective emotion work.

Assuming an adversarial posture

Much of the 'battling' in the US justice system takes place well before the hearing, when defence and prosecuting attorney agree on the plea. However, it is easier for the mark to accept the plea if the defence attorney gives the appearance of 'driving a hard bargain' with the prosecutor. The prosecutor cooperates by 'overcharging' – deliberately accusing the defendant of more crimes than are really justified – so that some charges can be used as bargaining chips. When the unnecessary charges are dropped, the client experiences relief, which is attributed to the attorney.

At the public hearing, when in plain sight of the defendants, most defence attorneys I observed adopted an aloof, emotionally neutral, sometimes even aggressive tone during 'on-stage' interactions with the prosecutor. The defence and prosecution remain on separate sides of the court. The defence attorney leads the defendant out of one door while the prosecutor leaves by another. Later, the defence attorney can exploit the adversarial illusion by suggesting that things would be 'even worse' if the prosecutor hadn't been forced to cut a deal.

Grim formality

The other courtroom actors assist the defence attorney in constructing a definition of the situation that seems especially grim, even frightening, to the defendant. The opportunity to observe the same judge presiding over both a plea hearing and a later vehicular homicide trial revealed that the judge was quite willing to joke, ask questions and make interjections in the trial setting. In the hearing, the judge looked solemn and spoke in only very serious tones. Similarly, in the trial setting, the attorneys would whisper to their clients, smile at jokes, enter and leave the courtroom, and use a variety of vocal tones as they addressed the participants in the trial. At the hearing, the attorneys were subdued and businesslike. The light-hearted banter characterizing the period before the hearing disappeared when it became evident that the judge was about to enter and that the performance should begin. An atmosphere of 'grim formality' apparently functions to legitimize the deal-making process and ensure that the defendant feels out of place. In Goffman's words, intimidated defendants are less likely to squawk when they learn they have been 'taken'.

Elaborate concern

By elaborate non-verbal demonstrations in open court, the defence attorney creates an impression of compassion for the client. One attorney who represented two young defendants in separate hearings was observed to elaborately pat his clients on the back in a fatherly fashion. He nodded vigorously when a client spoke to the always-solemn judge, and gestured expansively when encouraging the client to ask any additional questions of the court and explained how his client deserved 'special consideration'. The exaggerated display of concern contrasted markedly with the attorney's pre-trial banter with the prosecutor in which jokes were made about the client's alcoholism and inability to read. The exercise of elaborate concern may also convince the defendant's family and friends of the attorney's sincerity. These audience members, if won over, may eventually assist in convincing the defendant that the attorney 'did his best' to bring off a good deal. In cases where the judge has not joined 'the team', these displays of concern may be designed to convince the court that the defendant has not been coerced into a guilty plea.

Cooling the mark

When the reality of a jail sentence, fine or both set in, defendants may come to suspect that have been 'duped' by the court. My interviews with attorneys reveal that disappointed clients sometimes chose to express their displeasure rather than disappear quietly into jail. One increasingly popular form of recourse is to file a malpractice suit against the defence attorney. Other options include: publicly lying about being coerced into a plea bargain, embarrassing the attorney in front of the judge (a rare occurrence), showing defiant disrespect for the judge, asking the court for a new attorney (if the con is recognized early enough), backing out of the agreement at the last minute, and threatening to go to trial.

As the 'cooler', the defence attorney has primary responsibility for managing the client's anger during this crucial time. But all actors cooperate in this process. How do they do it? I overheard defence attorneys emphasizing their 'relief' at having certain serious charges waived in exchange for guilty pleas. One cooperative prosecuting attorney made a ritual of repeating loudly in front of the judge (but for the apparent benefit of defendant and family) the list of charges that had been waived as part of the deal. The defence attorney noted that the prosecutor must have been in a 'good mood today' and slapped the client on the back to emphasize his good fortune.

Stalling is a cooling out tactic that gives the defendant time to 'simmer down' after the con becomes clear. After a defendant has pleaded guilty to a judge, the attorney may request that a pre-sentencing investigation take place. During such investigations, defendants have time to accept their fate and attorneys can distance themselves from the client.

With the 'team-orientation' tactic, attorneys emphasize camaraderie and mutual obligation during the bargaining process. 'Team spirit' was instilled by an attorney who asked a defendant, before family and friends, if he had any questions or doubts about 'our strategy'. By publicly declaring support for the strategy, the client becomes more responsible for the outcome. The attorney may also involve family members or friends in the team effort ('We all need to support X in the courtroom today'). Later, when the defendant is experiencing bitterness or regret, it becomes much easier for the attorney to deflect the emotion. In one case I observed, the attorney announced to defendant and family that 'we are all disappointed' [with the sentence] but 'we can get through this together'. Guilt strategies are used when attorneys remind clients that it was 'your choice' to break the law and embarrass your family in the first place. And, 'we got the best deal we could for you, don't back out on us now'. Fear is used to remind the client that 'things could turn out much worse' if the deal case went to trial.

Conclusion

In this chapter I have explored how the experiences of emotion at work is influenced by the unique contextual features of work relationships. I have also suggested that emotion is a resource that, through language choices and social tactics, is used to define work relationships. And, finally, I have shared observations that illustrate how organization members collaborate to produce emotion as part of their work. Each of these three relational approaches to conceptualizing emotion raises interesting questions for researchers and organization members alike.

In the context of work relationships, some emotional experiences are 'flashpoints'. They signal that the delicate balance between public and private, organizational and personal realms, has been disturbed. More needs to be known about how members manage the tension between these relational 'dialectics' (Montgomery and Baxter, 1998; Rawlins, 1992). How do we know when we are friends and when we are co-workers and what does it mean to be both of these things simultaneously? Emotion is a barometer of moral and relational ethics. Emotion marks and expresses moral outrage and gives force to the relational obligations. Listening carefully to the emotional pulse of an organization should give researchers and members clues to its ethical health. Unemotional organizations, those where emotion is restricted to the private experiences of members, may be those that no longer debate matters of right and wrong.

The use of emotion is an important tool in defining work relationships. We know that emotion is an integral part of relational conflict and termination. But only recently have researchers come to appreciate the role of emotional expression and emotional editing in the maintenance and preservation of work relationships (Waldron, 1991; Tepper, 1995). Relationship maintenance, rather than relationship initiation or termination, is what most people do most of the time. Yet, the role of 'ordinary' emotional experiences (the sharing of jokes; the overlooking of embarrassment) in relationship preservation is not fully appreciated in the organizational literature. The positive and negative relational consequences of expressing intense emotion to peers and leaders also need to be further investigated.

Emotional abuse is an extremely memorable and strikingly common experience reported by the workers I have studied. I believe that co-workers and powerful members are too often ignorant of the painful emotional experiences they inflict on others. The signs of emotional distress are too infrequently the subject of organizational training and management education. Fear, humiliation, intense embarrassment, and emotional savagery of all kinds are too rarely the subject of organizational censure. The resulting desire for revenge and the potential for physical violence in the organizations I have studied is alarming. It appears that the sources of emotional distress have increased in the American workplace, whereas mechanisms for its expression, at least non-violent ones, have not. We must do more as researchers, leaders and co-workers to attend to the emotional needs of ourselves and others if the humanity of the workplace is to be reclaimed.

When we conceptualize work as a collaborative emotional performance, it directs our attention away from the individual person (the traditional performer of emotion labour). Instead, we ask how it is that the emotional experience is created by social systems: communication networks, dyads, teams, peer groups. Often, the products created by collectives are emotional, as when a team of sales people work together to calm an angered customer or when a teacher and school psychologist develop a plan to make a child more enthused about school. But, more than emotional services, many jobs require a kind of interpersonal emotional savvy if they are to be performed well. The attorneys I mentioned learn to recognize the emotional cues of judges and defendants and each other. They 'play off' their co-workers' emotional displays, coordinate their use of emotional 'props', signal each other with emotional key words. Emotional teamwork is essential if they are to achieve their jointly desired task goals.

Emotional teamwork is easy to observe in professions that perform it publicly or dramatically. The challenge for researchers is to rethink the behind-the-scenes work performed by office workers, managers, government clerks and countless others, where a large part of the task is, quite simply, getting along with others. How does emotional teamwork get done in these less dramatic settings? What are the emotional sensitivities, cues, performances that are essential in these jobs?

This chapter started with the observation that the discourse of popular culture is rich in descriptors of the emotional experiences that make personal relationships complicated and meaningful. The language reflects the importance of emotion in our ordinary interactions. What I hope to have made clearer in this chapter is that the emotional dimension of work relationships is just as important. However, the discourse of most organizational cultures must be expanded if we are to adequately understand what makes work relationships complicated and meaningful. Closer study of emotion promises to open a window to what workers find to be the most important, ethical and humanizing experiences in their working lives. That is something to get emotional about.

Notes

1 These accounts were obtained through interviews, focus groups and open-survey questions involving over 800 employees. To protect the identities of individuals and organizations I have altered names and identifying details. In some instances, quotes presented here combine answers from several survey or interview questions. I edited these to preserve continuity, eliminate redundancy and improve readability. However, in every case I have laboured to preserve the original language and meaning.

2 These comments are based on field observation of a single Common Pleas court. My comments are intended to stimulate thought about collaborative emotion work

in this setting. I do not claim that these observations generalize to all such courts or that they fully capture the 'reality' of the plea process. The process is complex, variable across jurisdictions, and therefore subject to numerous interpretations.

References

Barker, J.B. (1993) 'Tightening the iron cage: concertive control in self-managing teams', *Administrative Science Quarterly*, 38: 408–37.

Bies, R.J. (1987) 'The predicament of injustice: the management of moral outrage', in L.L. Cummings and B.M. Staw (eds), *Research in Organizational Behavior*, vol. 9. Greenwich, CT: JAI Press. pp. 289–319.

Day, D.V. and Crain, E.C. (1992) 'The role of affect and ability in initial exchange quality perceptions', *Group and Organization Management*, 17: 380–97.

Fineman, S. (ed.) (1993) *Emotion in Organizations*. London: Sage.

Goffman, E.G. (1952) 'On cooling the mark out: some aspects of adaptation to failure', *Psychiatry*, 15: 451–63.

Maynard, D.W. (1992) 'On clinicians co-implicating recipients' perspective in the delivery of diagnostic news', in P. Drew and J. Heritage (eds), *Talk at Work: Interaction in Institutional Settings*. Cambridge: Cambridge University Press. pp. 331–58.

Montgomery, M. and Baxter, L. (eds) (1998) *Dialectical Approaches to the Study of Personal Relationships*. Mahwah, NJ: Lawrence Erlbaum.

Morreall, J. (1991) 'Humor and work', *Humor*, 4: 35–373.

Neubauer, D. (1984) *America's Courts and the Criminal Justice System*, 2nd edn. Monterey, CA: Brooks/Cole.

Rawlins, W.K. (1992) *Friendship Matters: Communication, Dialectics, and the Life Course*. New York: Aldine.

Sharkey, W.F. (1997) 'Why would anyone want to intentionally embarass me?', in R. Kowalski (ed.) *Aversive Interpersonal Behaviours*. New York: Plenum Press. pp. 57–90.

Stenross, B. and Kleinman, S. (1989) 'The highs and lows of emotional labor: detectives' encounters with criminals and victims', *Journal of Contemporary Ethnography*, 17, 435–52.

Tepper, B. (1995) 'Upward maintenance tactics in supervisory mentoring and nonmentoring relationships', *Academy of Management Journal*, 38 (4): 1191–1205.

Trevino, L.K. (1992) 'The social effects of punishment in organizations: a justice perspective', *Academy of Management Review*, 17: 647–76.

Wagoner, R. and Waldron, V.R. (1999) 'How supervisors convey routine bad news: facework at UPS', *Southern Communication Journal*, 64: 193–210.

Waldron, V. (1991) 'Achieving communication goals in superior–subordinate relationships: the multi-functionality of upward maintenance tactics', *Communication Monographs*, 58: 289–306.

Waldron, V.R. (1994) 'Once more with feeling: reconsidering the role of emotion in work', in S.A. Deetz (ed.), *Communication Yearbook 17*. Thousand Oaks, CA: Sage. pp. 388–416.

Waldron, V.R. (1999) 'Communication practices of followers, members and proteges: the case of upward influence tactics', in M. Roloff (ed.), *Communication Yearbook 22*. Newbury Park, CA: Sage. pp. 251–99.

Waldron, V.R. and Catchings, B. (1996). 'Cooling the mark out'. Paper presented at the Annual Conference of National Communication Association, November. Chicago.

Waldron, V.R. and Krone, K.J. (1991) 'The experience and expression of emotion in the workplace. A study of a corrections organization', *Management Communication Quarterly*, 4: 287–309.

Waldron, V.R., Foreman, C. and Miller, R. (1993) 'Managing gender conflicts in the supervisory relationship: relationship-definition tactics used by women and men', in G. Kreps (ed.), *Sexual Harassment: Communication Implications*. Cresskill, NJ: Hampton Press. pp. 234–56.

Wayne, S.J., Kacmar, K.M. and Ferris, G.R. (1995) 'Co-worker responses to others' ingratiation attempts', *Journal of Managerial Issues*, 8: 277–89.

Wharton, A.A. (1993) 'The affective consequences of service work: managing emotions on the job', *Work and Occupations*, 20: 205–32.

5 EMOTION METAPHORS IN MANAGEMENT: THE CHINESE EXPERIENCE

KATHLEEN J. KRONE AND JAYNE M. MORGAN

The emotions of joy and anger are injurious to the spirit; cold and heat are injurious to the body. When joy and anger are without moderation, then cold and heat exceed all measure and life is no longer secure. Yin and Yang should be respected to an equal extent. (*The Yellow Emperor's Classic of Internal Medicine*; cited in Bond, 1993)

As the theoretic constraints and practical harms associated with treating emotion simply as something that interferes with rationality are increasingly understood, so is the need to reconceptualize a less contentious relationship between the two (Fineman, 1996; Putnam and Mumby, 1993). Alternative understandings and approaches to emotion in organizations can emerge from the assumption that reason and emotion are inextricably and more equitably entwined (Fineman, 1996). This chapter contributes to the development of such understandings by examining emotion in a culture rooted in an appreciation for the unity of opposites and whose language draws no distinction between mind and heart.

As revealed in the above sample of traditional medical discourse, for the Chinese, emotional processes intersect with spiritual and bodily processes in depicting what it means to be in 'good health'. Similarly, while emotion and reason tend to be depicted as distinct and competing processes in the West (Putnam and Mumby, 1993), they are conceptualized as continuous processes in China (Sun, 1991; Wong, 1991). Indeed, the Chinese term *xin* (heart) reflects a unitary concept of mind-heart rather than a bifurcation between the two (Sun, 1991). Thought–feeling continuity is reflected in Chinese expressions such as 'thoughts are felt in the heart' (Young, 1994: 118) and in conceptualizations of effective argument as convincing others to 'think feelingly' (p. 46), or to 'sway another's thinking by touching a responsive chord in his or her heart' (p. 118). Thought–feeling continuity also is reflected in everyday conversational expressions in which Chinese will place their hand over their heart when saying 'I think . . .' or when saying 'I've been thinking in my heart that . . .' (p. 118).

Thus, a language-centred approach to the study of emotion in China is compatible with attempts to construct alternative understandings of how emotion and rationality entwine (Abu-Lughod and Lutz, 1990; Fineman,

1996; Harré, 1986). In the West, when thought and feeling are positioned as being connected, either emotion is depicted as serving thought, or thought is otherwise privileged over emotion (Fineman, 1996). For instance, cognitive appraisals and reappraisals of emotions are advised in order to better manage overly emotional responses. In particular, this thinking 'about' or 'over' feelings strikes us as conceptually distinct from thinking 'with' or 'through' them. Thinking about feelings can be akin to using thought to harness, tame or otherwise dominate feelings, while thinking feelings through implies listening with feelings and being instructed by them (Krone, Chen, Sloan and Gallant, 1997). Only rarely are emotions thought of as a sign of maturity and intelligence (Lutz, 1987, 1988). Finer-grained understandings of what it means to conceptualize emotion and thought as continuously related can be revealed through the language Chinese managers use to describe their day-to-day emotional experience and can inspire us to go further in reconceptualizing the reason–emotion relationship.

Toward that end, we offer an interpretation of Chinese managers' metaphorical expressions of emotion. In general, metaphors explain one experience in terms of another experience. Typically, physical experiences are paired with and organize more abstract experiences (Johnson, 1987; Lakoff and Johnson, 1999). Both experiences share some characteristics, but not others. Metaphors express something about the whole of an experience that would be difficult to express using more literal language (Lakoff and Johnson, 1980; Ortony, 1975). This appears to be especially true for the expression of emotional experience – experience which might be inexpressible without the use of metaphor (Fainsilber and Ortony, 1987; Ortony, 1975). How Chinese managers understand and reason about emotion should be evident in the metaphors they use to describe their emotional experiences (Kovecses, 1990; Lakoff and Johnson, 1980, 1999).

Our approach stands in contrast to two others taken to understand Chinese emotional processes (Bond, 1993). First, some scholars have adopted a textual approach in which they have examined representations of emotion in various types of literary and medical texts (Klineberg, 1938; Lin, 1980; Wu, 1982; Yu, 1995). Other scholars have employed a highly empirical, cross-cultural comparative approach which tends to depict all Chinese as being the same (Hofstede, 1980; Trompenaars, 1993). Neither approach reveals much about how individual Chinese people experience and understand emotion in their day-to-day lives. A metaphor analysis of Chinese managers' descriptions of their emotional experience holds great promise for instructing us about the nature and meaning of their inner feelings, and about their reasons for responding as they do in emotional situations (Fineman, 1993). Our intention also is to avoid as much as possible squeezing the whole of an emotional experience through a single metaphorical expression, but instead to locate Chinese managers' emotion metaphors within a larger cultural and organizational milieu that plays a significant role in producing and reproducing these conceptual constructions (Abu-Lughod and Lutz, 1990). How emotion is experienced, interpreted and responded to is both a linguistic and a cultural construction (Heelas, 1986; Lutz and White, 1986; Middleton, 1989; Oatley, 1993). Thus, in the sections that follow we briefly describe how individuals are socialized to experience and manage emotion in China and the conditions under which Chinese managers in state-owned enterprises currently work.

The self and emotion in China

Understanding the meaning of emotional experience in China requires an understanding of the Chinese conceptualization of self. According to Chinese thought, human life is realized in the larger social group. Throughout childhood, the family inculcates ideals of loyalty and obedience within a clearly defined network of roles. It is within the family unit that children first learn to maintain harmony by restraining themselves and overcoming their individuality (Hofstede and Bond, 1988). Rather than learn to understand themselves as autonomous units with clearly defined boundaries, children learn to understand their place within a network of interdependent but clearly defined role relationships. Family values and relationships appear to go on to serve as the prototype for thought and behaviour in all social organizations including the workplace (Chen and Chung, 1994).

The cultural cultivation of an interdependent sense of self has several consequences for the experience and expression of emotion. First, in order to maintain face, group harmony and stability, the Chinese appear to neutralize intense inner feeling and to restrain its expression. Individuals are expected to subdue their emotions in the process of fulfilling their role-related responsibilities within their social networks (Sun, 1991). Second, getting in touch with inner feelings in order to express them to others appears to be relatively unimportant, especially if doing so would threaten to disrupt harmonious systems of relationships (Markus and Kitayama, 1991). Third, practising emotional restraint on behalf of a larger social network is not considered self-sacrificial. Rather than being troubled by not expressing their authentic inner feelings or by behaving in ways that contradict them, the Chinese appear to understand such practices as a necessary part of spiritual development that only can come from displaying their sensitivity and responsiveness to others (Chang and Holt, 1991; Hu and Grove, 1991; Sun, 1991; Tu, 1985). Perhaps as a result, while the expression of emotion may be subdued in China, feelings themselves do not appear to be suppressed or made unconscious (Krone, Chen and Xia, 1997). Fourth, in communicating with those who are positioned outside one's social networks, uncontrolled emotional outbursts can and do occur (Sun, 1991). It seems less important to restrain the expression of hostile emotion with out-group members (Chang and Holt, 1991; Hu and Grove, 1991; Sun, 1991). Thus, restraining oneself emotionally is not only necessary in developing oneself as a person and in maintaining group harmony, but also in acquiring support for the accomplishment of practical, instrumental ends (Chang and Holt, 1991).

Managing state-owned enterprises in China

Like the management of organizations everywhere, the management of state-owned enterprises in China has always been shaped by larger political and economic forces. These dynamics are far too complex to be addressed in detail here; however, we will briefly discuss two that seem most important to developing an understanding of managerial emotional experience: the shift to a 'factory director responsibility system', and the shift from a planned economy to a market economy.

Beginning in 1979, a factory director responsibility system was instituted in nearly all Chinese state-owned enterprises. This system was designed to restructure the relationship between three influential units that had been governing the factories since 1949: the Communist Party, business management and the workers' union. The institution of the factory director responsibility system signalled a redistribution of power between the Communist Party and business management. Between 1949 and 1979, management had been subordinate to the Communist Party, a relationship which sometimes meant that 'ideological purification' was emphasized at the expense of production. In 1979 factory directors were repositioned as coordinators of all three units and made more responsible for the productivity and economic performance of their operations (Chamberlain, 1987; Walder, 1989; Warner, 1991). This change supports the Chinese government's movement from a planned economy, in which factories were assured of governmental support regardless of their level of profitability, to a market-driven economy, in which managers are held more accountable for the economic success of their factories (Child, 1994). It also is challenging managers to at least consider greater employee participation in certain kinds of decisions (Krone, Chen and Xia, 1997). While little is known about how these changes are affecting the emotions of practising managers today, others have persuasively demonstrated a strong relationship between the dynamics of Chinese culture, politics and emotion (Kleinman and Kleinman, 1985). Similarly, while little is written about the emotional lives of the bureaucratically powerful, managing the day-to-day implementation of these types of changes strikes us as emotionally demanding. While we might assume that powerful organizational actors enjoy greater latitude to break or negotiate existing emotion rules, for Western male managers at least, managerialism appears to intersect with masculinity in ways that marginalize the expression of emotions such as fear or worry (Messerschmidt, 1996), and privilege the appearance of invulnerability and emotional self-control (Hearn, 1993). And in traditional China at least, the ability to restrain oneself emotionally has been considered a virtue and a cultural ideal to which all powerful officeholders must aspire (Yang, 1959).

Metaphor and emotion

Metaphor is much more than figurative language. It is the very way we organize and express thought. 'Metaphor is our most striking evidence of *abstractive seeing*, of the power of human minds to use presentational symbols. Every new experience, or new idea about things, evokes first of all some metaphorical expression' (Langer, 1967: 141). In this sense, metaphors are constitutive of reality (Ortony, 1979). Found in everyday experience and in everyday talk, metaphors structure our sense-making and guide our everyday responses in the world.

Three types of metaphors have been developed, each having its own structuring properties (Lakoff and Johnson, 1980). *Orientational* metaphors appear to organize a whole system of concepts with one another and are typically spatial in nature (for example, happy is up, sad is down: 'My spirits rose', 'I fell into depression'). *Ontological* metaphors allow us to understand experiences through objects and substances. These metaphors quantify, group and categorize experience to the extent that they appear to us now as straightforward, literal description (for example, mind as brittle object: 'He is going to crack'). *Structural* metaphors go beyond naming and quantifying concepts – they allow us to build meaning of one concept in terms of another (for example, argument is war; time is money). All metaphors are grounded in sensorimotor and cultural experience, although some are arguing that the relationship between physical experience and metaphor is much stronger (Lakoff and Johnson, 1980, 1999).

Used in organizations, metaphors give us systematic ways of thinking about how we can or should act in a given situation (Morgan, 1997). Metaphors provide a concise yet holistic image of a given organizational experience. Metaphors can be understood as 'problem-setting' devices as they reveal how our understanding of a problem, our naming and framing of it, shapes the strategies we ultimately adopt to address it (Schon, 1979). Used in organizations, metaphors are not neutral constructions of reality. They also express ideology – what exists, what is good and what is possible (Deetz and Mumby, 1985: 374). Metaphors, then, have the power to amplify dominant interests and mask those of less powerful groups. Through the use of metaphor, consensual social realities are produced and reproduced (Koch and Deetz, 1981) and/or resisted and challenged. Metaphor analyses can be useful in revealing an array of worldviews in organizations and the extent to which one worldview contends with or overpowers others.

We believe that metaphor analyses also can be useful in studying the subtleties of emotional meaning and expression in organizations. While numerous emotion metaphors have been identified, the *container* metaphor appears to dominate conceptualizations of emotion, at least in the West. Within this metaphor, emotions are conceptualized in terms of some sort of metaphorical *substance in a container*, with the container corresponding to the body (Kovecses, 1990). According to Kovecses (1990), the container metaphor consists of two variants: *emotions are fluids in a container* (for example, 'He was full of emotion'), and *emotions are the heat of a fluid in a container* (for example, 'She was seething with emotion'). In the first version, the container is filled or filling up with emotion; empty or emptying out the emotion. In the second version, the fluid in the container is seething, bubbling or simmering. Because of the heat, the fluid can be in constant motion. The emotion also may grow so intense that the pressure can cause the container to burst ('He poured out his feelings to her'). Alternatively, the pressure can be released in controlled ways ('He let out his emotions slowly'), or controlled by containing it or keeping it in ('She managed to bottle up her feelings'). Thus, images of the container metaphor conceptualize emotion as a mass entity that can exist separately from a person and exert considerable power over him or her. Emotion is a dangerous force that needs to be controlled, and requires a considerable amount of energy to do so (Kovecses, 1990). Evoked in organizations, the container metaphor of emotion complements the container metaphor of communication (Putnam et al., 1996). Both imply an ability and desire to draw distinct boundaries between an entity and some larger social system in which it is located so as to better control what goes on inside it. While understanding emotion as a dangerous force that must be cognitively contained can lead to positive outcomes for individuals and organizations (Conrad and Witte, 1994; Tolich, 1993), such containment can also lead to burnout (Van Maanen and Kunda, 1989), self-estrangement (Hochschild, 1983), or the suppression of protest messages that the organization needs to hear (Waldron and Krone, 1991).

The language of the container metaphor further suggests that emotions are fluids inside a bodily container, while ideas or thoughts are contained in the mind. The mind is the 'upper container' that acts as a lid to prevent the dangerous contents of the lower, bodily container from overflowing (Kovecses, 1990). Ironically, for the most part, the *heart* is notably absent from the dominant conceptual structure of the container metaphor of emotion. Only in one study, a comparison of emotion metaphors in English and Chinese, does the heart appear and it does so as a container within the bodily container (Yu, 1995).

While the container metaphor is evoked to make sense of a large number of emotional experiences, the language of it tends to reinforce a contentious relationship between thought and feeling in which reason eventually reigns. Still, linguistic and cultural dynamics combine to constrain the development of alternative conceptualizations. Clearly, while the container metaphor may be the dominant way to conceptualize emotion, it is not the only way (see Kovecses, 1990). Non-Western cultural understandings of emotion can inspire us to think beyond the constraints imposed by our own linguistic and cultural communities. We now turn our attention more fully to how the Chinese conceptualize emotion. What are the emotion metaphors used within this group of Chinese managers and what do they teach us about the ways in which Chinese managers experience and manage emotion? What conceptual structure of emotion is evident in their descriptions of their emotional experience?

The Chinese managers and their factories

As part of a larger study, 48 executive and deputy executive directors of state-owned enterprises in the People's Republic of China responded to our survey concerning pleasant or unpleasant emotional experience in their work. All respondents were members of two successive trade delegations participating in business meetings in the midwestern United States. Permission to collect data was secured from the Chinese State Council of Mechanical and Electrical Products in exchange for a training workshop on cross-cultural managerial styles.

All of the respondents in our study were male. While feminist activism in China has from time to time combined with other cultural/political movements to challenge traditional gender roles both in the family and at work (Kristeva, 1993), public life has been traditionally dominated by males. While it is not at all unusual for women to be employed as factory workers or perhaps to serve as leaders in the workers' union, most business managers are male (Kristeva, 1993). Our respondents had held their current positions from between 4 months to 21 years and their ages ranged from 29 to 55. Their levels and types of education varied: 2% had completed postgraduate education, 38% had completed undergraduate studies, 44% had completed technical college, 8% had completed high school, and 8% had completed vocational school training. The factories ranged in size from 50 to 38,000 employees and manufactured a variety of small products including tools, locks, watch casings and watches. Some 58% of the respondents reported having the authority to hire their employees while 29% reported having the authority to fire an employee, if necessary. In contrast to the assertion that emotion is experienced less intensely in China (Bond, 1993), this group of managers reported having been strongly affected by their emotional experiences (M = 1.87, with 1 = very strongly affected, 5 = weakly affected). Pleasant and unpleasant events appear to have been experienced equally intensely (M = 1.9 for pleasant events; M = 1.8 for unpleasant events).

Procedures for collecting and interpreting data

A questionnaire was developed that asked participants to describe a pleasant or unpleasant emotional event they had experienced through their work. They then were asked to describe how they were feeling during the event. Next, the managers responded to a series of questions regarding their relationship with the other person, and what they said or did not say during the emotional event. Last, they were asked to describe the best way to handle feelings during this type of emotional event in general.

Because all of the respondents were Chinese-speaking, a back-translation procedure was used to prepare the questionnaire (Brislin, 1970). Following the survey administrations, the Chinese responses were translated back into English. Three bilingual research assistants, one of whom is a Berliz-certified

English–Chinese translator, worked together to complete the translations. When necessary, their interpretations of responses were discussed until agreement could be reached on a final translation. Every effort was made to maintain the respondents' exact expressions rather than to simply convey their general ideas.

To analyse the data, one of us first carefully examined the original data for instances of metaphorical expressions in the broadest of senses – including ontological metaphors that look like straightforward description (Lakoff and Johnson, 1980). She then created a separate file for the metaphorical expressions and catalogued them according to delegation (A or B), respondent (1–24 in delegation A, and 1–24 in delegation B), and questionnaire item number (1–14). Next, she used a sorting procedure to group metaphors around themes to delineate recurring or 'main' metaphors (Koch and Deetz, 1981: 7). Metaphorical expressions were colour-coded to help vividly demonstrate the occurrences of these themes as they emerged naturally from the data.

Both of us then used matching sets of the colour-coded data as a basis for discussing the extended meanings or 'entailments' of the metaphors. Using Lakoff and Johnson's (1980) descriptions as a guide, we analysed the main metaphors in terms of the categories and underlying logics that they seemed to reveal. We considered most strongly those metaphors that were the most striking and pertinent to the immediate context. In this sense, frequency of metaphor usage did not so much determine the results as much as the depth of impact and coherence of certain metaphors (Smith and Eisenberg, 1987). To further analyse the metaphors, we often referred back to the original data to understand the placement and purpose of metaphorical expressions within their broader narratives.

Metaphorical expressions of emotion

The way in which these managers experience and process emotion is much like a sophisticated form of 'homeostasis'. Through homeostasis, an open system is able to coordinate the responses of its subsystems in ways that allow it to maintain its internal stability. Through homeostatic processes, open systems are able to register fluctuations in the environment and respond adaptively. Similarly, the managers in this study appear to understand disruptive emotional experience as a temporary loss of equilibrium and once this occurs, they actively work to regain it in their bodies, thoughts and feelings. They strive to 'cool' hot tempers and 'calm' agitated feelings through a conscious, perhaps even methodical, process. They then seek to 'draw a lesson' from their emotional experiences in ways that enhance their own well-being and that of their organization. We believe the metaphor of homeostasis acts as a kind of root image that can guide our exploration of Chinese managers' understanding of emotion and that also can stimulate the construction of alternative understandings of emotion in the workplace.

Three interrelated groupings of metaphorical themes emerged in support of the image of homeostasis: moderating the intensity of what is felt, restoring inner balance, and learning from emotional experiences.

Moderating feelings

The moderating process was best revealed in how the managers expressed they should first de-intensify their pleasant and unpleasant feelings by 'cooling down' or 'calming down'. The high and low metaphorical orientations suggest that extremely unpleasant or pleasant feelings do occur and need to be moderated and brought back up or down to their normal levels. In fact, the most common expressions in the data were 'calm down' and 'cool down', which reveal orientational metaphors at their base (Lakoff and Johnson, 1980). Especially when describing how unpleasant emotional situations ought to be handled, managers indicated that bringing emotions 'down' was a necessary first step. Being 'down' (but not too down or 'passive') in this case is the managers' preferred orientation, as opposed to being 'up' – either 'excited' or 'hot' in their temperament. At the same time, they referred to the importance of keeping others' emotions 'up'.

It is in the language of moderating feelings that the container metaphor is most evident. It appears that the managers do liken their strong inner feelings to 'fluid in a container' or the 'heat of a fluid in a container' – common metaphorical expressions of emotional experience (Kovecses, 1990). As a fluid is heated, it becomes not only higher in temperature, but increasingly rough and agitated. If not processed properly (cooled and calmed), the fluid may overflow uncontrollably, relieving the container of pressure. This idea was illustrated in one manager's description of an angry confrontation in which 'a severe criticism came pouring out'. It would make sense, then, that the managers' most common response to their pleasant and unpleasant inner emotional states was to 'cool' and 'calm' their feelings in order to bring the fluid, corresponding to the metaphor, back to a moderate temperature and an even, smooth surface within the bodily container. Regulating their feelings in order to moderate them requires considerable energy, though, and here is where the language of homeostasis comes into play. Strong inner feelings are not contained automatically, but stabilized through an effortful process of moderation. In doing so, managers mentioned how they had to 'constrain' or even 'overcome' themselves, suggesting that they viewed controlling their emotions as a kind of developmental challenge. These images refer to a conscious inner struggle that must be seriously engaged to reclaim, as one manager stated, an 'even temper'. Managers mentioned how they work to 'collect', 'restrict', 'correct' and 'control' themselves – suggesting an effortful and mindful emotion management process. For example, one manager indicated how he and his colleagues would 'try to overcome emotional upheaval and collect themselves in order to consider problems calmly'. Stabilizing an 'even temper' strikes us as a type of homeostatic process in which the body, thoughts and feelings intelligently work together to adjust the temperature and excitement of the overall emotional experience, which in turn will enable a more adaptive response to the environment.

Restoring inner balance

Restoring inner balance is almost equivalent to homeostasis, and has the end result of what three managers term achieving a 'clear mind'. Achieving a clear mind involves developing a stable understanding of the emotional experience that then enables managers to respond adaptively. Once emotions are properly calmed or elevated through the moderation process, clarity of mind-heart can then be regained. In a similar fashion, when the managers calm their feelings, they can achieve a certain clarity within and about their emotional experiences. To facilitate and perhaps reserve a space in which to achieve 'clear minds', managers referred to the need to be 'away' from the emotional situation. Being 'away' indicated not a psychological but an actual physical distancing from the person who sparked the 'high' emotion with the manager. Managers noted how they needed to simply 'avoid' the other person for a while. However, this is not to say that the managers wanted to avoid their feelings; in fact, it's quite the opposite. They indicated that being 'away' provided opportunities to experience an emotion as it happens, essentially allowing it to run its course. One manager said that he would simply 'let time pass' to 'get things over with naturally'.

To help them restore their inner balance, the managers would often retreat to their homes to 'encounter' their emotions in private. Metaphorical expressions involving 'home' inspire images of a sanctuary or an emotional refuge, perhaps a 'safe' place in which to truly experience the whole of the emotion. One manager, for example, stated that only his wife could comfort him, so he would 'go home' to cope with his emotional experience. Another manager stated that he would 'go home and entertain one's self with the family, and try to put one's mind in a different environment so that the negative emotions will not get worse'. In all of these cases, the home provides a different physical environment in which to experience the emotion.

While a few of the managers mentioned how they would use the home environment to 'occupy one's self with something else' for a while, they seemed to always return to the feeling at some point. Returning to the impetus of their emotional states, the managers could then reflect upon their own behaviour as well as that of their employees. Developing an understanding of the emotional experience restores inner balance and enables a more adaptive response to one's environment.

Learning from emotional experiences

Reflecting upon and learning from past emotional thoughts and behaviours is revealed in the managers' descriptions of how they (or their workers) should 'draw a lesson' from the experience. Managers indicated they should 'reflect upon', 'analyse', or 'seriously summarize' their role in the emotional upset. At the same time, subordinates needed to learn 'lessons' to 'improve' themselves, and in turn improve organizational functioning. For example, one manager who experienced an 'explosive burst of temper' with a subordinate told the employee: 'This is a lesson of blood. You should learn it by heart and improve yourself.'

The process of reflection also applied to pleasant feelings. One manager even stated that one should 'Reflect on one's own work and behaviour to see if there is anything worthy of positive emotions.' Even good times call for careful thought, introspection and analysis. Lessons learned from positive experiences can then be used as motivational resources to inspire employees to work harder. From his positive emotional experience, one manager, who had successfully persuaded employees to work overtime in excessive heat in order to meet an important production goal, learned that he was able to 'use a heart to change a heart'. Another manager, who lacked the resources to materially reward workers, summed up his approach to motivating employees by saying 'My way is to spiritually encourage with the appropriate good word.'

As in any systemic process, the managers strive to learn from both positive and negative emotional experiences in order to adapt, and in the end, thrive in both personal and organizational realms of living. It appears, in fact, that learning 'lessons' serves multiple purposes. Managers and employees can reflect on their actions and personally improve for the future. They may 'encounter' their feelings to make gains in self-knowledge and awareness. In this sense, organizations can be sites in which emotional development can continue to occur throughout one's working life (Averill, 1986). At the same time, though, these 'lessons' are taught and learned in the classroom of organizational efficiency and productivity. Emotional lessons are intimately tied to economic gains and losses, such that what improves the individual should also improve the business.

Alternative emotion metaphors based on the Chinese experience

How do images of emotion rooted in the Chinese experience instruct us in alternative ways to understand the relationships between thinking and feeling? The homeostatic metaphor suggests that the Chinese do not regard emotion as temporary or abnormal, but rather as an ongoing feature of their experience and of business. Many managers wrote not of emotional 'outbursts' but of lingering 'moods', suggesting the greater presence of emotion more generally. Emotion is always present and is a natural part of doing business. Emotions are not merely isolated experiences that should be contained. Instead, it is as if emotion surrounds them, as reflected by one manager who said 'never forget one's responsibility and places that can be improved in work, even in the *middle* of such good moods'.

Moderating the intensity of inner feeling, restoring balance and finding lessons in emotional experiences all require recognizing and validating feelings. Rooted in an appreciation for the unity of opposites, these images all illustrate how reason and emotion cannot exist apart from one another. Integrating feeling and thought is necessary to achieving and maintaining homeostasis. Doing so, however, is not easy and in fact appears to require some struggle, perhaps because both are given equal weight.

In moderating the intensity of their inner feelings, thoughts are infused in a way that keeps managers from 'losing themselves' in their emotional experience. As one manager stated: 'While feeling excited, also try to be stable. Be encouraging and at the same time, try to be restrictive.' Careful reasoning is used to return intense emotion back to a 'centre point'. Similarly, in restoring inner balance by achieving a 'clear mind', the managers do not deny or try to suppress the emotional components. Indeed, the experience of a clear mind may only be known in relation to a cloudy or troubled one. To be rational requires knowing and having experienced both.

Finally, the metaphor of 'lesson' suggests that the managers believe emotions have substance – not fleeting, intangible 'blips' in their thinking, but real entities that may be approached, reflected upon, analysed and ultimately understood. For this reason, emotions are valued as sources of information. Managers 'think through' their feelings to gain self-knowledge, perspective about other people, and insight into organizational functioning. The metaphor of lesson inherently suggests that critical thinking is employed, but it is used to understand and learn from emotional situations.

Managerial uses of emotion metaphors

All metaphors represent ideologically charged constructions of reality, and emotion metaphors are no different. In their use of the language of homeostasis, including moderating emotion, restoring inner balance, and the lesson, managers convey a clear perspective that mandates how employees should regard their inner emotional states and outward behaviour. In their view, failing to frame emotion this way threatens the stability and profitability of the overall organization. Clearly, managers have a disproportionate amount of power to construct and reinforce their perspectives on emotion, and to do so in ways that protect and naturalize their interests and the economic interests of their factories. Even when one manager appeared to break the emotion norms by referring to a time when he argued with a superior until they both were 'blue in the face', he still was aware of the 'best' way to treat such an experience: 'First of all, keep calm, then each should try to reflect upon what happened.' This manager could easily articulate, as could most of the others, what the 'appropriate' response should be. In doing so, the homeostatic imagery is maintained and held up as the correct way for everyone to manage emotion.

In addition, these managers leave no doubt that they hold themselves to the same stringent standards that they demand of their employees. Several reported engaging in self-criticism regarding their own emotional upsets – even when it is with employees who have behaved 'selfishly' or who have in other ways undermined the profitability of the factory. This pattern may be due to a cultural and organizational 'duality of structure' (Giddens, 1984) that constructs understandings of 'ideal' emotion processes that then become self-sustaining. Having conceptualized emotion as a strict process of homeostatic control, managers have little choice but to publicly aspire to that ideal.

Managers also may have a heightened sense of emotional awareness and need for emotional control because they recognize the power of their emotional displays. This may be one reason why this group of managers chose to stabilize their internal states away from the source of their agitation. The managers recognize that they need to first achieve a 'clear mind' so that they may then manage others around them. As one manager stated, 'First try to stabilize one's own emotions and internal activities, and then set out to influence and encourage people around.' While the managers may validate felt emotion, they link emotional upset with bad business. The key is to have an even, balanced, emotional experience that is felt at a moderate or 'normal' level of intensity so that business can be conducted as usual. The same manager continued: 'As a leader of an enterprise, anything *unusual* in emotion, moods, appearance, or even in mind, will easily bring some economic losses to the organization.'

While the managers claim to take responsibility for subduing their own emotional responses for the good of the organization, they clearly expect subordinates to do the same. Indeed, several of the managers' stories reflect anger at subordinates who put their own needs above the organization's needs. As one manager stated about a selfish employee: 'People like that are not worth our sympathy. He would sell out anybody for his own interest.' A second manager reported having 'an explosive burst of temper' with a buyer who had mistakenly purchased low quality materials that undermined their level of production for the next six months. The managers believed that just as they work to 'draw a lesson' from the emotional experience, subordinates should likewise reflect on their actions. In response to the careless buyer, the manager reported saying 'This is a lesson of blood. You should learn it by heart and improve yourself.' Emphasis is on learning how to 'correct oneself' to benefit the organizational operation.

Managing organizations is managing emotion. While homeostatic images of emotion imply an openness in system boundaries, it is managers who largely determine how permeable those boundaries will be. In doing so, they may be silencing or at least marginalizing emotional expression among organizational members who pay a disproportionate price for maintaining the status quo (Jaggar, 1989). System boundaries can be managed in ways that secure space for the articulation of managerial interests, while invalidating the expression of emotion among those who likely would be viewed as threats were they to articulate more freely their feelings of social and moral discontent.

On the surface of it, the ways in which this group of Chinese managers conceptualize emotion appears consistent with what seems to be some universal code of managerialism. The code makes clear that emotion should be managed in ways that do not disrupt organizational efficiency and productivity. However, only in the Chinese version do managers appear to take their emotion management responsibilities quite seriously, even going so far as to position themselves as instructors in the emotion management process.

Conclusions

Without question, emotion is heavily controlled among this group of Chinese managers. However, their discourse about emotion suggests that emotional control is an ongoing process of adaptation and learning similar to *homeostasis* and *lesson* rather than distinct episodes of confining feelings in a *container*. The container metaphor consists of two discrete dimensions, the mind container positioned over the bodily container. No such split appears to be implied in the language of *homeostasis* or *lesson*. Homeostatic processes require the body, mind and heart to work together in a coordinated fashion to regain emotional equilibrium. As the source of thought *and* feeling, the heart is at the *centre* of self-restraint, but it does not dominate the other parts of the system.

Understanding emotion as homeostatic process and lesson has interesting implications for managerial emotional labour. Moderating the intensity of strong feelings, regaining inner balance and learning from emotional experience strike us as effortful emotional labour. However, they also strike us as a type of emotional labour that is *less* self-estranging than that of containment. Rather than sacrificing emotion to reason, both are necessary in order to recognize the significance of a disruption, to restore a sense of equilibrium and balance, to learn from the experience, and to respond effectively. While emotions are definitely restrained in this form of emotional labour, they are not denied. In compartmentalizing or denying emotion, the language of containment not only dulls the expression of emotion, it simultaneously stifles the formation of an understanding of oneself as an emotional being. In contrast, a kind of emotional consciousness is constructed through the language of homeostasis and lesson. Within the language of homeostasis the emotional self is not removed or suppressed, but instead engaged in the entire learning process. This tendency toward self-engagement over self-estrangement is evident in the language of one manager who said that he would slow down to learn a lesson from the experience even in the middle of his 'moods'. Emotion becomes understood as an inevitable and ongoing source of individual and organizational renewal. Recognizing, reflecting upon and restraining emotion combine to transform emotional experience into lessons that can further develop and refine an understanding of what it means to be human. And, in the case of high-level managers, a heightened sense of emotion consciousness also is put to work on behalf of organizational survival.

This sample of managerial discourse has taught us what it looks like to conceptualize emotion in terms that go beyond 'containment'. At the same time, while Chinese managers believe in their own feelings as a kind of homeostatic process, they may deploy the language of homeostasis and lesson in ways that result in the simple containment of employee emotion in organizations. Exhorting a problem employee to learn from the consequences of his or her mistakes is not equivalent to providing the employee time and space in which to do so. Our sense is that the Chinese are attempting to operate according to some combination of what they consider to be 'best' socialist and capitalist principles. We wonder if the demands of participating in a Western, market-driven economy ultimately will have a homogenizing effect on managerial emotional labour. Even though the Chinese experience and understand emotion in homeostatic terms, a universal code of managerialism is rooted in Western capitalistic ideals that privilege concerns for productivity, speed and efficiency over concerns for careful thought, reflection and learning. With their country's shift toward a market-driven economy, Chinese managers may be constrained to present an orientation toward emotion that conforms to this unwritten code. To the extent that this occurs, emotion may run the risk of being returned to its more traditionally Western position of serving rationality. Amidst this drift toward Western managerialism, it would be interesting to learn more about unconventional expressions of emotion in Chinese work settings and the extent to which they are effective in challenging, resisting or negotiating the emerging managerial code (Clark, 1990; Jaggar, 1989; Sugrue, 1982; Trawick, 1990). We are intrigued by the possibility that a homeostatic understanding of emotion – moderating intense feelings, regaining inner balance and learning from emotional experiences – will linger on among members of more marginalized groups and become useful in resisting pressure to contain and commodify emotion.

All intercultural encounters are complicated and enriched by cultural differences, but those between the Chinese and North Americans are understood to be particularly problematic (Young, 1994). The Chinese skill of restraining emotion may be misinterpreted by non-Chinese as simply being unemotional. Those who operate largely according to a 'container' metaphor are unlikely to appreciate the sophistication involved in a more 'homeostatic' orientation toward emotion. Becoming conscious of cross-cultural metaphorical expressions of emotion in everyday life can help us realize the provisional nature of what we think we know about emotion, and the possibility of reconceptualizing thought and feeling as equally compelling forces in our lives.

References

Abu-Lughod, L. and Lutz, C. (1990) 'Emotion, discourse, and the politics of everyday life', in C.A. Lutz and L. Abu-Lughod (eds), *Language and the Politics of Emotion*. Cambridge: Cambridge University Press. pp. 1–23.

Averill, J.R. (1986) 'The acquisition of emotions during adulthood', in R. Harré (ed.), *The Social Construction of Emotions*. Oxford: Basil Blackwell. pp. 98–118.

Bond, M.H. (1993) 'Emotions and their expression in Chinese culture', *Journal of Nonverbal Behavior*, 17: 245–62.

Brislin, R.W. (1970) 'Back-translation for cross-cultural research', *Journal of Cross-Cultural Psychology*, 1: 185–216.

Chamberlain, H.B. (1987) 'Party-management relations in Chinese industries: some political dimensions of economic reform', *China Quarterly*, 112: 631–61.

Chang, H.C. and Holt, G.R. (1991) 'More than relationship: Chinese interaction and the principle of "kuan-hsi"', *Communication Quarterly*, 39: 251–71.

Chen, G.-M. and Chung, J. (1994) 'The impact of Confucianism on organizational communication', *Communication Quarterly*, 42: 93–105.

Child, J. (1994) *Management in China during the Age of Reform*. Cambridge: Cambridge University Press.

Clark, C. (1990) 'Emotions and micropolitics in everyday life: some patterns and paradoxes of "place"', in T.D. Kemper (ed.), *Research Agendas in the Sociology of Emotions*. Albany: State University of New York Press. pp. 305–33.

Conrad, C. and Witte, K. (1994) 'Is emotional expression repression oppression? Myths of organizational affective regulation', in S.A. Deetz (ed.), *Communication Yearbook 17*. Thousand Oaks, CA: Sage. pp. 417–28.

Deetz, S. and Mumby, D. (1985) 'Metaphors, information, and power', in B.D. Ruben (ed.), *Information and Behavior*, Vol. 1. New Brunswick: Transaction Books. pp. 369–86.

Fainsilber, L. and Ortony, A. (1987) 'Metaphorical uses of language in the expression of emotions', *Metaphor and Symbolic Activity*, 2: 239–50.

Fineman, S. (ed.) (1993) *Emotion in Organizations*. Newbury Park, CA: Sage.

Fineman, S. (1996) 'Emotion in organizing', in S.R. Clegg, C. Hardy and W.R. Nord (eds), *The Handbook of Organization Studies*. Thousand Oaks, CA: Sage. pp. 543–64.

Giddens, A. (1984). *The Constitution of Society*. Berkeley: University of California Press.

Harré, R. (1986) 'The social construction of emotions', in R. Harré and R. Finlay Jones, *The Social Construction of Emotions*. Oxford: Blackwell. pp. 2–14.

Hearn, J. (1993) 'Emotive subjects: organizational men, organizational masculinities and the (de)construction of "emotions"', in S. Fineman (ed.), *Emotion in Organizations*. Newbury Park, CA: Sage. pp. 142–66.

Heelas, P. (1986) 'Emotion talk across cultures', in R. Harré and L. Finlay Jones (eds), *The Social Construction of Emotions*. Oxford: Basil Blackwell. pp. 234–66.

Hochschild, A.R. (1983) *The Managed Heart: Commercialization of Human Feeling*. Berkeley: University of California Press.

Hofstede, G. (1980) *Culture's Consequences: International Differences in Work-Related Values*. Beverly Hills, CA: Sage.

Hofstede, G. and Bond, M.H. (1998) 'The Confucius connection: from cultural roots to economic growth', *Organizational Dynamics*, 16: 4–21.

Hu, W. and Grove, C.L. (1991) *Encountering the Chinese: A Guide for Americans*. Yarmouth, ME: Intercultural Press.

Jaggar, A.M. (1989) 'Love and knowledge: emotion in feminist epistemology', in A.M. Jaggar and S.R. Bordo (eds), *Gender/Body/Knowledge*. New Brunswick, NJ: Rutgers. University Press. pp. 145–71.

Johnson, M. (1987) *The Body in the Mind: The Bodily Basis of Meaning, Imagination, and Reason*. Chicago: The University of Chicago Press.

Kleinman, A. and Kleinman, J. (1985) 'Somatization: the interconnections in Chinese society among culture, depressive experiences, and the meaning of pain', in A. Kleinman and B. Good (eds), *Culture and Depression: Studies in the Anthropology and Cross-Cultural Psychiatry of Affect and Disorder*. Berkeley: University of California Press. pp. 429–90.

Klineberg, O. (1938) 'Emotional expression in Chinese literature', *Journal of Abnormal and Social Psychology*, 33: 517–20.

Koch, S. and Deetz, S. (1981) 'Metaphor analysis of social reality in organizations', *Journal of Applied Communication Research*, 9: 1–15.

Kovecses, Z. (1990) *Emotion Concepts*. New York: Springer-Verlag.

Kristeva, J. (1993) *About Chinese Women*. New York: Marion Boyars.

Krone, K.J., Chen, L., Sloan, D.K. and Gallant, L.M. (1997) 'Managerial emotionality in Chinese factories', *Management Communication Quarterly*, 11: 6–50.

Krone, K.J., Chen, L. and Xia, H. (1997) 'Approaches to managerial influence in the People's Republic of China', *Journal of Business Communication*, 34: 289–315.

Lakoff, G. and Johnson, M. (1980) *Metaphors We Live By*. Chicago: University of Chicago Press.

Lakoff, G. and Johnson, M. (1999) *Philosophy in the Flesh: The Embodied Mind and its Challenge to Western Thought*. New York: Basic Books.

Langer, S.K. (1967) *Philosophy in a New Key: A Study in the Symbolism of Reason, Rite, and Art*. Cambridge, MA: Harvard University Press.

Lin, K.M. (1980) 'Traditional Chinese medical beliefs and their relevance for mental illness and psychiatry', in A. Kleinman and T.Y. Lin (eds), *Normal and Abnormal Behavior in Chinese Culture*. Dordrecht, Netherlands: D. Reidel. pp. 95–111.

Lutz, C. (1987) 'Goals, events, and understanding in Ifaluk emotion theory', in D. Holland and N. Quinn (eds), *Cultural Models in Language and Thought*. Cambridge: Cambridge University Press. pp. 290–312.

Lutz, C. (1988) *Unnatural Emotions: Everyday Sentiments on a Micronesian Atoll and their Challenge to Western Theory*. Chicago: University of Chicago Press.

Lutz, C. and White, G.M. (1986) 'The anthropology of emotions', *Annual Review of Anthropology*, 15: 405–36.

Markus, H.R. and Kitayama, S. (1991) 'Culture and the self: implications for cognition, emotion and motivation', *Psychological Review*, 98: 224–53.

Messerschmidt, J.W. (1996) 'Managing to kill: masculinities and the space shuttle *Challenger* explosion', in C. Cheng (ed.), *Masculinities in Organizations*. Thousand Oaks, CA: Sage. pp. 29–53.

Middleton, D.R. (1989) 'Emotional style: the cultural ordering of emotions', *Ethos*, 17: 187–201.

Morgan, G. (1997) *Images of Organization*. Thousand Oaks, CA: Sage.

Oatley, K. (1993) 'Social construction in emotions', in M. Lewis and J.M. Haviland (eds) *Handbook of Emotions*. New York: The Guildford Press. pp. 341–52.

Ortony, A. (1975) 'Why metaphors are necessary and not just nice', *Educational Theory*, 25: 45–53.

Ortony, A. (1979) 'Metaphor: a multidimensional problem', in A. Ortony (ed.), *Metaphor and Thought*. Cambridge: Cambridge University Press. pp. 1–16.

Putnam, L.L. and Mumby, D.K. (1993) 'Organizations, emotion and the myth of rationality', in S. Fineman (ed.), *Emotion in Organizations*. Newbury Park, CA: Sage. pp. 36–57.

Putnam, L.L., Phillips, N. and Chapman, P. (1996) 'Metaphors of communication and organization', in S.R. Clegg, C. Hardy and W.R. Nord (eds), *The Handbook of Organization Studies*. Thousand Oaks, CA: Sage. pp. 375–408.

Schon, D.A. (1979) 'Generative metaphor: a perspective on problem-setting in social policy', in A. Ortony (ed.), *Metaphor and Thought*. Cambridge: Cambridge University Press. pp. 284–324.

Smith, R.C. and Eisenberg, E.M. (1987) 'Conflict at Disneyland: a root-metaphor analysis', *Communication Monographs*, 54: 367–80.

Sugrue, N.M. (1982) 'Emotions as property and context for negotiation', *Urban Life*, 11: 280–92.

Sun, L.-K. (1991) 'Contemporary Chinese culture: structure and emotionality', *Australian Journal of Chinese Affairs*, 26: 1–41.

Tolich, M. (1993) 'Alienating and liberating emotions at work – supermarket clerks performance of customer service', *Journal of Contemporary Ethnography*, 22: 361–81.

Trawick, M. (1990) 'Untouchability and the fear of death in a Tamil song', in C.A. Lutz and L. Abu-Lughod (eds), *Language and the Politics of Emotion*. Cambridge: Cambridge University Press. pp. 186–206.

Trompenaars, F. (1993) *Riding the Waves of Culture: Understanding Diversity in Global Business*. Burr Ridge, IL: Irwin.

Tu, W.-M. (1985) 'Selfhood and otherness in Confucian thought', in A.J. Marsella, G. DeVos and F.L.K. Hsu (eds), *Culture and Self: Asian and Western Perspectives*. New York: Tavistock. pp. 231–51.

Van Maanen, J. and Kunda, G. (1989) '"Real feelings": emotional expression and organizational culture', in B.M. Staw and L.L. Cummings (eds), *Research in Organizational Behavior*, 11: 43–103. Greenwich, CT: JAI.

Walder, A.G. (1989) 'Factory and manager in an era of reform', *China Quarterly*, 118: 242–64.

Waldron, V.R. and Krone, K.J. (1991) 'The experience and expression of emotion in the workplace: a study of a corrections organization', *Management Communication Quarterly*, 4: 287–309.

Warner, M. (1991) 'Labour–management relations in the People's Republic of China: the role of the trade unions', *International Journal of Human Resource Management*, 2: 205–20.

Wong, D.B. (1991) 'Is there a distinction between reason and emotion in Mencius?' *Philosophy East & West*, 41: 31–44.

Wu, D.Y.H. (1982) 'Psychotherapy and emotion in traditional Chinese medicine', in A.J. Marsella and G.M. White (eds), *Cultural Conceptions of Mental Health and Therapy*. Dordrecht, Netherlands: D. Reidel. pp. 285–301.

Yang, C.K. (1959) 'Some characteristics of Chinese bureaucratic behavior', in D.S. Nivison and A.F. Wright (eds), *Confucianism in Action*. Stanford, CA: Stanford University Press. pp. 134–64.

Young, L.W.L. (1994) *Crosstalk and Culture in Sino-American Communication*. Cambridge: Cambridge University Press.

Yu, N. (1995) 'Metaphorical expressions of anger and happiness in English and Chinese', *Metaphor and Symbolic Activity*, 10: 59–92.

PART II
APPROPRIATING AND ORGANIZING EMOTION

6 COMMODIFYING THE EMOTIONALLY INTELLIGENT

STEPHEN FINEMAN

I've performed or commissioned several new scientific analyses of data from hundreds of companies to establish a precise metric for quantifying the value of emotional intelligence . . . The business case is compelling: Companies that leverage this [emotional intelligence] advantage add measurably to their bottom line. (Goleman, 1998b: 5,13)

The idea of Emotional Intelligence is sweeping the country. Science itself is proving that it is Emotional Quotient, EQ, more than IQ or raw brain power alone, that underpins many of the best decisions, the most dynamic businesses and the most satisfying and successful lives. (Publisher's claims for Robert Cooper's and Ayman Sawaf's book, *Executive EQ*, 1997)

The flow and rhetoric associated with emotional intelligence has grown with extraordinary speed. Salovey and Mayer (1990) are said to have coined the term, but its popularization is associated with Daniel Goleman's book *Emotional Intelligence* ('The Number One Best Seller') in 1996. This was fast followed in 1998b by his *Working with Emotional Intelligence*, produced with a clear eye on industry, a market for his emotional intelligence training package. In the same year a *Harvard Business Review* article on the subject linked emotional intelligence to leadership (Goleman, 1998a). Goleman has his own web site to promote a 'four phase' approach to raising emotional intelligence. Emotional intelligence has taken root as the new 'answer' to a whole range of organizational performance problems, a supposed antidote to our customary cognitive preoccupations.

The diffusion of emotional intelligence into popular and professional literature, particularly in the United States, has been remarkable. Feature articles are evident in publications as diverse as *American Nurseryman*, *Parents*, *Mademoiselle* ('Never lose it at work again'), *Better Homes and Gardens*, *Learning*, *Newsweek*, *Cosmopolitan* ('The lowdown on high EQ'), *Academy of Management Review*, *The Southern Journal of Philosophy*

('Emotional intelligence and wisdom'), *Journal of Personality and Social Psychology*, and *HR Magazine* ('The smarts that count'). American Express has 'tapped into the power of emotional intelligence' (Hays, 1999). We are further informed, by Ann Beatty (1996) in the *St Louis Business Journal*, that Bill Clinton was voted as having a particularly high EQ compared with his co-runners in the 1996 US presidential election (a somewhat ironic observation in the light of his subsequent impeachment for lying to the US Congress). In the UK, emotional intelligence is, according to the *Times Higher Educational Supplement* (14 May 1999) 'reshaping business school research programmes'. The national Sunday newspaper the *Observer* takes a similar upbeat line in suggesting that emotional intelligence could be the 'final frontier for performance improvement in companies' (14 March 1999).[1]

How are we to appreciate such a phenomenon? One way is positivistically. Are the claims scientifically valid? Is there really such a construct as emotional intelligence and can it predict? Are the measures well developed? What are the samples and the statistics? Cooper and Sawaf (1997), for example, offer an EQ questionnaire comprising 21 subscales. Goleman speaks of 'five dimensions of emotional intelligence' and 'twenty-five emotional competencies'. How do these square up to traditional psychometric criteria?

This line of questioning has been taken up with some vigour by applied psychologists (including Schutte et al., 1998; Davies et al., 1998; Sternberg and Kaufman, 1998; Huy, 1999; Abraham, 1999). Indeed, some of these writers cast considerable doubt on the wisdom of trying to measure emotional intelligence (see for example Jones, 1997). However, my interest in this chapter is rather different. It lies in the commodification of emotion – transforming emotion into a marketable product. It is a process that goes beyond the niceties of academic debate and the psychologist's particular rendition(s) of truth. The popularization of emotional intelligence presents emotion in a form that can be contained and 'sold', especially to the corporate world. It does this through a set of rhetorical devices which privilege a certain, restricted, notion of emotion – which are themselves emotionally appealing. Its manifest instrumentality and elitism (it can produce 'stars') and its supposedly mutability ('raise your EQ') play on classic anxieties and promises, often with a clear managerialistic agenda. These, I will argue, are key ingredients for an emerging management fad, if not fashion. The extent to which the claims for emotional intelligence are scientifically 'true' is less of an issue here than how they are made to appear true, using social science and other means. Crucially, if emotional intelligence is embraced in this manner, what moral and practical consequences follow?

Selling emotion

The notion that certain work relationships require emotions as skills or competencies is not new. Counsellors, teachers, therapists, social workers, nurses and related medical professionals, as well as some sales and customers' services agents, have long been regarded as requiring sensitivity in their work, such as empathy, sympathy, the management of own feelings, as well as skills in anger and distress management. Many such jobs include focused training courses aimed at teaching incumbents appropriate emotional skills or 'face work' and ways of 'reading', controlling and re-presenting feelings (see Sturdy, 1998). There are management/organizational consultants who specialize in delivering generic, or bespoke, programmes of these sorts.

In one sense, emotional intelligence revolves around such well rehearsed issues, but is presented as something new – what Roy Jacques (1996) would terms a procrustean revolution. Procrustes, in Greek mythology, had a predilection for fitting guests into his bed by modifying the size of the guest. Yet emotional intelligence may be seen as 'discovering' and 'coming out' of emotions on an unusually wide scale. It is presented as central to just about all features of managerial and executive performance; the 'intelligent' deployment of emotions is crucial to successful performance. The traditional emphasis on intellectual ability in organizations has, goes the argument, eclipsed the role and value of emotions. Both need to be respected in equal measure:

> Emotional intelligence is the ability to sense, understand, and effectively apply the power and acumen of *emotions* as a source of human energy, information, connection, and influence. (Cooper and Sawaf, 1997: xiii, original emphasis)

For Goleman (1996: 43–4) (borrowing from Salovey and Mayer,1990), the emotionally intelligent have abilities in five main domains: *they know their emotions, manage their emotions, motivate themselves, recognize emotions in others*, and *handle relationships*. This is what helps them to be 'stars' in their occupation or calling.

A management idea that catches on does so because of psychological, cultural and rhetorical factors (Huczynski, 1996). Psychological features include a fear of losing ground to competitors and the urgency thus generated to find an authoritative fix, especially one that high prestige competitors already have adopted (see for example Gill and Whittle, 1992). Cultural factors concern how organizational and institutional stakeholders are thinking and feeling, creating more or less favourable conditions for the development and propagandization of the new idea. Emotional intelligence, therefore, needs to be perceived by its potential managerial users as attractive, firmly connected to organizational success and in tune with wider social pressures. Rhetoric connects these various processes; that is, the way different consultants, business academics and the business press craft emotional intelligence to appear cogent and indispensable to organizations and management (Hucznyski, 1996; Keiser, 1997; Sturdy, 1997). Pithy one-liners, such as, 'Generally speaking, it is IQ that gets you hired but EQ that gets you promoted' (Beatty, 1996: 43) illustrate the form.

The promise

> Modern science is proving everyday that it is emotional intelligence, not IQ or raw brain power alone that underpins the best decisions, the most dynamic organizations and the most satisfying and successful lives. (Cooper and Sawaf, 1997; xii)

> I was lucky enough to have access to competence models for 181 positions drawn from 121 companies and organizations worldwide, with their combined workforce numbering millions . . . I found that *67 percent* – two out of three – of the abilities deemed essential for effective performance were emotional competencies. (Goleman, 1998b: 31, original emphasis)

The promise of emotional intelligence is that it provides 'what employers want'; it is 'profitable' for business outcomes, it creates clear leadership – and, importantly, social science can support these claims. The titles/subtitles of the managerial books in the field immediately signal the promise, such as: *Hidden Dynamics: How Emotions Affect Business Performance and How You Can Harness their Power for Positive Results* (Ralston, 1995); *Executive EQ: Emotional Intelligence in Leadership and Organizations* (Cooper and Sawaf, 1997); *From Chaos to Coherence: Advancing Emotional and Organizational Intelligence through Inner Quality Management* (Childre and Cryer, 1999); *Emotional Intelligence at Work* (Weisinger, 1998).

Appeals to 'studies' and 'psychology' are frequently made to reinforce the credibility of emotional intelligence. Goleman, the dominant figure in the field, is fond of expansive claims. In *Working with Emotional Intelligence*, he speaks of 'landmark' studies which show, for example, that people with self-confidence are more successful, self-controlled people think clearly and stay focused under pressure, and innovative people generate new ideas. These are some of the findings from 'twenty-five years' worth of empirical studies that tell us with a previously unknown precision just how much emotional intelligence matters for success' (Goleman, 1998b: 6). Such hyperbole, which would unnerve characteristically cautious social scientists, is further embellished with frequent mention of 'big names' in industry, CEOs Goleman has spoken with, his former 'Harvard professors', and snappy tales of 'stars' in industry who purportedly embody facets of emotional intelligence.

Goleman indulges (indeed wallows) in aspiring-guru rhetoric (see Eccles et al., 1992). His book is structured with short, eye-catching sections (such as 'A Different Way of Being Smart', 'A Coming Crisis: Rising IQ, Dropping EQ', 'What Exactly Is A Star Worth?'). Sentences are short, the journalese is often direct and personal, and bold tables offer key summaries as the book progresses. The book's front cover is virtually identical in design to his previous 'international best seller', *Emotional Intelligence: Why It Can Matter More Than IQ*, offering ease of association for existing converts.

There is a growing industry of consultants and academics devoted to emotional intelligence, several of which involve Goleman himself. For example, there is the web-based 'Emotional Intelligence Consortium', and 'Linkage Inc.' of Massachusetts, a consultancy which assesses the 'impact of emotional competence on technical work' and features Goleman at conferences. Other, non-Goleman, web sites selling emotional intelligence services are 'Pro Philes', the 'unparalleled leader in emotional intelligence testing, profiling, training, coaching . . .' It eulogizes Dr Reuven Bar-On and his book *Optimizing People* (1999a), 'the last corporate secret . . . a practical guide for applying EQ'. Less flamboyant is Robert Cooper's and Ayman Sawaf's site, EQ.ORG, 'the online source for emotional intelligence' promoting their book *Executive EQ* and EQ training. The influence of virtual communications is significant here, offering accessible, 'instant', images to whet the managerial appetite.

The purveyors of emotional intelligence stress its performance benefits and mutability, a bait for performance-hungry, competitively anxious, managers and executives:

> our level of emotional intelligence is not fixed genetically, nor does it develop only in early childhood. Unlike IQ, which changes little after our teen years, emotional intelligence seems to be largely learned and it continues to develop as we go through life and learn through our experiences – our competence in it can keep growing. (Goleman, 1998b: 7)

Presenting emotional intelligence as a learned competence or set of competencies is a key ingredient of the sell. Competencies, more broadly, are now commonly associated with high-performance job behaviours in management (for example, Boyatzis, 1982; Mullins, 1999), and it is in this spirit that emotional intelligence is taken as a 'must' for team leadership, for wielding influence, for persuasion, networking, dealing with difficult co-workers, improving morale and sales performance (for example, Weisinger, 1998; Goleman, 1998b). Its promoters dispel any 'misconception' that that emotional intelligence is 'simply' about giving free rein to feelings. Typically, emotional intelligence is stripped of any 'irrational', 'feminine', even 'feeling' connotations that could worry or alienate managers. It is less a celebration of feeling than a resource to enhance managers' 'intelligent', rational control.

It is hard to deny that Goleman et al. have pulled off a significant rhetorical feat in the marketing of emotional intelligence. It has the appearance of a prize worth paying for, despite the somewhat fragmented and over-reverential style of Goleman's book, *Working with Emotional Intelligence*. As one reviewer comments:

> It reads like a cross between an introductory text on Human Resource Management and a Tom Peters book. It seems to have been thrown together in a rushed attempt to capitalise on the term EI and the name and recognition of the author. (Hein, 1999)

Measuring it

A management technique or fashion is made especially palpable, or real, if it is amenable to measurement and quantification. Popular management 'packages', from Management by Objectives to Total Quality Management, have capitalized on the attraction of calibration to management, and the sense of predictability and control that that brings. Emotional intelligence is no exception.

IQ-type acronyms, such 'EQ' and 'Emotional IQ' have become catchy shorthands for the emotional intelligence metric. It has been fed and formalized by applied psychological consultants and academics who have reduced emotional intelligence to an easy pencil-and-paper format, often with impressive-looking standardization data. For example the Bar-On Emotional Quotient Inventory claims to have been tested on 'over 14,000 individuals worldwide' and is the 'first scientifically validated test of "emotional intelligence"'. It is advertised as only available from the author, described ingenuously as 'not written to be another faddish "pop" hit . . . thus not sold in the bookshops' (Bar-On, 1999b). Bar-On, nevertheless, takes pains to stress the 'bottom-line' benefits of his tests in familiar 'SWOT' format: the strengths and weaknesses associated with specific EQ factors, the opportunities for improvement, and the threats that go with some low EQ scores. 'Instant' EQ tests have appeared in popular media. *USA Weekend*, for example, published a Goleman-derivative of twelve self-report questions, such as 'Bad moods overwhelm me' and 'I can sense the pulse of the group or a relationship and state unspoken feelings' (11 September 1995).

The readout format of the major EQ tests – subscale grids, maps, factor scores – adds to the appearance of an authoritative, scientific product which should be taken seriously. Its association with the familiar IQ reinforces the impression of something that is psychologically important – for job performance and self-image.

The right time for emotion?

The above rhetorical processes capture and define emotional intelligence in product form, worthy of managerial attention and purchase. But why should managers be receptive to such overtures? What wider social circumstances, if any, predispose emotion narratives to be received favourably?

At one level, there are plausible reasons why such narratives should *not* be well received. Feelings, certainly in British/northern European work cultures, historically have been a matter of individualization and privatization (see Newton et al., 1995). Rationality (that is, non-emotionality) of decision making and thought has long been prized in Western social conduct. 'Interfering' emotions – such as anger, fear, infatuation and stress – are regarded as hindering adaptation and progress in many organizations (see for example Robbins, 1998; Stearns and Stearns, 1986). Rational models of planning, performance and change continue to saturate management textbooks. Indeed, emotional restraint has become the hallmark of civility within and beyond organizations; the boundary between the private and the public is carefully protected and only cautiously tested (Elias, 1994). More locally, 'emotion' and 'feeling' talk in management and organizations is often highly circumscribed by subcultural mores, such as what is appropriate to express or show – in the school classroom, the aircraft galley, restaurant kitchen, corridor, washroom, executive board meeting, or hotel reception foyer (Fineman, 1999).

But there is another, rather different picture we can paint, signs of a new emotionality at large. For example, it is now regular practice for journalists to seek instant emotional reactions at disasters, tragedies or celebratory events, making public a range of intimate emotions, from embarrassment, love and exuberance, to despair and grief (Walter et al., 1995). In the UK the untimely death of Diana Princess of Wales in 1997 triggered an extraordinary, open, expression of grief in the UK. The media images of public distress and shock were played, and replayed, to a world audience.

In the USA, the camera now has voyeuristic access to the major courtroom trials, offering close-ups of the tears, anger and anguish of participants. TV and radio soap operas are often explicit about the emotional lives of their characters – their angst, depression, suicide, marital infidelity and sexualities. We have camera 'diaries' of individuals facing major emotional events, such as hospitalization or an incurable disease, some tracking the sufferer to his or her death. The emotional drama of emergency services – police work, fire fighting, ambulances, sea rescue – is captured in live footage. Chat shows of the Oprah Winfrey variety explore the sorrows, trials and tribulations of 'guests', often in remarkable emotional detail, lifting, for full public gaze, traditional taboos on incest, jealousy, polygamy, matricide and abandonment. Tears, anger or pain are part of the 'show', a commodification of emotion that can be translated into viewer rating figures.

Stress and stress-related illness have become part of public, organizational, medical and legal discourse. It is now 'OK' to feel and admit stress. For two decades feminism has eroded some of the crudest signs of male patronage and blurred some of the dichotomized 'female' and 'male' emotions. Sportsmen can now cry publicly, as well as whoop for joy. 'New men' who are willing to express their feelings, admit their failings and cross the gender-role divide, feature in popular magazines and films. 'Men's groups' have migrated from the West Coast of California to most major UK cities, places where men can talk semi-publicly about their feelings and personal concerns. Psychological counselling for a whole range of personal/emotional issues has become something of a mini-industry and is openly advertised in doctors' surgeries, health clinics and on workplace noticeboards.

In other arenas, the customerization of services such as banking, fast food, hotels, airlines, insurance companies, car service agents and theme parks has brought the 'smile industry' to the hitherto indifferent, or even grudging, face of customer services (Sturdy, 1997; Hochschild, 1983). Indeed, engendering enthusing emotions has been central to the much vaunted (and much criticized) organizational cultures of 'excellent' companies. The shaping of such emotions continues to feature in organizations where 'positive bonds' and 'shared visions' are valued (Brown, 1995).

All these processes suggest that emotions are finding different *forms* and *arenas* of social legitimization and expression. Such shifts are not unproblematic, nor necessarily uncontested, but they diffuse a belief that (a) emotion can be exposed in new ways, and (b) some of those ways can be productively harnessed to commercial ends. Both are key props to the propagation of, and receptivity towards, emotional intelligence.

A good thing?

The moral and value territory on which emotional intelligence treads is, typically, unquestioned. Like most managerial fixes, high emotional intelligence is good because it (supposedly) produces winners or stars in a competitive market system that values winners and stars. Its instrumental purpose requires no further justification, offering smooth entry for emotional intelligence consultants. Emotion is thus appropriated to shape and sustains a particular managerialistic perspective (see Kamoche and Mueller, 1998). The moral appeal of emotional intelligence is further embellished by the spectre it raises of the 'emotionally honest' ('indispensable for insight and good judgement'), the 'emotionally energetic' and those who have 'authentic presence' (see Cooper and Sawaf, 1997).

Given such a warm constellation of attributes it seems churlish to raise doubts about what emotional intelligence represents. Nevertheless, there are some important questions to consider.

What of the emotionally unintelligent?

The seduction of emotional intelligence is that it presents a plausible basic rationale: that emotions and cognitions often work in tandem, or intertwine, and that is a better base for examining all manner of decisions and interpersonal processes than exclusively cognitive formulations. This is what Goleman popularized in his first book, *Emotional Intelligence*, derived from a number of different 'respectable' sources, including Damasio's (1994) *Descartes' Error: Emotion, Reason and the Human Brain* (see also Chapter 1). But when such a rationale is used to argue that the emotionally intelligent have a special resource that will help them succeed organizationally while the rest will fail, or have 'fatal flaws' (Beatty, 1996), the prescription's import is as much moral as political. It is not unlike that associated with the use of IQ tests in streaming children towards different educational or occupational experiences. Indeed, historically the application of IQ has been shown to reflect the prejudices and predilections of the psychologists who have controlled the technique (such as their assumptions about the relative superiority of some racial groups (Kamin, 1974)). IQ labelling has been accused of causing 'immense damage to individuals and groups who are stigmatized as intellectually inferior by psychological tests that are given more credibility than they deserve' (Fox and Prilleltensky, 1997: 121). Emotional intelligence falls into IQ's shadow. Its mixed, often vague measures, are employed as a 'discourse technology' (Fairclough, 1989), where appropriated social scientific, or quasi-scientific, knowledge is used to powerfully disseminate a particular creed about emotions.

The issue is sharpened when the emotionally less-intelligent are defined as rescuable, but exclusively through the consultant-cum-guru's training programme. Constructing emotional intelligence in the benign language of 'competencies' and 'training' may lessen the personal anxiety of being categorized as low on emotional intelligence, but it does not release the manager from contrived dependence on the consultant to improve matters. Nor is there any guarantee, in a field where different authors offer different cocktails of attributes and competencies to define emotional intelligence, that 'appropriate' and enduring change will take place.

When social science findings are arranged to serve specific social-economic aims or interests (such as competitiveness, leadership, profit, corporate growth), there is always a risk of oversell, fashion-fade or outright failure. We may argue the moral import of such events in terms of the intentions of the fashion-setters (for example, their honesty, integrity, professionalism) and the effects on those who purchase the product or idea (helped, manipulated, confused, hurt, deceived, exploited . . .). Yet the moral dice are loaded when the very technique or concept creates distinctions that immediately relegate, with apparent force and authority, some people to a less worthy or less 'competent' personal condition. Emotions may be finding new avenues for 'coming out', but they are characteristically poised delicately within private and public domains. Negative judgements about emotional competence can be suggestive of all manner of personal 'disorders' which, when exposed to market-place demands, fashionable manipulations and powerful consultant-interventions, may exploit or harm (intended or unintended), much the same as has been found in jobs where emotional labour proves to be unduly onerous or personally damaging (Hochschild, 1983; see also this volume, Chapter 1).

The ingredients of executive stardom are somewhat volatile, reflecting (amongst other things) the social and economic times, as well as sectoral and functional differences. Furthermore, the search for key, universal, characteristics of managerial success has a long history of futility. If emotionally intelligent managers succeed, so do/have managers who seem to make no conscious choice about how to express their emotions – be they typically kind, charismatic, impassive, volatile, aggressive, autocratic, even ruthless. On this basis it would, at times, be emotionally intelligent to be uncompromising, inflexible, angry or pessimistic. Indeed, the 'tough love' corporate regimes of the late 1990s could be very much characterized as an emotionally stringent, controlling, response to harsh and competitive economic times

(Legge, 1995). But Goleman's emotionally intelligent managers are not offered this route. Goleman favours a more 'virtuous American', 'positive mental attitude' image of the emotionally intelligent manager, a person who displays 'emotional' traits of enthusiasm, optimism, hope, initiative and persistence.

What happens to feelings?

The emotionally intelligent manager is able 'read' and 'control' 'inner states', feelings, 'subjective currents' and 'body sensations', sort them and apply them selectively and 'appropriately' to management situations. Contrary perhaps to first impressions, it is the intellectualization process that makes feelings and emotions worthy of attention – because it is more amenable to articulation and consultant intervention. Cooper and Sawaf explain: 'When you are conscious of your emotional states you gain valuable *flexibility of response* . . . with some practice, you can begin to distinguish between the many different emotions and feelings' (1997: 13, original emphasis). Processes such as intuition and 'gut feeling' are celebrated by EI writers, but only insofar as they can be captured for EI purposes and instrumentation. They are, according to Goleman, 'at the heart' of 'vital foundation skill' for emotional competencies (1998b: 54). Or, in Cooper and Sawaf's terms, 'you can consciously guide your intuitive feelings . . . towards seeking solutions . . . into being more attentive and perceptive' (1997: 59).

As one progresses into the literature it becomes apparent that emotional intelligence is far more about intelligence than emotions. In other words, it is processes of thinking and judgement that are being targeted – and refocused on emotions to enhance control of self and others. The inchoateness and 'natural wisdom' of feelings are carefully dissected and harnessed for 'executive purposes'. This raises a number of issues.

- If feelings inform thoughts and thoughts inform feelings – that is, they interpenetrate – then making decisions about feelings and emotions is of itself a feeling/emotional process. Emotional intelligence promises a form of rationality and control by the actor that is illusory or, more pointedly, a fake.
- Describing and labelling one's sensations and feelings (to self or to others) does something 'to' them. It gives them a social and political context; a contextualized meaning. 'Real' feelings, in these terms, are inevitably social/language constructs amenable to whatever signs and symbols are familiar, or amenable, to the actor (see Chapter 1). When emotional intelligence consultants colonize this arena, their preferred language of feelings is exposed, shaping what managers 'ought' to be focusing on. Bad feelings or states for Goleman (1998b) include impulsiveness, abrasiveness, arrogance, preoccupation with image. Good feelings or states embrace empathy, composure and self-assurance. And good emotional presentation dramatizes these good feelings. Jealousy, rage, desire, envy, fear, guilt,

boredom, vindictiveness, shame, disgust, hurt, are not specifically addressed. One must presume that the emotionally intelligent manager can acknowledge such feelings and then turn away from those that fail to translate into effective managerial action or stardom. What happens to the rejected impulse is not clear.

- Consciousness and awareness are a leitmotiv throughout emotional intelligence theorizing. In *Emotional Intelligence*, Goleman (1996) acknowledges and endorses a Freudian view of an unconscious emotional life, but he does not dwell on the matter. He prefers to stress the behavioural signs and symptoms of feelings 'simmering beneath the threshold of awareness' (p. 55) which, once brought into conscious awareness, can be evaluated and if necessary 'shrugged off' (p. 55) and changed at will. Whether such evaluations can take place dispassionately has already been touched upon. Notwithstanding the socially desirable appeal of, say, replacing hate, envy and anxiety with love, admiration and joy, it is questionable whether cognitive control over private feelings (contrasted to emotional display) is achievable as suggested. But, significantly, what is missing from emotional intelligence formulations is a way of grasping the psychoanalytic reality that we very often do not know what emotions are impelling us (that is, why we are doing what we are doing) because of the variety of defensive, displacement and screening processes that add complexity and richness to emotional life. From this perspective many of our emotions defy conscious control.
- A phenomenological 'reading' of feelings would suggest that they are often experienced as mixed and changing. Emotional intelligence writings imply the opposite – that one's feelings are mostly identifiable (after appropriate training) in a clear, discrete form, ready for manipulation, such as re-facing, suppression or embellishment, towards managerial/ corporate ends.

An emotionally intelligent future?

For students of the diffusion of management knowledge – how management fashions are shaped and popularized – emotional intelligence is instructive in that it is the first fashion to take emotion *per se* as its 'product'. Its closest rival is the T-group, or sensitivity training, popular with many large corporations in the 1960s and 1970s – a time when human relations programmes and worker participation were emerging as important ways of democratizing work (and society). Unlike the T-group era, though, emotional intelligence is highly focused, specific in its outcome-claims and makes no pretence that feelings are of themselves 'good to get into the open'. It is the way some feelings are 'intelligently' directed that counts. We all, at times, ponder about what we should 'do' with our feelings; emotional intelligence consultants boil this down to a skill that can be improved and aimed at the best (in their terms) managerial behaviours.

For advocates of emotion in organizations there is, perhaps, something to celebrate in the widening interest in emotional intelligence. It directs attention to organizations which have, hitherto, been criticized for emotional illiteracy (for example, in supervision, appraisal, training, customer relations) and the difficulties that that can produce within and beyond the organization (see Gabriel, 1998; Kets de Vries, 1991). It challenges the dominant model of rationality in organizational effectiveness and, in doing so, exposes some of the traditional organizational oppressions which have emotional under-pinnings and consequences – such as sexism, harassment, lack of compassion, prejudice and exploitation.

But such potential gains should be regarded cautiously. To a large extent, emotional intelligence has become what its popularizers have wanted it to become – a commodifiable emotion funnel, profitable to sell, which promises a fast route to organizational success, even individual fame. It is able to engage its audiences because of the rhetorical force of this assertion and because feelings and emotions are now much more widely situated in common discourse as an important part of life. However, while commodi-fication helps to distribute and sell an idea, it is also its trap. Emotional intelligence is imprisoned in a sales gloss that makes extravagant claims and promises, exercises its own tyranny by over-idealizing one particular form of psychological being over another (and a prescribed route to change), and is highly contingent upon a certain sociocultural frame of organizational success.

Acknowledgements

My thanks to Martyn Pitt and Andrew Sturdy for their helpful comments on the ideas in this chapter. A version of this chapter was initially presented at the British Academy of Management's Annual Conference, Manchester, September 1999.

Note

1   The 'final frontier' is challenged by Zohar et al. (2000) who claim that 'spiritual intelligence' (SQ) is a richer form of emotional intelligence, capturing 'humanity's need for meaning'.

References

Abraham, R. (1999) 'Emotional intelligence in organizations: a conceptualization', *Genetic Social and General Psychology Monographs*, 125 (2): 209–24.

Bar-On, R. (1999a) *Optimizing People*. New Beafles, TX: Pro-philes.

Bar-On, R. (1999b) 'Pro-philes' web site: http://www.pro-philes.com

Beatty, A. (1996) 'Emotion quotient': a different kind of smart', *St Louis Business Journal*, 16 (April): 43–4.

Boyatzis, R. (1982) *The Competent Manager*. New York: Wiley.

Brown, A. (1995) *Organisational Culture*. London: Pitman.

Childre, D. and Cryer, B. (1999) *From Chaos to Coherence: Advancing Emotional and Organizational Intelligence through Inner Quality Management*. Boston: Butterworth Heinemann.

Cooper, R. and Sawaf, A. (1997) *Executive EQ*. London: Orion Business.

Damasio, A.R. (1994) *Descartes' Error: Emotion, Reason and the Human Brain*. New York: G.P. Putnam's Sons.

Davies, M., Stankov, L. and Roberts, R.D. (1998) 'Emotional intelligence: in search of an elusive construct', *Journal of Personality and Social Psychology*, 75: 989–1015.

Eccles, R., Nohria, N. and Berkeley, J.D. (1992). *Beyond the Hype: Rediscovering the Essence of Management*. Boston, MA.: Harvard Business School Press.

Elias, N. (1994) *The Civilizing Processes, Vols 1 and 2*. Oxford: Blackwell.

Fairclough, N. (1989) *Language and Power*. Harlow: Longman.

Fineman, S. (1999) 'Emotion and organizing', in S. Clegg, C. Hardy and W. Nord (eds), *Studying Organizations*. London: Sage.

Fox, D.R. and Prilleltensky, I. (1997) *Critical Psychology: An Introduction*. London: Sage.

Gabriel, Y. (1998) 'Psychoanalytic contributions to the study of the emotional life of organizations', *Administration and Society*, 30 (3): 291–314.

Gill, J. and Whittle, S. (1992) 'Management by panacea: accounting for transience', *Journal of Management Studies*, 30 (2): 281–95.

Goleman, D. (1996) *Emotional Intelligence*. London: Bloomsbury.

Goleman, D. (1998a) 'What makes a leader?', *Harvard Business Review*, 76 (6): 92–103.

Goleman, D. (1998b) *Working with Emotional Intelligence*. London: Bloomsbury.

Hays, S. (1999) 'American Express taps into the power of emotional intelligence', *Workforce*, 78 (7): 72–4.

Hein, S. (1999) Emotional Intelligence home page: http://eqi.org/busi.htm

Hochschild, A. (1983) *The Managed Heart*. Berkeley: University of California.

Huczynski, A.A. (1996) *Management Gurus*. London: Thompson.

Huy, Q.N. (1999) 'Emotional capability, emotional intelligence, and radical change', *Academy of Management Review*, 24 (2): 325–45.

Jacques, R. (1996) *Manufacturing the Employee*. London: Sage.

Jones, M.M. (1997) 'Unconventional wisdom: a report from the ninth annual convention of the American Psychological Society', *Psychology Today*, Sept/Oct: 34–6.

Kamin, L.J. (1974) *The Science and Politics of I.Q.*. Harmondsworth: Penguin.

Kamoche, K. and Mueller, F. (1998) 'Human resource management and the appropriation-leaning perspective'. *Human Relations*, 51 (8): 10–33.

Keiser, A. (1997) 'Rhetoric and myth in management fashion', *Organization*, 4 (1): 49–74.

Kets de Vries, M.F.R. (ed.) (1991) *Organizations on the Couch: Clinical Perspectives on Organizational Behavior and Change*. San Francisco: Jossey Bass.

Legge, K. (1995) *Human Resource Management*. Houndsmills, Basingstoke: Macmillan.

Mullins, L. (1999) *Management and Organisational Behaviour*. London: Pitman.

Newton, T., Handy, J. and Fineman, S. (1995) *'Managing' Stress: Emotion and Power at Work*. London: Sage.

Ralston, F. (1995) *Hidden Dynamics: How Emotions Affect Business Performance and How You Can Harness their Power for Positive Results*. American Management Association.

Robbins, S.P. (1998) *Organizational Behavior*. New Jersey: Prentice Hall.

Salovey, P. and Mayer, J.D. (1990) 'Emotional intelligence', *Imagination, Cognition and Personality*, 9: 185–211.

Schutte, N.S., Malouff, J.M., Hall, L.E., Haggerty, D.J., Cooper, J.T., Golden, C.J. and Dornheim, L. (1998) 'Development and validation of a measure of emotional intelligence', *Personality and Individual Differences*, 25: 167–77.

Stearns, P Z. and Stearns, P.N. (1986) *Anger: The Struggle for Emotional Control in America's History*, Chicago: University of Chicago Press.

Sternberg, R.J and Kaufman, J.C. (1998) 'Human abilities', *Annual Review of Psychology*, 49: 479–502.

Sturdy, A.J. (1997) 'The consultancy process – an insecure business?', *Journal of Management Studies*, 34 (3): 389–413.

Sturdy, A.J. (1998) 'Customer care in a consumer society', *Organization*, 5 (1): 27–54.

Walter, T., Littlewood, J. and Pickering, M. (1995) 'Death in the news: the public invigilation oration of private emotion', *Sociology*, 29 (4): 579–96.

Weisinger, H. (1998) *Emotional Intelligence at Work*. San Francisco: Jossey Bass.

Zohar, D., Mitchell, I. and Calder, L. (2000) *Spiritual Intelligence*. London: Bloomsbury.

7 BOUNDED EMOTIONALITY AT THE BODY SHOP

JOANNE MARTIN, KATHY KNOPOFF AND CHRISTINE BECKMAN

Impersonal criteria for making decisions and restraints on emotional expression at work have long been the hallmarks of organizational life (for example, Weber, 1946, 1981). Recent work has broken this emotional taboo (for example, Fineman, 1996), exploring how certain organizations require the expression of particular emotions at work in order to maximize organizational productivity, an aspect of job performance that has been labelled emotional labour (see for example Hochschild, 1983; Van Maanen and Kunda, 1989). Sutton (1991) and his colleagues (for example, Sutton and Rafaeli, 1998) have explored discrepancies between outward behaviour and inward feelings experienced by smiling flight attendants and nasty bill collectors. In contrast, feminist organizational theorists have developed an idealized view of the role of emotions in organizations, unencumbered, for the most part, by concerns about productivity, customer satisfaction, or profitability (see for example Marshall, 1984; Calas and Smircich, 1989; Hearn et al., 1989; Mills and Tancred, 1992; Gherardi, 1995; Meyerson, 1998). The feminist premise 'the personal is political', legitimates exploration, through self-disclosure, of how aspects of work affect home life, and vice versa (Olsen, 1983; Frug, 1986; Okin, 1989; Bologh, 1990; Martin, 1990; Wharton and Erickson, 1993). This refusal to try to dichotomize the public and the private legitimates the expression and exploration of a wider range of emotions at work, including sexual attraction, affection, vulnerability, fear, sadness and joy, dismantling many barriers between what is felt and what is expressed.

Bounded emotionality

Putnam and Mumby (1993) offered a modification of the feminist position on these emotional issues. They introduced bounded emotionality as a limited and pragmatic approach to the problem of emotional control in organizations. Mumby and Putnam focused on work-related emotions, which they defined as 'feelings, sensations, and affective responses to organizational situations' (1992: 471), although they acknowledged that such work feelings stem from and affect emotions arising from one's personal history and home life. Bounded emotionality encourages the expression of a wider range of emotions than is usually condoned in traditional and normative organizations, while stressing the importance of maintaining interpersonally sensitive, variable boundaries between what is felt and what is expressed. At the risk of extending Mumby and Putnam's (1992: 471) ideas with a specificity they did not intend, bounded emotionality has six defining characteristics, each of which is discussed below: intersubjective limitations, emergent (rather than organizationally ascribed) feelings, tolerance of ambiguity, respect for individual differences in values, authentic self-expression, and community building.

Intersubjective limitations   Emotional expression in organizations should be bounded, Mumby and Putnam argued, because individuals should constrain emotional expression in order to function effectively in interpersonal relationships in ways that are sensitive to other people's emotional needs and competencies. In work settings, bounded emotionality should begin with a recognition of another person's subjectivity, acknowledging potential differences as well as commonalities and working within whatever emotional limitations both individuals bring to the relationship (Mumby and Putnam, 1992: 478; see also Putnam and Mumby, 1993: 51–2; Meyerson, 1994, 1998). Such limitations would include an individual's preferred modes and range of emotional expression. For example, one person might have a hot temper, needing to express anger before calming down, while another might be more restrained and self-contained, preferring public expression of a narrower range of emotions. Intersubjective responsiveness to such individual limitations, or preferred modes of emotional expression, would presumably have as a prerequisite some intimate knowledge of the other obtained through careful observation and voluntary self-disclosure.

Meyerson (1998) observed that bounded emotionality presents a stark contrast to bounded rationality. Emotions are to be bounded voluntarily, to protect interpersonal relationships, while rationality is bounded (see for example Simon, 1976) because of inevitable human limitations in information processing ability, producing such short cuts as cognitive heuristics, satisficing, and standard operating procedures. Mumby and Putnam's formulation of the bounding of emotional expression at work drew on feminist deconstructions of the false dichotomy between rationality and emotionality and delineated ways organizational theory and research have privileged cognitive functioning, leading to a neglect of emotional issues and an over-emphasis on cognitive aspects of decision making. To highlight these issues, Mumby and Putnam chose to frame bounded emotionality as a concept of resistance to bounded rationality.

Spontaneously emergent work feelings   The goal of bounded emotionality is to build interpersonal relationships through improved mutual understanding of work-related feelings, primarily in order to foster community rather than further the efficiency or productivity goals of the organization. Work feelings should emerge spontaneously from the performance of tasks; they should not be organizationally ascribed. Several studies show how emergent work feelings can surface in a manner which is not controlled by an organization's management or initiated primarily for the organization's benefit. For example, Morgen (1994, 1995) found that staff in feminist health clinics emphasized self-disclosure and openly discussed work-related and personal feelings. Cohen and Sutton (1995) found that, for their own enjoyment, hair stylists encouraged salon clients to talk about personal matters.

Mumby and Putnam (1992: 479) acknowledged that emotions can sometimes be bounded both for intersubjective reasons and to serve the organization's instrumental purposes – simultaneously: 'Organizations do not need to sacrifice or lose sight of technical efficiency, but they should embed instrumental goals within a larger system of community and inter-relatedness.' This means that, in spite of their conceptual distinctiveness, bounded emotionality and emotional labour may be empirically difficult to distinguish. It may be that bounded emotionality will be more situationally variable, as the need to exercise respect for intersubjective limitations may vary depending on the individual and the context, while emotional labour norms (for example, you should smile) may be more stable. When instrumental concerns foster emotional labour, Mumby and Putnam argue that resulting felt emotions such as anxiety or frustration are to be expected and should, within intersubjective limits, be expressed in accord with bounded emotionality.

Tolerance of ambiguity   Tolerance of ambiguity is an essential component of bounded emotionality because it permits contradictory feelings, positions and demands to coexist. Given the discussion above regarding the complex mix of feelings likely to emerge in situations where emotional labour is required, the enactment of bounded emotionality necessarily entails some tolerance of ambiguity, including contradictions and irresolvable tensions (Meyerson, 1998).

Respect for individual value differences   No one set of values should take precedence over all others. Enacting value priorities must, according to bounded emotionality, depend on individual preferences and context. Therefore, for example, management must not attempt to enforce, or even generate commitment to, a single set of 'shared' values. Instead, the value priorities of individuals must be respected, allowing a heterarchy rather than a single hierarchy of value priorities.

Authentic self-expression   Bounded emotionality should facilitate a person's ability to express him or herself 'authentically' (without distortion) at work. This presumes that a person has a single self that, transcending context, can be known. Without such a concept of self, the idea that bounded emotionality can facilitate the experience of being 'authentically oneself' at work would be meaningless. This conceptualization of a unified self supersedes notions of mind–body dualism and presumably, alienated or fragmented labour. Mumby and Putnam are assuming an integrated, unitary and probably knowable self.

Community   One purpose of enacting bounded emotionality is to facilitate strong feelings of community among organizational members. Evidence supporting this contention has been found in a series of studies of bounded emotionality in feminist organizations (Ferree and Martin, 1995), including a record company (Lont, 1988), a female weavers' guild (Wyatt, 1988), and dyadic tutoring teams at a university (Nelson, 1988). Studies such as these, of organizations exhibiting norms of bounded emotionality, have all focused on relatively small, usually non-profit organizations.

Exploring the bounds of bounded emotionality

This chapter works with and extends, a bit, the idea of bounded emotionality. Rather than refer to an integrated self we argue, drawing on post-structuralism and social psychological research (such as Flax, 1990; Kitayama and Markus, 1996), that the self is fragmented, composed of overlapping, nested identities that become activated in a context-specific manner, without assuming clarity or consistency over time. Definitions of the self and the potential for authenticity are important, particularly because this chapter addresses questions of diversity in emotional preferences. Mumby and Putnam seem to advocate bounded emotionality as a singular and more desirable alternative to the usual ways of organizing work, remaining silent about how to treat diversity. This silence raises some questions. How does a group or an organization foster bounded emotionality without creating conformity pressures that undermine or counteract commitment to being sensitive to individual limitations and respecting a heterarchy of values?

Some people prefer more impersonality and emotional reserve. If an ideal bounded emotionality is enacted, such differing subjectivities should be recognized, listened to, and treated particularistically, so that multiple patterns of reaction to bounded emotionality are treated as normal and acceptable (Meyerson, 1998). Alternatively, those who differ could simply be pressured to conform to accepted, bounded emotional behaviour, suppressing, repressing or subordinating their subjectivities. This would entail a departure from authenticity, whether one defines this in integrated or fragmented terms. Without enacting respect for those who differ, bounded emotionality may carry the risk of becoming simply a revised claim for conformity, albeit with a different definition of what is desirable. Further, if it is the case that more women than men have been socialized to prefer emotional expressiveness and self-disclosure, then bounded emotionality may become a claim for conformity to reversed gendered standards of behaviour that disproportionately disadvantage men.

Prior research on bounded emotionality has focused on a limited set of small, often non-profit, organizations. We don't know if it is possible to enact bounded emotionality in one of the large for-profit organizations that dominate so much of industrialized society. The efficiency and financial pressures of the competitive marketplace, compounded by the pressures toward growth that come, particularly, when a company is publicly owned, would work against the time consuming, non-instrumental orientation of bounded emotionality. Feminist theory advocates explorations of the intersections of public (work) and private (home) concerns (see for example Hochschild, 1989), yet because of the pressures of a competitive marketplace, there is always the danger that performance concerns will take precedence over other priorities. Given these tensions, bounded emotionality may be difficult to enact in a large for-profit organization, creating pressures toward reversion to more familiar forms of emotion management in organizations: impersonality or emotional labour, reinforced by traditional bureaucratic or normative control mechanisms.

Bounded emotionality would have a better chance of surviving in such a context if facilitating factors were present. Two such factors are: (1) the proportion of women in various parts of the organization's hierarchy, and (2) the organization's ideology. First, if more women than men have been socialized to prefer expressing the kinds of emotions and engaging in the kinds of self-disclosure on which bounded emotionality is based, this form of emotional management might be more likely to flourish in an organization that employed a relatively large proportion of women, provided that some of those women held high-level management positions and were willing to influence the development of these kinds of emotional norms. Second, the enactment of bounded emotionality might have a greater chance of success in an organization that has an ideology congruent with some of the fundamental elements of bounded emotionality. Although it is doubtful that any organization has deliberately incorporated bounded emotionality into its strategy and goals, an organization might endorse goals or values congruent with some of its attributes.

Method

The organization and its employees

As part of a larger project, we studied a large for-profit organization that had an unusual prevalence of women employees in the managerial ranks and that endorsed an ideology that supports a subset of the elements of bounded emotionality. The Body Shop International (BSI) is a publicly owned firm in the cosmetics industry, with retail outlets scattered across the globe. The company is known for its commitment to using naturally based products, protecting the environment, and promoting various social and political causes. This chapter is based on data collected between December 1992 and November 1993; during this interval BSI employed over 6,000 people internationally. At that time there were just under 1,000 retail outlets in 42 countries, with new stores, both franchised and company-owned, opening every two to three days. Between 1 March 1990 and 28 February 1992, total revenues had risen from £208.1 million to £265.4 million (company memo dated 16 September 1992). In these years, BSI was a large and successful private sector organization. Recent growth had been so rapid that current structures, job definitions, employee statistics, and even records of names and telephone numbers were unavailable or seriously out of date. Because rapid change both preceded and extended beyond the period of investigation, this study is an in-depth snapshot of a particular period in the company's life cycle, rather than a longitudinal study.

We interviewed and observed approximately 575 employees, drawn from all levels of the hierarchy, in all five parts of the company in the United States and the UK. (A breakdown of the characteristics of the employees observed and interviewed, and a fuller description of the variety of methods used is available in Martin et al., 1998.) Most of our data collection time was spent in observation, participant-observation and informal conversations. Duration of observations ranged from two hours to several weeks (periodically), with greater time spent in observations of and informal conversations with non-managerial employees, particularly on shop floors. We conducted in-depth structured interviews with 57 employees, representing all five parts of the firm, including most levels of management; 16 (28%) of these interviewees held non-managerial positions. Because most of our interactions with non-managerial employees involved extensive observation and informal conversations, we have more confidence in our understanding of non-managerial perspectives than these structured interview numbers would suggest. However, the informality of our interactions with non-managerial employees means we do not have as much in-depth material from these levels of BSI as we would like.

Titles, employee lists, and statistics were often viewed as a low priority at BSI, so these kinds of information were difficult to find, often out of date, and sometimes in error. For this reason, any numbers below should be regarded as the best, good faith estimates we could obtain. At our request, company officials estimated the percentage of women employees during this period (for the UK only, because US offices were growing so rapidly that employee listings were unavailable at the time). Although men held a considerable proportion of the very highest level jobs at BSI, the company was staffed at upper-middle, middle and lower levels largely by women and served mostly women customers. In the UK, of 167 people at the middle to upper management levels, 134 (80.2%) were women. This was an unusually high percentage of women in relatively high levels of management, compared to national averages in both the United States and the UK (see for example Marshall, 1984, 1995; Morrison et al., 1987; Collinson et al., 1990). Such a percentage is large enough to create dramatic changes in organizational practices (Pettigrew and Martin, 1987).[1] (More detailed breakdowns of the percentages of women in various parts of the corporation are given in Martin et al., 1998.) It is rare to find a large multinational corporation where such a large proportion of female employees holds middle and upper level managerial positions. However, women were not close to a majority at the highest ranks, and in the months the study was conducted there was a widely shared perception that increasing numbers of men were starting to be hired from outside the company into top executive positions.

Several limitations of our focus merit mention. This is a study of a single organization. The company is similar to many others in its large size, financial solvency, international scope and rapid growth. We also chose it because of the distinctiveness of its ideology and the proportion of women in its managerial ranks. Our goal was to examine an outlier – a corporation that was unusual on these two dimensions – to help us explore bounded emotionality in a large for-profit organization subject to the efficiency pressures of a competitive marketplace. This is a cross-sectional study, rather than a longitudinal account that would permit us to address questions about the origin and evolution of bounded emotionality.

Data collection and analysis

The first and second co-authors used a variety of methods, including: the study of archival materials published by the company and others; observation in offices, manufacturing plants, distribution centres, and especially on retail shopfloors; participant-observation in employee training programmes and on the shampoo bottling line; on-site structured interviews, described above; informal conversations on- and off-site, in pubs, parking lots, cafeterias and restaurants; and public events at BSI and elsewhere. We used this variety of methods not to triangulate (use different methods to show evidence supporting the same conclusions), but because these various approaches permit us to address different questions and find different kinds of answers. Inconsistencies across employees, contexts and research methods were therefore anticipated. For example, we saw contradictions between the practices we could observe and the interpretations of behaviour offered in some interviews. When such inconsistencies occurred, these issues were explored, whenever possible, in subsequent interviews and observations.[2] We took extensive notes regarding all interviews, lectures and seminars, and archival material. For off-site and informal conversations, we took no notes during the interactions but, at the end of each session, prepared field notes with as much accuracy as possible, preferring to omit rather than misquote. Each night, or as soon as possible, the researchers transcribed these research notes. We sorted the data captured in over 400 pages of field notes, inductively developing new and subdividing or discarding old categories, as suggested by proponents of grounded theory (Glaser and Strauss, 1967). One of the first new categories to emerge, unanticipated when we planned our study, was the topic of this chapter, the management of emotions.

Emotion at BSI

Although origins of a company's emotional management practices cannot be attributed solely, or perhaps even substantially, to a leader's actions or preferences, these can be contributing factors.[3] For this reason, it is important to include in this account, as a piece of the puzzle, a statement from BSI's founder, Anita Roddick, regarding the company's goals and values which were institutionalized in the form of the company's charter. Focusing on emotional values, Anita Roddick explained:

> I am mystified by the fact that the business world is apparently proud to be seen as hard and uncaring and detached from human values ... the word 'love' was as threatening in business as talking about a loss on the balance sheet. Perhaps that is why using words like 'love' and 'care' is so difficult in today's extraordinarily macho business world. No one seems to know how to put the concept into practice ... I think all business practices would improve immeasurably if they were guided by 'feminine' principles – qualities like love and care and intuition. (Roddick, 1991: 17)

Anita Roddick's use of the word 'feminine' in conjunction with qualities like love and care signals an attempt to revalue emotionally expressive characteristics, such as caring, stereotypically associated with women. She does not explicitly endorse bounded emotionality, although love and caring are congruent with it. Her language, however, intertwines instrumental objectives with emotional concerns, making it difficult to determine if she is giving priority to emotional labour over bounded emotionality. Because a leader's rhetoric and employees' reality can differ, it is essential to examine how and if these ideas are enacted.

Enacting bounded emotionality

Although the company does not explicitly advocate discussing home, family and friendship concerns at work, Body Shop employees switched easily between task-oriented concerns and the more intimate self-disclosures that provide a basis for bounded emotionality. This shifting, which blurred distinctions between public and private concerns, was evident in observations of employees at all levels of BSI, in the relative privacy of tête-à-têtes, and in the more public arenas of meetings, casual conversations among tour guides, or chatter in a manufacturing plant.

We regularly heard employees discussing a wide range of emotional topics such as sexual orientation, violence in the home, and sadness and joy about work-related matters, as well as fears and psychiatric difficulties. Non-verbal communication was affectionate and intimate (although seldom obviously sexual), with hugs, kisses and touching evident in both public and private settings, to an extent that surprised us. Although we cannot offer verbal quotations of this more intimate, individualized material because of our promises of anonymity, the following quote suggests that intimacy was a way of life at work for many Body Shop employees: 'There's lots of gay men and women in the company. In all the shops we know the ins and outs of each other's personal lives' (Frederick, Shop Clerk, Company Shop, UK).

Such self-disclosure provides a basis for assessing the subjective state of an individual. The next step in enacting bounded emotionality, according to Putnam and Mumby, is to take that information into account and adjust one's task-related interaction to fit the other's emotional preferences and limitations. For example, one employee was having trouble being filmed for a Body Shop video: 'He fucked it up half way through, but he was so stressed out, I couldn't ask him to do it again. Really, I thought he would burst into tears' (Ursula, Lower Management, Headquarters, UK). Some Body Shop employees described their working relationships in terms that suggested such interpersonal emotional calibration was a habit. Sally, a middle manager in the marketing division (a pseudonym) in the UK, showed her understanding of one of her co-workers

> William works in (our group). He sees things in terms of right and wrong, numbers, prices, quantities. There is no middle ground. Figures are either right or wrong. A staff situation right now, however, has William agonizing. Difficult feedback is needed. It will hurt a person. William worries; should he give feedback now, before his vacation? He worries that he wouldn't be there after the feedback, when the pieces will need picking up. William has a high degree of sensitivity for a man.

Another aspect of bounded emotionality involves recognizing a heterarchy of values, by allowing others to have a different set of values, or a different priority of values, from oneself, not giving precedence to either person's view. This is a difficult objective to attain, and even more difficult for a researcher to see. We did note, repeatedly, that Body Shop employees of both sexes tended to portray men and women as having stereotypically different emotional preferences and styles of interaction, differences which they tried to be sensitive to: 'There are differences between men and women. Women have more emotion; (it's) not just hidden in some corner. Guys use delaying tactics while women say, "Let's just go for it." A complete over-balance either way is a problem' (Winston, Upper Management, Headquarters, UK). Strong emphasis was placed, throughout the company, on informal subjective assessments of performance, sometimes supplemented by more formal evaluation procedures. Managers, in particular, were assessed on their emotional competency, which including letting work-related feelings emerge spontaneously. Here too sex, or sexual stereotypes, were seen as creating a heterarchy of values and goals in the emotional domain: 'I manage an all-female team. I was appraised as keeping well with women's emotions; I use empathy. Women have more tears, sensitivities, PMS (pre-menstrual syndrome), more personal conflicts' (Tim, Middle Management, Headquarters, UK). Other more individuated or less stereotypical ways of respecting a heterarchy of values reflected sensitivities to differences in job responsibilities, age and personal circumstances.

According to Mumby and Putnam, these practices of intimate self-disclosure, blurring boundaries between public and private, showing sensitivity to another person's subjective state, allowing work feelings to emerge spontaneously, and respecting a heterarchy of values and goals should allow employees to feel a kind of authenticity at work. Some Body Shop employees reported such feelings:

> BSI is nice because I don't feel like I have to fit some kind of mold . . . At BSI I feel I can be more myself. (Lorie, Shop Clerk, Company Shop, USA)

> Emotion is not frowned on. People have no separate work personality. You are accepted as who you are. A 'normal' corporate culture requires that you put on the personality of the company while you are at work. Not here. There are negatives (associated with this); it makes management more difficult. There is no instant obedience. People debate, then agree about what needs to be done. There are also positive (effects); people own the decision. Emotional work is sometimes a negative. There are always compromises. It would be bad not to have it, though. (Winston, Upper Management, Headquarters, UK)

It is difficult to discern from such remarks whether these feelings of authenticity are, as Mumby and Putnam assert, reinforcing a sense of an integrated self. The prevalence of sex stereotyping suggests that it may be difficult to express some aspects of a fragmented self, particularly those aspects that contradict existing sex stereotypes. Taken as a whole, the data presented above suggest that many but not all elements of bounded emotionality were enacted at BSI.

Coexistence of emotional labor and bounded emotionality

At BSI, emotion was frequently managed for instrumental purposes, although it was difficult to decipher whether such instrumentality took priority over bounded emotionality. For example, shop staff were well trained to hide emotions that might impede a sale, using emotional labour techniques similar to those in previous studies of cashiers, flight attendants and bill collectors:

> A customer wanted to buy two identical baskets of Body Shop products. Two similar baskets had already been made up, but they were not exactly the same; the washcloths were different colors. Karen said, 'OK, I'll make you one exactly the same.' As Karen turned away from the customer, she rolled her eyes and smiled at the observing researcher. (Researcher, Observation in Franchise Shop, USA)

Although this behaviour could indicate bounded emotionality if the shop clerk were worried that the customer might find it difficult to deal with the clerk's feelings about the extra work being required, the researcher observing this incident was assured, in a subsequent conversation, that the clerk was simply feeling impatient with the customer's demands.

The emotionally charged atmosphere of BSI was intensified by the firm's attempt to avoid bureaucratic modes of operation. Employees had to show extreme forms of emotion, positive and negative, in order to complete essential tasks. As one manager told us, 'It's amazing because there are loads of things that stink. It's not a sharp organization. You can't get things done easily. You don't just make a proposal. You have to pitch it – be emotional and argue it. There aren't clear channels and structure' (Martha, Upper Management, Franchise and Company Shops, UK).

Emotional labour at BSI was used to further the firm's political and environmental objectives, as well as its productivity-related concerns. For example, Roddick (1991: 170–1) explained how she used emotions to encourage employees to join in the company's various community and political action projects.

> Whenever we wanted to persuade our staff to support a particular project we always tried to break their hearts. At the next franchise holders' meeting we put on a real tear-jerking audio-visual presentation, with wonderful slides of the children against a background of Willie Nelson's version of 'Bridge over Troubled Water'. And to enable members of staff to experience what we had experienced, the next edition of 'Talking Shop', the monthly video distributed throughout BSI organization, was devoted to Boys' Town and what we could do there. The response was a joy. Everyone wanted to get involved in raising money and sponsoring boys, and from that moment onwards the International Boys' Town Trust more or less became an integral part of BSI's extended family.

Roddick also encouraged employees to use emotional expression for more conventional instrumental purposes, 'Sally doesn't support women much. But she's the one who breaks down in tears with frustration. She can cry so easily. I told her it has to be used. I said, "Here, cry at this point in the ... meeting"' (Roddick, Interview, Researcher's house, 17 November 1993). Thus, Roddick and other Body Shop employees frequently and self-consciously used emotion management techniques for instrumental organizational purposes. This combination of emotional labour and bounded emotionality created a close knit, intimate community where employees were deeply involved with each other and passionately committed to their work. (Subcultural variations at the BSI are discussed in Martin et al., 1998.)

Impediments to the implementation of bounded emotionality

Several factors made it difficult to enact bounded emotionality consistently at BSI. Some of these factors stemmed from corporate policies, such as pursuing rapid international expansion, while others were environmental causes, such as characteristics of the labour market. Other difficulties stemmed from employees' internal states and preferences, which in turn were affected by their home circumstances.

Effects of growth Expanding into 42 countries in a short time created enormous logistical problems that strained the company's ability to enact bounded emotionality. This can be seen in a conversation among several employees at a 'values meeting' convened to generate commitment to the company's mission and social change agenda:

> 'We have no time to meet. The department is run by phone and deadlines.'
> 'You can find time.'
> 'We don't have time. We don't.'
> 'Individuals are islands, sidetracked because we're so busy. Sad.'
> 'This is a normal effect of quick growth.'
> 'In the old days, we were moving just as fast.'
> 'Everyone had the same pressure then.'
> 'And cared for each other more.'

The company's commitment to avoiding bureaucratic red tape exacerbated the confusion caused by growth. New hires proliferated, jobs were changed, and offices and desks were shuffled. Emotional sensitivity to another's emotional needs or work feelings required, at the very least, a knowledge of who people were and what they were supposed to be doing. This crucial information sometimes was hard to find. '(We need) pictures and names in departments. They would help us know who people are. Now we're so big we don't know the people in our own department' (Lisa, Values meeting, Headquarters, UK). Sometimes the open expression of emotion, in the midst of all this ambiguity, was clearly insensitive to employees' emotional needs, as one employee reported: 'I got called a fucking dickhead the other day. I don't know people any more. There's less friendliness. I'm scared that I know less than half the people. We need a system to build social introductions to know people – not just a voice on the phone, but a person' (Chris, Values meeting, Headquarters, UK). Under such conditions, face-to-face interactions among all or even many employees were impossible and knowledge of the subjectivities of others was scarce, as so many of the others were now strangers. The lack of interpersonal closeness due to the company's growth made it more difficult to follow through on commitment to the company's espoused values of caring and nurturance, creating instead conditions which fostered impersonality. Although it is an achievement to enact the goal of bounded emotionality, even partially, in a large for-profit organization, it is clear that BSI's rapid growth placed strains on its ability to do so.

Limitations of the labour market   These problems were exacerbated by the influx of new hires. Growth created a need to expand the managerial staff at the headquarters in Littlehampton, on the coast of southern England. There was a shortage of qualified candidates with the requisite managerial-level retailing experience who lived within commuting distance. Experienced female managers were said to be especially hard to find. And, given that employment at BSI entailed showing evidence of prior deep commitment to the company's political, community and environmental agendas, the local labour market had been exhausted. Some of the new hires, especially at the managerial level, were criticized as lacking some of the political commitments, gender sensitivity and emotional management skills of the 'old guard' employees. When some employees complained about a growing lack of community at BSI, they attributed it not to a lack of time or to the pressure of work to be done, nor to growth *per se*, but rather to the influx of high-ranking men hired from more traditional retailing organizations:

> Now more senior males have been brought in (from the outside) and it is more male macho, more 'go get it'. Some individuals and some of these outside hires do not have empathy. (In contrast) take George (an 'old guard' employee). Janet says, 'He's an honorary female.' As the company has grown, gender comes in. Men haven't got the feminine instinct that the company was founded on. They are brought up through the company by osmosis. Caring and sharing are expressed physically in the company. People give a hug and a kiss. This is anathema for certain individuals; they tend to be those who were brought in during the last couple of years. (Tim, Middle Management, Headquarters, UK)

Dealing with emotional diversity Those Body Shop employees who found intimate self-disclosure and emotional expressiveness at work to be comfortable and desirable were often unsympathetic when other employees, such as some new hires, had different emotional preferences. For example, in response to an observation about managers at other companies, who avoided getting really personal or emotional at work, Sally objected: 'That's a cop out. It's like refusing to love if you've been hurt once. Don't let anyone get too close? This is crazy. If good friends can and do work together, tough stuff comes up. It's something we can handle' (Sally, Middle Management, Marketing division, UK). Those who had difficulty complying with demands for emotional openness encountered verbal hints or informal requests for conformity; threats of punishment for refusing to comply were usually latent, such as the tacit threat of withdrawn warmth and friendliness.

There were also a few formal bureaucratic procedures that encouraged compliance. For example, part of the job application process at BSI was a group interview by a panel of current employees who sought evidence of the applicant's commitment to Body Shop values and its political agendas. Morris was a Body Shop manager who had suggested that one of his acquaintances be interviewed for a managerial job. According to Morris, the panel members interviewing his acquaintance had asked, 'If BSI doesn't offer you a job, would you take a job elsewhere if you didn't know the company's policies on human rights and the environment?' When the applicant answered affirmatively, the panellists rejected him, in part, according to Morris, because they thought that if he were really committed to BSI values, he would not accept a job anywhere without investigating the company's policies in these key areas. But Morris knew that his friend was too emotionally reserved to reveal that he would accept the other job because he needed money badly to support his wife and child. The child had a severe disability and needed constant, expensive care. The rejected job applicant had intense emotions about his son and wanted to keep these feelings private. The panellists, in contrast, considered the applicant's political commitments to be of paramount importance, so that self-disclosure about the applicant's intimate problem became an essential prerequisite for becoming a Body Shop employee. The applicant's silence was congruent with his individual emotional preferences, but he was not hired. This kind of emotional diversity creates a contradiction for bounded emotionality. Compliance pressures are used to support bounded emotionality, by sanctioning or excluding those uncomfortable with its tenets. This process contradicts bounded emotionality, by requiring acts of intolerance that fail to recognize as legitimate the emotional preferences of people with differing subjectivities and values.

Resistance   Some Body Shop employees enacted bounded emotionality, yet simultaneously expressed some limited discomfort with it. For example, some expressed impatience with the time required to respond to the needs of others:

> At an afternoon meeting in Supply, a male warehouse packer complained passionately about PZP's (Peak Zone Pallets[4]). His manager responded, 'Don't get emotional; let's just deal with it.' (Mike, Warehouse Manager, Supply, UK)

> Sometimes there is too much talk about emotion. Right now (I wish I could say), 'Let's get on with it', but I don't. Usually people use their boss as a confidant. They aren't constrained by (the lack of privacy in an office with) open space and desks. (Tim, Middle Management, Headquarters, UK)

Sometimes employees questioned whether intense emotional expression was authentic. A supervisor apologized for a mistake and his supervisor responded: 'Don't get over-contrite' (Researcher, Observation, Supply, UK). Other employees expressed discomfort with emotional practices by joking about them. For example, at an afternoon coordination meeting, one man's complaint was countered with an unsympathetic 'I'm an emotional man here; I'm welling up', as the speaker pretended to wipe an imaginary tear from his eye. These signs of resistance were observed most frequently among men, both non-managerial employees and high-ranking managers.

Attempts to separate public and private   The company's emotional practices, including its advocacy of merging personal and working life, sometimes met with opposition from the families of Body Shop employees. Theresa, a middle manager in UK retail operations, told us: 'And my Mum said, "Don't let (BSI job) change your character".' Jeff, a manager of a company shop in the UK, had a similar reaction: 'When I started work (at BSI) my brother said, "Don't bring your leftist vegetarian bullshit home".' It is difficult to respond to intersections between work and home when members of a family have differing opinions about what is personally and politically desirable and when some family members want to separate home and work concerns.

Stress at work   Whenever private emotional concerns are mixed with an organization's instrumental objectives, there is a danger – particularly in a firm struggling to survive in a highly competitive market – that instrumental concerns will take priority over an individual's personal or family needs (see for example Newton et al., 1995). Signs of physical and emotional stress were evident at BSI, particularly in some parts of the headquarters, where claims of being understaffed and overworked were common. Although we heard complaints in various parts of the company, the problems of stress were particularly visible among the tour guides who scheduled and delivered tours of the headquarters. Their feet hurt, their necks ached, the phones were ringing off the hook, visitors were clamouring for attention, and everyone was very busy. Several tour guides talked openly about the physical and emotional effects of work stress. One told us: 'I was on the phone 22 hours between Monday morning and Wednesday night. Betty (a new employee) told another Body Shop employee to piss off, and she's only been here (a very short time).' Another reported, 'Nadine is the third person to hurt her foot. You get tired and fall over – just not concentrating.' Some employees felt that working very long hours, rather than demands for emotional expressiveness and self-disclosure, made their personal and work lives merge, to the detriment of the former. This problem was evident in some shops, as well as in headquarters and some other working sites. For example:

> I have no personal life . . . Each of (these particular) shops is evacuated two times a week due to terrorist threats. Each time this happens I get phone calls. It's hard on marriage. There's no way I could do my job with a child . . . To do this you need a partner who understands. The quality of life is ridiculous. At 4 am I'm up north; at 11 pm I come home, but then I have two more hours of work to do at home. I work like a maniac during the week. On Saturday I watch (Body Shop videos) at home and go through the post. I put aside one hour for the post. Sunday I do my weekly report. I try to ignore it and keep clear, but I live with a dread of the phone because I'm always on call . . . When I'm in Littlehampton (headquarters) I can't get over their hours. It seems more relaxed. I resent it a bit. (Martha, Upper Management, Franchise and Company Shops, UK)

The company's concern about stress was sufficiently strong that the headquarters provided (anonymous) counselling for those employees who wished to take advantage of this resource. As noted in Meyerson's (1994) analysis of the work stress literature, though, however helpful such a counsellor may be, the implicit message is that the work stress is an abnormal response which must be 'fixed' by fixing the individual. The blame for the problem and the responsibility for fixing it resting primarily with the individual experiencing the stress. Such an analysis overstates the case in the BSI example, as the company took the initiative to relieve the organizational sources of stress, offering paid leave to some employees, providing child care on site for some employees, and sometimes adjusting work content and working hours. Allocation of these sources of help was facilitated by the company's norms of emotional openness and self-disclosure:

> People know if you are sick (from stress) or depressed from nervous exhaustion. Someone is off the team now from stress and depression. The reaction was 'Take whatever time you need to re-evaluate your life.' (Question: 'Is she paid?') Of

course. Another company might say, 'If you can't take the heat get out of the kitchen.' We (at BSI) have a full-time counsellor for us overworked people. (Tim, Middle Management, Headquarters, UK)

Roddick openly and repeatedly discussed, with evident worry, signs of stress among Body Shop employees. She was particularly concerned about the disturbing number of female employees who reported violence at home. Whereas the employees generally attributed their stress to long hours of work, Roddick stressed that the company had provided an exciting, aesthetically pleasing and emotionally supportive environment which empowered employees, and in this, most of them agreed. Roddick believed that the empowerment of female employees – economically and personally – upset the balance of power at home.

> The company talks about the body, having relaxed forms of interaction. (People are) frisky, touch, hug, kiss. Women are so excited by their work. They have an emotional support system. They are valued. They have new ways of communicating. The company counselor says that employees' worst problem is domestic violence. Littlehampton is a working class town, where there are few college degrees. The men aren't prepared for the changes their wives go through after working for us. After a full day of being valued and listened to at work, they want to be valued and listened to at home. I don't know what to do about it. What is never said: do women really need a domestic relationship? (Roddick, Interview, Researcher's house, 17 November 1993)

Whether caused by overwork or a discrepancy between an exciting, empowering work environment and a more mundane, less empowered home life, both male and female employees of BSI sometimes reported considerable emotional and physical work stress. Although BSI emphasized integrating emotional concerns into the working environment, in ways that were unusual and went beyond the usual 'act nice' or 'act tough' demands of instrumental emotional display, their version of bounded emotionality provided little protection from the experience of aversive emotional stress on the job.

Conclusion

Enacting bounded emotionality

We found considerable evidence of the enactment of bounded emotionality. The employees of BSI frequently discussed intimate personal issues with co-workers. Work feelings emerged spontaneously, often with no apparent instrumental motivation. Sensitivity to the emotional limitations of co-workers tempered the expression of these emotions, as did respect for a heterarchy of values. Ambiguity, primarily caused by the firm's disdain for standardized bureaucratic procedures, was tolerated, if not enjoyed, and ensuing feelings of frustration were freely expressed. Employees often expressed delight at the extent they felt they could 'be themselves at work', reflecting a sense of personal authenticity, although we could not determine, from our data, whether this reflected an integrated or fragmented self. Although morale varied across individuals, across time, and across parts of the organization, most employees shared a strong sense of being part of the BSI community. Thus, we found all six of the elements of bounded emotionality enacted regularly, in a large for-profit organization. This approach to the management of emotion, then, is not too idealistic for implementation in a highly competitive, large scale business context.

Conformity pressures

This enactment of bounded emotionality, however, fell short of the ideal described by Putnam and Mumby. Sometimes, for example, employees failed to listen to each other's emotional concerns, or expressed impatience with emotional needs, thereby eroding mutual understanding and perhaps, to some extent, undermining the company's well developed sense of community. Such shortfalls, we believe, are inevitable in any interpersonal context, and are especially likely to occur in a task-oriented context, such as a corporation. Of greater theoretical interest are the ways that success in enacting bounded emotionality carried seeds of its own erosion, in that pressure to conform to the ideals of bounded emotionality paradoxically undermined some of its premises. Such pressures to conform came from Anita Roddick, in her role as leader of the company, from informal pressures to conform from other employees, and from the encapsulation of bounded emotionality in formalized rules and procedures. For example, job applicants were screened for value homogeneity in group interviews, performance appraisals included assessments of a manager's demonstrated ability to express emotional empathy and sensitivity within a sex-stereotypical heterarchy of values, and company-sponsored social events fostered community building. As a package, this mix of leadership, informal emergent practices, and formal bureaucratic mechanisms of control encouraged conformity with bounded emotionality norms.

Although bounded emotionality requires respect for individuals whose values differ, employees who preferred more restrained forms of emotion management were sometimes pressured to display more open emotionality. Sometimes these conformity pressures were relatively subtle (such as gentle jokes), but in other cases, the pressures were enforced by formal procedures. It was difficult for Body Shop employees to find a balance between commitment to a form of bounded emotionality and the needs of some employees who preferred more emotional distance. These conformity demands present a dilemma that is perhaps inherent in bounded emotionality: how can a variety of emotional preferences be honoured in a heterarchy of values, without eroding bounded emotionality itself?

Coexistence of bounded emotionality and emotional labour

Bounded emotionality did not displace more conventional forms of emotion management at BSI. Employees also freely and frequently engaged in emotional labour – for example, smiling to increase productivity or using tears to help get a task completed. In addition, even apparently non-instrumental behaviour at BSI may have indirectly served instrumental organizational purposes – for example, by increasing loyalty and commitment to the firm or by reinforcing the sense that this was a uniquely desirable place to work. In addition, it is likely that feelings of authenticity created productivity benefits for the company because of reactions such as: 'I can do my best work when I can be myself.' Although the bounded emotionality model draws a conceptual distinction between instrumental emotional labour and non-instrumental work feelings, in practice it is virtually impossible to maintain such separation, particularly in a high-commitment organization like BSI, where many employees expressed a deep satisfaction with their work and saw congruence between their values and those of the company. Mumby and Putnam draw attention to the possibility of such congruence, and in most parts of BSI we found that emotional labour and bounded emotionality were indeed hard to separate.

Obstacles to implementing bounded emotionality

Several factors threatened BSI's ability to continue implementing bounded emotionality. The organization's increased size had detrimental effects because it increased both the amount of work and the number of employees who did not know each other or each other's job responsibilities. The company's growth also made it more difficult to hire and retain a demographically and ideologically homogeneous group of employees from the local labour market. Many job applicants with the requisite retailing experience came from more traditional organizations, lacked an intense commitment to BSI's political agenda, and were uncomfortable with the emotional expressiveness required by bounded emotionality. In addition, most of these job applicants were men, making it more difficult to maintain the company's commitment to providing opportunities for managerial positions to women. Further, many of BSI's long-term employees, who had been hired when they were young and single, were now married and anticipating caring for children or ageing parents. The goals and attributes of an ageing workforce did not mesh easily with the company's predilection for extremely long working hours and high-pressure performance. Many of the long-term employees were women, a fact that exacerbated these anticipated difficulties, because women would do so much of the dependent care within the family. Such difficulties were intensified by the fact that BSI was subject to the pressures of a highly competitive marketplace. BSI's financial success and public stock offering created demands for rapid growth, and that growth exacerbated the effects of local labour market limitations. BSI was in danger of losing its distinctiveness and becoming imprisoned, with so many other formerly innovative organizations, in the iron cage of bureaucracy, with its traditional and normative emphases on impersonality and emotional labour.

Despite the obstacles, however, the company had so far managed to maintain two distinguishing features that may have facilitated the continued implementation of bounded emotionality: a relatively high proportion of women employees, some with high-level managerial positions, and a relatively strong ideological commitment to finding ways of doing business differently. The presence of one or both of these factors may be key to resisting bureaucratic isomorphism, at least in the domain of bounded emotionality. In large for-profit organizations, would the presence of a high proportion of women, with a significant minority at the highest ranks, be enough to sustain bounded emotionality? Or, would ideology alone suffice, perhaps in the firms that have joined the Social Venture Network, a network of organizations with ideologies similar, in some ways, to that of BSI? Or, because so many women do not seek to do business differently, must both factors be present? If studies addressing questions such as these could show that bounded emotionality is more pervasive than we thought, or that emotional labour need not be as pervasive as it is, such research would be an important contribution to organizational theory and practice.

Bounded emotionality: a more dangerous form of control?

Because this firm is, to a large extent, successful in enacting bounded emotionality, it provides an opportunity to question the desirability of this approach to managing emotions. Is bounded emotionality a better way of doing business, from employees' points of view, or is it a more effective, more invasive, and therefore potentially more dangerous control mechanism? Answers to this question represent a matter of opinion, and opinions will differ. Below we analyse both sides of the question and offer our own judgements.

A pro-bounded-emotionality interpretation of these data would echo Mumby and Putnam's enthusiasm for the advantages of personal authenticity at work. Generally, most Body Shop employees appreciated the chance to 'be themselves' at work, to share their personal joys and sadnesses, and to join in a community with others who shared their political and communitarian convictions, as well as intimate knowledge of their personal lives and emotional ups and downs. To the extent that BSI did not provide a perfect working environment, it was, in the eyes of most of the employees we studied, better than the available alternatives, where the same conflicts of interest between employee and employer might surface, often in a more alienating or exploitative form. When conflicts between individual and organizational interests did occur, the emotional and physical needs of employees were often given priority, as when stressed employees were given paid leave or tasks were left incomplete in order to spare an employee emotional turmoil.

An anti-bounded-emotionality interpretation would note that when organizational commitments to profit making conflicted with individual interests or other organizational interests that had been democratically chosen by employees, organizational tasks often took precedence over 'personal' concerns. For example, tour guides experienced physical as well as emotional work stress (their necks and feet ached), and some shop staff worked such long hours that their physical needs for sleep and relaxation, and their emotional needs for family life, were not met. When work encroached on family and personal time, BSI did not change organizational practices, for example by reducing chronic long hours; instead it provided formal mechanisms to alleviate the resulting stress on individuals, through private counselling, time off and day care, in effect blaming individuals for organization-caused difficulties (Meyerson, 1994). From this perspective, bounded emotionality can be interpreted as emotional exploitation.

There is no conclusive empirical means of disconfirming or supporting one of these interpretations at the expense of the other. The authors of this chapter differ in our opinions. One of us worries that, while most people at BSI sincerely believed in the company's espoused values, the rhetoric may have been stronger than the implementation. According to this co-author, sometimes the leftist political, environmental and humanitarian rhetoric (such as stated commitments to elements of bounded emotionality) seemed to be used primarily to sell cosmetics for a profit, living up to promises only when such promises did not conflict with commercial objectives. From this perspective, the physical and emotional signs of employee stress, outlined above, are convincing evidence of a lack of good faith.

The other two co-authors of this chapter take these signs of stress very seriously, and see them as an area meriting serious ameliorative action, but nevertheless believe that this company was trying hard to enact its ideals, including bounded emotionality. One of these co-authors feels that large firms in the private sector have more difficulty enacting bounded emotionality because such firms are more likely to employ people with divergent emotional preferences. In such contexts, bounded emotionality may also be more needed, because pressures for growth and profit may make emotional labour, and emotional exploitation, more likely. In comparison with other large firms in the private sector, this co-author thinks that BSI was more effective in enacting bounded emotionality. Many employees of BSI, including Anita Roddick, made a point of trying to respect differences in emotional preferences, in accord with bounded emotionality's emphasis on a heterarchy of values – perhaps the most difficult aspect of bounded emotionality to enact. However, BSI did not enact bounded emotionality as well as small, non-profit or feminist organizations have done. In part, this shortfall may have occurred because small, feminist organizations may attract and hire people with similar emotional preferences rather than people with a variety of emotional profiles. According to this co-author, bounded emotionality may represent an unattainable ideal for most large for-profit firms, unless they deliberately set out to hire people with similar emotional preferences – making respect for individual differences in values less difficult to attain but also less needed.

The last of the co-authors did not disagree with these descriptions of the ways BSI failed to attain the ideal of bounded emotionality, but was more forgiving. She noted that the company had never set out to attain this, or any other emotional ideal, other than to be a 'caring' company where expressions of words like love would not be inappropriate. From this perspective, BSI was like Ivory soap – certainly not perfect but '98 percent pure'. Although our estimates of the purity of the company's motives varied, all three of us thought that the company deserved credit for its efforts to do business differently within the constraints of a highly competitive industry. In contrast to the constrained emotional expression norms of most large for-profit organizations, BSI was attempting to move, and to a substantial extent succeeded, toward a form of bounded emotionality – one that, perhaps inevitably, coexisted with conventional forms of emotional labour.

Acknowledgements

Portions of the research reported here were supported by the Graduate School of Business, Stanford University and, for Kathy Knopoff, the Cate Muther Fellowship for doctoral research on women entrepreneurs. Exceptionally helpful comments were offered by Debra Meyerson, Robin Ely, and the reviewers and editor of this journal. We give special thanks to Anita Roddick and the employees of The Body Shop International. This chapter is based on an earlier article, entitled 'An alternative to bureaucratic impersonality and emotional labor: bounded emotionality at The Body Shop', *Administrative Science Quarterly*, 1998, 43: 429–69.

Notes

1　There are studies that suggest that women are more likely than men to engage in self-disclosure, express a wider range of emotions, and seek ways to acknowledge the inseparability of work and personal lives without letting work concerns take priority over family needs (see for example Allen and Haccoun, 1976; Eagly and Johnson, 1990; Ely, 1995; Fletcher, 1995). A few researchers attribute such differences to biology, but most argue they are an effect of socially or culturally constructed differences – for example, differential socialization of men and women or differential recruitment and control mechanisms (see for example Ekman, 1973; Acker and Van Houten, 1974; Zajonc, 1985; Harding, 1993; Kitayama and Markus, 1996).

2　A brief description of feminist methodology might be useful in the context of this volume, as such methods are particularly helpful in studying emotions in field contexts. We used a variety of qualitative methods, some of which were more detached and traditional, such as observation, while others were more congruent with feminist approaches, such as the in-depth interviews described above. Feminist methodology requires that researchers not conduct themselves, or write, as distanced, objective, neutral disembodied experts, but rather that they seek to establish mutual trust and understanding between researchers and study participants (see for example Oakley, 1981; McRobbie, 1982). We are white women, as were most of the study participants. According to feminist theory, intimacy, demographic similarity and subjective rapport with study participants should elicit more honest self-disclosure, an approach that some consider more ethical and more informative (such as Laws, 1978; Oakley, 1981) and others see as a manipulative way for researchers to collect better data (Stacey, 1996). Feminist methods allow the participant's experience to come through in her own voice (Laws, 1978), shifting the relationships between the researchers and participants toward mutual understanding (Bernard, 1982; McRobbie, 1982), and the pre-rogative of interpretation and analysis from the researcher to the participant (Graham, 1984). Such an approach evokes a more interactive, personalized and intense form of talk in which respondents become conversational partners, capable of structuring and directing the interviews more on their own terms. In accord with these premises, we began each scheduled interview with some information about ourselves, encouraging questions. After promising anonymity, we began with relatively non-threatening questions about the interviewee's career path in the company and current job responsibilities. As soon as possible (we watched for signs of self-disclosure, comfort and physical ease) we encouraged interviewees to tell stories about specific recent events. Graham (1984) argues, and we concur, that the self-structured format of story telling enables free-flowing narrative and can counter some of the privileging of the researchers' role in generating knowledge. To keep the conversation going, and to deepen our contextual under-standing, we used planned, relatively non-directive probes for details (What happened next? Why? Who else was involved?) and then asked for emotional reactions (How did you feel about that? What problems did that cause?). After each specific event history, we probed for the meanings of events and processes, asking study participants for their interpretations (What did that mean to you? What lesson did you draw from that event?). If we had an interpretation, we would check with study participants to see if we had misunderstood or not fully comprehended their viewpoints. During the majority of the interviews, gender issues were raised spontaneously by the employee; when this did not happen, the investigators opened the subject at the end of the interview with a question tailored to the respondent's job and responsibilities.

3   The origins of an organization's practices regarding the management of emotion are difficult to decipher. Some researchers argue that leaders can control practices, even in such domains as emotion, by articulating goals and values that organ-izational members will come to share and enact (see for example Schein, 1985). Other scholars are sceptical of all claims about the power of managerial rhetoric and stress that members will react differently to leaders' value statements – some members 'buying in' and others reacting negatively or neutrally. From this point of view, organizational members develop and maintain their own goals, values and practices, with as much independence from managerial priorities as they can manage (see for example Van Maanen and Barley, 1984; Kunda, 1992). This conflict of views may be overdrawn, as there is evidence that cultural consensus can emerge from both top-down and bottom-up origins; in addition, it is important to distinguish managerial value rhetoric from employees' values and employees' practices, as these all may differ (see Martin, 1992, for a review).

4   Peak Zone Pallets are more readily accessible, containing high turnover products.

References

Acker, J. and Van Houten, D.R. (1974) 'Differential recruitment and control: the sex structuring of organizations', *Administrative Science Quarterly*, 19: 152–63.

Allen, J. and Haccoun, D. (1976) 'Sex differences in emotionality: a multidimensional approach', *Human Relations*, 29 (8): 711–22.

Bernard, Jessie (1982) *The Future of Marriage*, 2nd edn. New Haven, CT: Yale University Press.

Bologh, R.W. (1990) *Love or Greatness: Max Weber and Masculine Thinking: A Feminist Inquiry*. Boston: Unwin Hyman.

Calas, M.B. and Smircich, L. (1989) 'Using the f-word: feminist theories and the social consequences of organizational research'. Paper presented at the annual meeting of the Academy of Management, Washington, DC.

Cohen, R.C. and Sutton, R.L. (1995) 'Clients as a source of enjoyment on the job: how hair stylists shape demeanor and personal disclosures'. Stanford, CA: Unpublished manuscript.

Collinson, D.L., Knights, D. and Collinson, M. (1990) *Managing to Discriminate*. New York: Routledge.

Eagly, A.H. and Johnson, B.T. (1990) 'Gender and leadership style: a meta-analysis', *Psychological Bulletin*, 108 (2): 233–56.

Ekman, P. (1973) 'Cross cultural studies of facial expression', in P. Ekman (ed.), *Darwin and Facial Expression: A Century of Research in Review*. New York: Academic Press. pp. 169–222.

Ely, R.J. (1995) 'The power of demography: women's social constructions of gender identity at work', *Academy of Management Journal*, 38 (3): 589–634.

Ferree, M.M. and Martin, P.Y. (eds) (1995) *Feminist Organizations*. Philadelphia: Temple University Press.

Fineman, S. (1996) 'Emotion and organizing', in S. Clegg, C. Hardy and W. Nord (eds), *Handbook of Organization Studies*. London: Sage. pp. 543–64.

Flax, J. (1990) *Thinking Fragments: Psychoanalysis, Feminism, and Postmodernism in the Contemporary West*. Berkeley: University of California.

Fletcher, J.K. (1995) 'Radically transforming work for the 21st century: a feminist reconstruction of "real" work', *Academy of Management Journal*, 1995 Best Papers Proceedings: 448–52.

Frug, M.J. (1986) 'The ideology of bureaucracy in American law', *Harvard Law Review*, 97: 1276–1388.

Gherardi, S. (1995) *Gender, Symbolism and Organizational Cultures*. London: Sage.

Glaser, B. and Strauss, A. (1967) *The Discovery of Grounded Theory: Strategies for Qualitative Research*. Chicago: Aldine.

Graham, H. (1984) 'Surveying through stories', in C. Bell and H. Roberts (eds), *Social Researching: Politics, Problems, Practice*. London: Routledge.

Harding, S. (1993) 'Rethinking standpoint epistemology: what is "strong objectivity"?', in L. Alcoff and E. Potter (eds), *Feminist Epistemologies*. New York: Routledge.

Hearn, J., Sheppard, D.L., Tancred-Sheriff, P. and Burrell, G. (eds) (1989) *The Sexuality of Organization*. Newbury Park, CA: Sage.

Hochschild, A.R. (1983) *The Managed Heart: The Commercialization of Human Feeling*. Berkeley, CA: University of California Press. pp. 89–136.

Hochschild, A.R. with Machung, A. (1989) *The Second Shift*. New York: Avon Books.

Kitayama, S. and Markus, H.R. (eds) (1996) *Emotion and Culture: Empirical Studies of Mutual Influence*. Hyattsville, MD: American Psychological Association.

Kunda, G. (1992) *Engineering Culture: Control and Commitment in a High-tech Corporation*. Philadelphia: Temple University Press.

Laws, J.L. (1978) 'Feminism and patriarchy: competing ways of doing social science'. Paper presented at the Annual Meeting of the American Sociological Association.

Lont, C. (1988) 'Redwood records: principles and profit in women's music', in B. Bate and A. Taylor (eds), *Women Communicating: Studies of Women's Talk*. Norwood, NJ: Ablex. pp. 233–50.

Marshall, J. (1984) *Women Managers: Travelers in a Male World*. New York: John Wiley.

Marshall, J. (1995) *Women Managers Moving On*. London: Routledge.

Martin, J. (1990) 'Deconstructing organizational taboos: the suppression of gender conflict in organizations', *Organizational Science*, 1: 339–59.

Martin, J. (1992) *Cultures in Organizations: Three Perspectives*. New York: Oxford University Press.

Martin, J., Knopoff, K. and Beckman, C. (1998) 'An alternative to bureaucratic impersonality and emotional labor at The Body Shop', *Administrative Science Quarterly*, 43: 429–69.

McRobbie, A. (1982) 'The politics of feminist research: between talk, text, and action', *Feminist Review*, 12: 46–57.

Meyerson, D.E. (1994) 'Interpretations of stress in institutions: the cultural production of ambiguity and burnout', *Administrative Science Quarterly*, 39: 628–53.

Meyerson, D.E. (1998) 'Feeling stressed and burned out: a feminist reading and re-visioning of stressed-based emotions within medicine and organizational science', *Organizational Science*, 9: 103–18.

Mills, A.J. and Tancred, P. (eds) (1992) *Gendering Organizational Analysis*. Newbury Park, CA: Sage.

Morgen, S. (1994) 'Personalizing personnel decisions in feminist organizational theory and practice', *Human Relations*, 47: 665–83.

Morgen, S. (1995) '"It was the best of times, it was the worst of times": emotional discourse in the work cultures of feminist health clinics', in M.M. Ferree and P.Y. Martin (eds), *Feminist Organizations*. Philadelphia: Temple University Press.

Morrison, A.M., White, R.P., Van Velsor, E. and The Center for Creative Leadership (1987) *Breaking the Glass Ceiling: Can Women Reach the Top of America's Largest Corporations?* Menlo Park, CA: Addison-Wesley.

Mumby, D.K. and Putnam, L.L. (1992) 'The politics of emotion: a feminist reading of bounded rationality', *Academy of Management Review*, 17 (3): 465–85.

Nelson, M. (1988) 'Women's ways: interactive patterns in predominantly female research teams' in B. Bate and A. Taylor (eds), *Women Communicating: Studies of Women's Talk*. Norwood, NJ: Ablex. pp. 199–232.

Newton, T. with Handy, J. and Fineman, S. (1995) *'Managing' Stress: Emotion and Power at Work*. London: Sage.

Oakley, A. (1981) 'Interviewing women: a contradiction in terms' in H. Roberts (ed.), *Doing Feminist Research*. London: Routledge and Kegan Paul.

Okin, S.M. (1989) *Justice, Gender and the Family*. New York: Basic Books.

Olsen, F. (1983) 'The family and the market: a study of ideology and legal reform', *Harvard Law Review*, 96: 1497–1578.

Pettigrew, T.F. and Martin, J. (1987) 'Shaping the organizational context for black American inclusion', *Journal of Social Issues*, 43: 41–78.

Putnam, L.L. and Mumby, D.K. (1993) 'Organizations, emotion and the myth of rationality', in S. Fineman (ed.), *Emotion in Organizations*. London: Sage.

Roddick, A. (1991) *Body and Soul*. New York: Crown.

Schein, E.H. (1985) *Organizational Culture and Leadership*. San Francisco: Jossey-Bass.

Simon, H.A. (1976) *Administrative Behavior*, 3rd. edn. New York: Free Press.

Stacey, J. (1996) 'Can there be a feminist ethnography?', in H. Gottfried (ed.), *Feminism and Social Change: Bridging Theory and Practice*. Urbana, IL: University of Illinois Press.

Sutton, R.I. (1991) 'Maintaining norms about expressed emotions: the case of bill collectors', *Administrative Science Quarterly*, 36: 245–68.

Sutton, R.I. and Rafaeli, A. (1988) 'Untangling the relationship between displayed emotions and organizational sales: the case of convenience stores', *Academy of Management Journal*, 31: 461–87.

Van Maanen, J. and Barley, S.R. (1984) 'Occupational communities: culture and control in organizations', in B. Staw and L. Cummings (eds), *Research in Organizational Behavior*, vol. 6. Greenwich: JAI Press. pp. 287–366.

Van Maanen, J. and Kunda, G. (1989) 'Real feelings: emotional expression and organizational culture', *Research in Organizational Behavior*, 11: 43–103. Greenwich, CT: JAI Press.

Weber, M. (1946) 'Bureaucracy', in H.H. Gerth and C. Wright Mills (eds and trans), *From Max Weber: Essays in Sociology*. New York: Oxford University Press. pp. 196–244.

Weber, M. (1981) 'Bureaucracy', in O. Grusky and G.A. Miller (eds), *The Sociology of Organizations: Basic Studies*. New York: Free Press. pp. 7–36.

Wharton, A.S. and Erickson, R.J. (1993) 'Managing emotions on the job and at home: understanding the consequences of multiple emotional roles', *Academy of Management Review*, 18 (3): 457–86.

Wyatt, N. (1988) 'Shared leadership in the Weavers Guild', in B. Bate and Anita Taylor (eds), *Women Communicating: Studies of Women's Talk*. Norwood, NJ: Ablex. pp. 147–75.

Zajonc, R.B. (1985) 'Emotion and facial efference: an ignored theory reclaimed', *Science*, 5 April: 15–21.

8 AESTHETIC SYMBOLS AS EMOTIONAL CUES

VARDA WASSERMAN, ANAT RAFAELI AND AVRAHAM N. KLUGER

This chapter draws a connection between aesthetic symbols in organizations and emotions of organizational participants. Perhaps because both these notions maintain an unclear link to productivity and efficiency they have not been centre-stage issues in organizational research. Yet both are clearly recognized as essential elements of organization (cf. Cacioppo and Gardner, 1999; Fineman, 1996; Gagliardi, 1990; Strati, 1992). We believe that the two notions are tightly related. We wish to assert and illustrate in this chapter that aesthetic symbols can and do generate a predictable pattern of emotional scripts. We begin with a brief review of pertinent research and then describe an empirical study that integrated qualitative and quantitative data to illustrate our thesis.

Aesthetic symbols

The concept 'aesthetic' originates from the Greek notion *aisthētikos*. It is sometimes used to describe a sense of the pleasant or the beautiful, but in actuality is broader, and connotes any sensual perceptions (*Webster's Seventh New Collegiate Dictionary*). Both natural or artistically created stimuli can elicit aesthetic reactions (Carritt, 1931), and any sensual experience is an aesthetic experience.

Organizational scholars have recently begun to recognize the importance of aesthetics or an aesthetic point of view to organizations and organizational studies (Strati, 1992, 1996; Ramirez, 1996; Dean et al., 1997; Gagliardi, 1990; Ottensmeyer, 1996; White, 1996; Kuhn, 1996; Schmitt and Simonson, 1997). The message in such recent work is that aesthetics are important to organizational research because they have an enormous – though potentially unnoticeable – influence on behaviour (Norberg-Schulz, 1971; Schmitt and Simonson, 1997). As the definition suggests, any and all physical surroundings elicit an aesthetic experience. It is therefore likely that multiple aesthetic experiences exist in any organizational context and that variation among such experiences influences constituents' emotion and behaviour.

Of particular interest to us here is the aesthetics of physical cues or symbols in and of organizations. Given the amount of time that human beings spend in various physical structures in which organizations operate, questions regarding the impact of these structures are noticeably missing from organizational discourse (Bitner, 1992; Davis, 1984). Indeed, organizations are becoming more interested, and invest more resources, in layout design. But scholarly research is still lacking about such expenditures. How should they be channelled? What is their impact? We propose an initial framework to answer such questions.

Aesthetic symbols and participant emotions

Some research has documented the meanings, ergonomic implications and behavioural effects of environmental symbols (Gibson, 1979; Canter, 1997; Davis, 1984; Ornstein, 1986, 1989, 1992; Trice and Beyer, 1984; Knez, 1995; Evans et al., 1996). Scholars have specifically dealt with philosophical aspects of aesthetics (White, 1996), and a few have focused on the physical layout of service organizations (Bitner, 1986, 1990, 1992).[1] But only limited attention has been given to the link between emotions and aesthetics in organizations (for some exceptions see Strati, 1992, 1996; White, 1996; Kuhn, 1996).

Of specific interest to us is the relationship between emotions and aesthetics in service organizations. In this context Bitner (1992) and Mehrabian and Russell (1974) offer broad theoretical frameworks, upon which we rely in this analysis. Bitner (1992) suggests a concept that she labelled the 'servicescape' of service organizations, and a framework for analysis which comprises a mapping of environmental dimensions, participant mediating responses (cognitive, emotional and physiological) and participant (employee and customer) behaviours. Bitner's (1992) analysis considers emotions as varying on a single dimension of positive to negative. As Zeithaml and Bitner (1996) recently recognized, this treatment ignores the complexity of emotional responses as documented by Mehrabian and Russell (1974).

Mehrabian and Russell's (1974) analysis presents a more complex view of emotions. They propose a three-dimensional view of emotion, in which three dimensions – pleasantness, arousal and power – are cardinal to the understanding of any emotion. The framework argues that these three dimensions can map *any* emotional responses to any environment (see also Babin and Darden, 1995; Takahashi, 1995). Yet most of the research on emotional reactions within organizations (including Bitner, 1992) continues to focus on only one dimension (pleasant–unpleasant) or on resulting behaviours (such as attitudes of approach or avoidance). For example, Donovan and Rossiter (1982) considered the influence of feelings of pleasantness on behaviours of spending time and money. The goal of our conceptual and empirical analysis is to extend these initial efforts toward establishing the link between environmental cues (or aesthetic stimuli) and the more complex and complete picture of participants' emotions proposed by Mehrabian and Russell (1974).

Aesthetic symbols, emotions and the service environment

The sensual character of aesthetics suggests that the aesthetics of an organization will affect the emotions of all individuals conducting various responsibilities within organizations (managers, employees or clients). In Foucault's spirit (1979),[2] we view aesthetics as a form of knowledge (see Strati, 1992; Dean et al., 1997), which can be controlled in order to gain power. The combination of our two arguments thus far – that aesthetics influences emotions, and that aesthetics is a form of knowledge – leads to the inevitable conclusion that it is possible to control and manipulate emotions through aesthetics. In other words, an understanding of the different possible meanings of aesthetic aspects of an organization provides a source of power and control over both participants' (clients' and employees') emotions. Organizations trying to evoke certain emotions in participants may therefore be able to do so by manipulating aesthetic symbols (see also Goodsell, 1977).

Control over the aesthetic discourse has a particular importance in service organizations, where survival can depend on successfully presenting an image expected by clients (Schmitt and Simonson, 1997). Such presentations, we propose, rely on eliciting desirable emotions in clients. Hence, our study describes an analysis of the effects of aesthetic symbols on emotional reactions in typical service establishments. We examine this process in the context of bars and restaurants.

We chose to focus on restaurants and bars because of their practical importance in fulfilling a variety of human needs yet their significant variation in aesthetic appearance. This variation is partly a reflection of organizational attempts to control clients' emotions (as implied by Foucault's theory), and partly a result of the consumerism trend in which restaurants and bars are commodities that, like any other commodity, consider atmosphere and design as a key part of their sell. In this sense, restaurants are not only places that supply clients with food and nutrition. Restaurants are also used to satisfy other needs. For example, restaurants may be used as a 'stage' for clients to 'show off' or to both establish and reinforce social status (Goffman, 1959). The appearance of a restaurant or a bar may therefore be no less important than the food or drink that they sell.

It is specifically the design or style of a restaurant or bar that determines the kind of 'stage' presented by a particular restaurant. This design (or aesthetic cues) can have a significant influence on the type of clientele visiting in the restaurant, their behaviour and their emotions. Individuals may choose to visit a restaurant according to what they think it represents. In entering the restaurant, they buy not only the food itself, but also the social image that the restaurant projects. Even before stepping into the restaurant, people examine the extent to which its design (or aesthetic symbols) fits their self-image.

Cherulnik (1991) offers one of the most extensive studies on restaurants. He demonstrated that people maintain vast cognitive attributions concerning price, service conditions, food quality, and customers' occupations related to a restaurant. This chapter is an attempt to broaden Cherulnik's (1991) research beyond the cognitive schemes, by considering the emotional elements of responses to restaurants. Thus, our first goal in the chapter is to document that three dimensions of affect (pleasantness, arousal and power) can be discerned in subjects' evaluation of aesthetic symbols of restaurants. Following Takahashi (1995) we specifically expect to find the three dimensions of affect to underlay associations with physical appearance of restaurants.[3] Hence, our first, overarching proposition of study is:

P1   Emotional responses to physical surroundings of service organizations contain the three basic dimensions of pleasantness, arousal and power.

Aesthetic design: monomorphic or eclectic

Our second goal is to further enhance our understanding of aesthetic symbols in organizations. Toward this goal we seek to identify the influence of particular aesthetic designs on the three dimensions of emotion. Only scant literature is available on conceptualizations of different aesthetic styles (Canter, 1997). Building on what we could find, we posit that a key issue for such conceptualization is the legibility of the design (Nasar, 1987; Pederson, 1986). Legibility of aesthetic design can bear at least two values: monomorphic and eclectic. A design that is *monomorphic* is *clearly legible and can be easily labelled and identified*. Monomorphic designs contain aesthetic elements that represent *only one consistent style*. The monomorphic design may be 'baroque', 'modern', 'Chinese', or 'efficient', but in all these and similar cases it is clearly identifiable.

In contrast, a design can be *eclectic*, in which case it is not clearly identifiable. The eclectic design style is a style that has *no one clear direction* and contains a blend or amalgam of styles (Nasar, 1987). For example, the coffee shop frequented by the characters in the American TV show 'Seinfeld' or any other coffee shop that cannot be succinctly described by a single descriptor is likely to bear an eclectic design. The categorization of monomorphic versus eclectic can be applied to any aesthetic dimension. For example, if we focus on the distinction between an old versus modern style, then clearly old or clearly modern styles would be labelled 'monomorphic'. In contrast, a style characterized by a blend of old-style elements and modern-style elements would be labelled 'eclectic'.

Our conceptual analysis of the emotional impact of eclectic designs suggested that such designs *would not evoke extreme emotions (either positive or negative) among participants*. This expectation draws from the following logic. The eclectic style allows for a larger number of and more varied elements. Such variety increases the probability that there will be elements that any participant may find attractive. Eclectic designs can be expected to provide more space for imaginative fantasies. Even if the match to one's taste is not exact, an eclectic style offers some probability that certain aspects will be appealing. Therefore, this style can be expected to evoke less antagonism and less extreme emotions in participants. Consequently, this style can be expected to yield mildly positive reactions of pleasantness among most people.

In contrast, we expect the monomorphic design to be more emotionally committing, yielding either highly positive or highly negative emotions. Such styles are clearer, and likely to create distinct associations that can be expected to provoke more antagonism as well as greater enthusiasm among participants. Hence our second broad hypothesis was as follows:

> P2　Monomorphic designs (that is, non-eclectic designs) will evoke more extreme emotions than eclectic designs. Eclectic designs will evoke fewer extreme positive or negative emotions and will produce mild positive reactions among a majority of people.

Empirical study

We examined these two propositions in an empirical study that combined both qualitative and quantitative data. In a pilot study we first used expertise (opinions of architects and frequent customers) to identify the salient dimensions that separate monomorphic from eclectic designs in restaurants. We then applied these dimensions in an inductive (qualitative) study of emotional reactions to the aesthetic design of similarly priced restaurants. To broaden the representation of the dimensions identified in the pilot study we expanded the set of stimuli to include bars as well. In a deductive (quantitative) study we analysed the nature of emotions elicited by different types of aesthetic environments.

Method

Pilot study: classifying aesthetics

Our first goal was to construct a conceptual structure that would allow us to distinguish between different design styles of restaurants. Toward this end we collected pictures of a variety of similarly priced restaurants (see below). We showed the pictures to 20 experts (architects, interior designers and people who regularly frequent restaurants) and asked them how they would classify the pictures. We also asked these experts about relevant dimensions for drawing distinctions between the physical (aesthetic) appearance of different restaurants.

These interviews suggested two key categories of our stimuli: an ethnic dimension and a warm–cold dimension. The first dimension – ethnicity – contrasted, for example, French designs with Chinese or Middle Eastern styles. This dimension has been recognized in previous theoretical works (for example, Baraban and Durocher, 1988). The second dimension – warm or cold – is less familiar in theoretical literature, but is frequent in architects' discourse and the majority[4] (19 of the 20) of the experts we interviewed agreed that this is an essential dimension for distinguishing among restaurants.

Once these dimensions were recognized, our conceptualization suggests that each of the restaurants in our sample could be categorized as either monomorphic or eclectic on both of these dimensions. Hence, a restaurant can theoretically be classified as monomorphic (when clearly cold or clearly warm), or as eclectic (when neither clearly cold nor clearly warm). We therefore asked our 'experts' to classify the pictures on these two dimensions. Experts had no problem in classifying the restaurants on either dimension. However, these classifications revealed that none of the restaurants was perceived as clearly (monomorphically) cold. This occurred although our subjects were the ones who originally suggested the warm–cold dimension for classifying the pictures.

It could be that cold restaurants used to exist and could theoretically exist, but are no longer in vogue and therefore were not a part of our initial set of stimuli. To obtain complete representation of the warm–cold dimension of design we searched for additional food service locations in which this dimension will be more completely represented. We found it in bars (a similar service industry), and hence added pictures of 35 bars to our set of potential stimuli. The experts were then contacted again and asked to classify the complete set of pictures of restaurants and bars. This time the classification yielded six categories of pictures, which represented both monomorphic and eclectic designs, as shown in Table 8.1.

Pictures of equally priced bars represented the warm–cold dimension, while pictures of equally priced restaurants represented the ethnic dimension. A satisfactory level of agreement was apparent among the experts regarding the classification of all pictures. Experts were then asked to select one picture that would prototypically represent each of the categories. Thus, they had to choose six pictures to represent each of the six categories in the table. The modal choices were the stimuli used in the following study.

Table 8.1   *The six categories of pictures*

	Monomorphically designed establishment	Eclectically designed establishment	Monomorphically designed establishment
Ethnic dimension	Restaurant with mostly European elements	Restaurant with both European and Middle Eastern elements	Restaurant with mostly Middle Eastern elements
Warm–cold dimension	Bar with mostly cold elements	Bar with both cold and warm elements	Bar with mostly warm elements

Study: emotional reactions to aesthetic cues

Stimuli

As noted above, from an initial pool of 85 photographs of restaurants and bars six were selected. Two photographs represented monomorphic values on the ethnic dimension: One represented a European style design (Figure 8.1 (a)), and one a Middle Eastern style (Figure 8.1 (c)). A third picture represented an eclectic (combined or indistinct) style, which is neither European nor Middle Eastern, and may contain elements of both styles (Figure 8.1 (b)).

Figure 8.1 *Pictures of restaurants: ethnic dimension*

(a) European restaurant (monomorphic)

(b) Eclectic restaurant

(c) Middle Eastern restaurant (monomorphic)

In addition, three photographs were chosen to represent the warm–cold dimension. One represented the monomorphic-cold design (Figure 8.2 (a)), another represented the monomorphic-warm design (Figure 8.2 (c)), and a third represented an eclectic design, which contains both warm and cold elements (Figure 8.2 (b)). Thus this set of stimuli provided a comparison of two monomorphic styles dimensions: ethnicity and warm or cold.

Figure 8.2 Pictures of bars: warm–cold dimension

(a) Cold design bar (monomorphic)

(b) Eclectic bar

(c) Warm design bar (monomorphic)

Subjects

Israeli subjects (n=200, 105 business-school students and 95 non-students) of different ages participated in a study that was described to them as an attempt to explore the influence of design on emotions. Half the subjects (51%) were men. Students participated in the study for experimental credit; non-students participated as a gesture of goodwill to the first author.

Procedure

Each subject was asked to write an imaginary story regarding a plausible visit to each of the establishments in the pictures. Subjects had no problem with this task. Three examples of stories written by three different subjects are included in the Appendix.

Two judges then coded all the stories collected with regard to the emotions that they embodied. This coding process provided data regarding the emotions that each story contained. The coding allowed for quantitative analyses to bolster the qualitative analyses of the narratives. Judges specifically coded the following aspects of the stories: the category of each emotion, the direction of each emotion, and the intensity of each emotion.

1. *Category of each emotion* Each emotion was coded regarding the salient category it represented from the three categories identified by Mehrabian and Russell (1974). A *pleasantness* code was assigned when a story contained terms such as appraisal, enjoyment or unpleasantness. An *arousal* code was assigned when stories contained terms such as overload, activity or relaxation. A *power* code was assigned when stories contained terms such as dominance, control, submission or threat. The codes were not mutually exclusive, so each story could be coded as containing any or all of these categories.

The coding process was as follows. Judges first identified all emotional terms in each story, and then classified each term into one out of the three emotional categories. Judges were instructed to classify emotions on the basis of the most salient feature of each emotion. Thus, this classification identifies the most salient dimension of each emotion, although according to Mehrabian and Russell's (1974) dimensional view all three dimensions characterize each and any emotion.

2. *The direction of emotion* Next, judges were asked to determine the direction of each emotion. For example, an emotion coded as 'pleasantness' could be coded as negative (for example, ugliness) or as positive (for example, beauty). Similarly, an emotion coded as arousal could be coded as low (for example, boredom or relaxation) or as high (for example, excitement). In the power dimension, weakness is an example of low power whereas control is an example of high power. The direction of the evoked emotions was used both as input for a qualitative analysis (see Results section) and as an input to the next measure.

3. *The intensity of emotions*   Two indices of intensity of emotion were developed. First, we assumed that designs that evoke extreme emotions are likely to yield disagreements among the viewers of the photographs. That is, we assumed that clear (monomorphic) styles evoke extreme emotions, but that they will be extreme in one direction for some subjects and in the other direction for others. Thus, intensity of emotion was assessed by the distribution of the direction of emotions between subjects. When responses were more or less evenly split between low and high values we assumed they were extreme. When responses were clustered in one location, we assumed they were not extreme. Second, we asked judges directly to code the intensity of emotions in a story. Judges were specifically asked to identify both narratives that revealed strong emotions of the writer and narratives that evoked strong emotions in the reader. These two indicators of intensity were used to test our second proposition. Reliability of judges' coding was verified, though minor discrepancies between the judges were excluded from all analyses.

Results

Table 8.2 presents the frequency of stories that contained at least one emotional term in each of the three dimensions. As is evident in Table 8.2, all three emotional dimensions were found in the narratives. The dimension of pleasantness is the most prominent dimension, but both the arousal dimension and the power dimension are also evident. These findings are consistent with our first hypothesis, confirming that subjects' reactions to aesthetic stimuli can be mapped using Russell's emotional map.

Table 8.2   *Percentages of texts containing emotional expression by design and type of emotion*

Design	Dimension	Category of emotion (%)		
		Pleasantness	Arousal	Power
Monomorphic	European	81	57	67
	Middle Eastern	80	61	51
Eclectic	Nondescript	86	52	31
Monomorphic	Cold	79	48	31
	Warm	82	77	36
Eclectic	Nondescript	82	70	16
Mean		81.66	60.83	38.66

Table 8.3 summarizes the direction and intensity of the emotions categorized in Table 8.2. As shown in Table 8.3, and as expected in our second proposition, monomorphic styles (European and Middle Eastern, cold or warm) yielded an even split in the pleasantness dimension. That is, whereas eclectic designs largely evoked pleasant emotions, monomorphic design styles evoked emotions that were, more or less, equally divided between high and

Table 8.3 *Percentages of texts containing emotional expression by design and direction (negative or positive) of emotion*[a]

| Design | Dimension | Category of emotion (%) | | | | | |
| | | Pleasantness | | Arousal | | Power | |
		Positive	Negative	High	Low	High	Low
Monomorphic	European	40	41	17	40	24	43
	Middle Eastern	41	39	7	54	49	2
Eclectic	Nondescript	8	78	20	32	21	10
Monomorphic	Cold	35	44	25	23	15	16
	Warm	41	41	10	67	4	32
Eclectic	Nondescript	15	67	49	21	5	11

[a] Only stories that included a clearly negative or positive emotion were included in this table. Hence percentages do not add up to 100%.

low pleasantness (half expressed dislike and half enjoyment, while only about 20% did not express clear emotions of pleasantness).

Eclectic designs: moderate yet pleasant experiences

The narratives (stories) generated by subjects in reaction to the eclectic designs further confirmed that the experience of visiting such locations is typically associated with pleasant yet moderate (*not* extreme) emotions. This sentiment was evident in narratives such as:

This is a very regular place, there is nothing special about it.

The moderate (non-extreme) emotions generated by these locations were reflected in texts such as:

I didn't feel anything special, it was OK, not more, not less.

There is nothing special about the bar, it's nice, but similar to other bars.

Behaviours and relationships embedded in stories associated with the eclectic design revealed a similar pattern. They comprised references to 'average' ('nothing special') relationships. For example:

I would come to this place with people who are not very close to me but also not strangers.

Topics of conversation, or service received, in such (eclectic) establishments were also more mundane. To illustrate:

We talked about daily affairs: gossip, politics, problems at work and general things. Nothing special.

Finally, the quality of service received seemed to be moderate – not excellent but not awful either:

> The waitress was nice, but she made a lot of mistakes.

> The service wasn't 100%, but the atmosphere didn't leave us enough time to consider the food.

> Service was a little bit slow, but no one was angry when food arrived 25 minutes late.

A prominent element of narratives generated by the eclectic designs was the frequent reference to blind dates.[5] This is insightful because it may help unravel the unique merit of eclectic designs. Some subjects noted that such places would be appropriate for blind dates because they enable them 'to impress women'. Others noted that the eclectic places could please many (different) people and are therefore appropriate for blind dates. For example:

> It's a mixture of many styles, and therefore, it suits everybody.

Consistently, respondents indicated that they were not likely to be regular customers of the eclectic institution. And most subjects suggested that the eclectic institutions provide anonymity. One subject explicitly noted:

> There is no regular clientele in this place, only passers-by.

The greater anonymity of eclectic designs may reduce the face cost in case of a failure of a blind date, which, as we discuss later, may be why eclectic styles are judged more suitable for blind dates.

Monomorphic designs: extreme experiences

In contrast to the eclectic styles, narratives evoked by the monomorphic designs contained unusual events and extreme emotions. These effects were evident in all monomorphic stimuli. In both qualitative and quantitative analyses, the monomorphic designs evoked strong positive reactions among some respondents and strong negative reactions among others. Importantly, each design elicited a different set of associations, but all associations were extreme.

Our analyses further revealed that subjects made similar associations to the restaurants classified as monomorphic-European and those bars classified as monomorphic-cold: both places were noted as 'civilized places'. Similar associations were also made to places classified as warm and those classified as Middle Eastern; both of these were noted in stories as representing 'primal instincts'. Below, we therefore first describe subjects' reactions to the cold and European designs and then describe subjects' reactions to warm and Middle Eastern designs.

Monomorphic cold and European designs: distant and cool emotions

Narratives concerning cold and European design styles evoked distant and extreme emotions. As summarized by one subject:

[As I walked in] a feeling of chilliness engulfed me.

Attributions of 'correctness and coolness' prevailed in these stories. Such attributions were evident both with respect to service representatives and with respect to clients. For example:

Our behavior in the bar was restrained; the other clients looked sophisticated.

The waitress's manner was very correct.

Subjects also identified the cold design as being sophisticated, civilized and snobby.[6] These sentiments were often translated into places being noted as fashionable and popular among 'up and coming' crowds. Terms such as 'in' and 'yuppies' were popular in these narratives. And, as may be expected in presumably 'sophisticated' places, conversations focused on weighty affairs rather than daily affairs. For example:

We talked about philosophy.

We had a deep conversation about life and its meaning.

We talked about mergers of companies.

Consistent with the prestige association, the cold and European design seemed to be associated with greater expense. This is particularly interesting since all pictures were intentionally selected to represent locations that are equally priced. Status symbols such as fancy or delicate china and furnishings were often mentioned (Fussel, 1983). These symbols were sometimes translated into a feeling of intimidation and concern both for the actor and for other customers:

[I was worried.] Would I behave properly as expected from me?

Everybody was busy showing they belonged to the place. I wasn't sure.

I arrived with a few architect friends, who were dressed properly and I wasn't. I didn't fit in.

I was impressed by the friendly attitude of the waitress towards the regular clients. But towards strangers like me, her attitude was just polite.

Subjects who reported a sense of belonging to such places reported a sentiment of pleasure in the cold and high status place. To illustrate:

I felt like a princess in a palace. I was dressed properly, and I ordered the best dish as the waiter recommended.

I felt I was floating in a wonderful dream, cut off from reality . . . food was magnificent!!!.

Monomorphic warm or Middle Eastern designs: sensual and impulsive

As opposed to the 'high-brow' atmosphere at cold and European locations, the warm and Middle Eastern locations elicited passionate and sexual attributions. This was evident in descriptions of clients, employees and topics of conversation. Subjects noted that the 'warm' bar was more appropriate for men or that few women would feel comfortable there. This attribution of masculinity was tightly associated with sexuality:

It's a place of passion and impulses [sexual excitement and desire].

It was a hall of sex . . . waitresses dressed provocatively.

The smell, the atmosphere, everything called for sex.

After a few minutes, a woman sat near me. I immediately understood her intentions.

Attributing masculinity to the bar was at times felt as threatening, especially to female subjects. At the same time, it was reported as free and liberating:

The atmosphere here is more liberated.

The bar is designed in such a way that it gives a feeling of freedom, which is important to most men.

In the case of the Middle Eastern design, the feeling of freedom was one of 'social freedom' regarding who could frequent the place and how they could behave. Narratives suggested a lack of tightly imposed norms to be complied with. For example:

We sat together, laughed and spoke freely, because the place was so disordered, that we could feel comfortable.

In this restaurant you can wear any clothes you want.

Such feeling of freedom were accompanied with a high degree of sensual arousal involving multiple senses:

The restaurant was noisy, it was hot and the flies came onto my plate.

There was an acrid smell of fish in the air.

Tables were sticky . . .

The floor was dirty . . .

These high degrees of arousal were also evident in the quantitative analyses, as can be seen in Table 8.3.

In sum, both the qualitative and quantitative results confirm, as we predicted (P2) that monomorphic designs (non-eclectic) evoke extreme emotions that may be either positive or negative. In contrast, eclectic design styles are preferred by more subjects, but do not evoke distinct feelings.

Discussion

This effort is part of a stream of research on the relationship between environmental cues and the emotions experienced by organizational members.[7] Drawing on both qualitative and quantitative data we illustrated a link between the appearance of organizations and the emotions felt by potential participants. Our results pertain to imaginary rather than actual experiences, but they do confirm our (albeit broad) propositions. First, the results show clear evidence for all three emotional dimensions of emotion in stories evoked by aesthetic factors. Second, the results document that affective reactions can, to some extent, be predicted with a systematic analysis of the aesthetics of environmental cues. Our analyses contribute to theoretical understanding of both aesthetics and emotions in organizations in multiple ways. They help explain previously unaccounted preferences for eclectic over monomorphic designs, they reveal the importance of considering power in analyses of emotion, and they help position two dominant social science frameworks as pertinent to the study of aesthetics and designs. We discuss each of these implications separately.

People prefer eclectic over monomorphic designs

Our conceptual analysis of the difference between the two designs extends Pederson's (1986) contention that subjects prefer eclectic designs by offering an (albeit tentative) explanation for such preferences. The eclectic design comprises a combination of multiple and varied elements. Such variety can be expected to increase the probability that any and all people will find some elements of the design attractive. In contrast, monomorphic designs are more likely to create distinct associations that can be expected to provoke either more antagonism or greater enthusiasm. The implication is that when a select target audience can be identified, and a specific design that will appeal to this audience can be planned, a monomorphic design of that nature may be managerially powerful. In contrast, when the target audience comprises multiple and potentially varied individuals an eclectic design may be more effective.

Future research is essential, however, regarding the concepts of eclectic versus monomorphic designs. First, the constructs themselves deserve further inquiry. Such research may focus not only on eclecticism in aesthetics, but also on eclecticism and monomorphism of restaurants and bars. We believe the constructs deserve further attention in the broader context of exploring the impact of physical cues on individual emotion and behaviour (Pratt and Rafaeli, 1999; Rafaeli and Worline, in press). Such research may gain by looking into research on eclecticism in other domains, such as psychotherapy, organizational consulting, or social work.

Second, additional empirical documentation is essential regarding individuals' preferences for eclectic design. It is plausible that both individual and context differences may moderate this effect. For example, individual differences in goal directed behaviour (action orientation versus state orientation) were found by Kluger et al. (1999) to moderate the influence of service environments on participants' emotions and behaviours. In this study, customers who are action oriented (who can be expected to maintain a rational and planned decision making and shopping process) did not react positively to shops eliciting a high level of arousal.

Power as a central tenet in the study of emotion

Our somewhat unconventional methods – of coding qualitative narratives (rather than reliance on structured measures) may be of merit above and beyond the theoretical findings. Previous research – which relied on structured, quantitative measures – could not confirm the power dimension. Consequently, researchers tended to neglect the issue of power in affect research (see for example Russell and Barrett, 1999). Our data position such neglect as not justified, suggesting that power should be integrated into studies of emotions in organizations. Even within our data fewer associations are made to power than to pleasantness (see Table 8.2). But many narratives did include references to power, suggesting that totally ignoring it is inappropriate. Considering power in analyses of emotion is consistent with the importance of power to organizational members (see for example Pfeffer, 1981, 1992). It is specifically important in the context of relating aesthetics to emotion, given the important role attributed to power in messages communicated by aesthetic symbols (cf. Molloy, 1975; Rafaeli et al., 1997).

One proposition that our data suggest is that the power dimension is prominent only in those relatively less frequent situations in which strong emotions are evoked (see also Kluger and Rafaeli, in press). In our data the narratives solicited in association with the monomorphic design contained more references to power than those elicited by the eclectic designs, and our analysis suggested that monomorphic designs are construed as more extreme than eclectic designs. Thus, power appears to be a dominant element of reactions to design when the design is more, rather than less, provocative.

Our effort demonstrates that the sensation of power is so fundamental in our lives that it may be evoked by physical as well as social stimuli transmitted by aesthetics.

Theoretical (social sciences) lenses for the study of aesthetics and emotions

In the context of a volume such as this one, an additional goal of this chapter is to suggest novel theoretical lenses for studying and understanding emotional reactions in organizations. We see our study as suggesting two such lenses. First, we suggest that the preference of eclectic styles over mono-morphic styles may be afforded by Lévi-Strauss's (1963) suggestion that the distinction between nature and culture bears core implications for human social construction. Second we suggest a link between aesthetic designs and the psychoanalytic theory advanced by Freud (1940). As we explain below, both of these theoretical lenses are pertinent to our unexpected findings wherein monomorphic designs that were warm elicited forbidden sexual desires, while monomorphic cold designs were associated with intellectual attributes.

Aesthetic design as a distinction between nature and culture

A claim maintained by the school of structural anthropology is that the tension between nature and culture is central to human thought and action (Lévi-Strauss, 1963). In this school of thought, primitive thought is argued to be a reconstruction of nature while the thought and action of modern cultures involves abstract models constructed to represent the world. Human behaviour is argued to be governed by this tension between natural and abstract paradigms. According to Lévi-Strauss (1963), the primitive modes of action (which can be described as wild or untamed) are primary in human mentality, and are what all humans have in common. These modes of action stand in contrast to the civilized (tamed or domesticated) thought patterns, which are central to modern societies. Modern or cultured thought is argued to be primarily intellectual and rational, while primitive or natural thought is argued to be emotional and instinctive (Geertz, 1973). This frame-work suggests a potential modification to our conceptualization of different aesthetic designs because it predicts unexpected links in our data.

Specifically, our analyses found that in response to a design that we defined as European and cold, subjects made attributions of constrained, civilized and intellectual behaviour. In contrast, in response to designs we labelled monomorphic Middle Eastern and warm, subjects made attributions of impulsive and unconstrained behaviour.[8] Thus, the associations elicited by different designs were split on a nature–culture continuum: the cold and European design elicited associations that can be categorized as tamed or cultural, while the warm and Middle Eastern design elicited associations that can be categorized as 'natural'.

Applying this conceptual framework to our analysis of different designs suggests a new variable for studying aesthetic cues, namely the extent to which a design reflects cultural manipulation versus mimicking natural compositions. This conceptualization suggests insightful new propositions regarding the pattern of emotions that different designs will yield. Specifically, based on Lévi-Strauss's (1963) analyses we predict that designs that more strongly reflect cultural manipulation will trigger emotions loaded on the power dimension because the cultural manipulation embedded in the design would be a symbol of social power. In contrast, designs that are more natural, or less constrained, are predicted to be more arousing because the natural elements of the design would be symbols of instinctive or unconstrained behaviour.

Indeed, a close look at our quantitative findings reveals precisely this pattern. A closer look at Table 8.3 confirms that the two monomorphic designs (European and Middle Eastern) elicited very different patterns of both arousal and power. In response to the Middle Eastern style a proportionately far greater number of high-arousal stories was generated than in response to the European style (54% versus 7% of stories for the Middle Eastern design reflected high arousal as compared to 40% versus 17% for the European style). Similarly, the gap in the power felt by subjects was greater in the Middle Eastern style than in the European style (2% versus 49% of stories for the Middle Eastern style reflected high power as compared to 43% versus 24% for the European style; see Table 8.3).

Thus, the European design, which was construed in the narratives as relatively more civilized and socially constraining, was also construed as less arousing but more empowering or domineering. The Middle Eastern style, which was construed in the narratives as relatively less constraining, was also construed as more arousing. The mechanism underlying these emotional associations may have to do with the materials used in the different monomorphic styles. A closer look at our stimuli reveals that the materials used in the European and the cold designs tended to be cultivated (such as concrete, iron and artificially coloured wood). In contrast, the materials used in the European and warm styles were natural materials (such as stone and untreated dark wood). Thus, when manipulation of nature is evident in a design, attributions of culture and civility are made. When nature is maintained in a design, attributions of impulsiveness are made.

The eclectic design may also be interpreted in this conceptualization. Following Lévi-Strauss (1963), eclectic designs may be styles that offer a compromise between the extremes of nature and culture. Eclectic styles maintain a mixture of natural materials and artificial elements. For example, in our stimuli both the eclectic restaurant and the eclectic bar contained both wood and earth colours (natural elements) and metal, steel, plastic and artificial colours (cultivated elements). This mixture allows for two sets of attributions to emerge (natural or free, and cultural or constrained). The hybrid may help to make the eclectic design liked by more people. Hence, as our data reveal, the eclectic design was associated with a feeling of pleasantness for a large number of people (78% and 67% of subjects, respectively, saw the eclectic restaurant and bar as pleasant, while only approximately 40% of subjects saw any of the monomorphic designs as pleasant). In short, both aesthetically and emotionally the eclectic design appears to combine nature with culture.

Aesthetic design and emotion as psychoanalytic processes

A second theoretical lens that helps advance our understanding of our data is that of psychoanalytic theory. Sandstrom (1974) advanced an initial implementation of psychoanalytic concepts to the study of aesthetics. Extending Sandstrom's (1974) line of thought, our focus on aesthetic design as emotional cues suggests that conceptually distinct designs can be associated with distinct psychoanalytic constructs (Freud, 1940). Freud (1940) differentiated between the superego, which represents cultural norms, and the id (or libido) which represents bare instincts. The ego in Freud's theory contains the adaptation of libidinal impulses to cultural norms. It may therefore be that cold designs are agents of the superego, while warm designs are agents of the id. Along this line of thought the eclectic design represents the ego, as it is a combination of aspects of the id and the superego. Consistently, in our study cold designs were considered relatively more civilized, while warm designs were considered relatively more natural and impulsive.

Freud's (1940) theory further asserted that the id reflects basic human impulses that demand immediate satisfaction, and especially sexual instincts. In contrast, the superego reflects culture and society, both of which restrain human impulses to cultural norms. Indeed, our findings are that warm designs – that we now suggest are more libidinal – evoked sexual and impulsive associations. In contrast, cold designs – which we now suggest to be representations of the superego – evoked narratives and emotions that reflect controlled and civilized aspects of social life. In this analysis the eclectic design may be construed to represent the ego: it combines the satisfaction of both basic needs (those of the id) and social needs (those of the superego). The eclectic design is preferred and judged to be more pleasant by subjects precisely because it offers a response to two basic yet conflicting sets of psychoanalytic human needs – the basic drives of the id and the social requirements of culture. Eclectic designs in a sense offer a middle ground between two extremes.

The psychoanalytical lens on the study of design helps explain the pattern of feelings with regard to social threat, which were not predicted by our propositions but were nonetheless noticeable in our data. The pattern was of social deviance being construed as anxiety provoking in the cold designs and as an opportunity for self-fulfilment in the warm design. Although unexpected, these findings suggest a potentially valuable direction for future research. Specifically, our qualitative findings revealed that on one hand, narratives relating to the cold (European) restaurants contained repeated references to the anxiety associated with social norms. To illustrate, subjects voiced concerns about understanding the menu, being appropriately clothed for the place, or really belonging in the place and with its clientele. In contrast, stories elicited by the warm design contained a subtle but consistent theme of the opportunity to deviate from social norms, and be oneself. Subjects saw the warm design as offering an opportunity to be a little different from others, do something different for the first time, or act more naturally.

Complementary to this pattern is the finding that in the eclectic designs, subjects fantasized far more about blind dates and similar social situations which can be viewed as social daring that is within reasonable limits. The eclectic designs elicited narratives that can be argued to be representations of the ego because they reflected a version of guarded freedom: they simultaneously violated certain social boundaries, but did not reach a point of total lack of restraint. For example, in the blind date narrative that we received primarily (yet unexpectedly) in response to the eclectic styles, subjects appeared to construct in their minds a version of daring behaviour that is within given limits. Emotionally, there is a certain violation of social norms in going for a date with someone you have never met before. But the mere fact that there is an acceptable social term for such behaviour suggests that it is socially (albeit marginally) acceptable. Thus, the blind date represents a pattern of behaviour that combines social constraints that would be too imposing on their own with personal instincts which would be inappropriate on their own.

We did not predict this conceptual link at our point of departure, so these analyses are but post hoc propositions that should be empirically supported in future research. However, our data do suggest that, as suggested by Sandstrom (1974), considering the psychoanalytic meanings of aesthetic cues may help us understand the narratives, emotions and behaviours of participants.

Summary

Building on an empirical study of subjects' reactions to aesthetic cues we illustrated that subjects associate distinct emotions with aesthetic cues, and that designs that are conceptually distinct (eclectic rather than monomorphic, warm rather than cold) are preferred by most subjects. We further offered two conceptual lenses for future research, which we found useful for making sense of unexpected patterns in our findings: the nature–culture framework proposed by Lévi-Strauss and the psychoanalytic framework proposed by Freud. Clearly, these frameworks provide post hoc explanations that require further empirical testing. However, they cannot but add to the overarching message of this chapter – that there is managerial power embedded in the management of aesthetic cues. Unravelling the nuances of the use of such power is an important and fascinating avenue for future research. Such research is essential for a more complete understanding of emotions in organizations.

An aesthetic understanding of organizational life has been of recent interest (Dean et al., 1997; Strati, 1992). Our analysis brings forth the emotions that aesthetics evoke as a new form of knowledge of both aesthetics and organizations. Historically, scholarly work in organizational behaviour focused on the functional aspects of aesthetics, addressing questions regarding the effects of different colours or designs on productivity. Little attention was placed on how different plans or designs make people feel in organizations. As in many other realms, emotions were historically left out of the discourse regarding organizational aesthetics. We argue these two aspects are not necessarily contradicted. Specifically, understanding the emotional interpretations people place on their surroundings can help organizations design their appearance in a manner that will manage the emotions experienced by both employees and customers. Such management can also improve productivity. In the cases we studied – of restaurants and bars – eliciting particular emotions can lead to better sales, more frequent customer visits, and bigger tips for waiters and waitresses.

Yet viewing aesthetics as a tool for the management of participant emotions raises a set of ethical questions. Building on Foucault (1979), this thesis positions aesthetics as a form of social power, which raises two ethical problems. First, aesthetics may be misused toward dictating the 'right' way that people should feel. Hochschild (1983) and Rafaeli and Sutton (1989) noted this problem with respect to the management of emotions of employees. We extend the ethical dilemma to the management of emotions of all participants, making it more acute since customers are less likely to be aware of the emotional manipulation. Perhaps a new concept can be suggested – 'emotion engineering' – and as with any other form of engineering the outcomes need to be monitored to avoid misuse.

Second, our analysis may be interpreted as suggesting that there is one perfect design for any set of clientele. This would leave little space for creative design imagination, as well as no place for heterogeneity in clientele. We caution against both of these outcomes. A controlled world where everything – including aesthetic design and participant emotions – is known in advance seems scary and alienating.

Acknowledgement

This chapter was partially funded by a grant from the German Israel Fund (# 485) and a grant to the third author from the Recanati Fund of the School of Business Administration at the Hebrew University. The chapter is based on the MA thesis of the first author.

Notes

1 For a broader mapping of the environmental research, see Saegert and Winkel, (1990).

2 Foucault suggested that any kind of knowledge is power, which is enforced by the people who possess it and who connote the 'right' discourses for a given area. Knowledge and control over the discourse becomes a power resource. Social relations in a given area become controlled by 'specialists' in the area, since these function as agents of power and knowledge.

3 We also extend Takahashi's (1995) analysis, which was of abstract pictures, to more complex but also more familiar stimuli, namely pictures of real organizations.

4 For the discrepancy between the theoretical language and the architects' practice, see Canter, 1997.

5 This may be argued to be due to the young ages of approximately half our subjects. However, we did not find a relationship between the age of subjects and the mention of blind dates.

6 This association between 'European' and prestige may represent values in the Israeli context where anything European is considered more prestigious than anything Middle Eastern, and Jews of European (Ashkenazy) origin are often considered snobby as compared to Jews of Middle Eastern (Sephardic) origin (Eisenstadt et al., 1993). These values have been sharply criticized, but may still prevail.

7 See http://iew3.technion.ac.il:8080/~anatr/main.html

8 This may appear odd, given perceptions of Middle Eastern cultures as conservative and constraining (Schwartz, 1999). It is important to note, however, that these were the perceptions of Israeli subjects of local Middle Eastern restaurants.

Appendix: Examples of stories reported by subjects

A story elicited by a picture of a monomorphic (cold design) bar

We went to this place to discuss our students' film, a film with a very poor budget. Everyone was sitting. They seemed very pleased with themselves, feeling disgustingly 'in', smoking and talking about the film angles and about philosophical issues. In this post-modern design, with its shocking colors, you can easily find the best coffee in town. But its clients are only famous people, architects, lawyers and other yuppies. Of course, I didn't fit in, because I wasn't dressed properly with my T-shirt and jeans. Most people knew each other, but I didn't feel good, especially due to the cold correct attitude of the waitresses toward me. They also noticed that I don't belong in this place.

A story elicited by a picture of an eclectically designed bar

I set a meeting with a guy, and we were supposed to meet at this place. I felt quiet good at the beginning since the place was intimate enough, and there were all kind of clients. I didn't know anyone there, and it seemed also that nobody else did. I didn't know this place before, and neither did my date. We met at 21:00 o'clock [early] in order to avoid the crowded hours of the pubs. The atmosphere was calm, and we could enjoy the privacy and the nice conversation. The place was full of couples in their twenties and thirties, talking quietly. So we could also feel comfortable. The design of the place is not very unique, but it is romantic (not too much), warm (but not too much), intimate and nice. I won't come back to this place unless I am with people who are not too close to me, because the place is not very beautiful. There is a combination of beautiful and ugly elements. Moreover, the service is OK, but not very good (we waited for 30 minutes for our Greek salad!). On that particular evening I wasn't angry about the slow service. The problems came later after I dated the same guy again . . .

A story elicited by a picture of a monomorphic (warm) designed bar

We were in a huge cavity, a real sex den. The waitresses were dressed provocatively and they caught my eyes. This was good because we didn't get any service. The smell, the atmosphere, everything called for sex. In the corner a couple was enthusiastically kissing, beside the bar a bunch of scary men – with high levels of testosterone in their blood – were sitting and smoking. After a while we felt exhausted and went out. This was a very difficult mission since at this stage people were dancing on the tables, and there was not a single free centimeter to be found. Using our elbows, we went out to the fresh cool air, tired, angry, and thirsty and not satisfied at all.

References

Babin, B. and Darden, W.R. (1995) 'Consumer self-regulation in a retail environment', *Journal of Retailing* 71 (1): 47–70.

Baraban, R.G. and Durocher, J.F. (1988) *Successful Restaurant Design.* New York: Van Nostrand Reinhold.

Bitner, M.J. (1986) 'Consumer responses to the physical environment in service settings', in M. Venkatesan, D.M. Schmalensee and C. Marshall (eds), *Creativity in Services Marketing.* Chicago: American Marketing Association. pp. 89–93.

Bitner, M.J. (1990) 'Evaluating service encounters: the effect of physical surroundings and employee responses', *Journal of Marketing,* 54: 69–82.

Bitner, M.J. (1992) 'Servicescapes: the impact of physical surroundings on customers and employees', *Journal of Marketing,* 56: 57–71.

Cacioppo, J.T. and Gardner, W.L. (1999) 'Emotion', *Annual Review of Psychology,* 50: 297–332.

Canter, D. (1997) 'The facets of place', in G.T. Moore and R.W. Marans (eds), *Advances in Environment, Behavior and Design.* New York: Plenum Press. pp. 109–47.

Carritt, E.F. (1931) *Philosophies of Beauty from Socrates to Rob.* London: Bridges.

Cherulnik, P.D. (1991) 'Reading restaurant facades: environment inference in finding the right place to eat', *Environment and Behavior,* 23: 150–70.

Davis, T.R.V. (1984) 'The influence of physical environment in offices', *Academy of Management Review,* 9 (2): 271–83.

Dean, J.W., Jr, Ottensmeyer, E. and Ramirez, R. (1997) 'An aesthetic perspective on organizations', in C.L. Cooper and S.E. Jackson (eds), *Creating Tomorrow's Organizations.* New York: John Wiley. pp. 419–37.

Donovan, R. and Rossiter, J. (1982) 'Store atmosphere: an environmental psychology approach', *Journal of Retailing,* 58: 34–57.

Eisentadt, S.N., Lissak, M. and Nahun, Y. (1993) *Communities in Israel and Their Social Location.* Jerusalem: Jerusalem Institute for the Study of Israel (in Hebrew).

Evans, G.W., Lepore, S.J. and Schroeder, A. (1996) 'The role of interior design elements in human response to crowding', *Journal of Personality and Social Psychology,* 70 (1): 41–6.

Fineman, S. (1996) 'Emotion and organizing', in S.R. Clegg, C. Hardy and W. Nord (eds), *Handbook of Organization Studies.* London, Sage. pp. 543–65.

Foucault, M. (1979) *Discipline and Punish.* New York: Vintage Books.

Freud, S. (1940) *Jenseits des Lustprinzips.* Frankfurt: S. Fischer Verlag.

Fussell, P. (1983) *Class.* New York: Ballantine Books.

Gagliardi, P. (1990) *Symbols and Artifacts: Views of the Corporate Landscape.* New York: Walter de Gruyter.

Geertz, C. (1973) *The Interpretation of Cultures.* New York: Basic Books.

Gibson, J.J. (1979) *The Ecological Approach to Visual Perception*. Boston: Houghton-Mifflin.

Goffman, E. (1959) *The Presentation of Self in Everyday Life*. New York: Doubleday.

Goodsell, C.T. (1977) 'Bureaucratic manipulation of physical symbols: an empirical study', *American Journal of Political Science*, 21: 79–91.

Hochschild, A. (1983) *The Managed Heart*. Los Angeles: University of California Press.

Kluger, A. and Rafaeli, A. (in press) 'The three dimensions of affective reactions to physical appearance', in N. Ashkenasy (eds), *Emotions and Organization Life*. Westport, CT: Quorum Books.

Kluger, A., Rafaeli, A. and Greenfield, I. (1999) 'Emotions, cognitive guides and service delivery landscape: the influence of service context on the quality of service transactions. Paper presented at the Annual Meeting of the SIOP, Dallas, Texas.

Knez, I. (1995) 'Effects of indoor lighting on mood and cognition', *Journal of Environmental Psychology*, 15: 39–51.

Kuhn, J.W. (1996) 'The misfit between organizational art: a comment on White and Strati', *Organization*, 3 (2): 219–24.

Lévi-Strauss, C. (1963) *Structural Anthropology*. New York: Basic Books. pp. 206–31.

Mehrabian, A. and Russell, J.A. (1974) *An Approach to Environmental Psychology*, Cambridge, MA: Massachusetts Institute of Psychology.

Molloy, J. (1975) *Dress for Success*. New York: Warner Books.

Nasar, J.L. (1987) 'Effect of sign complexity and coherence on the perceived quality of retail scenes', *Journal of the American Planning Association*, 53 (4): 499–509.

Norberg-Schulz, C. (1971) *Existence, Space and Architecture*. London: Studio Vista.

Ornstein, S. (1986) 'Organizational symbols: a study of their meanings and influence on perceived psychological climate', *Organizational Behavior and Human Decision Processes*, 38: 207–29.

Ornstein, S. (1989) 'Impression management through office design', in R. Giacalone and P. Rosenfeld (eds), *Impression Management in Organizations*. Hillside, NJ: Lawrence Erlbaum. pp. 411–26.

Ornstein, S. (1992) 'First impression of the symbolic meanings connoted by reception area design', *Environment and Behavior*, 24 (1): 85–110.

Ottensmeyer, E.J. (1996) 'Too strong to stop, too sweet to lose: aesthetics as a way to know organizations', *Organization*, 3 (2): 189–94.

Pederson, D.M. (1986) 'Perception of interior designs', *Perceptual and Motor Skills*, 63: 671–6.

Pfeffer, J. (1981) *Power in Organizations*. Boston: Pitman.

Pfeffer, J. (1992) *Managing with Power*. Boston: Harvard University Press.

Pratt, M. and Rafaeli, A. (1999) 'Symbols in relating work in organizations'. Paper in progress, School of Business, The University of Illinois at Urbana-Champaign.

Rafaeli, A. and Sutton, R.I. (1989). 'The expression of emotion in organizational life', in L.L. Cummings and B.M. Staw (eds), *Research in Organizational Behavior* vol. 11, Greenwich, CT: JAI Press. pp. 1–42.

Rafaeli, A. and Worline, M. (in press) 'Symbols in organizational culture', in N. Ashkenasy (ed.), *Handbook of Organizational Culture*. Beverly Hills: Sage.

Rafaeli, A., Dutton, J., Harquail, C.V. and Mackie-Lewis, S. (1997) 'Navigating by attire: the use of dress by female administrative employees', *Academy of Management Journal*, 40 (1): 9–45.

Ramirez, R. (1996) 'Wrapping form and organizational beauty', *Organization*, 3 (2): 233–42.

Russell, J.A. and Barrett, L.F. (1999) 'Core affect, prototypical emotional episodes, and other things called emotion: dissecting the elephant', *Journal of Personality and Social Psychology*, 76 (5): 805–19.

Saegert, S. and Winkel, G.H. (1990) 'Environmental psychology', *Annual Review of Psychology*, 41: 441–77.

Sandstrom, S. (1974) 'The sociocultural theory on aesthetic visual estimation and use', in R. Kueller (ed.), *Architectural Psychology*. Sweden: Studentliteratur ab.

Schmitt, B. and Simonson, A. (1997) *Marketing Aesthetics: The Strategic Management of Brands, Identity and Image*. New York: Free Press.

Schwartz, S. (1999) 'A theory of cultural values and some implications for work', *Applied Psychology: An International Review*. 48 (1): 23–49.

Strati, A. (1992) 'Aesthetic understanding of organizational life', *Academy of Management Review*, 17 (3): 568–81.

Strati, A. (1996) 'Organizations viewed through the lens of aesthetics', *Organization*, 3 (2): 209–18.

Takahashi, S. (1995) 'Aesthetic properties of pictorial perception', *Psychological Review*, 102 (4): 671–83.

Trice, H.M. and Beyer, J.M. (1984) 'Studying organizational cultures through rites and ceremonials', *Academy of Management Review*, 9: 653–69.

White, D.A. (1996) '"It's working beautifully!" Philosophical reflections on aesthetics and organization theory', *Organization*, 3 (2): 195–208.

Zeithaml, V.A. and Bitner, M.J. (1996) *Services Marketing*. New York: McGraw-Hill.

PART III
WORKING WITH EMOTION

---

9 IF EMOTIONS WERE HONOURED: A CULTURAL ANALYSIS

DEBRA E. MEYERSON

I recently attended a professional development workshop that started out much like other professional workshops. Midway through the second day I was roused by some of my (mostly male) colleagues' comments about working mothers. I took a deep breath, stood up, and challenged the premise of their arguments. What I had to say was not popular and some of my fellow participants seemed eager to shift the conversation. I did not oblige. I was offended by my colleagues' comments. The conflict escalated until the dinner break. I felt angry and misunderstood, and I contemplated not returning for the evening session. I suspected that many people were angry at me and resented the time we spent talking about the pulls on working moms. The more I thought about it, the angrier I became at my colleagues for not 'getting it'.

For no clear reason, I decided to stick it out through dinner. As I waited in line, a man who had taken a rather vocal stand among the 'opposition' approached me, put his hand on my shoulder, and said 'Thank you. It must have been awful for you because I'm sure this hits you very close to home. I really appreciate your struggles and wish I could completely understand.'

Through the dinner break, I engaged with this man in a different way. We both shared how we felt and what we thought, and we listened to each other. I felt validated in this conversation and gained the courage to return to the session.

That conversation transformed me; it shifted my intent and gave me the capacity to re-engage. But more important, it helped me encounter my feelings of guilt and inadequacy that lurked just beneath my surface anger. That evening, I revealed some of my own struggles and feelings of guilt as a working, travelling mother. My colleagues listened and I sensed they began to empathize. Some told their own stories, revealing their own sense of inadequacy as they tried and failed to live up to their ideals of being active fathers and good providers. As the conversation deepened, we began to bridge some unexpected divides. That evening, we all learned.

Contrast this story with what typically occurs. In an escalation of this type, I typically remain angry and struggle on in a no-win battle about who is right and why they just 'don't get it'. I ignore the others' feelings and struggle to manage my own. Others control their feelings and ignore mine as they persist in trying to prove me wrong and resentful. No one gets beyond the surface feelings of anger and resentment, and everyone thinks of themselves as right and righteous. We continue to talk past each other and the gulf widens.

What if emotions were honoured? That is, what if people regularly *attended to* and *engaged* others' feelings? In the above example, my colleague's desire to know the full range of my experience, helped me access the feelings that lurked beneath my anger. In doing so, he transformed my experience, which enabled me to engage with others more fully and honestly. What if this kind of interaction – where human beings engage a fuller and deeper range of their own and others' feelings – was the norm rather than the exception?

In this chapter, I draw from my own and others' research to develop a snapshot of how profoundly different the social world and social science would be if emotions – in all their depth and complexity – were honoured as the 'stuff' of social experience (Sandelands, 1998). I draw initially on an ethnographic research project on social workers' experiences of burnout in two distinct cultural settings: one in which emotions were expected to be controlled and one in which emotions were honoured as a legitimate part of professional experience. In the latter case, honouring meant that social workers attempted to access and engage their own and others' feelings. I take social workers' emotional experiences of burnout as the particular experience in contrast. I then revisit my central question: Why does this matter? How would professional practice, social interactions and social science be different if emotions in general were honoured? Finally, I address why – why we live, work and research from the standpoint of our heads not hearts. I look at the ways in which social interactions in most contexts are culturally predisposed to suppress all but a few human feelings (Mumby and Putnam, 1992). I'll begin by describing the research on which my primary contrast is based. (The research is described in detail in Meyerson, 1994 and 1998.)

Study and methods

The research involved a 14 month ethnographic study of medical social workers in two distinct cultural contexts. I studied social workers because members of this occupation, like those in other caregiving occupations, report unusually high levels of stress and burnout (Cherniss, 1980; Maslach, 1982).

I was also, at the time, interested in experiences of ambiguity, and the work of social work is in many ways ambiguous.

To understand how social workers' experiences were shaped by institutional and cultural conditions, I studied social workers in organizations that were culturally distinct. The two organizations in which I did most of my research were similar in many ways, but they varied in the extent to which the institution of medicine – the ideology, norms, and way of thinking – defined the culture of the organization. Both sites were large Veterans Administration hospitals. Due to their client populations, both hospitals employed an unusually large number of social workers.

The first hospital, Acute, was an acute-care teaching hospital that divided social workers between the departments of Medical Social Work and Acute Psychiatric Social Work. I focused on social workers in the former group who were divided between the departments of Medicine, Surgery, Kidney Dialysis, Neurology, Spinal Cord, and Geriatric. The second hospital, Chronic, was a non-teaching rehabilitation hospital. Social workers were assigned to one of several groups. I studied social workers in Geriatrics and the Chronic Psychology Ward.

Social workers in the two hospitals possessed similar interests and qualifications. Much of their work involved assessing patients' psychological and social conditions, including diagnosing patients' material and emotional resources, support systems and family environments as well as conducting initial assessments of patients' psychological states. Social workers in both contexts spent a good deal of time developing support systems for patients and families. Since tasks were in many ways comparable, social workers in the two settings regularly transferred back and forth between hospitals ruling out self-selection as a primary explanation for the distinct nature of their experiences in the two hospitals.

I used several methods of data collection, including participant and non-participant observation, structured interviews, pen and paper exercises, and archival research. Data analysis involved an iterative process whereby I moved back and forth between data collection and analysis.

'Burnout' is a term used and often misused to describe an extreme form of stress. The term was originally intended to capture an emotional condition that was typically embedded in the context of caregiving relationships (Maslach, 1993). According to the widely accepted definition of the concept, the construct of burnout captures three related experiences: emotional exhaustion, depersonalization, and reduced personal accomplishment. I explored in this study how social workers experienced burnout in the two different cultural settings. The differences are suggestive of more general patterns in the way social workers in the distinct contexts relate to their own and others' emotions.

Experiences of burnout

Case 1: Acute

Social workers in Acute described burnout as a disease of the individual. They blamed individuals for not properly coping and described people who burned out as flawed professionals. One social worker in Acute summarized this sentiment:

> I think that the people who burn out will have the same problem wherever they go. They probably had the problem before they came here. I see it as an internal problem. I don't see it as job situated at all.

Social workers in Acute talked about burnout as a lapse of emotional control and as a symptom of professional weakness. As one social worker put it, as professionals 'we are not allowed to burn out'. Others suggested that even the admission of burnout was a sign of professional weakness. One social worker claimed:

> That's my professional job to fight off burnout. I would consider that if somebody said to me, 'I'm burned out' then I would call them a very non-professional person. I wouldn't deal with them anymore because they should quit. That's part of my professional task too, to avoid burnout.

The social work supervisor at Acute offered professional workshops on avoiding burnout. He described burnout as a debilitating disease to be cured. According to the supervisor, burnout meant 'gone to ashes, all burned out'. When I asked about staff burnout, he claimed that none of his staff had been burned out. People could not be professional and burned out. These were mutually exclusive terms and he vigorously defended the professionalism of his staff.

The notion that to be a professional one must avoid, control or, if all else fails, deny their experiences of burnout is not unique to social workers. A recent study of physicians revealed a skyrocketing level of stress and emotional exhaustion among doctors (Neuwirth, 1999). Yet doctors are notoriously unwilling to acknowledge their stress, despite growing evidence that physician stress has a dramatic impact on their ability to empathize with their patients and care for them adequately, which in turn has been shown to impact patient outcomes.

Case 2: Chronic

Social workers in Chronic described a qualitatively different experience of burnout. In general, social workers in Chronic viewed burnout as a normal consequence of their work:

> It's part of our life. There is no way not to have occasional bouts of burnout when you do this kind of work.

Some even talked about burnout as a healthy response:

> Burnout is the need to detach and I think that there is something healthy about
> letting yourself occasionally detach. . . . When people are feeling the symptoms
> and they go on vacation or they just come in an hour late, that's just taking care
> of themselves and honoring how they are feeling. And just like stress, it's not a
> bad thing when you start to feel the signs and symptoms of stress. It's a warning
> signal to take care of yourself, and it can be a very positive thing.

The social workers who interpreted burnout as normal, as 'part of the
cycle', also tended to see burnout not as an individual condition, but as a
condition endemic to their occupation:

> It [burnout] means what we do here is stressful, that we are asked to always give
> and sometimes there simply isn't anything left to give, so we take a break and then
> we are okay.

Others suggested that feeling burned out was normal and inescapable. They
would say things like the following:

> If people do not burn out occasionally in this job, they must not be working hard
> enough.

In short, the social workers in Chronic talked about their capacity to let
themselves and their colleagues feel burned out, which they understood as
part and parcel of allowing each other to care for their clients.

Two different experiences

In the first case, social workers in the predominantly medical cultures talked
about burnout in the language of control and treatment. In this context,
burnout was a lapse of emotional control. Because medical professionals are
expected to control emotions, the admission of burnout signalled professional
weakness. In the extreme, burnout was considered a failure and a disease
that one must cure.

In Chronic, social workers described burnout as a normal experience –
part of the ebb and flow of their emotionally consuming work. Some viewed
burnout as endemic to the caregiving role. People talked openly about their
feelings of being depleted and they collectively developed ways to care and
cover for each other. In this context, emotional control was viewed as
impossible and even undesirable because social workers were supposed to
use their emotions as a source of connection and insight. The capacity to feel
for clients and develop empathy was viewed as a professional competence
rather than weakness, which meant that social workers had to feel, and often
feel badly. Moreover, it meant that social workers regularly lost 'control' of
their emotions and were therefore prone to burn out. It was therefore up to
the community to 'cope' with this collective reality and to ensure that they

each stay 'whole', which translated into a practice of helping one another experience fully the pain and joy of their work.

I attributed the social workers' different experiences of burnout and emotions more generally to the different cultural conditions in which the social workers were embedded (Meyerson, 1994). Beliefs and norms in the highly medical culture of Acute encouraged social workers to suppress and otherwise control their emotions. Their talk about emotions reflected the beliefs and norms of traditional medical practice: the emphasis on finding cures, the mandate of detachment and rationality, the focus on individuals as the locus of disease and cure, and the valuing of technical skill and knowledge as the criteria of competence (Friedson, 1970; Larson, 1977; Starr, 1982).

In contrast, the beliefs and norms operating in Chronic encouraged social workers to access their emotions and respect and engage the feelings of others. In this context, their experiences of emotions reflected a psychosocial ideology (see for example Toren, 1975): the belief in self-determination and thus placing control with clients rather than professionals, the emphasis on the social and situated nature of clients' conditions, the respect for multiple ways of knowing, and the valuing of social and emotional expertise as well as technical knowledge (Huntington, 1981). Portraits of the social work profession make explicit the importance of developing the skill of empathy as a basis of caregiving.

What if emotions were honoured?

Work and professional practice

I begin with the suggestion that the norms about emotional experience displayed in Chronic carry several implications about social interactions inside and outside of work. The norms I observed illustrate what I believe Bill Kahn (1993) describe as a system of organizational caregiving. Caregiving systems provide recurring patterns of care to members of a community who provide care to others. In Chronic, for example, people cared for and filled in for the person who felt burned out; they permitted the person to feel, rest and heal. However, the caregiving system I described did not enable caregivers to avoid burnout, as Kahn predicted. Instead, the system enabled members to burn out, because it allowed them to give fully to their work, to feel and to heal. For social workers, the capacity to experience their full range of feelings and to have their feelings honoured by others was personally and professionally fulfilling, even if exhausting. Social workers are in the business of caring for human beings; to legitimate their capacity to feel, to feel for others, and to create communities to support their feelings is to give them the capacity to do their work (Meyerson, 1998). Yet this capacity is not legitimate within most professional or bureaucratic contexts, even ones that purport to be in the business of human service and support. Moreover, because burnout was understood as a normal experience of work, burnout seemed to be less disruptive to the community as a whole, because the community permitted members to feel, care for, and fill in for one another. The community absorbed and worked through the pain, and this work became an essential component of community (Turner, 1974).

I believe Chronic was unusual. What if it wasn't? What if norms of professional practice regularly encouraged people to access and respect emotional experience? What if the work of doing this was valued and visible? The transformational possibilities of this normative shift would derive from many sources and are documented by a growing body of related research (Fletcher, 1998a, 1999; Frost et al., this volume; Jacques, 1996).

First, to acknowledge the effort involved in accessing and 'joining' (Frank, 1992) others' emotions as 'real work' that requires developed skill would be to develop a radically different language of 'work' and 'competency' (Fletcher, 1998a, 1999). Since there exists no readily available vocabulary to describe this work in terms of competency (as opposed to women's natural traits), it largely remains invisible. However, if the work involved in honouring and encountering emotions 'counted' as real work, more people would learn to do it well and would be rewarded for doing so (Fletcher, 1998a; Jacques, 1993; Kolb, 1992).

Peter Frost and Sandra Robinson's (1999) work on 'toxic leadership' suggests the second way work might shift. Frost and Robinson studied people who act to absorb, disperse and dissipate pain and suffering in a system – people whose efforts require extraordinary acts of courage and compassion. Though essential to the organization, these acts are typically invisible. However, if the work of tapping into, engaging and absorbing the emotions of an organization was valued, I suspect that organizations would take better care of their toxic handlers, and, more to the point, the work of handling pain and suffering could be distributed more widely throughout a community. As in Chronic, communities could be strengthened by collectively taking up the work and supporting the people who do it. Individuals would no longer need to suffer in silence.

Third, when the work of honouring others' experiences, including their feelings of being devalued, is absent in a system, it is sorely missed. Dutton et al.'s (1999) observations of hospital cleaners makes this point in their description of the pain and loss of dignity that results when a context is void of compassion and concern. They also show how small mundane acts of compassion can make a big difference in how individuals feel about their work and their worth as human beings. Small acts can go a long way in enabling individuals to retain their pride and feel valued. If workplaces put a premium on the work of compassion, we would undoubtedly see more humane workplaces.

Social interactions

Not only would the nature of work be different if peoples' emotional experiences were regularly honoured in a culture, but the nature of social interaction would also shift. This shift would resemble what psychiatrists Jean Baker-Miller and Irene Stiver (1997) have called for in their book *The Healing Connection*. They begin with the notion that the capacity to connect with one's own feelings and the feelings of others is a precondition to growth fostering relations. But the capacity to connect with one's feelings is dependent on others' capacity to join in these feelings:

> we believe that all people need this resonance and response in order to even experience their important feelings in all of their depth and complexity. . . . when we talk about being in connection, we mean being emotionally accessible, and how to learn how to be emotionally accessible, we need the experience of being in connection. Without this interplay with others, we cannot know and understand our own thoughts and feelings. (Baker-Miller and Stivers, 1997: 45)

The example that opened this chapter revealed the ways in which such an interplay helped me acknowledge the anxiety that lurked beneath my surface anger. The conversation with my colleague helped me feel and think clearly and enabled my colleague to encounter his own feelings. By helping each other access the feelings beneath our superficial expressions, we developed a mutual appreciation that transformed our motives and relationship. These kinds of connections validate individuals, foster learning and create community (Noddings, 1984; Turner, 1974).

Unfortunately, these types of interactions are far more the exception than the norm, particularly in work contexts (Goleman, 1995). People learn early on to create connection and acceptance by concealing feelings, particularly feelings that are culturally illegitimate, like fear, jealousy, shame and hurt. In doing so, they learn to mask large parts of themselves, often with the intent of gaining social acceptance (Brown and Gilligan, 1992). Ironically, in seeking connection, they avoid the prerequisites of real connection (Fletcher, 1998b).

Social science

A social science that honours emotional experience would treat emotions as a legitimate realm of social experience. Narrative accounts that detailed the texture of human feeling in organization – joy and pain, fear and suffering, hate and love – would be central in social science, rather than relegated to special volumes or critical discussions (see for example Fineman, 1993; Mumby and Putnam, 1992; Sandelands, 1998).

A social science that honoured emotions as a legitimate realm of experience would mark nothing less than a pedagogical and epistemological revolution. In his critique of traditional psycho-oncology research, Arthur Frank calls for a shift from a clinical to a narrative mode of practice, which would entail a change in epistemology from a social science based on detachment and judgement to one based on empathy and engagement (Frank, 1992). Furthermore, social science would need to adopt a pedagogy that lends itself to teaching people about themselves and others, helping them to encounter and know their feelings: 'To witness ill persons' experiences as embodied, angry, contingent, eccentric, interrelated, and suffering, and to communicate what has been witnessed to a larger group, is a genuine pedagogy . . . to witness suffering in all its depth and commonality' (1992: 483).

A social science that honoured emotions would develop a language to name emotional engagement as a form of work and provide a legitimate and recognizable vocabulary to evaluate the competency involved in these efforts. It would create a language to describe feelings as an essential part of human experience in public and private spheres of life.

Consider a typical report on work and family balance – a literature one might think would be filled with accounts of emotional experiences. I recall reviewing a colleague's paper that seemed typical of this genre. Using her own experience as an illustration, the paper laid out a typology of coping approaches; it described a person who strategically allocated her time across conflicting demands. But I knew from talking with my colleague that a more accurate description of her lived emotional experience of work and family – of trying to be a competent professional and good mother – would convey her feelings of anguish, guilt and burnout. I knew that she routinely felt 'out of control' and emotionally spent. I also knew that she experienced great joy and satisfaction from living such a full life. Yet she wrote her experience in the familiar and seemingly neutral vocabulary of coping and control. She talked about her clever allocation of time, her strategies for managing stress, and the division of labour in her home. Surely, these were parts of her experience, but not the essence. The suppression of emotions in her written account reinforced the myth of control, which in this case meant the myth of achieving 'balance'. It also created an inaccurate portrait that no doubt perpetuated others' sense of inadequacy for being unable to cope as well as this mythical 'supermom'.

Is the portrait of the clever and in-control woman a constructive portrait? What would an alternative look like that more accurately portrayed her emotional experience of work–family? It might portray her simultaneous joy and anguish, her feelings of being out of control, torn in too many directions. Might this not be a more humane and full portrait? Had my colleague had the language to write a narrative that reflected her feelings of being torn and out of control, she might have helped others by legitimating these feelings, saying 'you are not alone and it is understandable that you feel this way'. Had she legitimately been able to access and represent a deeper range of emotions, her colleagues, friends and families may have honoured her experience and possibly even stepped in to help her. At the very least, writing these experiences into her account may have created an alternative understanding of the stresses on working parents, which could trigger a dialogue about community level solutions. Such conversations could suggest ways people can care for each other as they struggle to straddle multiple roles. To be sure, this kind of portrait would generate a different kind of conversation about 'balance'.

A social science that viewed organizations as the site of feelings would ask different questions about human experience in organizations. Different knowledge would be sought, for example, about the experiences of burnout. Rather than viewed as a problem for an individual to control, feelings of burnout would be understood as a lens into the nature of work. Research might investigate how members of communities respond to others' feelings, the kinds of emotions people feel as they perform the work, the depth of feeling engaged in the course of the work, the kinds of interactions and relationships engaged, and the learning fostered through these relations. Informed by this social science, a community might then ask itself how it can best support its members. It might inquire into how it might organize itself to engage its members' feelings and enable them to act in the face of pain and suffering. Research on burnout might ask about how members of an organization can fill in for each other so that people can ride the ebbs and flows of their emotions. Or, studies may attempt to surface big and small acts of compassion and caring in organizations (see for example Frost et al., this volume). These are very different questions from those currently asked within most caregiving communities, and certainly different from the ones being offered up by social science.

If social science is to produce knowledge that enables communities to care for their members, it must become self-conscious of how its texts conspire to suppress feelings in organizations. Through experimental forms of writing and pedagogy, such as the narrative mode called for by Arthur Frank and as represented by some work in this volume (Frost et al.), social science can help reflect and create forms of work, professional practice and human interaction that honour feelings.

Emotional control as a dominant ethic

Having argued for a transformation to forms of social science, human interaction and professional practice that would honour emotions, I turn to the institutional and cultural mechanisms within each of these domains that mitigate against such a shift.

Work and professional practice

Elsewhere, I have argued that the ethic of emotional control has surfaced consistently throughout a variety of disciplines, but perhaps nowhere as vividly as in medicine (Meyerson, 1998). The emphasis on emotional control within medicine can be traced to the discipline's reliance on science as the basis of professional knowledge and legitimacy (Starr, 1982). As the authority of medicine became linked to scientific thought, objectivism took on the status of a moral code, and along with it, its cornerstones of detachment and rationality. Couple this stance with the reductionist practice of turning whole people into bodily parts and diseases, a practice that follows directly from medical specialization (Friedson, 1970; Larson, 1977), predefined diagnostic categories, and standard clinical practice (Stone, 1991).

To illustrate the effects of this ethic of emotional detachment and reductionism, I draw again from Arthur Frank's critique of the ways in which oncology treats emotions and human suffering. Frank describes a situation in which a 29-year-old woman was diagnosed with breast cancer a week after her wedding. Frank critiques the sense of detachment conveyed in the entire report, but the last sentence, in particular, conveyed the stance of detachment and the emphasis on control: 'The patient adjusted to her new marriage and work, accepting the temporary disruption of her life related to treatment'. The key words are 'adjusted', and 'accepting' and 'temporary disruption'. Adjustment and acceptance are what psychological work ancillary to medical treatment specializes in. The patient's fears and history are explored, but for the instrumental purpose of securing her adjustment and acceptance. Treatment can then proceed with as much compliance and as little disruption as possible. Frank continues:

> nothing is wrong with providing the back-up to get the woman through chemotherapy . . . But the language of the case suggests that treatment muted the young woman's feelings. . . . The Massie and Holland case study makes no effort to enter the perspective of the young woman calling herself 'half a person'. Instead, this is only an 'attitude' to be changed. Case 'management' does not consist in helping her to have her feelings; rather success seems to mean getting her over such feelings. (Frank, 1992: 469)

Psychologists have long known that to heal grief and other painful feelings it is first crucial to experience them fully. This notion is supported in a woman's personal account of her experience following an abortion. Recalling what she told her psychologist after he prescribed sleeping pills to calm her down: 'I don't want sleeping pills, I need to have my feelings, not mute them. Not being able to have my feelings is what is wearing me down' (Frank, 1992: 469). This institutionalized emphasis on control translates into a practice that even the most humane efforts of practitioners have difficulty in overcoming. Within the institutional context of traditional medicine, efforts to help patients through traumatic conditions typically get practised as helping people get through their feelings, work out their anger, and manage their suffering.

Within the traditional contexts of medicine, when caregivers do work to engage the emotions of patients and families, their efforts often go unrecognized and remain outside of the parameters of what is considered their 'real work' (Fletcher, 1998a; Jacques, 1996). Earlier, I drew on Peter Frost's (1999) account of a nurse's skilful acts of compassion that the author observed as an essential part of a patient's healing process. But as Frost notes, in this case and others like it, the acts were subtle and virtually invisible to most eyes looking to account for the content of professional work. This caring work does not fall within conventional parameters of professional practice.

The work of Joyce Fletcher and Roy Jacques further explains the institutionalized disappearance of work that engages emotions, as well as other forms of 'relational practice'. Fletcher (1999) points to three processes, which I alluded to in an earlier discussion of professional practice, that occur in a range of professional contexts that create what she calls a 'disappearing dynamic': the attribution of inappropriateness of this work to professional contexts, the lack of language to describe the work in terms of skills or competencies, and the conflation of the work with stereotypical images of femininity.

Related to these dynamics, the general subordination of emotion to reason is reinforced by the gender associations of these two forms of experience (Mumby and Putnam, 1992). The cultural construction of men as rational and women as emotional helps to enforce the oppositional nature of these two characteristics, where emotionality is thought to be synonymous with 'irrationality'. The resulting images preserve the preference for the 'rational man' in contrast to the 'emotional' (irrational) woman (Meyerson, 1998; Mumby and Putnam, 1992).

The privileging of reason and the mandate of emotional control are built into the bureaucratic ideal (Weber, 1946). Efficiency and fairness are thought to be best served through the detached and impartial mechanisms of bureaucracy. Emotions are to be engaged to serve instrumental ends – 'coopted and alienated in a form known as emotional labor' (Mumby and Putnam, 1992). Emotional displays become part of the work, or emotions become targets to manipulate for instrumental and social ends (Fineman, 1996). Even when management enforces norms to support the expression of spontaneous rather than manufactured feelings, these norms can become instruments of managerial control (Martin, Knopoff and Beckman, 1998).

Social interactions

Daily interactions are governed by similar cultural mechanisms. Baker-Miller and Stiver (1997) attribute the preponderance of emotionally detached interactions to the general emphasis on self-gratification rather than growth. They suggest that the emphasis on individual achievement and other mechanisms of self-gratification substitute for the learning and sense of connection that would be accomplished through more emotionally authentic interactions.

The work of Claire Nuer (1999) and her team of colleagues at the firm LAL provides another way of thinking about the mechanisms that inhibit people from engaging fully their own and others' emotions. Their work reveals people's overwhelming drive to quench the thirst of what they lump into the notion of the ego system. Because this thirst is never quenched, people constantly seek momentary relief, which comes in quick fixes – proving that one is 'best', 'right', or 'important'. Though the interactions that provide these ego 'fixes' are temporarily satisfying, they also deprive people of emotionally authentic connections – the very thing that could provide a deeper sense of satisfaction. But in an individualist, achievement oriented culture, living outside of this ego system requires the support and engagement of others, which is itself inhibited by traditional emotionally detached patterns of interaction.

Social science

Social science knowledge legitimates language and reproduces norms of detachment and control (Maslach and Goldberg, 1998). This surfaces in how we engage in research and our choice of research titles. Researchers are supposed to be objective, dispassionate observers outside the systems we observe. Thus, empathy is not supposed to be employed as a source of understanding, and connections with those we are observing threatens the integrity of the 'data.' Even anthropologists – the consummate observers of human experience – are supposed to remain outside the systems they are studying, even as they attempt to gain access to the experiences of people within a culture. This has always been understood as a central dilemma of anthropological research, expressed as the dilemma of 'going native'. Ruth Behar articulates the challenge of witnessing the intimacies of human experience – and feeling them – while remaining detached from them:

> Loss, mourning, the longing for memory, the desire to enter the world around you and having no idea how to do it, the fear of observing too coldly or too distractedly or too raggedly . . . Life after all, is bountiful. But surely this is not the anthropology being taught in our colleges and universities? It does not sound like the stuff of which PhDs are made. And definitely it is not the anthropology that will win you a grant from the National Science Foundation. (Behar, 1996: 2–3)

Because the language of social science makes little room for emotions, and certainly has no place for the emotions of social scientists, it contains no language to articulate the real work of anthropology. Even Geertz recognizes there is a problem: 'We lack the language to articulate what takes place when we are in fact at work' (Geertz, 1995: 44, quoted in Behar 1996: 9).

How, then, are researchers able to empathize with those they study when social scientists are not supposed to feel? An increasing array of researchers, including some authors in the present volume (for example, Frost et al.), join Arthur Frank in his critique of traditional social science and his plea for an alternative: 'In the objectivist cycle of observation, assessment, and intervention, there is no necessity of encounter in the existential sense of one person encountering the humanity of an other. If anything, clinical practice invokes norms against "self-disclosure".' Frank attributes the suppression of emotions to nothing less than the moral code of social science that implicitly prescribes a response to emotional pain and suffering. Other social sciences are no less adamant in their mandate of emotional detachment.

It should come as no surprise that when social scientists claim to be studying emotions, they mostly study emotional labour or 'managed' emotions. Organizational reports tend to focus on emotional displays manufactured to produce intended outcomes among clients or customers, such as displays of happiness at Disneyland (Van Maanen, 1991), anger by bill collectors (Rafaeli and Sutton, 1991), or cheerfulness by flight attendants (Hochschild, 1983). Even reports of burnout focus on controlling burnout, or, as Maslach argued, since much of the burnout work presumes 'that it is some flaw or weakness of the individual that leads him or her to burnout. And if that is the case, then individual treatment strategies are the only reasonable solution to the problem' (Maslach and Goldberg, 1998: 70). The management of the experience – not the texture of it – has become the focus of this and other bodies of research on emotions (Patrick, 1984a, b).

Whether it is the suffering of patients, the emotional experiences of organizational participants, the experience of burnout, or the encounters of field workers, much of the substance of social experience is lost in the construction of theory (Sandelands, 1998). Instead, research tends to serve the instrumental ends of the relevant institutions. The problem with this approach is that the people and their humanity may be lost in this pursuit.

Conclusion

Social science contains the possibility of creating knowledge that recognizes, expresses and honours feelings. With new questions, categories and language may come the possibility of alternative forms of professional practice and social interaction. These alternatives could legitimate and enable the emergence of communities that care for their members and provide conditions for human connection and autonomy (Turner, 1974). This alternative social science would encourage social scientists to encounter emotions, to engage them and to record them. But to encounter emotions, social scientists would need to access their own feelings and build on them as a source of insight and connection. This is a risky enterprise. It requires forfeiting some control over the research process and shifting how social scientists engage in it (Behar, 1996). It would also require an alternative epistemology and, as Frank has asserted, a new pedagogy of practice that would allow researchers to know, display and describe emotions.

While I believe that this form of knowledge will continue to be relegated to the margins of social science, it is still essential to ask what is missed by a social science that ignores and suppresses emotional experiences, among both those studied and those who do the studying. It also seems important to reflect on the consequences of these systemic omissions – how, for example, do dominant texts and categories of research conspire to suppress feelings and to reproduce norms of emotional control? And, as Frank suggested, how do social science texts legitimate a particular form of response to human pain and suffering and, implicitly, de-legitimate other possibilities? Social science might also be served by developing a healthy scepticism about what current research does capture, and more vigilantly question whether social science, as it is currently practised, adequately accomplishes its objective of understanding human experience.

I've described ways in which professional practice could be transformed, including shifts in what counts as 'work', what is considered competency, and what gets valued and rewarded in these calculations (Fletcher, 1999), as well as changes in the way communities and organizations engage and care for their members. I have also suggested that if emotions were honoured in the course of everyday social interactions the nature of these interactions and their consequences would also be transformed. I have suggested that these forms of interactions may be an essential component of communities. But for many people, these human experiences feel fleeting and inappropriate to the public domain of work. It may be time to look at what can be gained by honouring our own and others' range of feelings and to examine the role of social science in creating language, categories and questions that would legitimate alternative ways of working and interacting.

Acknowledgements

I would like to thank Stephen Fineman and Jane Dutton for their very thoughtful comments on this chapter. I would also like to acknowledge the foundational work of Joyce Fletcher and Roy Jacques, as well as Peter Frost who contributed directly to my understanding of the organization of 'emotion work'.

References

Baker-Miller, J. and Stiver, I. (1997) *The Healing Connection*. Boston, MA: Beacon Press.

Behar, R. (1996) *The Vulnerable Observer: Anthropology that Breaks your Heart*. Boston: Beacon Press.

Brown, L. and Gilligan, G. (1992) *Meeting at the Crossroads*. Cambridge, MA: Harvard University Press.

Cherniss, C. (1980) *Professional Burnout in Human Service Organizations*. New York: Praeger.

Dutton, J., Debebe G. and Wrześniewski, A. (1999) 'Being valued and devalued at work: a social valuing perspective'. Working paper, University of Michigan, Ann Arbor.

Fineman, S. (1993) *Emotion in Organizations*. London: Sage.

Fineman, S. (1996) 'Emotional subtexts in corporate greening', *Organization Studies*, 17: 479–500.

Fletcher, J. (1998a) 'Relational practice: a feminist reconstruction of work', *Journal of Management Inquiry*, 7: 163–86.

Fletcher, J. (1998b) 'Developing an interactive self: transforming social institutions', *Social Policy*, summer: 48–51.

Fletcher, J. (1999) *Disappearing Acts*. Cambridge, MA: MIT Press.

Frank, A.W. (1992) 'The pedagogy of suffering: moral dimensions of psychological therapy and research', *Theory and Psychology*, 2: 467–85.

Friedson, E. (1970) *The Profession of Medicine: A Study in the Sociology of Applied Knowledge*. New York: Harper and Row.

Frost, Peter F. (1999) 'Why compassion counts', *Journal of Management Inquiry*, 8 (2): 127–33.

Frost, P. and Robinson, S. (1999) 'The toxic handler: organizational hero and casualty', *Harvard Business Review*, July–August: 96–106.

Geertz. C. (1995) *After the Fact: Two Countries, Four Decades, One Anthropologist*. Cambridge, MA: Harvard University Press.

Goleman, D. (1995) *Working with Emotional Intelligence*. New York: Bantam Books.

Hochschild, A.R. (1983) *The Managed Heart: Commercialization of Human Feeling*. Berkeley: University of California Press.

Huntington, J. (1981) *Social Work and General Medical Practice: Collaboration or Conflict*. Boston: Allen and Unwin.

Jacques, R. (1993) Untheorized dimensions of caring work: caring as structural practice and caring as a way of seeing', *Nursing Administration Quarterly*, 17 (2): 1–10.

Jacques, R. (1996) *Manufacturing the Employee*. London: Sage.

Kahn, William A. (1993) 'Caring for the caregivers: patterns of organizational caregiving', *Administrative Science Quarterly*, 38 (4): 539–63.

Kolb, D. (1992) 'Women's work: peacemaking in organizations', in D. Kolb and J. Bartunek (eds), *Hidden Conflict in Organizations*. Newbury Park, CA: Sage.

Larson, M. (1977) *The Rise of Professionalism: A Sociological Analysis*, Berkeley: University of California Press.

Martin, J., Knopoff, K. and Beckman, C. (1998) 'An alternative to bureaucratic impersonality and emotional labor: bounded emotionality at the Body Shop', *Administrative Science Quarterly*, 43: 429–69.

Maslach, C. (1982) *Burnout: The Cost of Caring*. Englewood Cliffs, NJ: Prentice Hall.

Maslach, C. (1993) 'Burnout: a multi-dimensional perspective', in W. Schaufeli, C. Maslach and T. Marek (eds), *Professional Burnout: Recent Developments in Theory and Research*. Washington, DC: Taylor and Francis. pp. 19–32.

Maslach, C. and Goldberg. J. (1998) 'Prevention of burnout: new perspectives', *Applied and Preventative Psychology*, 7: 63–74.

Massie, M.J. and Holland, J.C. (1989) 'Common psychiatric disorders and their management', in *Handbook of Psychooncology: Psychological Care of the Patient with Cancer*. New York: Oxford University Press. pp. 271–323.

Meyerson, D.E. (1994) 'Interpretations of stress in institutions: the cultural production of ambiguity and burnout', *Administrative Science Quarterly*, 39: 628–53.

Meyerson, D.E. (1998) 'Feeling stressed and burned out: a feminist reading and re-visioning of stress-based emotions within medicine and organizational science', *Organizational Science*, 8: 103–18.

Mumby, D.K. and Putnam, L.L. (1992) 'The politics of emotion: A feminist reading of bounded emotionality', *Academy of Management Review*, 17: 465–86.

Nathanson, D.L. (1989) 'Denial, projection and the emphatic wall', *Research*. New York: Plenum Press. pp. 37–59.

Neuwirth, Z.E. (1999) 'The silent anguish of the healers', *Newsweek*, 13 Sept. 79.

Noddings, N. (1984) *Caring: A Feminine Approach to Ethics and Moral Education*. Berkeley: University of California Press.

Nuer, C. (1999) 'Eco-system leadership', *Perspectives on Business and Global Change*, 13: 43–50.

Patrick, P.K.S. (1984a) 'Organizational strategies: promoting retnetion and job satisfaction', *Family and Community Health*, 6: 57–67.

Patrick, P.K.S. (1984b) 'Preventing burnout: coordinating the employee health function', *Family and Community Health*, 6: 76–92.

Rafaeli, A. and Sutton, R. (1991) 'Emotional contrast strategies as a means of social influence: lessons from criminal interrogators and bill collectors', *Academy of Management Journal*, 34: 749–75.

Sandelands, L.E. (1998) *Feeling and Form in Social Life*. Lanham, MD: Rowman and Littlefield.

Starr, P. (1982) *The Social Transformation of American Medicine*. New York: Basic Books.

Stone, D.A. (1991) 'The transformation of political conflict through medical gatekeeping'. Paper presented at the conference on the Impact of Public Policy on the Capacity of Citizens, University of Arizona.

Toren, N. (1975) 'Deprofessionalization and its sources', *Sociology of Work and Occupations*, 2: 323–36.

Turner, V. (1974) *Dramas, Fields, and Metaphors: Symbolic Action in Human Society*. Ithaca, NY: Cornell University Press.

Van Maanen, J. (1991) 'The smile factory: work at Disneyland', in P. Frost, L. Moore, M. Louis, C. Lundberg and J. Martin (eds), *Reframing Organizational Culture*. Newbury Park, CA: Sage. pp. 58–76.

Weber, M. (1946) 'Bureaucracy', in Hans Gerth and C. Wright Mills (eds and trans), *From Max Weber: Essays in Sociology*. New York: Oxford University Press. pp. 196–244.

10 EMOTIONAL LABOUR AND AUTHENTICITY: VIEWS FROM SERVICE AGENTS

BLAKE E. ASHFORTH AND MARC A. TOMIUK

Research on emotions in organizational life seems to be on the rise. Part of what makes the topic so intriguing is that emotions appear at first blush to be the very antithesis of organizations: emotions are stereotypically thought to be spontaneous and unruly whereas organizations are stereotypically thought to be planned and ordered. The upshot, rightly or wrongly, is that organizations are often regarded as arenas for an epic struggle between emotionality and rationality.

In this chapter, we focus on one such arena: the *emotional labour* of front-line service agents. Emotional labour is defined here as the act of conforming (or attempting to conform) to display rules (Ekman, 1973) or affective requirements (Bulan et al., 1997) that prescribe on-the-job emotional expression (cf. Hochschild, 1979, 1983). Affective requirements enjoin service agents to display a certain range, intensity and frequency of emotions for a given duration, whether or not the display matches the agents' internal feelings.

More specifically, we focus on agents' self-perceptions of *authenticity* during service encounters. Unfortunately, as Erickson (1995: 123) notes, 'there are as many definitions of authenticity as there are those who write about it'. Given our interest in agents' own constructions of authenticity, we will sidestep the semantic debate and define authenticity simply as the extent to which one is behaving according to what one considers to be their true or genuine self – who one 'is' as a person.

We recognize that many theorists question whether contemporary individuals have a true self, arguing instead that individuals are a shifting montage of many selves associated with specific social domains and relationships (see for example Gergen, 1991; Lifton, 1993; Sande, 1990). Thus, feelings of authenticity may depend on what identities are most salient in a given context. As identities become differentially salient, so too might the basis for feelings of authenticity (Erickson, 1995; Ryan, 1995). For example, authenticity at the office may well differ from authenticity in the home. Nonetheless, the service agents interviewed for the present study had very little difficulty speaking about whether or not their work behaviour reflected their true selves. In short, it appears that people tend to *believe* they have an authentic self that displays strong cross-situational consistency (cf. Abiala,

1999: Table 4; Sheldon et al., 1997) – assuming, of course, that they have some behavioural discretion across roles.

Some scholars have posited an authenticity motive; that is, a desire to affirm and express one's real self (Erickson and Wharton, 1997; Gecas, 1986). Authentic behaviour enables individuals to immerse themselves in a valued self-conception, thereby deriving intrinsic pleasure from 'being themselves' and reinforcing the worth of the self-conception (Ashforth, 2000). Moreover, a valued self-conception may assume a moral cast. The goals, values, beliefs and so on that constitute the self-conception may be seen not as an incidental self-description but as the 'right way' for oneself to be. The self-conception may become an imperative such that to behave authentically is to be 'good,' whereas to behave inauthentically is to be 'bad' – even if one's behaviour garners social approval and rewards (cf. Higgins, 1987).

Indeed, it has been argued that service agents are affected more by *emotional dissonance* than by emotional labour *per se* (Ashforth and Humphrey, 1993; Morris and Feldman, 1996a, 1996b; cf. Wharton, 1999). Emotional dissonance occurs when one's displayed emotions differ from one's actual emotions (Abraham, 1998; Hochschild, 1983; Morris and Feldman, 1996a, 1996b) or 'true feelings' (Morgan and Averill, 1992) – when one is behaving inauthentically.[1] Like cognitive dissonance, emotional dissonance is an aversive state that one typically seeks to avoid or escape (Richman, 1988). Thus, emotional dissonance was positively associated with emotional exhaustion and job dissatisfaction among customer service representatives from a variety of industries (Abraham, 1998), and among members of debt collection agencies, a military recruiting battalion and a nursing association (Morris and Feldman, 1996b). Emotional dissonance was also positively associated with work alienation and job dissatisfaction among waiters and waitresses (Adelmann, 1995), and perceptions of inauthenticity at work were associated with depressed mood among bank and hospital employees (Erickson and Wharton, 1997).

What makes authenticity and inauthenticity a compelling topic is that many organizations seek to manufacture authenticity. Erickson and Wharton (1997) argue that because customers are often able to discriminate between authentic and inauthentic emotions, many organizations expect service agents to not only display prescribed emotions but to actually feel them. In short, many organizations are interested in creating a work context that routinely evokes the desired emotions. Thus, a battery of control techniques have been developed to foster internalization of service roles or at least to compel convincing displays of the prescribed emotions (see for example Fineman, 1996; Hochschild, 1983; Leidner, 1993, 1999; Van Maanen and Kunda, 1989; Waldron, 1994).

The present study explores the nature and experience of authenticity. As described below, we interviewed frontline service agents from a variety of service occupations. Our interviews were guided, in part, by the following research questions: (1) To what extent do service agents believe they behave authentically during service encounters? (2) What aspects of service encounters make agents feel authentic, and what aspects make them feel inauthentic?

We begin by briefly describing our research method. We then present some tentative answers to the research questions. We close by considering the implications of our findings for authenticity in service encounters.

Method

Ninety-six interviews were conducted with individuals from a variety of service occupations as part of a larger study on emotional labour. Larsson and Bowen's (1989) typology of 'service interdependence patterns' was used to provide an initial basis for selecting occupations. Larsson and Bowen categorize service occupations according to the diversity or range of customers' demands (that is, the need for customization) and customers' disposition to participate (that is, to play an active role in the service encounter). An example of a low diversity and low disposition occupation is a bank customer service representative; an example of a low diversity and high disposition occupation is a retail salesperson; an example of a high diversity and low disposition occupation is a dentist; and an example of a high diversity and high disposition occupation is a lawyer.

Our intent was to sample widely from Larsson and Bowen's (1989) domain of occupational types, but to couple the resulting breadth with depth in particularly promising occupations. Thus, four or more individuals were interviewed from certain occupations (high depth), and one or two individuals were interviewed from other occupations (high breadth). The high depth occupations included consultant, dentist, funeral home director or employee, hockey referee, nurse, real estate agent, café/hotel/restaurant/ store owner, salesperson and sales manager, supply agent/manager, teacher, and waiter/waitress. The other occupations included account manager, accountant, airline customer service representative, art agent/curator, bank customer service representative, chef, club doorman/bouncer, daycare worker, dietician, food service manager, hairstylist, lawyer, librarian, letter carrier, marketing manager, medical technologist, mortgage broker, optician, pharmaceutical company representative, police officer, portrait photographer, property manager, psychiatric clerk, school principal/vice-principal, social worker, tax investigator, and taxi driver.

The interviews were conducted by the two authors and a graduate assistant. Most interviews resulted from industry contacts, and some from cold calls. In the high depth occupations, the snowball technique was used where one interviewee is asked to nominate other potential interviewees. The interviews were semi-structured in that the interviewers had a protocol of 41 open-ended questions, but often deviated from the protocol to pursue interesting leads. On average, interviews lasted about one hour.

Interview transcripts were content analysed. The data for the current chapter are drawn primarily from four questions. Using grounded theory techniques (for example, Strauss and Corbin, 1998), we moved iteratively between the data and emergent theory, developing conceptual categories and then linking these categories to make sense of the data.

Results

The results are presented in two parts. First, we examine the interaction of acting and authenticity. Second, we examine the aspects of service encounters that make service agents feel authentic versus inauthentic.

Acting and authenticity

Two interview questions investigated the link between acting and authenticity: (1) 'To what extent do you have to be a good actor to be a [job title]?' (2) 'If a good friend were to watch you working, would they say, "That's the [interviewee's name] I know", or "Who is this person?"' Responses to the first question were classified as either 'No, you don't have to act' or 'Yes, you do have to act'. Responses to the second question were classified as either 'Yes, that's him/her' or 'No, that's not him/her'.

Thirty-four responses were not classifiable, either because the questions were not asked directly (recall the interviews were semi-structured) or the interviewee did not provide a reasonably clear answer to both questions. Of the remaining 62 responses, 42 (68%) answered 'Yes, you do have to act', and 52 (84%) answered 'Yes, that's him/her'. What is most intriguing is that about half (32) responded 'Yes' to *both* questions, implying that one must adopt a persona to perform one's role but that one's authentic self is still apparent.[2] How is it possible for one to be simultaneously inauthentic and authentic? To shed some light on this paradox, we will explore the notions of acting and authenticity below and, later in the chapter, offer a theoretical explanation for the paradox.

'No, you don't have to act' – 'No, it's not him/her'   None of the 62 responses fell in this quadrant. This is not surprising: if one perceives no need to act, then one's authentic self, by default, is likely to inform how one enacts the role. One's perception that acting is not necessary may derive from job autonomy or 'display latitude' (Kruml and Geddes, 1998; Morris and Feldman, 1997), or from a belief that one genuinely feels and expresses what is expected (however, as discussed below, respondents who said they did not act generally revealed that they often did). Either way, one's friends are very likely to say 'Yes, that's him/her'.

That said, there were some glimmers in the interviews of a possible exception. For example:

Q: When you're here at work doing your job versus when you're at home . . . would someone say that you're still essentially the same person . . . or do you somehow come across differently?

A: I'm very different . . . you will find that people in the funeral business are quite humorous. There's quite a few comedians in the business. That's at home, in their social life. In the business it's not the case at all. They're very serious . . . I've had some [say], 'I can't believe you're the same person' . . . but I'm at the office now and I'm at work. (funeral director, 6 years of experience)

When I'm talking to a client I feel that I am the same person, although it's my business side, my professional side. It's more than my normal feeling. Sometimes I'm in front of a guy and I like him a lot as a friend. But the way I act is that I'm here to do business – I'm not the same person you know. (accountant, 3 years)

The funeral director and accountant are being authentic in their work and other roles, but because the display rules differ so drastically between these roles, each *appears* to be a different person to those who know them well. The different roles call forth different, but possibly equally authentic, facets of the self. Thus, the greater the differentiation in role identities and display rules between two roles, the greater the likelihood of a differentiated self. Given the context-specific nature of many role identities (Ashforth, 2000; McCall and Simmons, 1978), one may be able to internalize and enact even contradictory identities.

'No, you don't have to act' – 'Yes, it's him/her'   Twenty of the 62 responses (32%) fell in this quadrant. These respondents typically prided themselves on what they regarded as their honest and straightforward manner. For example:

I don't put on a performance for anybody. I am . . . who I am, and that's what you get . . . because if you do [act], you have to try to remember what part you played with that client, what part you played with another client . . . If you have a standard [you're OK]. (art curator, 15 years)

. . . someone has to be a good actor, but I'm not. I am a plain guy. And I play plain. Sometimes you have to use a few curves, but I'm not acting really . . . I'm very easy to recognize. I'm not a bluffer, unless I play poker. (government tax investigator, 25 years)

Many of these respondents appeared to reject the appellation of 'actor' because they interpreted the term negatively, as being phony. However, as the following quote suggests, subsequent discussion generally revealed that they did indeed engage in acting to influence service encounters.

Good actor? . . . I never accepted it as a good term . . . if you're an actor it's because you're really not being honest. You're really out to fool someone you know.

[Later, in response to a question about managing a difficult situation:]

It's almost like how well can you control your emotions and help people . . . it's how well you can control all those aspects of your personality, how people perceive you, the messages you're sending out. (supply agent, 2 years)

Aside from respondents' reactions to the term 'actor', it is undoubtedly true that individuals differ in the degree to which they routinely engage in acting. There are probably a host of situational and individual factors that affect the perceived need to act (for example, display rules are clear, inflexible, and enforced; individuals have relatively low power and status) as well as the motivation to act, given a perceived need (such as organizational support; high role identification, self-monitoring, and acting ability).

'Yes, you have to act' – 'No, it's not him/her' As noted, over two-thirds of the classifiable interviewees (42 of 62) said that they had to act in their job, and those who denied having to act often implied just the opposite. The prevalence of acting in service roles is not surprising, given the ubiquity of display rules and the fact that even service agents who identify strongly with their role will not always feel precisely what is expected of them. However, only 10 of the 42 (24%) self-perceived 'actors' said that a close friend would *not* recognize them in the role – that their behaviour was so different from their natural propensity that it was unrecognizable. For example:

Q: Now, if a close friend were to watch you dealing with customers, would that friend say 'Yes, this is the person that I know?'

A: . . . No . . . of course you're gonna act differently . . . you have to have that persona that you take on and that's it . . . it's not the same person that you are, obviously . . . You have to be a Madame, the hostess, or the barmaid, or Mrs. Restaurant person. (waitress, 2 years)

This disavowal of the role identity appeared to be somewhat more prevalent among roles that entailed the expression of negative emotions. A particularly clear example is the following:

. . . good acting is to keep the serious face on different situations. Not necessarily show that you're tough, but you gotta portray a role like a sheriff. Very serious. No joking around. If you're a joking type, then nobody will take you serious. They step all over you . . . I'm myself when I'm friendly . . . But when I have to get physical, that's not me. That's somebody else that's taken over . . . It doesn't happen often but when it happens, it's ugly . . . it's like I almost don't know who that person is. (club doorman, 11 years)

Because the experience and expression of negative emotions tends to be aversive – almost by definition – to both the service agent and client, it is not surprising that agents might distance themselves from the role identity. This suggests that emotional dissonance and, therefore, job dissatisfaction and turnover, will be particularly pronounced in service roles that require the expression of negative emotions (such as bill collector, police interrogator; cf. Rafaeli and Sutton, 1991).

Moreover, Ashforth and Humphrey (1993) argue that strong emotional dissonance is not tenable over the long run. Because inauthenticity is aversive, individuals tend to either exit the role or gradually internalize it as a means of reducing the dissonance. Further, following Salancik's (1977) notion of behavioural commitment, acting as if one were an exemplar of the role tends to bind one to the role such that identification may occur so as to 'make sense' of the implied commitment. For example, one interviewee sounded the following cautionary note:

Q: Do you have to be a good actor to be in your occupation?

A: Yeah, definitely. They like melodrama.

[Later] *Q*: Now, if a friend were to watch you talking to a client, would that friend say this is the man that I know or . . . ?

A: Definitely not the person I know . . . [But] it becomes you at some point in time. You put on a mask and you wear it long enough, it becomes you. (security consultant, 25 years)

'Yes, you have to act' – 'Yes, it's him/her' As noted, about half (32 of 62) of the classifiable interviewees fell in this final quadrant. What was surprising was that individuals simulated a wide range of emotions (across interviews far more than within interviews) and yet continued to feel authentic in the role ('Yes, it's him/her'). The following examples convey the flavour of the positive, neutral and negative affective tones – or, in Wharton and Erickson's (1993) framework, the integrative, masking and differentiating emotions – that were simulated:

You have to put on a smile when you don't feel like putting on that smile. You have to ask those questions when you don't feel like hearing the answers – you *do* have to be a good actor. And you don't care about the weather, you couldn't care less how it is outside but you've got to keep asking. And you don't care *how* they're feeling because *you're* feeling miserable – you've got to still go out there and ask them – you're there for that. (medical technologist, 6 years)

Q: What does good acting entail?

A: When it comes to the time that there's an offer being negotiated, you have to sometimes hide your feelings a lot. And you also have to keep yourself under control because . . . you're dealing with situations where emotions become very inflamed. So you have to try to keep calm and keep everybody calm. Yeah, there's a lot of play-acting going on. (real estate agent, 6 years)

. . . in a hockey game at any time there could be conflict so I'm always prepared and I've got this aggressive nature that my fiancé's seen . . . but it's completely different . . . I view myself as a situational [person], depending on the situation I'm in I act differently. I find myself very adaptive. In terms of hockey I tend to have this aggressive nature when refereeing. (hockey referee, 11 years)

We explore this paradox of inauthenticity/authenticity later, but one potential clue arising from some interviews is the central role of identity. It appears that individuals are less likely to perceive a contradiction between the statements 'Yes, I act' and 'Yes, I'm authentic' when they identify either with the role *per se* or with specific aspects of the role (such as being nice, being professional). In such cases, being true to the display rules is being true to oneself – even if one is not currently feeling the displayed emotion:

Q: Do you have to be a good actress to be a good dietician?

A: Sometimes you do because . . . you have to convince the person that they're going to be successful – that they can do it . . . So you have to be very convincing.

[Later] *Q*: If a good friend of yours was watching your work with a client, would they say, 'Yeah, that's the [person] I know – that's her', or would they say, 'Gee, who's that?'

A: No . . . it's me . . . I'm a caring person and that's why I went into the health care profession – I want to help people. And that comes across. I think that's what clients like about me – that they know I'm being sincere and genuine and that I do want to help them. I don't see them as a dollar sign. (dietician, 3 years)

. . . I'm typically not acting. If acting is interpreted as telling a story or delivering something that you don't truly believe in, then that's not you. However, if acting means kind of emphasizing points and being energetic if the situation desires it or putting on some sort of a show to make a point or something like that, then I would say I do a lot more acting . . . a lot of our work is communication and you need to communicate effectively and if acting is putting on a show then to some extent you do that. You need to. But you do it because you believe in it. (consultant, 2 years)

The dietician and consultant are putting on an act to uphold aspects of their roles that they believe in. In this sense, inauthenticity serves the cause of authenticity.[3] Again, we will revisit the inauthenticity/authenticity paradox later.

What aspects of service encounters make agents feel authentic versus inauthentic?

Two questions directly probed the nature and bounds of authenticity: (1) 'What kinds of service interactions make you feel like you're really being yourself, that your behaviour reflects who you really are?' and (2) 'What kinds of interactions make you feel false?' The responses were quite varied, ranging from the very general (such as working with people, being helpful) to the very specific (such as cocktail parties, negotiating). However, four major motifs were evident, aside from the role of identity discussed above.

Affective disposition of customer   The most common motif was the affective disposition of the customer. Service agents felt authentic when dealing with customers who were friendly, upbeat, open, honest and cooperative, and felt inauthentic when dealing with customers who were the opposite or were simply not liked. For example:

Q: What kinds of interactions with customers make you feel like you're really being yourself? Like, that you're behavior reflects who you are?

A: I would say customers that are friendly, cause I'm fairly easygoing. I don't like stress. I don't like antagonistic people. I prefer the people that have a sense of humor . . .

Q: And, likewise, in what kinds of interactions do you feel like you're being false?

A: Sometimes when customers . . . are abusive or feeling negative. Sometimes you would really like to tell them off. But you can't so then I feel false when I try to calm them down and try to get them to another track. Just sometimes you'd really like to tell them to grow up. (salesperson, 3 years)

Q: In what kinds of interactions do you feel like you're being false?

A: When I'm dealing with a client that I don't like and have to be pleasant . . . you almost feel like a hypocrite. You've got to be the same basically to him or her as anybody else, but it's very . . . hard . . . when I have to spend time with people that I don't like at work well, I don't feel I'm being my true self because in my personal life I wouldn't be spending any time with those people. (librarian, 6 years)

This link between customers' affective disposition and agent authenticity meshes with Kruml and Geddes's (1998) research. Based on a sample of service agents from various occupations, Kruml and Geddes found that customers' positive affect was negatively related to agents' experience of emotional dissonance.

Upholding the sanctity and conventions of the role or organization   Another common motif was the need to affirm the sanctity and conventions of the role or organization; that is, the image and manner of doing business – even if the image and manner are dubious in the eyes of the agent or the public. Service agents mentioned feeling false when they had to defend conventions with which they disagreed, such as denying a customer's wishes because of organizational regulations or exigencies, lying to customers on behalf of the organization (such as about the availability of a product or delivery dates) or to expedite interactions, defending a co-worker who did something questionable, skirting issues because of organizational politics, and so on. For example:

We had a young man with quite a very serious cancer, and the oncologist has more of a tendency to think they'll be cured more than they will be. And I think that probably comes from working with cancer all the time – you have to have some kind of hope. But then he relayed that message to this young man, and the palliative care social worker was trying to make this young man see how serious his condition was . . . And yet the oncologist . . . was saying, 'Ah, you know – there's an 80% chance you'll be cured from this therapy' . . . it can be very hard, because if he [the oncologist] really believes that, you can't really go against [him]. One of the really important things is to never divide in front of the patient and the family. They have to get the same message, otherwise it must be very difficult – hopefully the right message, though. (nurse, 20 years)

Q: Now, are there interactions with clients that make you feel like you're being false . . . ?

A: You do feel sometimes as a liar. You have to lie sometimes to be able to get a sale . . . Sometimes I feel bad when I see that the person is very vulnerable. I feel really bad. But sometimes I say to myself, 'Wow, I did a good job'.

Q: So it's . . . part of the job and you accept that?

A: Of course. (shoe salesperson, 1 year)

Mood and attention The third motif was the transitory mood and attention of the service agent. Service agents reported feeling false when they had to perform their role while in an incompatible mood or while distracted by personal or work-related problems. For example:

I would say to work in a place like this you've got to be a good actor, because even though you might be in a bad mood – because of problems at home, or with a friend, or family, or something like that – when you come to work . . . you've got to show that smile, you've got to fake it . . . sometimes you don't feel like discussing, so you'll agree with whatever the person [says] just to not cause any further discussions. (café manager, 7 years)

Tenure of relationship The fourth motif was the tenure of the agent–customer relationship. Service agents felt that their interactions tended to become more authentic as they got to know a particular customer, whether during the course of a single service encounter or over multiple encounters. For example:

Q: In what kinds of interactions do you feel you're being false?

A: I think the only time we tend to be false is on our initial introduction. We tend to be overly polite . . . our behavior is modeled as opposed to being free and open, initially. We're modeling what we believe we're supposed to be modeling during the initial encounter.

Q: And what do you base yourself on for that modeling?

A: Accepted behavioral norms, like 'Hello, how are you, very pleased to meet you. Isn't it a nice day today' and all that stuff – the standard bullshit exchange between people who don't know each other and are being introduced. I think everybody tends to be a little bit phony initially. (real estate agent, 10 years)

Q: Now, are there certain interactions with customers that make you feel like you're being really you? Where you can sort of just be yourself?

A: . . . The client that I feel like I'm really being me [with] is the one that I've known for a while and that . . . know where their place is. So therefore when you know that person, you can joke around and chitchat with them on the phone or in person and even go to lunch with them, but when it comes to business they can switch and talk about business and not mix everything together. (salesperson, industrial equipment, 2 years)

The notion of relationship tenure may help explain a paradox hinted at by Himmelweit (1999). She notes that paid caregivers often develop highly personalized attachments to their clients, such that they may freely offer help that goes well beyond the employment contract and may decline transfers to more convenient clients. Rather than suffer the emotional exhaustion often associated with the helping professions, the caregivers felt energized and authenticated by caregiving. Perhaps a long-term service relationship is potentially authenticating precisely because it enables the agent to overlay a personal and mutual relationship on an otherwise impersonal and one-way relationship (cf. bounded emotionality; Martin et al., 1998). In support, Kruml and Geddes (1998) found that service agents' emotional attachment to customers was negatively associated with the experience of emotional dissonance.

Similarly, some service agents in the present study also reported feeling most authentic when interacting in settings that connoted a personal rather than purely business relationship, such as at a restaurant or on a golf course. Such settings may help agents and customers relax, thereby facilitating authenticity, and may signal growth in the interpersonal relationship, thereby sanctifying further authenticity. However, one danger of conducting business on more personal turf is that it may blur the boundaries of work and home such that both role identities are compromised (Ashforth et al., 2000).

Implications for authenticity

Our data thus suggest a paradox. On the one hand, our service agents generally believed that their role enactments reflected their 'true selves', that a close friend would indeed recognize their behaviour and say 'That's the person I know'. On the other hand, our service agents also generally believed that they had to be a 'good actor' to do their job well, that faking emotions was a routine part of their job. How can we reconcile this paradox of simultaneous authenticity (cross-situational consistency) and inauthenticity (good actor)?

Surface authenticity and deep authenticity

We speculate that there are two levels of authenticity, *surface authenticity* and *deep authenticity*. The former is concerned with behaviour in a given service encounter whereas the latter is concerned with identity. More specifically, surface authenticity occurs when one's emotional expression or display reflects one's current emotional experience, when the expression genuinely reflects actual feelings. For example, an obstetrics nurse with 11 years of experience talked about 'getting just as much joy out of [a] delivery as the couple'.

Deep authenticity occurs when one's emotional expression or display is consistent with the display rules of a specific identity that one has internalized (or wants to internalize) as a reflection of self – *regardless of whether the expression genuinely reflects one's current feelings*. In internalizing the service role (that is, identifying with the role) or aspects of the role (such as being helpful), one defines oneself at least partly in terms of the role. Thus, as noted earlier, being true to the role is tantamount to being true to oneself (Ashforth, 2000). For example, if the role calls for friendly service, then acting in a friendly manner is being true to the role and oneself – even if one is currently in a foul mood. As the consultant that was quoted earlier put it, 'you do it' – you act – 'because you believe in it'.

Surface acting and deep acting We should distinguish surface and deep authenticity from Hochschild's (1979, 1983) constructs of surface and deep acting. Hochschild argued that service agents comply with display rules through either surface or deep acting. Surface acting involves simulating emotions that are not actually felt, typically through a combination of verbal and non-verbal cues (such as facial expression, posture, gestures, voice tone). Deep acting involves actively inducing, suppressing or shaping one's actual emotions so that one's expression of emotions is consistent with one's experience of emotions. Thus, surface acting focuses on outward behaviour, whereas deep acting focuses on inner feelings.

How do surface and deep acting relate to surface and deep authenticity? Surface acting is associated with surface *in*authenticity because the individual is displaying emotions that are not actually felt, whereas deep acting is associated with surface authenticity because the individual is summoning emotions such that the display does conform to the experience. Conversely, surface acting and deep acting may each be associated with *either* deep authenticity *or* deep inauthenticity. If one identifies with the role (deep authenticity), then surface and deep acting can each be used to uphold the valued role identity when one does not currently feel what is expected; however, even if one does not identify with the role (deep inauthenticity), surface and deep acting can still be used to conform to display rules and thereby meet one's performance obligations.

Linking surface authenticity and deep authenticity Figure 10.1 links the concepts of surface and deep authenticity into a flowchart. The flowchart depicts three questions that individuals implicitly ask themselves. We say 'implicitly' because it is very unlikely that individuals consciously and routinely ask these questions in a sequential, lock-step manner. The process is probably more intuitive, holistic and automatic. Thus, the flowchart should be viewed as a heuristic for exposition purposes. The three questions are numbered, as are the potential choices.

Given that a role identity has been cued, the first question is: 'Do I identify with the role?' As noted, identification is associated with deep authenticity (arrow 1A), whereas a lack of identification is associated with deep inauthenticity ('This role is not me'; 1B). Regardless of one's level of role identification, emotions are inevitably experienced and displayed in the course of a service encounter. This leads to the second question: 'Do my displayed emotions in this situation reflect display rules?' If the displayed emotions do reflect the display rules, then one is conforming to role expectations (2A); if they do not reflect display rules, then one is not conforming (2B).

This leads to the third question: 'Do my displayed emotions in this situation reflect my experience of emotion?' Following the 2A fork, if the displayed emotions also reflect one's actual experience of emotion, then surface authenticity is attained ('This display is real'; 3A). Conversely, if the

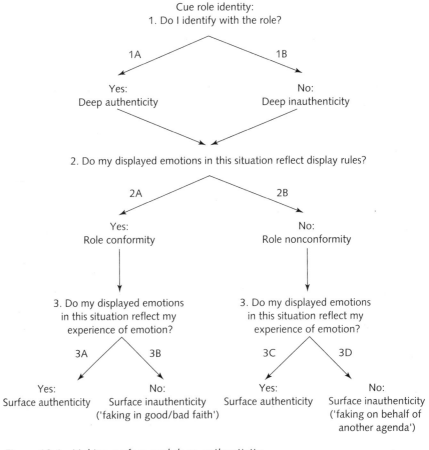

Figure 10.1 *Linking surface and deep authenticity*

displayed emotions do *not* reflect one's experience, then surface inauthenticity is the outcome (3B). In the case of 3B, if one believes that the display rules are appropriate – even though one is not actually experiencing the expected emotion – one is said to be 'faking in good faith' (Hochschild, 1983; Morris and Feldman, 1996b; Rafaeli and Sutton, 1987). In the words of one interviewee:

Sometimes I feel hypocritical or like I'm lying to my client [by being very positive about their chances of losing weight]. But then I say, 'Well, if this over-enthusiasm is going to help them lose weight, then it's actually beneficial to them' so I'm not being that bad. You have to make yourself believe that you're not bad. (dietician, 3 years)

Note, then, that a service agent may incur surface inauthenticity as the price of upholding a role identity. Alternatively, if one believes that the display rules are inappropriate, one is 'faking in bad faith'. Rafaeli and Sutton (1987: 32) quote a check-out clerk who resented acting friendly because 'pasting on a smile should not be part of the job'. Whether one is faking in good faith or bad faith, one is nonetheless simulating the expected emotions.

Following the 2B fork, where one is *not* conforming to the display rules, we return to the third question: 'Do my displayed emotions in this situation reflect my experience of emotion?' If the displayed emotions do reflect one's experience, then surface authenticity is achieved (3C), albeit at the expense of the role. For example:

[When I get very angry] I don't really care any more how the other person feels. All I care about is getting what I want and having my objectives met. When it gets to that point, I have very little regard left for the client . . . So anything goes. It's a total war, basically. (property manager, 7 years)

Conversely, if the displayed emotions do not reflect one's experience, then surface inauthenticity is the outcome (3D). In this case, one is thus behaving in a manner that is not only contrary to the role identity, but to one's current emotional state. Such incidents are likely to be relatively rare, but may occur if one is trying to control an encounter in ways that are not sanctioned – if one is 'faking on behalf of another agenda'. For example, a store salesperson may feign impatience so that a customer will not ask questions.

What is the causal relation between surface and deep authenticity?   Surface and deep authenticity are conceptually independent, but likely to be weakly to moderately correlated in practice. Assume a teacher strongly identifies with her role (1A). Because she has defined herself in terms of the role (at least in the school context), she is more likely not only to conform to display rules (thus affirming the identity) (2A), but actually to feel the expected emotions (3A). Thus, deep authenticity fosters surface authenticity. However, incidents may occur periodically that require her to display emotions that are not actually felt (for example, a student makes a very amusing but off-colour remark that requires a stern rebuke; she is very worried about an impending parent–teacher meeting but must appear attentive and positive with her students). In such cases, she employs surface acting for the sake of her role identity, such that surface inauthenticity (3B) exists against a backdrop of deep authenticity.

Conversely, assume another teacher does not identify with his role (1B). Because he is required to conform to display rules (2A), despite his disengagement from the role, he may be forced to express emotions that are not actually felt (whether through surface or deep acting) (3B). Thus, deep inauthenticity fosters surface inauthenticity. However: (1) given his disengagement from the role, he is more likely than the highly identified teacher to deviate from display rules and express his real feelings (for example, being rude to students) (3C), and (2) incidents may occur from time to time that cause him to actually feel and express the emotions that are normatively expected (for example, a student gives an inspirational presentation, causing him to praise the student) (3A). In such cases, surface authenticity exists against a backdrop of deep inauthenticity.

In the long run, surface inauthenticity in the service of the role (3B) may actually foster deep authenticity. As suggested earlier, because surface inauthenticity is often aversive, individuals may come to identify somewhat with the role as a means of 'getting into' the role and actually feeling some of the expected emotions, thereby reducing the dissonance. However, it is likely that individuals will continue to feel at least somewhat ambivalent about the role, fluctuating between moments of identification ('This is me') and disidentification ('This is not me') (Ashforth and Mael, 1998; Sturdy, 1998).

Authenticity and emotional dissonance

How does the distinction between surface and deep authenticity relate to the experience of emotional dissonance? Figure 10.2 provides an answer by crossing surface authenticity and surface inauthenticity with deep authenticity and deep inauthenticity, thereby creating a 2 × 2. In cells 1 (surface authenticity and deep authenticity) and 2 (surface authenticity and deep inauthenticity), emotional dissonance is absent because, by definition, one's emotional expression is consistent with one's emotional experience. Cell 2 may be nonetheless associated with work alienation (for example, low job satisfaction and organizational commitment) because of the deep inauthenticity.

In cells 3 (surface inauthenticity and deep authenticity) and 4 (surface inauthenticity and deep inauthenticity), emotional dissonance is experienced because, by definition, one's emotional expression is not consistent with one's actual feelings. However, emotional dissonance is likely to be much lower in cell 3 than cell 4. In cell 3, because the individual identifies with the role (deep authenticity), he or she is more likely to conform to display rules such that the surface inauthenticity would likely reflect faking in good faith (3B). In such cases, surface inauthenticity may actually *support* a valued role identity,

	Deep authenticity	Deep inauthenticity
Surface authenticity	Cell 1 No emotional dissonance	Cell 2 No emotional dissonance
Surface inauthenticity	Cell 3 Low – High emotional dissonance [a]	Cell 4 Low – High emotional dissonance [a]

[a] The magnitude of dissonance depends on the particulars of the encounter. However, the underlined term (that is, low or high) is the modal tendency.

Figure 10.2   *Authenticity and emotional dissonance in a service encounter*

thus greatly muting the experience of emotional dissonance. (That said, if one disagrees with a particular display rule (faking in bad faith; also 3B) or has a difficult time summoning the appropriate verbal and non-verbal cues during a particular service encounter (for example, due to an abusive client or personal problem), then emotional dissonance may be high.) There is some circumstantial evidence from the literature supporting a negative link between identification and emotional dissonance. Morris and Feldman (1996b) found a negative correlation of $r=-0.41$ between 'role internalization' (sample item: 'With my job I sometimes have to act in ways that are not completely consistent with my true values' [reversed], p. 23) and emotional dissonance. Similarly, Bulan et al. (1997) found that job involvement was negatively associated with inauthenticity (however, only for men).

In cell 4, because the individual does not identify with the service role (deep inauthenticity), he or she is less likely to endorse the display rules and conform to them, such that the surface inauthenticity is more likely to reflect either faking in bad faith (3B) or faking on behalf of another agenda (3D) than was the case in cell 3. Because surface inauthenticity does *not* support a valued identity, the experience of emotional dissonance may be quite acute. However, the intensity of dissonance is likely to vary across service encounters, depending on the particulars of the situation (for example, the cued display rules, agent's mood, client's demeanour).

Summary

Our analysis suggests a number of speculative conclusions:

• Job autonomy is likely to be associated with authenticity.

- The greater the differentiation in role identities and display rules between two roles, the greater the likelihood of a differentiated self. Differentiated roles may evoke different, but possibly equally authentic, facets of the self.
- Although many individuals react negatively to the notion of being an 'actor', most individuals do engage in impression management activities from time to time.
- Individuals are more likely to disavow role identities that involve the expression of negative emotions. Thus, emotional dissonance, job dissatisfaction, and turnover will be greater in such roles.
- Acting is less likely to be perceived as a sign of inauthenticity when one identifies with the role or with specific aspects of the role. One may act to affirm a valued identity (that is, by simulating or summoning expected emotions that are not currently felt). Thus, inauthenticity may facilitate authenticity. More specifically, although surface acting is associated with surface inauthenticity, surface acting and deep acting may support deep authenticity.
- Service agents feel most authentic when: dealing with customers who are friendly, upbeat, open, honest, cooperative, or are otherwise liked; not upholding role or organizational conventions with which they disagree; not experiencing an incompatible mood or distraction; dealing with customers whom they have come to know such that a more personalized relationship has developed.
- Deep authenticity fosters surface authenticity, and deep inauthenticity fosters surface inauthenticity. However, deep authenticity may at times be supported by surface inauthenticity (as formalized below), and deep inauthenticity does not preclude instances of surface authenticity.
- Surface inauthenticity fosters emotional dissonance, particularly when coupled with deep inauthenticity.
- Over time, however, surface inauthenticity in the service of the role (see Figure 10.1, arrow 3B) may foster deep authenticity, although it may be coupled with ambivalence.

In closing, the requirement to display certain emotions during service encounters challenges the self-perceived authenticity of service agents. However, when service agents identify with their roles they tend to construe good acting as supporting – rather than challenging – their authenticity.

Acknowledgements

We thank Blair Templeton for conducting some of the interviews, and Stephen Fineman and Glen Kreiner for their constructive comments on an earlier draft of the chapter. This study was funded by grants from the Dean's Award of Excellence Program, College of Business, Arizona State University, and the Social Sciences and Humanities Research Council of Canada (#410-96-0770).

Notes

1 Morris and Feldman (1996a) argue that emotional dissonance is not an outcome of emotional labour but a component of it because the experience of dissonance means that one has to put more effort into complying with affective requirements. A lawyer who is surprised by her client's courtroom testimony has to work harder to display affective neutrality or approval than one who is not. However, because emotional dissonance is necessarily a function of a person–situation interaction, including dissonance in the emotional labour construct means that emotional labour cannot be operationalized in purely objective or situational terms.

2 It should be noted that we are assuming that individuals are generally authentic – are more or less true to themselves – when interacting with close friends (see for example DePaulo and Kashy, 1998).

3 Granfield (1991) came to a similar conclusion in his study of law students at a prestigious law school. Granfield found that working-class students attempted to hide their background and blend in by acting like other students, a tendency he dubbed 'making it by faking it'.

References

Abiala, K. (1999) 'Customer orientation and sales situations: variations in interactive service work', *Acta Sociologica*, 42: 207–22.

Abraham, R. (1998) 'Emotional dissonance in organizations: antecedents, consequences, and moderators', *Genetic, Social, and General Psychology Monographs*, 124: 229–46.

Adelmann, P.K. (1995) 'Emotional labor as a potential source of job stress', in S.L. Sauter and L.R. Murphy (eds), *Organizational Risk Factors for Job Stress*. Washington, DC: American Psychological Association. pp. 371–81.

Ashforth, B.E. (ed.) (2000) *Role Transitions in Organizational Life: An Identity-Based Perspective*. Mahwah, NJ: Erlbaum.

Ashforth, B.E. and Humphrey, R.H. (1993) 'Emotional labor in service roles: the influence of identity', *Academy of Management Review*, 18: 88–115.

Ashforth, B.E. and Mael, F.A. (1998) 'The power of resistance: sustaining valued identities', in R.M. Kramer and M.A. Neale (eds), *Power and Influence in Organizations*. Thousand Oaks, CA: Sage. pp. 89–119.

Ashforth, B.E., Kreiner, G.E., Fugate, M. and Johnson, S.A. (2000) 'Micro role transitions', in B.E. Ashforth (ed.), *Role Transitions in Organizational Life: An Identity-Based Perspective*. Mahwah, NJ: Erlbaum.

Bulan, H.F., Erickson, R.J. and Wharton, A.S. (1997) 'Doing for others on the job: the affective requirements of service work, gender, and emotional well-being', *Social Problems*, 44: 235–56.

DePaulo, B.M. and Kashy, D.A. (1998) 'Everyday lies in close and casual relationships', *Journal of Personality and Social Psychology*, 74: 63–79.

Ekman, P. (1973) 'Cross-cultural studies of facial expression', in P. Ekman (ed.), *Darwin and Facial Expression: A Century of Research in Review*. New York: Academic Press. pp. 169–222.

Erickson, R.J. (1995) 'The importance of authenticity for self and society', *Symbolic Interaction*, 18: 121–44.

Erickson, R.J. and Wharton, A.S. (1997) 'Inauthenticity and depression: assessing the consequences of interactive service work', *Work and Occupations*, 24: 188–213.

Fineman, S. (1996) 'Emotion and organizing', in S.R. Clegg, C. Hardy and W.R. Nord (eds), *Handbook of Organization Studies*. London: Sage. pp. 543–64.

Gecas, V. (1986) 'The motivational significance of self-concept for socialization theory', in E.J. Lawler (ed.), *Advances in Group Processes*, vol. 3. Greenwich, CT: JAI Press. pp. 131–56.

Gergen, K.J. (1991) *The Saturated Self: Dilemmas of Identity in Contemporary Life*. New York: Basic Books.

Granfield, R. (1991) 'Making it by faking it: working-class students in an elite academic environment', *Journal of Contemporary Ethnography*, 20: 331–51.

Higgins, E.T. (1987) 'Self-discrepancy: a theory relating self and affect', *Psychological Review*, 94: 319–40.

Himmelweit, S. (1999) 'Caring labor', *Annals of the American Academy of Political and Social Science*, 561: 27–38.

Hochschild, A.R. (1979) 'Emotion work, feeling rules, and social structure', *American Journal of Sociology*, 85: 551–75.

Hochschild, A.R. (1983) *The Managed Heart: Commercialization of Human Feeling*. Berkeley, CA: University of California Press.

Kruml, S.M. and Geddes, D. (1998) 'Exploring the dimensions of emotion labor: the heart of Hochschild's work'. Paper presented at the annual meeting of the Academy of Management, San Diego.

Larsson, R. and Bowen, D.E. (1989) 'Organization and customer: managing design and coordination of services', *Academy of Management Review*, 14: 213–33.

Leidner, R. (1993) *Fast Food, Fast Talk: Service Work and the Routinization of Everyday Life*. Berkeley: University of California Press.

Leidner, R. (1999) 'Emotional labor in service work', *Annals of the American Academy of Political and Social Science*, 561: 81–95.

Lifton, R.J. (1993) *The Protean Self: Human Resilience in an Age of Fragmentation*. New York: Basic Books.

McCall, G.J. and Simmons, J.L. (1978) *Identities and Interactions: An Examination of Human Associations in Everyday Life*, rev. edn. New York: Free Press.

Morgan, C. and Averill, J.R. (1992) 'True feelings, the self, and authenticity: a psychosocial perspective', in D.D. Franks and V. Gecas (eds), *Social Perspectives on Emotion*, vol. 1. Greenwich, CT: JAI Press. pp. 95–123.

Morris, J.A. and Feldman, D.C. (1996a) 'The dimensions, antecedents, and consequences of emotional labor', *Academy of Management Review*, 21: 986–1010.

Morris, J.A. and Feldman, D.C. (1996b) 'The impact of emotional dissonance on psychological well-being: the importance of role internalisation as a mediating variable', *Management Research News*, 19 (8): 19–28.

Morris, J.A. and Feldman, D.C. (1997) 'Managing emotions in the workplace', *Journal of Managerial Issues*, 9: 257–74.

Rafaeli, A. and Sutton, R.I. (1987) 'Expression of emotion as part of the work role', *Academy of Management Review*, 12: 23–37.

Rafaeli, A. and Sutton, R.I. (1991) 'Emotional contrast strategies as means of social influence: lessons from criminal investigators and bill collectors'. *Academy of Management Journal*, 34: 749–75.

Richman, J.A. (1988) 'Deviance from sex-linked expressivity norms and psychological distress', *Social Forces*, 67: 208–15.

Ryan, R.M. (1995) 'Psychological needs and the facilitation of integrative processes', *Journal of Personality*, 63: 397–427.

Salancik, G.R. (1977) 'Commitment and the control of organizational behavior and belief', in

B.M. Staw and G.R. Salancik (eds), *New Directions in Organizational Behavior*. Chicago: St Clair Press. pp. 1–54.

Sande, G.N. (1990) 'The multifaceted self', in J.M. Olson and M.P. Zanna (eds), *Social Inference Processes: The Ontario Symposium*, vol. 6. Hillsdale, NJ: Lawrence Erlbaum. pp. 1–16.

Sheldon, K.M., Ryan, R.M., Rawsthorne, L.J. and Ilardi, B. (1997) 'Trait self and true self: cross-role variation in the big-five personality traits and its relations with psychological authenticity and subjective well-being', *Journal of Personality and Social Psychology*, 73: 1380–93.

Strauss, A. and Corbin, J. (1998) *Basics of Qualitative Research: Grounded Theory Procedures and Techniques*. Newbury Park, CA: Sage.

Sturdy, A. (1998) 'Customer care in a consumer society: smiling and sometimes meaning it?', *Organization*, 5: 27–53.

Van Maanen, J. and Kunda, G. (1989) '"Real feelings": emotional expression and organizational culture', in L.L. Cummings and B.M. Staw (eds), *Research in Organizational Behavior*, vol. 11. Greenwich, CT: JAI Press. pp. 43–103.

Waldron, V.R. (1994) 'Once more, *with feeling*: reconsidering the role of emotion in work', in S.A. Deetz (ed.), *Communication Yearbook*, vol. 17. Thousand Oaks, CA: Sage. pp. 388–416.

Wharton, A.S. (1999) 'The psychosocial consequences of emotional labor', *Annals of the American Academy of Political and Social Science*, 561: 158–76.

Wharton, A.S. and Erickson, R.J. (1993) 'Managing emotions on the job and at home: understanding the consequences of multiple emotional roles', *Academy of Management Review*, 18: 457–86.

11 AMBIVALENT FEELINGS IN ORGANIZATIONAL RELATIONSHIPS

MICHAEL G. PRATT AND
LORNA DOUCET

concepts [like ambivalence] emerge when they are needed to make sense out of
life's situations . . . [and] the rapidity, complexity, precariousness, and intensity
of today's world are likely to generate increasing burdens of ambivalence . . .
(Weigert and Franks, 1989: 224)

Depictions of organizational life have ranged from depictions of extreme
alienation (Erikson, 1986) to extreme commitment (Butterfield, 1985; Kunda,
1992). However, the emotional portrait of workers may not be so easily
captured by simple shades of positive or negative feelings. Rather, the rapid
rate of change, the ever-increasing complexity, and the seeming incom-
pleteness characteristic of social life in the twentieth century suggest that
this is an 'age of ambivalence' (Weigert and Franks, 1989). In the workplace,
individuals confront the realities of hypercompetitive marketplaces, tech-
nologically mediated relationships, inconsistent empowerment, and economic
insecurity. These and other issues have become embedded in the social
structure of organizations and affect the bonds between individuals and
between individuals and their organization. The result, we argue, is that
individuals often experience ambivalence: 'overlapping approach-avoidance
tendencies' (Sincoff, 1990) characterized by 'mixed feelings' about their work
groups and organizations.

Despite the fact that ambivalence is inherent in modern life, and is a central
concept in many social sciences (cf. Boehm, 1989; Freud, 1950/1920; Bowlby,
1982; Merton, 1976; Smelser, 1998), our understanding of ambivalence in
organizations is limited. In this chapter, we examine the topic of *emotional
ambivalence* in the context of work relationships. We have four major goals
in this regard: (1) to briefly review the concept of ambivalence, especially
emotional ambivalence; (2) to argue for the prevalence of ambivalence in
individuals' relationships both with and within organizations; (3) to propose
two major sources of ambivalence in these relationships; and (4) to offer
a typology of responses that individuals use to cope with emotional
ambivalence.

To illustrate these goals, we draw upon two different cases, rural doctors
whose practices have been recently bought out by a large managed care
organization (referred to hereafter as HealthCo[1]), and employees at bank
call-centres. These cases reveal two types of ambivalent relationships in

organizations. The case of the rural doctors principally illustrates how individuals can become *ambivalent with* their employing organization. Thus, it shows an individual's ambivalence with their collective. The call-centre, by contrast, primarily illustrates ambivalent relationships between bank call-centre employees and co-workers, as well as between employees and customers. Thus, it shows us ambivalent relationships *within* (rather than with) an organization.[2] We believe that both types of ambivalent relationships (both with and within) are likely to be common in modern organizations.

What is ambivalence?

While the notion of competing affective forces has been discussed for centuries, the term 'ambivalence' was coined by the psychoanalyst Eugen Bleuler in 1910. 'Ambivalence' was derived from the Latin *ambo* meaning 'both' and *valere* meaning 'to be strong' (Meyerson and Scully, 1995), and generally refers to opposing forces existing simultaneously within an individual.

In this chapter, our primary focus is on the sources of emotional ambivalence, and how people respond to the target of one's ambivalence. While Freud tended to view emotional ambivalence simply as the existence of both love and hate towards some person or object, we take a broader view here (cf. Merton and Barber, 1976). We define emotional ambivalence *as the association of both strong positive and negative emotions with some target (such as, a person or object/symbol).*[3] Two implications of this broader definition are noteworthy. First, the experience of emotional ambivalence may involve feeling a wide array of emotions. Thus, ambivalence may involve a whole combination of positive and negative feelings, such as when a person experiences intense happiness, anxiety, fear and pride about a new promotion. Second, ambivalence is always relational: one feels ambivalence towards something or someone. Thus, ambivalence should always be viewed in the context of a relationship (for example, self–object, self–other).

Ambivalence and its prevalence in relationships

Because of our interest in ambivalent relationships with and within organizations, we discuss the prevalence of ambivalence in self–other relationships that exist within the context of the workplace. However, before discussing how ambivalence has been conceptualized in work relationships, we first review how ambivalence can characterize interpersonal relationships, more generally.

Ambivalence in familial and other relationships

In psychology and related disciplines, ambivalence often forms and is expressed in the context of intimate interpersonal relationships such as familial or romantic relationships. Ambivalence is often experienced in *children* in their relationship with parents or with siblings (see Smelser, 1998). Bowlby (1982), for example, lists insecure/ambivalent (resistant) attachment as one of three major types of relationships that form between mother and infant, along with secure and insecure/avoidant. Insecure/ambivalent infants were characterized by both highly dependent behaviours (such as clinging) as well as angry or frustrated behaviours.

Ambivalence also occurs within *adult* relationships. In their review of insecure/ambivalent relationships, for example, Cassidy and Berlin (1994) note that such ties are characterized by adults, especially in their relationships with their parents and with romantic partners. Mikulincer (1998: 420) characterizes this style as 'insecurity concerning others' responses together with desire for intimacy and high fear of rejection'. Psychoanalysts also believe that ambivalence is common in adults. Their emphasis, however, are on more dysfunctional and pathological expressions of ambivalence. In their work, ambivalence has been linked to neuroses, especially obsessive-compulsive disorders, as well as to schizophrenia (Sincoff, 1990; Smelser, 1998). As such, strongly ambivalent individuals may be unable to form close, positive relationships as their ambivalence keeps them in a perpetual state of approaching then avoiding others (cf. Horney, 1945).

Ambivalence in work relationships

Traditionally, managerial treatments of work relationships, especially those that capture the 'psychological bond' between individual and organization – such as organizational commitment (see Meyer and Allen, 1997, for review), person–organization fit (see Kristoff, 1996, for review), and identification (see Pratt, 1998, for review) – have focused almost exclusively on individuals who do (or should) strongly and positively identify with their collectives. That is, they have looked at the causes and consequences of positive, secure individual–organizational relationships. Recently, however, there has been a renewed interest in exploring the ambivalent aspects of work relationships.

Ashforth and Mael (1998: 95), for example, suggest that the tension between individuation and conformity to organizational constraints is a prime cause of ambivalence in organizations:

> With regard to organizations, the ascendance of normative control – with its internalized claims on thought and feeling – makes it particularly difficult to differentiate self from system. The resulting tension gives rise to a sense of ambivalence toward the organization – of being simultaneously attracted and repulsed.

Pratt and Rafaeli (2000) make a similar claim and distinguish identity-based ambivalence from status ambivalence. In addition to the need of establishing one's own identity *vis-à-vis* a larger group (identity ambivalence), they note that individuals will often have mixed feelings towards the status level assigned to them by the collective (status ambivalence). As a result, individuals will use symbols to both confirm and deny identity and status designations imposed upon them by the organization.

Building on work on clinical and developmental psychology, organizational theorists have also constructed typologies that include ambivalent relationships, as well as secure and avoidant ones. To illustrate, Dukerich et al. (1998) suggest that one form of identification is 'conflicting identification', where individuals strongly identify and disidentify with an organization. Similarly, Pratt (1996) posits that ambivalent attachments can be produced as organizations manipulate members' ties with members and non-members, thus causing them to move both 'towards' and 'away from' the organization. Thus, organizational researchers are beginning to understand the importance of ambivalence in the individual–organizational relationship.

Illustrating ambivalence in organizational relationships

To help illustrate our points about ambivalence, we will use two cases throughout this chapter. We briefly introduce each case here.

Case 1: bank call centres – ambivalent relationships within organizations

Ambivalent relationships exist within organizations. Employees have love/hate relationships with their supervisors, their colleagues and their customers. Our first case illustrates these ambivalent relationships in excerpts from focus group interviews of front line workers in a retail bank call centre. These call centre workers answer phone calls from bank customers regarding financial products and services. Typically, they provide account balance information and perform troubleshooting for customers with banking problems such as lost cheques or malfunctioning ATM cards.

Call centre workers often join a bank with expectations of high professional status; yet they are often disappointed with the controlled, 'assembly line' mentality that is often applied to call centre work. Moreover, the controlled nature of their work does not take the pressure off the workers and allow them to mindlessly perform their duties. Rather, given the changes in the competitive landscape in financial services, these workers face increased pressure to provide more customized, higher quality service in a more timely fashion. Since call centres can cover larger geographical regions than 'brick and mortar' branches, workers face more diverse requests and are often less familiar with some products they are servicing. In addition, many customers are unfamiliar and uncomfortable with telephone banking which increases the pressure experienced by the call centre worker.

These sources of conflict and discomfort affect call centre workers' relationships within their organization. For example, workers may alternatively *enjoy* helping customers who are intimidated by telephone banking, yet they also express *frustration* with these same 'incompetent' customers who slow them down and ruin their productivity. Call centre workers also express ambivalence across relationships within the organization. For example, they express ambivalent attitudes towards authority – managers place conflicting demands upon workers, but are also sources of emotional support. Working in a call centre, therefore, provides workers with a dilemma. On the one hand, banks are prestigious organizations and call centre work allows for meaningful interactions with customers and co-workers. On the other hand, the position itself is not high status, and to maintain these (and other) benefits, workers must endure high-pressure jobs that are, at times, made more difficult by these very same customers and co-workers.

Case 2: rural doctors – ambivalent relationships with organizations

In addition to having ambivalent relationships within an organization, one might feel ambivalence in relationships with the organization itself. Our second case illustrates this point well. This case involves older rural primary care ('family') doctors whose clinics have just been bought out by a large managed care organization. Having spent a lifetime building up their practices, 'being their own bosses', and 'doing what they think is right for the patient', they are now employees who must not only treat patients but must also be financially accountable to their 'parent' organization, HealthCo. In interviews, physicians recognized that their relationship with HealthCo had many good aspects to it (for example, HealthCo allowed the doctors to keep their clinics' names and it provided them with good benefits).[4] However, they also noted that they joined with HealthCo because of what they saw as 'the inevitability of managed care': they did not want to find themselves without patients because they were not part of a larger integrated health care system. They were motivated by fear. As one physician put it, 'I'd be terrified if I was on the outside [not in a larger health care system] in private practice like the [other] internists in town.'

Interestingly, some described the relationship between them and their new parent organization as being like a marriage. They were 'courted' and now they were 'partners'. However, it was clear that this was a 'marriage of convenience': they would join because the linkage provided economic benefits for both sides. Thus, although there were some positive sentiments in joining with HealthCo, there was not a lot of 'love' in the relationship. This sentiment is nicely illustrated in the example given by one physician:

> We were a ma and pa grocery store, and we were doing just fine. But then they built a Meijer's[5] across the street. The options are we stay a ma and pa grocery store, or we join Meijer's. Now the food is just as good, the service may be a little different but it's adequate. And if the people are going to go more and more to Meijer's, you may as well jump on the bandwagon and smile and say, 'Here I am'.

You may miss the ma and pa food store, but they're gone now, so are the independent doctors going to be.

Inherent in these and many other conversations with these rural doctors was deep-seated ambivalence regarding how they related to their new parent organization. As we will discuss throughout the chapter, there were many sources of their conflicting feelings. It is to these sources that we now turn.

Sources of ambivalence

Since its coinage, ambivalence has been most extensively examined by psychologists and sociologists (cf. Freud, 1950/1920; Merton, 1976). Not surprisingly, these researchers suggest at least two primary sources of ambivalence: (1) individual differences/ambivalent attitudes; and (2) structural or environmental conditions, respectively.

Individual differences/ambivalent attitudes

While all individuals experience ambivalence, some individuals express stable patterns of ambivalence in their propensity to react to situations, such as the formation of intimate relationships (Ainsworth et al., 1978; Hazan and Shaver, 1987). Psychoanalysts, for example, note that while the source of ambivalence is often relationships (for example, parent–child), ambivalence can become internalized as a personality orientation. As Horney (1945: 46–7) suggests, personality and relationships are mutually reinforcing:

> It is not accidental that a conflict that starts with our relation to others in time affects the whole personality. Human relationships are so crucial that they are bound to mold the qualities we develop, the goals we set for ourselves, the values we believe in. All these, in turn, react upon our relationships with others and so are inextricably woven.

One way in which ambivalence becomes entrenched as an individual difference is through the formation of *ambivalent attitudes*. King and Emmons (1990), for example, offer evidence regarding the construct of ambivalence over *emotional expression*. Here, an individual has the propensity to have mixed feelings about expressing emotions. To illustrate, an individual may want to honestly express their emotions, but fear that such expression may cause them embarrassment or hurt.

More generally, Thompson and Zanna (1995) examine individual differences in ambivalent *social attitudes*. That is, they find that certain individuals are more likely to experience attitudinal ambivalence than others. Such attitudes combine ambivalent feelings, thoughts and behavioural choices. In describing attitudinal ambivalence, Thompson and Zanna (1995) explain:

We can all think of instances in which we have held different beliefs about the same issue, felt torn between two emotions or choices, or had our heart tell us one thing and our head another. The phenomenology of these attitudes is often quite distinct. With the positive and negative aspects seemingly equally significant concerns, our attitudes pull us in different directions. The result is often a highly polarized evaluation; an 'unstable dialectic' (Holmes & Rempel, 1989: 26) between positive and negative assessments. In short, we experience ambivalence. (p. 260)

Specifically, they note that individuals who tend towards attitudinal ambivalence tend to report lower 'Need for Cognition' and higher 'Personal Fear of Invalidity'.[6]

These individual differences in attitudinal ambivalence and ambivalence over emotional expression may be indicative of a generalized tendency to experience ambivalence and may carry over to relationships within and with organizations. To illustrate, the focus group methodology used to study the call centre workers made it evident that individuals disagreed about how to emotionally respond to work situations. These differences suggest that the experience of emotional ambivalence may be partially explained by individual differences. For example, the members of the focus group were discussing their mixed feelings in dealing with abusive customers when one employee said:

> You know, I don't understand. I don't get a lot of abusive customers. Yeah, they might be angry, but as long as you let them vomit it out (the employee makes a vomiting gesture), they don't get too abusive.

Thus, despite having the same types of customers, the aforementioned worker did not form ambivalent relationships with her customers.

Similarly, other workers also expressed some surprise and confusion regarding the emotional ambivalence expressed by other focus group members:

> See, I'm the complete opposite of [these other employees] . . . I enjoy the benefits of this place, the exposure to something new. My attitude or approach towards customers is not to yield [like these other employees who feel torn], but to be very nice.

Or, in response to a focus group discussion about the emotional ambivalence created when trying to be pleasant with abusive customers, one call centre worker distinguished herself from the others by stating:

> Regarding foul language, I will not let anyone talk to me that way. I say 'excuse me if you continue to curse I'll disconnect'. I don't care if I fail the call. I'm a person.

The call centre workers quoted above expressed fewer ambivalent feelings than other focus group members. This suggests that these call centre workers do indeed differ in their tendencies to experience emotional ambivalence. However, propensity to respond to situations with emotional ambivalence does not address the structural or environmental conditions that may trigger either an emotionally consistent or an emotionally ambivalent response.

Structural/environmental conditions

Sociologists have detailed several structural sources of ambivalence, and have even coined the term 'sociological ambivalence' to describe the study of ambivalence produced by normative contradictions embedded in a social structure (Coser, 1979; Merton and Barber, 1976). One common manifestation of these structural contradictions is *role conflicts*. Role conflicts can occur when the same role calls for conflicting behaviours (intra-role conflict), such as a manager of an empowered team who has to be both 'superior' and 'peer'; or when different roles put inconsistent demands on an individual (inter-role conflict), such as when you need to be at your children's soccer game *and* work late to attend a business meeting (Biddle, 1986; Katz and Kahn, 1978).

Inconsistent role demands were at the heart of many doctors' experiences of ambivalence. To illustrate, rural family care physicians who work in small practices need to be cognizant of their role as 'business person' and 'healer'. As one doctor described:

> When I started my practice, my teachers told me . . . 'Do a good job taking care of patients like you have in residency and the business will take care of itself.' You don't have to do anything with the business. And today it's exactly the opposite. You get up in the morning and the first thing you have to do is that you make sure that you have made the right business decision. Otherwise, you won't have a place to go to work during the day. You still have to take care of patients, but it has gotten to the point that if you don't actively take a role in making a decision about how your practice functions, then there is a significant risk that you won't have patients walking in the door because they will be directed some place else.

While embedded in their roles as doctors, being a member of a large health care organization often made the 'healer' versus 'business person' conflict even worse. As another physician opined:

> You may be in a position where you have to put your HMO [health maintenance organization] ahead of your patients, specifically financially where they may be asking you to limit care or putting you in a position where your financial well-being depends on how much you spend on your patient. We do have to watch the bottom line, but we should not be restricted unduly in determining what is best for the patient.

Still another noted:

> The only concern is that you hope [that in] no way you are affecting patient management because of concerns of the bottom line . . . the problem for the

physician is to decide what is efficient care versus what is proficient care. And reconciling the two can be a struggle.

Call centre workers also experience role conflicts with respect to meeting demands for both quality and productivity:

> I am here to provide customer service, not to please management (i.e. meet productivity statistics). So, that's what I do – I provide customer service. I tell them (management); 'Do you care if I provide customer service? You can't have it both ways.'

Even if not directly caused by role conflict, ambivalence can still be role-related. For example, call centre personnel may suffer from the emotional dissonance associated with *emotional labour* (see Morris and Feldman, 1996, for a comprehensive review). In studying the work of flight attendants, Hochschild (1983: 7) first proposed the concept of emotional labour and defined it as 'the management of feeling to create a publicly observable facial and body display'. She further explains that: 'This labor requires one to induce or suppress feeling in order to sustain the outward countenance that produces the proper state of mind in others.' Emotional labour is often required by service providers in their interactions with customers. Performing emotional labour can create emotional dissonance if the emotions *displayed* for the customer are different from the emotions *felt* by the service provider. Call centre personnel have to perform emotional labour. The most common type is masking unpleasant emotions and presenting a positive or at least calm face to the customer. To illustrate:

> It's hard to answer the phone when there is a customer who is screaming right from the start. It catches you off guard. You take offense. Then the customer says that they don't mean to vent on you. And you say 'I understand'. (The representative is gritting her teeth as a demonstration of holding back her anger.)

Similarly, another call centre worker noted how she suppressed her anger:

> You know, the natural, normal, human instinct is to lash back out when you're attacked. But, I [work to] stay calm [and make the customer happy].

Sometimes call centre personnel must perform emotional labour in the form of withholding pleasant emotions. As described below, often call centre workers experience pleasant feelings towards their customers and would like to have an extended social conversation with them. However, due to time constraints, they suppress these feelings and 'stick to business':

> Once I had this customer who had the same last name as me. I was weighing this in the back of my mind. We may be related. But, I didn't mention it. I just treated it like business.

Emotional labour may lead to emotional ambivalence in at least two ways. First, having to suppress positive feelings (such as attraction) may simultaneously evoke negative emotions (such as frustration). Second, the suppression of negative emotions (such as anger) may be a source of professional pride. In both these instances, emotional labour leads to the co-presence of positive and negative feelings.

More generally, sociological ambivalence can result from *societal changes* and increases in societal *complexity* (Weigert and Franks, 1989). Such changes may ultimately lead to role conflicts, but the very act of changing may be enough to spark ambivalence. For example, most of the physicians we interviewed noted the marked changes in practising medicine that had occurred in their lifetimes:

> There's a lot more interference from many organizations – government, insurance companies, and third party payers. Patients have changed. They want to know more about what's going on with their health care. Government determines what diagnoses physicians can and cannot treat, the appropriate time for treating diseases, and when you can and cannot see patients in the nursing homes.

Changes such as these made some physicians acutely aware that the 'golden age of medicine' was over. Instead of 'all-knowing' disseminators of health-related knowledge, they were now service providers who were questioned about their diagnoses. Moreover, instead of being their own bosses, they were now employees. These changes, however, also brought positive benefits such as potentially more meaningful interactions with patients as well as economic security. As such, these changes resulted in ambivalence.

Joining HealthCo also brought changes in how doctors were perceived by their peers. These changes, too, resulted in ambivalence. While physicians believed that they were 'doing the right thing' by joining a large health care organization, their colleagues saw them as 'having sold out our local community'. As one frustrated physician mentioned:

> a lot of people – even in the area where I practice – see what I am doing as sad because I have gone over to the other side of the enemy [by] cooperating with an integrated system, cooperating with a managed care plan and they see that as anti-patient, anti-profession . . . we face the friction and the antagonism of our cohort who still think we can maintain the status quo. [What drives me is] trying to balance that. Trying to convince them that they need to change [but] 'suffering the slings and arrows of their misfortune'.

Responses to ambivalence

Drawing on such diverse sources as psychoanalysis, developmental psychology, sociology and organizational behaviour, we suggest that there are two primary dimensions of responses to ambivalence: *attitude* and *movement*. From an attitudinal perspective, individuals can choose to emphasize the *positive aspects* of their relationships, the *negative aspects*, or *both simultaneously*. With respect to movement within the relationship, individuals can respond to emotional ambivalence by *approaching* the organization or organizational relationships, avoiding them, or doing *both simultaneously*. In the following section, we will describe combinations of attitudinal and movement responses identified in physicians and call centre workers including positive / approach, negative / approach, negative / avoidance, and mixed responses (vacillation and paralysis).

Positive / approach responses

Perhaps surprisingly, one of the most oft-discussed responses to ambivalent relationships is where individuals attempt to get closer to, and express positive emotions towards, the source of their ambivalence. To illustrate, sociologists Weigert and Franks (1989), building on the work of Merton (1957), suggest that one response to ambivalence is strong, even *fanatical commitment* whereby individuals accentuate the positive aspects of the ambivalent relationship:

> Merton suggested that the resolution of the pain of ambivalence between old and new ties felt by persons who change membership may explain why new recruits often become super members. Ambivalence leads to the amplification of commitment so that converts adhere to the new faith more strongly than born members (1957: 295) . . . Indeed we may hypothesize that conformity often results from an attempt to resolve ambivalence.

In this way, commitment becomes a source of coping with the ambivalence. As Pirsig (1974: 134) suggests, fanatical commitment helps one to resolve one's doubt:

> You are never dedicated to something you have complete confidence in. No one is fanatically shouting that the sun is going to rise tomorrow. They *know* it is going to rise tomorrow. When people are fanatically dedicated to political or religious faiths or any other kinds of dogmas or goals, it's always because those dogmas or goals are in doubt. (original emphasis)

Building on this logic, social psychologist Brickman (1987: 15) even goes as far as to assert: 'commitments are about ambivalence'.

Brickman explains the psychology behind the transformation of ambivalence to commitment in his conceptualization of the commitment process. To him, commitment is the 'binding' of the positive and negative elements inherent in a relationship or situation. That is, commitment allows individuals to resolve dissonances or tensions by emphasizing the positive (positive / approach) or negative (see negative / approach below) aspects of their relationships or situations (Pratt, 1994). Thus, he argues that even highly ambivalent people can express enthusiasm towards their relationships by emphasizing the positive aspects of their ambivalent relationships. This emphasis of one aspect of the ambivalence allows the individual to cope with the conflicting emotions that he or she feels.[7]

In a related vein, psychoanalyst Horney (1945) – who discusses extreme forms of ambivalence – suggests a similar positive / approach coping response. In her work on neuroses or inner conflicts, she suggests that individuals may respond to ambivalence by *moving towards* others. This response orientation, like that suggested by Weigert and Franks (1989), is manifested as compliance and by a strong need to affiliate with others. However, for Horney (1945: 42), the ultimate goal of 'moving towards' others is to feel safe:

> When moving *toward* people he accepts his own helplessness, and in spite of his estrangement and fears tries to win the affection of others and to lean on them. . . . he will attach himself to the most powerful person in the group. By complying with them, he gains a sense of belonging and support which makes him feel less weak and less isolated. (original emphasis)

Extrapolating from these theorists, we suggest that some individuals who both love and hate their organizations may express this ambivalence by expressing a positive / approach orientation towards their organization, or towards particular people (such as powerful people) in the organization. In the case of the rural doctors, some ambivalent physicians exhibited this orientation. To illustrate, one physician who feared that HealthCo was heading towards ' a system where the bottom line is important . . . [and] there is a risk that the physician will do less because of the reimbursement scheme', nonetheless idealized his relationship with the parent organization:

> *I don't see any down side* [to the relationship with the organization] *at all. I have no complaints at all about what is going on*. . . . I see us as being a team. . . . We have similar goals in providing good primary care to people and being sure that they are integrated into the health care system when they need referrals to specialists. . . . I think I will practice [here] until I am able to retire. And then in the last few years, engage in some administrative type jobs [with the parent company]. (emphasis ours)

Thus, despite expressing apprehension over where the organization was going, this physician not only had no complaints about HealthCo, but he also planned to continue to be involved with this organization as a doctor, and ultimately as an administrator. Thus, his orientation towards the organization was both positive and approaching.

Negative / approach responses

A second type of response to ambivalence is the negative / approach response. Here, individuals accentuate the negative aspects of their relationships, but not to such a degree that it causes them to leave the relationship. Rather, they attempt to retain the attachment, but react to the attachment with negative emotions such as anger, frustration or rage.

Psychoanalytically, this response type would be similar to *moving against* the target of one's ambivalence by attacking, being aggressive and feeling angry (Horney, 1945). Examples of extreme 'moving against' reactions would be *revolutions, sabotage, workplace aggression* or other *violent acts* that undermine the relationship (Martinko and Zellars, 1998; Neuman and Baron, 1998).

A less extreme form of 'moving against' where more of the positive aspects of the relationship are maintained would be responding with *voice*. According to Hirschman (1970: 30), voice involves 'any attempts to change, rather than to escape from, an objectionable state of affairs'. Thus one exhibits a negative orientation towards an organization by criticizing the status quo, while also choosing to remain attached, and thereby approach the organization. This type of response is the one predominantly used by Meyerson and Scully's (1995) 'tempered radicals' who espouse ideologies that are in conflict with their organizations (such as a feminist in a paternalistic Fortune 500 company). Being neither true insiders nor complete outsiders, these individuals work as 'outsiders within'. While not calling for revolutionary change, these workers *are* angry at their organizations but are motivated to work with organizational members to produce change.

Similar to voice, the use of *derogatory comments*, or even *humour* at the expense of the target of one's ambivalence, may also serve as a less extreme form of negative / approach response (cf. Coser, 1979[8]; Katz et al., 1973). This type of response is common in service organizations, especially those that cater to 'difficult' clientele (such as the mentally ill, socially disadvantaged people, prisoners). For example, Coser (1979) shows in great detail how psychiatric residents respond to ambivalence towards their clients by discounting their importance and referring to them as 'sick'. Similarly, in Pratt and Dutton's (2000) study of how librarians dealt with the presence of homeless patrons in their library, they found that some librarians dealt with their ambivalent attitudes towards these patrons by referring to them as 'bums'. We view these as approach responses because they are confrontational towards the organization or its constituents.[9]

Illustrations of these milder forms of negative / approach responses (such as derogatory comments and humour) were evidenced in our cases. Here, members expressed their anger and frustration with the organization by voicing resentments or otherwise acting out. Some physicians responded to their new employment situation with anger, and by going against the wishes of their new parent company. For example, one expressed resentment when his new 'bosses' decided that he should spend less time with his patients:

> They [HealthCo representatives] bring out the production numbers – 'this is what you're making, what I should make, and so forth.' [I then snap at them and say] 'yeah, but I don't want to make that much.' I want to take my time with my patients.

Still another remarked how the company was 'getting greedy' by raising patient fees and how he resonated with the anger of a patient who told him:

'You bastards need some competition!'

Call centre workers expressed (and acted out) their resentment of the lack of support from supervisors, especially when dealing with complex problems or difficult customers.

> Sometimes I press assist 'out of spite'. I don't expect help, but I press it anyways [to annoy my supervisor].

They also express revolutionary thoughts regarding employee–management relations. As one worker noted, 'My dream is a union'.

Call centre workers also use derogatory humour to deal with their ambivalence. Customers are often the targets of this humour, as the following three excerpts illustrate:

> I have a child with a disability. I just figured out that it helps me to treat every customer like they have a disability – 'Oh yeah, you're the one with the rude disability'. And 'you're the one with that disability where you can't balance your checkbook'. [This gets laughs from the other representatives present]

> [There are customers] at the ATM who think you are inside it – tapping on the machine – 'are you in there?' [Then, another rep says] Yeah, I had this woman call to complain that there is no deposit envelopes at the ATM – what did she think I could do, right then? I felt like saying, 'move over, here I come out the hole.' [Many of the focus group participants laugh . . . then another representative says] Yeah, I had this guy at the ATM who hadn't gotten his money. He's saying to me 'look, look, I have no money. Can you see me, I'm the guy waving – with the red hat.' He thinks I can see him through the security camera. [Everyone laughs]

> The customer tells you that 'all you are is a programmed paper pusher' [because you read this scripted information or because you quote policy], and your response is 'I am not a robot. If you say that again I will be forced to disconnect.' [The representative says this in a mechanical tone of voice and the rest of the representatives laugh]

The organization is also a target for derogatory humour:

> This system is designed to crack people. It's just like the military in a communist country. I am just waiting for the day that they start patrolling the center with machine guns. [The other representatives laugh]

Negative / avoidance responses

Individuals may also react to ambivalent relationships by detaching themselves from that relationship. In psychoanalytic terms, this would be akin to *moving away*, where individuals isolate themselves out of a need to establish 'emotional distance between themselves and others' (Horney, 1945: 75). Thus, unlike negative / approach responses, individuals who engage in negative / avoidance responses still retain negative feelings towards the organization, but respond to these negative feelings by physically or psychologically distancing themselves from the relationship rather than engaging in confrontational behaviours.

In the organizational literature, negative / avoidance responses can be expressed as psychological *escapist* behaviours, such as playing computer games while at work. Here, individuals respond to ambivalence by ignoring, avoiding, or otherwise engaging in behaviours that buffer the individual from the ambivalent relationship. Psychological negative / avoidance responses would also include what Coser (1979) refers to as *denial* or *evasion* of ambivalence whereby individuals refuse to acknowledge that ambivalence exists; as well as the notion of *neglect* (Farrell, 1983) whereby individuals respond to ambivalence by showing up late, missing work and so on.

There were some examples of escapist behaviours in the call centre. The following excerpts illustrate how some of these workers psychologically distance themselves from angry customers:

> While customers are venting [I suggest] distract yourself – file your nails.

> [When a customer starts venting at me] I try to figure out what's for lunch.

Call centre workers also describe the escapist behaviours used by other representatives:

> I hate it when you got this rep next to you baring her soul to the customer – talking about her divorce, her husband's drinking, the kids – it's not fair that I'm doing all this work, while she's goofing off [avoiding taking more calls].

> It's bad when you have reps that don't care – leave customers on hold while they're taking lunch orders.

At a more extreme level, these responses may result in *turnover* or *exit* from the organization (Hirschman, 1970). In our cases, everyone we interviewed was currently employed by the organization, thus none had yet exhibited exiting behaviours. Moreover, given that many of the physicians that we talked to had either founded or had worked several years to build up their practices, it was unlikely that they would have chosen this strategy. Many call centre workers, however, did have plans to exit the organization as soon as possible. Call centres are typically plagued with high turnover, and this particular centre consistently struggled to retain workers.

Positive and negative / approach and avoidance response: vacillation

Some individuals exhibit 'mixed' responses: they choose to alternately emphasize the positive and negative aspects of their relationships, and to alternately approach and avoid the targets of these relationships. The end result is vacillating behaviours that occur as members attempt to satisfy their conflicting orientations towards a target (Coser, 1979; Merton, 1976). To illustrate, Pratt and Dutton (2000) found that some librarians who felt ambivalence towards homeless patrons would alternate among engaging in behaviours *towards* them (for example, calling social service organizations), *against* them (for example, calling the police), or *away* from them (for example, ignoring them).

According to some psychoanalysts, vacillation may occur if individuals engage in the defence mechanism known as *splitting* (Sincoff, 1990). Splitting is often achieved by splitting *the targets* of their ambivalence so that the positive aspects of the relationship gets associated with one individual or object, and the negative aspects of the relationship get associated with another individual or object. Children, for example, resolve ambivalence with their parents by seeing one parent as 'good' and the other as 'bad'. In our data, three types of splitting were evident: temporal splitting, current versus ideal relationship splitting, and the construction of 'trade-offs'.

First, individuals responded to ambivalence via *temporal splitting*, whereby they like the target of their ambivalence at some points in time but not at others. Here, the individual can alternate between love and hate by viewing the relational target totally positively today, but totally negatively tomorrow. This type of splitting was evident among the rural doctors. Many doctors expressed positive emotions when discussing their current relationship with HealthCo. However, when viewing the future direction of HealthCo, they expressed anxiety and even anger. Thus, they shunted their negative feelings towards HealthCo into the future.

To illustrate, one physician talked about being free to make decisions about patient care, but then noted with apprehension that 'this could change in the future'. Similarly, another mentioned that he appreciated the protection offered by HealthCo, but did not like HMOs. When asked about the future of HealthCo, though, he noted that: 'I can see them trying to corral all of the physicians into the surrounding counties. They will eventually put together a large, integrated HMO-like system.' And still another otherwise satisfied physician complained about the threat of capitation, where health care organizations get a set fee to provide for all of the healthcare needs of a patient for an entire year:

> If you have a fee for service, you may have them come back every three months. If you have capitation, you may have them come back once a year . . . with capitation, there is the strong temptation or incentive to do less – to see people less often.

When asked if HealthCo will capitate, he said: 'It's just a matter of time before it happens to us.'

In addition to temporal splitting, physicians exhibited another type of splitting: *they split their ambivalence between current and ideal relationships*. That is, they talked positively about their current relationships with

HealthCo, but noted the negative aspects of their relationships by talking about how things would be different in an 'ideal world'. Thus, while not directly complaining about their relationship with HealthCo, they offer windows on their frustrations by saying how things 'should be different'. To illustrate:

> In an ideal world, all health care providers [like doctors] will be cost effective and knowledgeable and therefore not need input from a company telling them how to be more efficient. . . . the company wouldn't expect the doctor to have a lot of paper work, a lot of bureaucratic responsibilities, [and] wouldn't question him, for example, if he ordered an extra test if they knew the doctor was already cost effective. And they would have fair compensation [for doctors].

A third way that individuals split their ambivalence was by construing the ambivalent relationship as consisting of *trade-offs*. As suggested by our earlier discussions of the rural physicians, these doctors were able to deal with ambivalence by conceptualizing the positive and negative aspects of their relationship with HealthCo as a trade-off between economic security and professional freedom.[10] On the one hand, physicians felt positive affection towards their parent company because they offer them protection from an ever-increasingly competitive market place:

> As we looked to our future, it was easy for us to see that just because you worked hard and patients liked what you did . . . you could lose that if you got on the wrong side of some of the big insurance contracts. And we felt it was important for us to partner with somebody who could protect us from the marketplace.

However, it was clear to physicians that such protection came with a steep 'price tag':

> The worst [thing about our relationship] is the loss of autonomy. I think that they [people in the large health care organization] are certainly responsive to requests that physicians may have, but you do realize that someone else is running the show – that they ultimately make the decisions. And even though they try to be responsive to your needs, you don't have that final say.

Call centre workers also conceptualized their job as a series of trade-offs. Some saw a trade-off in having to endure an unsatisfying job in order to get work benefits. Some of these benefits were tangible:

> I only work here for the benefits. I am going to school too – getting ready for another career.

> I stay for the benefits. If my wife had benefits, I'd be out of here. But, now I am going to grad school and starting my own business. I will be going part-time. Then, I'll be happy.

Other benefits were intangible:

I'm taking voice lessons and my teacher tells me I have incredible range. I am convinced it is from working here. My teacher says that people work years to develop that sort of range. I can feel those muscles at work while I'm on the phone. You have to get something out of this.

Customer service is a tough job, but I love people. I even love working with difficult people. I love to develop my interpersonal skills – not just for [the bank], but for myself personally. I try things out on people and take notes in my personal notebook – what worked, what didn't, what I did and how someone reacted.

All of these forms of splitting serve to compartmentalize the sources of ambivalence. The result is that the good and bad aspects of a single relationship become separated and individuals subsequently engage in both approaching and avoiding behaviours in the context of that relationship (that is, vacillate).

Paralysis

Psychoanalysts note that ambivalent individuals often suffer from extreme *indecision* (Sincoff, 1990). Thus, a final response to ambivalence is *paralysis* or the inability to act (Weigert and Franks, 1989) or form a strong opinion. Individuals who become paralysed emphasize neither the positive nor negative aspects of their relationships, nor can they decide whether to approach or avoid the targets of these relationships. Therefore, unlike other responses, paralysis is a non-response or perhaps a 'pre-response' to action that occurs when individuals do not or cannot resolve ambivalence. According to Weigert and Franks (1989), 'Ambivalence must be resolved for action to occur.' Thus, paralysis may precede the other responses.

We did not find evidence of this response in our cases. However, this may have been due to the fact that interviewing makes demands for action (that is, responses to questions), and thus individuals may have been 'forced' to respond to the ambivalence in their work relationships. In addition, not acting is likely to be an impractical long-term option for people in work organizations. For example, call centre workers who are so paralysed in their relationships with clients that they cannot pick up the phone would quickly get fired. Thus, paralysis could lead to termination.

Summary and conclusions

We do not contest that there are individuals who experience primarily negative feelings in their organizational relationships (such as, alienation). Moreover, we do not deny that some may feel mostly positive feelings in this regard (such as joy or pride). Between these two extremes, however, is a more complicated – and perhaps more accurate – view of how some view their workplace relationships.

Our goal in writing this chapter was to make our readers think about the multiple and conflicting emotions that often accompany relationships both with and within organizations. Specifically, we have drawn upon existing theory to delineate the concept of ambivalence, and to map out some of the sources of and responses to this ambivalence. We also drew upon our experiences with bank call centre workers and rural physicians to illustrate our arguments, and to extend these arguments in places (for example, the different types of 'splitting'). Ironically, given the topic we discuss, we end our discussion with some ambivalence: while we are pleased with the goals we achieved, we are also made aware of how much we have left unexplored.

To illustrate, while we have talked about how individuals respond to ambivalence, we did not talk about the impact of this ambivalence on the mental and physical health of workers. Research suggests that there are human costs to emotional ambivalence, such as employee distress (King and Emmons, 1990) and high employee burnout (Maslach and Jackson, 1985). However, other research directly or indirectly suggests ambivalence – or the conditions that lead to ambivalence – may also bring positive benefits. Hirschhorn (1988), for example, argues that the increased complexity in the workplace provides an opportunity for workers to learn to face the inherent uncertainties of life and to deal constructively with both the pleasant and unpleasant aspects of work (and life). Similarly, researchers have found that individuals with multiple roles and identities – and thus with higher potentials for experiencing ambivalence – are more likely to be able to respond flexibly and more effectively in complex environments (cf. Sieber, 1974; Pratt and Foreman, 2000). Thus, future research should examine the conditions whereby ambivalence may be a help or a hindrance to the health of workers' minds and bodies.

Similarly, subsequent research should explore whether certain types of organizations might be more likely to spawn ambivalent relationships than others. Both of our examples draw upon service organizations.[11] Given the high potential for ambivalence in interpersonal relationships, service organizations may be seedbeds for conflicting emotions. By extrapolation, individuals in any organization with boundary-spanning roles may be potentially 'at risk' from experiencing workplace ambivalence.

Exploring these and other questions is likely to trigger still others. To illustrate, are certain individuals better equipped to constructively handle (that is, maintain mental and physical health during) ambivalent relationships? Do certain organizational characteristics encourage more constructive approaches? Alternatively, are certain responses (such as negative / avoidance versus splitting) more constructive in some organizations or in some status positions than others? For example, low status workers may use more types of escapist behaviours than high status workers, who in turn may use more types of splitting behaviour. Finally, what other sources and responses are there to ambivalence that we have not mentioned? Are there, for example, such things as positive / avoidance responses?

To close, these questions suggest that significant work remains to be done in exploring ambivalence. Contrary to much extant research, workplace ties need not be viewed as simply positive or negative. Rather, they often involve combinations of strong and conflicting emotions. This ambivalence, we argue, is a fundamental property of many relationships with and within organizations.

Acknowledgements

We thank Etty Jehn and Elizabeth Scott for their comments on an earlier draft of this chapter. We also appreciate the assistance of Peter Foreman and Shankar Nair who transcribed the interviews of the rural physicians mentioned herein. Moreover, we wish to acknowledge the financial support of the Wharton Financial Institutions Center and an anonymous retail bank in conducting research on the call centre workers.

Notes

1 'HealthCo' is a pseudonym for the large health care organization.

2 The two cases also illustrate how workers of different status levels can experience ambivalence. Physicians are often seen as high status. Call centre workers, by contrast, are of lower status.

3 While we focus on emotional ambivalence, we realize that the experience of ambivalence often intertwines feeling, thinking and doing (see Pratt and Barnett, 1997). Hence, Bleuler differentiated among three types of psychological ambivalence: (a) 'voluntary' / behavioural ambivalence, which involves conflicts over how to act in order to fulfil one's wishes; (b) 'intellectual' / cognitive ambivalence, which involves holding contradictory ideas; and (c) 'emotional' / affective ambivalence, which involves holding conflicting emotions, such as love and hate towards someone or something (see Freud, 1950/1920; Merton and Barber, 1976; Sincoff, 1990).

4 Although semi-structured interviews (Spradley, 1979) with physicians at four clinics were the main source of data used in this chapter (n = 16), the first author also interviewed the two company liaisons that HealthCo assigned to the physicians' clinics. In addition, he gathered archival data and engaged in unobtrusive observations of the clinics. Data analysis for both of our cases was done in a similar fashion. Following the iterative process recommended by Strauss and Corbin (1990) and Miles and Huberman (1984), we travelled back and forth between the data and an emerging structure of theoretical arguments. To begin, we initially scanned the data for dominant themes. This preliminary form of data analysis occurred concurrently with data collection. As themes began to emerge in the data, they were noted and continually compared against new, incoming data. We then organized the themes in light of existing theory. After developing, exploring and evaluating several combinations of theory and data, we arrived at a framework (for example, sources and responses to ambivalence) that we

believed contributed to theory without doing undue 'violence' to our experiences. That is, while it was important that our framework added to the understanding of organizational behaviour, we did not want it to unduly distort the actual experiences of the physicians and call centre workers.

5 Meijers is often referred to as a 'superstore' in the United States as it combines a grocery store with an automotive store, a hardware store, a clothing store, and so on. It attempts to provide 'one stop shopping'.

6 *Need for Cognition* refers to a propensity to 'engage in and enjoy effortful cognitive behaviors' (Cacioppo et al., 1986: 1033). *Personal Fear of Invalidity* is a 'concern with error or the consequences of a decision' (Thompson and Zanna, 1995: 265).

7 A less extreme, but similar form of positive / approach reactions would be notion of *loyalty* in Hirschman's (1970) typology. Here individuals respond to some dissatisfaction in their personal or organizational relationships by *passively* waiting and hoping that things will get better. Thus, loyalty does not involve extremely committed actions, nor strong 'moving towards' ones; rather, loyalists stick by their organization and take a 'wait and see' approach. Although Hirschman's concept of loyalty relates to a broader range of relationship dis- satisfactions than those stemming directly from ambivalence, Smelser (1998: 12) suggests that it may be viewed as a reasonable reaction to ambivalence as an individual 'represses the negative side of ambivalence and accentuates the positive'.

8 Coser (1979: 106) actually discusses the use of humour as a type of denying or avoidance technique. However, he also admits that humour has an 'implicit or explicit aggressive content' to it. Moreover, the use of humour in this way keeps the relationship central in the mind of the joker, unlike other avoidance techniques (such as watching television) which serves to put the ambivalent relationship outside of one's conscious awareness. Thus, we feel that humour is more of an attacking response than it is an avoiding response.

9 Jokes not directed at the organization – ones that are only used as a means of diversion – would be considered avoidant rather than approach responses.

10 Such a trade-off is not dissimilar to the one experienced by children in their relationships with their parents, which according to psychoanalysts is a primary source of ambivalent attachments.

11 The organizations we studied were also highly bureaucratic. There may also be a relationship between level of bureaucracy and the experience of ambivalence.

References

Ainsworth, M.D.S., Blehar, M.C., Waters, E. and Wall, S. (1978) *Patterns of Attachment: A Psychological Study of the Strange Situation*. Hillsdale, NJ: Erlbaum.

Ashforth, B. and Mael, F. (1998) 'The power of resistance: sustaining valued identities', in R. M. Kramer and M.A. Neale (eds), *Power and Influence in Organizations*. Thousand Oaks, CA: Sage. pp. 89–119.

Biddle, B.J. (1986) 'Recent developments in role theory', *Annual Review of Sociology*, 12: 67–92.

Boehm, C. (1989) 'Ambivalence and compromise in human nature', *American Anthropologist*, 91: 921–39.

Bowlby, J. (1982) *Attachment and Loss*, 2nd edn. London, Hogarth Press / Institute of Psycho- Analysis.

Brickman, P. (1987) 'Commitment', in C.B. Wortman and R. Sorrentino (eds), *Commitment, Conflict, and Caring*. Englewood Cliffs, NJ: Prentice Hall. pp. 1–18.

Butterfield, S. (1985) *Amway: The Cult of Free Enterprise*. Boston, MA: Southfield Press.

Cacioppo, J.T., Petty, R.E., Kao, C.F. and Rodriguez, R. (1986) 'Central and peripheral routes to persuasion: an individual difference perspective', *Journal of Personality and Social Psychology*, 51 (5): 1032–43.

Cassidy, J. and Berlin, L.J. (1994) 'The insecure / ambivalent pattern of attachments: theory and research', *Child Development*, 65: 971–91.

Coser, R.L. (1979) *Training in Ambivalence: Learning through Doing in a Mental Hospital*. New York: Free Press.

Dukerich, J., Kramer, R. and Parks, J.M. (1998) 'The dark side of organizational identification', in D. Whetten and P. Godfrey (eds), *Identity in Organizations: Developing Theory through Conversations*. Thousand Oaks, CA: Sage. pp. 245–56.

Erikson, K. (1986) 'On work and alienation', *American Sociological Review*, 51 (1): 1–8.

Farrell, D. (1983) 'Exit, voice, loyalty, and neglect as responses to job satisfaction: a multidimensional scaling study', *Academy of Management Journal*, 26: 596–607.

Freud, S. (1950/1920) *Beyond the Pleasure Principle*. London: W.W. Norton.

Hazan, C. and Shaver, P. (1987) 'Romantic love conceptualized as an attachment process', *Journal of Personality and Social Psychology*, 52: 511–24.

Hirschhorn, L. (1988) *The Workplace Within: Psychodynamics of Organizational Life*. Cambridge, MA: MIT Press.

Hirschman, A.O. (1970) *Exit, Voice and Loyalty*. Cambridge, MA: Harvard University Press.

Hochschild, A.R. (1983) *The Managed Heart: Commercialization of Human Feeling*. Berkeley: University of California Press.

Holmes, J.G. and Rempel, J.K. (1989) 'Trust in close relationships', in C. Hendrick (ed.), *Review of Personality and Social Psychology: Close Relationships*, Vol. 10. Beverly Hills: Sage. pp. 187–220.

Horney, K. (1945) *Our Inner Conflicts: A Constructive Theory of Neurosis*. New York, W.W. Norton.

Katz, D. and Kahn, R.L. (1978) *The Social Psychology of Organizations*, 2nd edn. New York: John Wiley.

Katz, I., Glass, D.C. and Cohen, S. (1973) 'Ambivalence, guilt, and the scapegoating of minority group victims', *Journal of Experimental Social Psychology*, 9: 423–36.

King, L.A. and Emmons, R.A. (1990) 'Conflict over emotional expression: psychological and physical correlates', *Journal of Personality and Social Psychology*, 58 (5): 864–77.

Kristoff, A. (1996) 'Person–organization fit: an integrative review of its conceptualizations, measurement, and implications', *Personnel Psychology*, 49: 1–49.

Kunda, G. (1992) *Engineering Culture: Control and Commitment in a High-tech Corporation*. Philadelphia: Temple University Press.

Martinko, M. and Zellars, K. (1998) 'Toward a theory of workplace violence and aggression: a cognitive appraisal perspective', in R. Griffin, A. O'Leary-Kelly and J. Collins (eds), *Dysfunctional Behavior in Organizations: Violent and Deviant Behavior*. Stamford, CT: JAI Press.

Maslach, C. and Jackson, S.E. (1985) 'The role of sex and family variables in burnout', *Sex Roles*, 12: 837–51.

Merton, R.K. (1957) *Social Theory and Social Structure*. New York: The Free Press.

Merton, R.K. (1976) *Sociological Ambivalence and Other Essays*. New York: The Free Press.

Merton, R.K. and Barber, E. (1976) 'Sociological ambivalence', in R.K. Merton (ed.), *Sociological Ambivalence and Other Essays*. New York: The Free Press. pp. 3–31.

Meyer, J.P. and Allen, N.J. (1997) *Commitment in the Workplace: Theory, Research and Application*. Thousand Oaks, CA: Sage.

Meyerson, D. and Scully, M. (1995) 'Tempered radicalism and the politics of ambivalence and change', *Organizational Science*, 6 (5): 585–600.

Mikulincer, M. (1998) 'Adult attachment style and affect regulation: strategic variations in self-appraisals', *Journal of Personality and Social Psychology*, 75 (2): 420–35.

Miles, M.B. and Huberman, A.M. (1984) *Qualitative Data Analysis*. Beverly Hills, CA: Sage.

Morris, J.A. and Feldman, D.C. (1996) 'The dimensions, antecedents, and consequences of emotional labor', *Academy of Management Review*, October: 986–1010.

Neuman, J. and Baron, R. (1998) 'Workplace violence and workplace aggression: evidence concerning specific forms, potential causes, and preferred targets', *Journal of Management*, 24 (3): 391–419.

Pirsig, R. (1974) *Zen and the Art of Motorcycle Maintenance: An Inquiry into Values*. New York: Bantam Books.

Pratt, M.G. (1994) 'The happiest, most dissatisfied people on earth: ambivalence and commitment among Amway distributors'. PhD dissertation, University of Michigan, Ann Arbor (University Microfilms).

Pratt, M.G. (1996) 'Creating commitment the AM(bivalence) way'. Paper presented at Carnegie Melon University (April; Pittsburgh, PA).

Pratt, M.G. (1998) 'To be or not to be: central questions in organizational identification', in D. Whetten and P. Godfrey (eds), *Identity in Organizations: Developing Theory through Conversations*. Sage. pp. 171–207.

Pratt, M.G. and Barnett, C.K. (1997) 'Emotions and unlearning in Amway recruiting techniques: promoting change through "safe" ambivalence', *Management Learning*, 28 (1): 65–88.

Pratt, M.G. and Dutton, J.E. (2000) 'Owning up or opting out: the role of emotions and identities in issue ownership', to appear in N. Ashkanasy, C. Hartel and W. Zerbe (eds), *Emotions in Organizational Life*. Quorum Books. pp. 103–29.

Pratt, M.G. and Foreman, P.O. (2000) 'Classifying managerial responses to multiple organizational identities', *Academy Management Review*, 25(1): 18–42.

Pratt, M.G. and Rafaeli, A. (2000) Symbols as a language of organizational relationships. Working paper.

Sieber, S.D. (1974) 'Toward a theory of role accumulation', *American Sociological Review*, 39: 567–78.

Sincoff, J. (1990) 'The psychological characteristics of ambivalent people', *Clinical Psychology Review*, 10: 43–68.

Smelser, N.J. (1998) 'The rational and the ambivalent in the social sciences', 1997 Presidential Address, *American Sociological Review*, 63 (February): 1–16.

Spradley, J. (1979) *The Ethnographic Interview*. New York: Holt, Rinehart and Winston.

Strauss, A. and Corbin, J. (1990) *Basics of Qualitative Research: Grounded Theory Procedures and Techniques*. Newbury Park, CA: Sage.

Thompson, M.M. and Zanna, M.P. (1995) 'The conflicted individual: personality-based and domain-specific antecedents of ambivalent social attitudes', *Journal of Personality*, 63 (2): 259–88.

Weigert, A. and Franks, D. (1989) 'Ambivalence: a touchstone of the modern temper', in D. Frank and E. McCarthy (eds), *The Sociology of Emotions: Original Essays and Research Papers*. Greenwich, CT: JAI Press. 205–27.

12 A DETECTIVE'S LOT: CONTOURS OF MORALITY AND EMOTION IN POLICE WORK

ROBERT JACKALL

Big-city police detectives work in several tangled worlds, each marked by its own peculiar rationality and morality. Their work provides them with a front-row seat ticket to private lives in turmoil and to gear-grinding institutional gridlock on whose order should prevail. As criminal investigators who unravel deeds already done, they roam the fastness of the streets, a world of masked identities, cloaked agency, relationships governed by particularistic norms, binding codes of honour, and, frequently, remarkable violence. All the while they labour in the interstices of the instrumentally rational, thoroughly bureaucratized milieux of their own semi-military police organizations and of procedure-driven district-attorney offices and courts, working to transform street knowledge into convincing proof that fixes responsibility for crime. As police officers, they stand as lightning rods in American society's endless authority-and-its-uses maelstroms. Their work shapes distinctive experiences, feelings, habits of mind, occupational self-images and moral rules-in-use. The moral ambiguity of their work sets them against the pieties of mainstream society; the dangers of their work, including the risks to their selves, bind them to one another. This chapter surveys this terrain.

Organizational incentives and emotional meanings

In the course of a typical four-day tour during 1991–1993, a 34th precinct squad detective of the New York City Police Department in the upper reaches of Manhattan might 'catch' two aggravated gun assaults, an armed extortion of a bodega owner balking at his creditor-controlled installation of illegal slot-machines in his store, a complaint about a knife-wielding derelict, a flim-flam operation connected to the Dominican lottery, a DOA (that is, dead on the detective's arrival), and a drug-related homicide.[1] Although initially reported to the squad, rapes, drug-possession and sales violations, and even robberies and burglaries, were all given to specialized units either at the precinct or in other organizational wings of the department. Each of the fifteen 'catching' detectives in the squad, organized in three teams of five, received about 300 criminal 'complaints' each year. Precinct squads are thus the principal, though not the only, institutional reception point for the fodder of the city's criminal justice system. Of such complaints, each detective 'took' between 200–250 'cases' each year; that is, he or she decided to investigate those complaints; six other detectives, all senior in rank, aided their junior colleagues.[2]

Cases are, first and foremost, bureaucratic entities. Each is reviewed by bosses several times at different intervals, first by detective sergeants and then by detective lieutenants. Each case must be 'closed' bureaucratically, though only those that are 'cleared' by arrest or by 'exceptional clearance' (the police have enough to arrest but, for reasons beyond the detective's control, such as the culprit's death, the arrest cannot be effected) count as 'hits' in the detective's 'batting average'. All other cases count as 'outs', with the occasional exception of those determined to be inappropriately assigned to the squad, which, as 'walks', do not count in one's overall average. A detective's batting average is one, though only one, important ingredient in promotion reviews in the steep hierarchy of detectives to move from third-grade to second-grade rank; first-grade rank depends, in most cases, on extraordinary success in celebrated cases.[3] Once caught, a case 'belongs' to a detective until it is resolved, thus producing at least formal investigative continuity, sometimes over long periods of time, and the 'chain of custody' of whatever evidence is obtained in an investigation. The unintended consequence of the catching system is a fragmentation of knowledge about squad cases and, among some squad detectives, an accompanying bailiwick mentality.

Bureaucratic incentives thus frame and ensure detectives' attention to their cases if, by chance, dedication to duty wavers or if detectives do not respond to the premium that their peers put on persistence (the highest occupational accolade is when one detective says of another: 'I wouldn't want that guy after me'). But, even for the most premium-responsive or duty-conscious, the emotional meaning of work for detectives depends on the construction of the moral status of victims. Suicides, numerous in the 34th precinct since men and women drive halfway across the country in order to jump off the George Washington Bridge, are regarded with a scorn ('What degree of difficulty was the dive?') that those who work with death reserve for those who throw away life, and the emotionally painful work of informing next-of-kin that suicide brings is resented. Homicides afford finer distinctions. Detectives shed few tears over a known robber's or drug-dealer's death because they see sudden demise as a warrior's fate in violence-ridden trades. They take grim satisfaction in these 'public service homicides' as 'street justice' that is far more uncompromising than the justice meted out by the legal system. For instance, one day in spring 1993, the 34th squad received a 'squawk' about a shooting at a bank; the victim was 'likely', that is, likely to die (he survived), and the shooter was in hand. But when the squad arrived at the scene, the uniformed police officers were cracking jokes and laughing loudly, while standing over the still bleeding, comatose body of the 'victim' in the company of the 'shooter' who was not in custody. The shooter presented the detectives with his gun and his carry-permit and explained that he had been going to the bank to make large cash deposits on behalf of local businesses when the victim tried to rob him at gunpoint, only to be shot himself. The victim turned out to be a career robber, wanted for several similar heists. The detectives took the shooter back to the station house to record his statement and then, in a mock ceremony, presented him with a trophy for good citizenship. But the sense of Old Testament meetness that attaches to such cases, indeed to most 'uptown murders' (cases where the victims, culprits and uncooperative witnesses are all criminals), is usually outweighed by the drudgery of cleaning up other people's messes.

Detectives almost always become quite emotionally involved in cases with an 'innocent' victim, one murdered through no fault of his or her own. Thus a stray bullet from a drive-by drug-related gang war kills a 'civilian' and provokes detectives' indignant wrath; urban marauders' wanton murder-for-sport of a college boy on a city highway fuels exhaustive investigative efforts; a boyfriend's child-battering-murder of a noisy baby afflicted with colic provokes icy rage against him and the mother who, out to 'cop' (buy) marijuana during the event, nonetheless went out again to get beer before calling the ambulance; the still unsolved murder of a to-this-day unidentified four-year-old girl, sexually violated, stuffed into a picnic cooler, and abandoned at a construction site in a sizzling July, triggers the deepest paternal grief and the squad's formal adoption and burial of the child, christened 'Baby Hope' by the men; and the murder of a brother officer in uniform while interrupting a drug-house robbery prompts fierce rage that spurs an international manhunt and a lingering sadness that lasts for more than a decade. Detectives make even career criminals into honorary innocent victims if they have died a particularly cruel or vicious death. A drug-dealer tortured to reveal the location of drugs or money before being executed, or a prostitute raped before being killed, invariably prompts detectives to say: 'No one deserves to die like that'. Innocent victims, whether real or honorary, allow detectives to assert publicly their most valued self-image: defender of the innocent and avenger of the social order. As it happens, such idealistic expressions are quite rare. For the most part, detectives talk about the Job.

Talking about the Job

The Job, first, is to contain the forces of disorder. This requires mastery of criminals' ways, wiles and habits of mind. Squad detectives continually discuss their cases, old and new, with their colleagues in the open-but-confined, metal-desk-cluttered forum of the squad room, sketching out their understandings of the logic of criminals' worlds through stories. These intricate tales are usually filled with rosters of names and aliases of street players, thickets that, while bewildering to most outsiders, detectives navigate easily since fixing identities is at the heart of criminal investigation. They present the wildly improbable ins-and-outs of life in the underworld ('You can't make this stuff up'), complete with all of its peculiarities and regularities – stories of robbers who repeatedly use the same routine with the same exact words; tales of extreme violence as a tool-in-trade; stories of the fatalistic bravado of the streets spurred by archaic codes of 'respect' (A young man says to a still younger man brandishing a gun: 'You wanna shoot me? Go ahead and shoot me. You wanna shoot me? Go ahead and shoot me.' So the younger man shoots him).

These are also unvarnished tales, completely unencumbered by the requisite disclaimers and sentimentality that burden middle-class discussions about those usually portrayed as 'disadvantaged'. Here, for example, is a detective's story about amateurs trying to break into the big-time:

> Didja ever hear the story of the Apple Dumplin' Gang? José and Ricky, two Spanish kids, decide they wanna be big-time taxi robbers. So they hail a livery cab and get in the back seat. José pulls a gun and Ricky announces the stickup. The driver snaps on the automatic door lock, starts driving like mad, and they end up in front of the precinct station house. They have to shoot their way outta the car. They figure they made a mistake getting in the car in the first place. So, next time, they both come up to the driver's side of a livery. They wanna show the driver they're serious, so José shoots him in the leg, and Ricky announces the robbery. The driver steps on the gas and squeals down the street, leaving the kids standing there. José shoots after the car and shatters the rear window. They figure they fucked up by not surrounding the cab. So, next time, José comes up on the passenger side of a livery, and Ricky on the driver's side. It's hot outside and the car's windows are open. José sticks the gun in the passenger window, Ricky announces the stickup, and José tries to shoot the driver. But he misses and ends up shooting Ricky, right in the chest. The driver takes off, leaving Ricky on the ground and José standing there. José goes over to Ricky. Ricky says to José: 'You shot me, José. You shot me.' And then he dies. That's the story of the Apple Dumplin' Gang.

Others might lament such violence as 'senseless' or 'tragic' but, to detectives, it makes perfect sense that the streets treat bumbling ineptitude mercilessly. In their view, stupidity turns all tragedy into parody.

Squad stories also provide detectives with a self-dramatizing venue to display their experiences and skills to each other in an entertaining way. Thus, a detective tells about a fabled day in the 34th squad when he and only two other colleagues handled a wild shooting spree that resulted in a double homicide and four seriously wounded victims, a drug-related homicide, and another gun assault, all occurring within a span of a few hours; a detective describes the thrill of confronting and arresting armed robbers, men at the top of the criminal prestige hierarchy, honoured even by police for their nerve; or a detective tells about his intensive search for the most feared, and elusive, hit man and getaway wheelman in New York City; or a detective gives a deadpan recitation of a statement that he elicited from a man who butchered his roommate, stabbing her thirty-seven times ('Honest to God, detective, she fell on the knife'); or a detective describes his trade-talk during a long extradition journey with a violent drug-dealer about the you-can-drive-a-truck-through-it loopholes in the criminal justice system ('That's why they call it *criminal* justice'). The stories contain a myriad of self-images. Detectives see themselves, and present themselves to each other, as men and women unafraid of confronting and immersing themselves in the ugly underside of modern society, a world from which most people turn away although, in private, they sometimes rue the emotional costs of such immersion. With important exceptions, they exult in the danger of their work, in the heart-pumping excitement that only the chase and mortal combat afford; one detective has prominently displayed on his desk the quotation from Hemingway: 'There is no hunting like the hunting of armed men, and those that have hunted armed men long enough and liked it, never care for anything else thereafter.' And they see themselves as men and women who can laugh, even with criminal adversaries, about working in an absurd world, and have heard and seen it all, not least human behaviour at its very worst.

The Job, second, is the New York City Police Department itself and the sprawling, bewilderingly complex congeries of bureaucracies that make up the criminal justice system. Detectives' talk here focuses on what they see as the irrationalities of their own bureaucracy and of a legal system geared toward procedural justice. Put briefly, the exigencies of detectives' work, as detectives themselves see them, clash with bureaucratic needs. One can mention only a couple of examples here. The police department and even more the legal system have formal, written rules and procedures for every conceivable situation in which uniformed or plainclothes police officers or detectives might find themselves. But containing the forces of disorder means successfully working the streets, work that, whether done in uniform, plainclothes, or as a criminal investigator, requires attributes and habits of mind completely different from those instituted and valued in bureaucratized systems. Only long street experience teaches police (though some officers never master the skills[4]) how to read the streets, how to understand the nuances of street argot, how to discern and exploit the peculiar moral frameworks of street players ('I mean, it's okay that he shot her 'cause these bitches need to be taught a lesson. But you don't shoot a woman *in the face*'), and how and when to act decisively, with force if necessary.

Yet, in the police bureaucracy, only written examinations determine one's path 'up the blue' to the civil-service ranks of sergeant, lieutenant and captain, the commanders of officers who work the streets. Detective commanders go through the same process and then are 'invited' or 're-invited' into the detective bureau. The bureaucratic premium is on the mastery of bureau-cratically sanctioned skills. Many men who excel in test-taking and gain civil-service promotion are not thought to have 'made their bones' on the streets. In addition, many policewomen in the New York City Police Department retreat from the streets as soon as possible after the police academy to the remove of desk jobs; they also far exceed their brother officers in test-taking skills, besides being the beneficiaries of affirmative-action pressures for more women in higher ranks. From the viewpoint of street warhorses, the police department is increasingly governed by 'house mouses'. Typically, the less experience such superiors have, whether they are male or female, the more they insist that their subordinates adhere closely to established procedures. In such a world, cops or detectives who aggressively pursue criminals or who, for that matter, demonstrate initiative beyond standard operating procedures become liabilities to ambitious bosses.

The increasingly bureaucratized recruitment of detectives, coupled with the case system, fragments occupational knowledge and undercuts the fabled *esprit de corps* of the detective bureau. Detective work used to be organized as an apprentice system. Detectives, who at bottom are simply uniformed patrolmen on special assignment, were selected solely by other detectives. As in any large organization, 'hooks' – that is, connections to powerful higher-ranking members of the detective bureau through familial ties, sexual liaisons or other informal associations – were and still are important. But, until the late 1980s, one also had to demonstrate investigative abilities to key authorities in the bureau. Thus, Detective Gennaro Giorgio, then (in the early 1960s) a uniformed officer, talked his sergeant into delaying for twenty-four hours the distribution of an already printed police-artist portrait of a rapist. Giorgio argued that he had seen the predator on his beat, that the rapist would 'book' if his face hit the street, and that he, Giorgio, could con him into coming into the 'house'. And con him the wily Giorgio did. He found and talked with the targeted suspect, suggesting that the police were investigating a series of robberies and that the suspect's name had come up in that investigation. He asked the suspect to talk to detectives to clear his name. After the rapist's identification by his most recent victim and his subsequent indictment, Giorgio received a personal invitation from the chief of detectives to join the bureau. Now, the path to the coveted detective's gold shield is, for the most part, governed by union contract.

Many young officers are made detectives after serving, say, eighteen months in buy-and-bust undercover narcotics work, which demands nerves of steel and remarkable physical courage, but no demonstration of investigative promise. The total number of officers with detective rank in the NYPD has thus ballooned in recent years. Many of these detectives are forever assigned to units such as narcotics and not to the detective bureau itself, let alone to precinct squads. Moreover, in the squads themselves, there are no formal mechanisms for experienced detectives to transmit their knowledge to green juniors, except for occasional, thoroughly standardized courses that most young detectives find boring. To be sure, some senior detectives in squads do 'adopt' favoured juniors and school them in investigative techniques. These ties are personally powerful and organizationally effective; but they also produce resentment among detectives not selected for such tutoring. The endless storytelling in precinct squad rooms serves to disseminate some occupational lore in a more widespread and equitable fashion, especially about the subterfuges of criminal investigation, a recurring theme in many narratives. But, generally speaking, knowledge is fragmented in squads. And the busier the squad, the more fragmented the knowledge.

Take, as an extreme example, two detectives, who served in uniform together where each saved the other's life on different occasions, who went through the narcotics bureau together, who came into the 34th squad together where they worked on the same team, their desks only a few feet apart. During the frantic year of 1992, one detective was looking for an identified suspect in a triple homicide; the other detective had just interviewed, and then sent on his way, the same man as a witness to another murder. Neither detective knew of the other's interest in the man. Such an incident spurs momentary impulses for reform, specifically calls for thorough communication of the details of all the cases in a squad; but bureaucratic inertia, and the malaise it generates, soon reasserts itself. Some detectives work on others' cases only reluctantly, since one's prosperity depends principally on how one handles one's own cases. But typically squads advocate and live by an ethos of teamwork even when details of others' cases are obscure.

The structural and moral anomaly of detective work

The perceived exigencies and subsequent practice of detectives' work regularly clash with the values and practices of lawyers and judges. For instance, all detectives rely on informants for secret information. Without informants, virtually all investigations come to a grinding halt. But the police department, at the insistence of the district attorney on the basis of court rulings in particular cases, requires detectives to register informants whom they use regularly. Officially, this allows a detective to go before a magistrate by himself, without his witness, in order, say, to obtain a warrant. But, detectives argue that, like most bureaucratic procedures, informant registration protects bosses first and foremost if things go wrong. Those with the deepest knowledge of criminal activity are most often criminals themselves; they are the least likely to submit to the formal bureaucratic process of official registration. The rule leaves detectives with the tricky problem of how to utilize the most detailed and arguably the most reliable information from the street.

Again, lawyers and courts place a great premium on written documentation of the investigation of events, an important procedural safeguard against false accusation, arrest and prosecution. Precisely because of this premium, detectives know that everything they record in writing will be subjected to extensive public interpretation and reinterpretation. But blind alleys are part of every major investigation. The street yields its secrets grudgingly and never straightforwardly. Even a seemingly open-and-shut case goes through many twists and turns before its telling in court; and even 'final' adjudication rarely closes a major case permanently. As detectives see it, their specific goal in a murder investigation is to identify a suspect on the basis of available evidence, and produce a coherent, compelling narrative, complete with a demonstration of the suspect's means, opportunity, and plausible motive linking him or her to the crime, a story that admits no alternate readings. Thus, detectives commit to writing as little as possible about their ongoing investigations until they know the final shape of their narratives in order to minimize later alternative exegeses of their work. The practice makes courts and defence attorneys deeply suspicious of detectives' methods. Prosecutors also have their doubts, but since they must work hand-in-glove with detectives, they usually adopt a knowing-and not-knowing stance ('I don't want to know what happens at the station house').

Similarly, the legitimacy of the courts depends on how successful they are in upholding the claim of being the impartial institutional arena in American society to establish 'truth' and fix responsibility for crime. Courts rely on sworn testimony from witnesses, some of whom are also victims, from accomplices, from experts of various sorts, and especially in criminal cases, from investigating police detectives. Prosecutors regularly call on detectives to introduce statements by accused criminals to build their cases. These statements may be, for instance, admissions about foreknowledge of a crime; exculpatory statements that, with requisite contradictory circumstantial evidence, can undercut credibility; or outright confessions. But the key issue, one always sharply contested, is: how did the detective obtain the statement? More often than not, to defence attorneys' advantage and prosecutors' chagrin, the answer is: through deception of one kind or another.

Detectives regularly use ruses of all sorts to outfox suspects and elicit statements. In cases with multiple culprits, for instance, detectives know that the concept of legal responsibility embedded in the notion of 'acting in concert' (the street phrase is 'acting in concrete') is a wholly foreign notion to most criminal suspects. On the street, one is responsible for, say, a shooting death during a robbery, if and only if one actually pulls the trigger; but if a detective elicits an admission that one was 'down for the robbery, but not for the shooting', he or she can nail the suspect for felony murder. Detectives also feign more knowledge than they have, suggesting the availability of other witnesses, even when none exists; they hint at possible betrayal from accomplices, even when this is unlikely; and they sow doubt in suspects' minds about possible residues of hard forensic evidence, even when there is none to be had. Detectives cajole, wheedle, insult, frighten, bully and tease information from suspects, even as they often establish remarkably deep emotional relationships with them, particularly with youths who, before being taken into custody, have often had no prolonged interaction of any sort with adults. But, in the end, detectives betray suspects to a thoroughly depersonalized system. In brief, detectives violate all the normal expectations (to be sure, even under the best of circumstances, more often honoured in the breach than in the keeping) of social relationships. But, in public at least, they are unapologetic about the moral ambiguity of their work. They argue that all criminals are thoroughly deceptive anyway ('They all lie all the time'); and they assert that the fantastically bureaucratized system in which they labour would collapse of its own weight unless they bend procedures or circumvent them entirely. In detectives' world, deception is the groundwork of whatever truth one can hope to attain. Detectives delight in the discomfort that such an anomalous role causes for those whose need for the appearance of moral probity outweighs any sense of justice. However, the legal system's dependence on the anomalous, morally ambiguous occupational role of criminal investigators does not confer any privileges on detectives. Indeed, when it comes to formal proceedings, the watchword in detectives' world is: 'It's always the detective that's on trial'.

The structural and moral anomaly of their work give detectives a marginal-native cast of mind in the world of intricate, interlocking bureaucracies that make up the criminal justice system. Of course, the system breeds a profound scepticism, indeed cynicism, in all of its occupational groups – prosecutors, defence attorneys, judges and police alike – as well in all of the other, smaller work groups that get a close day-to-day look at the system's machinations. But perhaps more than any occupational group, detectives regularly confront the system's extraordinary combination of functional rationality and substantive irrationality. Jurisdictional disputes between different law-enforcement bureaucracies are the paradigmatic example. In New York City, such disputes often make justice a pawn in heated rivalries or, more simply, a function of geography or even of the time of day. New York City has five different district-attorney jurisdictions and two federal-prosecutor juris-dictions. Each district attorney is connected to a branch of the New York State Supreme Court; the federal prosecutors are connected to federal courts either in the Southern District in Manhattan or in the Eastern District in Brooklyn. There is the gigantic New York City Police Department, into which in 1995 were merged the formerly separate authorities of the Housing Police and the Transit Police. But another dozen police authorities still flourish, ranging from the Metro-North Police, to the Amtrak Police, to the Port Authority Police. Every federal law enforcement agency, from the Federal Bureau of Investigation and the United States Marshals Service, to the Immigration and Naturalization Services, has major operations in the city, which has long been the national centre of organized crime, the principal east-coast port-of-entry for narcotics, and a prototypical site for youth-gang violence for more than 150 years. In this world, despite rational controls in place to monitor particularly vicious criminals, the left hand often does not know what the right hand is doing. Thus, a hit man, already on bail pending trial for a double murder in the Bronx, is released on cash bail for assault by a judge in Brooklyn's night court even though the man he wounded was a key witness to a Bronx quadruple homicide. Neither the assistant district attorney nor the night-court judge were legally able to take into account the pending Bronx double-murder trial, nor were they aware that the Brooklyn shooting victim was a witness to the slaughter of four people.

Moreover, one of the paradoxes of law-enforcement work is that police of all sorts need crime, the more vicious the better, the more innocent the victims the better, in order to demonstrate their prowess to their peers and to make a plausible public claim of the necessities of their services. The rivalry between and within all law-enforcement bureaucracies for 'good' cases is fierce, often producing extremely frustrating outcomes for detectives. Criminal investigators, for example, both detectives and investigating district attorneys in Manhattan, laboured long and hard to build a case against a remarkably vicious Harlem-based drug and extortion ring with cult-like overtones, responsible for at least forty murders over ten years. But FBI agents and prosecutors swept in at the last minute, stole the case, placed it under federal jurisdiction, and then offered a plea to the ringleader, by far the worst of the lot, in order to gain his testimony against his lieutenants in death penalty cases. Detectives consider such 'deals with the devil' a kind of moral leprosy and do not hesitate to say so, often provoking angry confrontations between themselves and their rival opposite numbers, here the FBI agents.

Class resentments

Criminal investigation also takes detectives behind respectable public faces. For instance, criminal enterprise is often intertwined with 'legitimate' businesses. Thus, young subway robbers sell the earrings and necklaces they rip off terrified riders, cowed by claw hammers, knives, box cutters, guns or Mike-Tyson-like biceps, to upper-middle-class midtown jewellery stores, which recycle stolen gold in their own products, often paying the youngsters with gold tooth-sleeves, oral attire made popular by rap stars. Insofar as they make a market for plunder, businesses provide an incentive for youthful crime. Drug dealers purchase bodegas, money-wire-transfer shops, or restaurants to launder the tons of small-bill profits from street-sales; or they loan out money at exorbitant rates of interest so immigrants can purchase such enterprises and labour their whole lives to repay the loans in clean money. Further, in the early 1990s, Washington Heights drug money brought great prosperity to many nightclubs, new car dealerships and car repair shops, especially those that sidelined in installing *clavos*, concealed compartments to hide guns and drugs. Indeed, the river of drug money in the precinct kept so many businesses afloat that community non-cooperation with the police in solving drug-related violence was the norm, not the exception. Sometimes, of course, businesses are out-and-out fronts for criminal commerce, such as the famous chicken shack in the Bronx that, until its break-up by police and prosecutors in 1995, sold surplus Soviet AK-47s along with fried drumsticks. Further, detectives regularly cross paths with some professionals who flirt with outright collaboration with criminals. With a high-minded occupational ideology sanctioned by law, some defence attorneys are afforded blind-eye-professional-courtesy by prosecutors and judges alike that enables them to maintain a publicly respectable knowing-and-not-knowing stance toward the depredations of their clients even as they excoriate the police in court for procedural infractions. Some journalists, who see their work as a vocation to 'comfort the afflicted and afflict the comfortable', frequently romanticize community activists who regularly blame police for the use of 'excessive force' in attempting to curb the violence that disproportionately afflicts African-American and Latino residential areas in New York City.

Their journeys behind respectable public façades, and the lightning-rod nature of their occupation, stir profound class resentments in detectives, who are overwhelmingly drawn from the working class. These sons and daughters of policemen, firemen, craftsmen, labourers, bus and truck drivers, and service workers of various sorts see themselves and their brother and sister officers constantly being blamed for the sorry outcomes of miserable social conditions that they had no hand in fashioning, states of affairs that indeed were created, and are now sustained, by elites of far higher social station than they. Moreover, as detectives see it, their principal critics are members, allies or servants of those same elites, the very people who benefit most from the order that police maintain, but who, far removed from the savagery of the streets, can indulge in the indignation that guards a cherished sense of moral probity.

The long arm of the Job

Detective work brings with it burdens. Despite their own tough public stance, detectives know that the moral ambiguity of their work taints them in the eyes of others. This includes even rule-oriented police officials who have never served in the detective bureau and who view with suspicion the subterfuge and skirting of procedures that are at the heart of criminal investigation and that, from detectives' standpoint, make a rigidly bureaucratized system work at all. These ambiguous exigencies of their work make detectives the targets of defence attorneys and sometimes zealous prosecutors alike, let alone those journalists who trade in moral outrage. Most detectives come to resent doing necessary work that is largely unappreciated and often pilloried. Further, detectives know that their regular interactions with criminals coarsen their views of human nature and create a general suspiciousness of others' actions and motives; they recognize that their constant encounters with the horrific results of predatory violence numb them and, indeed, sometimes terrify them. They cannot openly reveal such sentiments to their fellow officers since the whole construction of the police world depends on officers maintaining the appearance of a rugged emotional distance, especially from the most emotion-laden and draining experiences of their work. Only the murder of a completely innocent victim, such as the murder of a child or of a police officer killed in the line of duty, allows police officers to reveal to each other forlorn patches at the centres of their souls. Even more must detectives compartmentalize their work from their families, hiding the commonplace savageries that they encounter on duty from their loved ones. But compartmentalization never works entirely, because the Job has a very long arm. Its rhythms, its language, its images, its ugliness, its secrecy find their ways under tightly closed doors and come to stand between husbands and wives or between lovers, subtly eroding the delicate frameworks that sustain intimacy and trust. Detectives' divorce rates are high; alcoholism is an occupational hazard; as of late 1999, reports of domestic violence by police officers, including detectives, are on the rise; each year, a few detectives 'eat their guns', a sobering reminder to those who stay behind of the fragility of a seemingly robust world. The vast majority of detectives long for the day when they mark twenty years on the Job and, with a generous pension, can leave it behind for ever.

But leaving the Job behind is not easy because detective work is also exhilarating and links detectives to each other. Detectives have the licence to cross the chequerboard of little worlds that comprise modern bureaucratized society. Since their work depends principally on talking with people, the best detectives can place themselves on the level of any person at any social station, providing them with ethnographic access to many worlds, especially to the raw, coarse vitality of the streets, an undeniably fascinating panorama of violence, lust and aggression screened from the view of most. Their occupationally honed storytelling skills, coupled with the truth-is-stranger-than-fiction lore of their field, and their appreciation for the absurdities of bureaucratic systems, make them boon companions at bars or parties. The necessity constantly to assert authority and take charge in their work makes them magnets in such social gatherings, particularly to the opposite sex who flock around them like bees to alpha honey. When they 'make cases', they have the singular satisfaction of knowing that, often through their efforts alone, they take violent predators off the streets, helping to shape a civil social order that is the bedrock condition of a democratic society. And, despite all the bureaucratically structured rivalries between them, detectives share an increasingly rare sense of occupational solidarity that binds them one to another, and to other police officers, in a brotherhood of duty, of risk, of loyalty, and of death.

Acknowledgements

Special thanks to Janice M. Hirota and Duffy Graham for close readings and excellent critiques of a draft of this chapter.

Notes

1 This chapter is based on continuous fieldwork with the 34th precinct detective squad from January 1992 through early September 1993, with twice-a-week fieldwork continuing through 1994, and more sporadic contact with individual detectives continuing to the present. My work with the 34th squad was preceded by four months' fieldwork with the Central Robbery Squad of the then independent New York City Transit Police Department. My intensive work with the police was followed by extensive fieldwork in the New York State Supreme Court in late 1994 and through the spring of 1995, and then at the office of the District Attorney of New York from the summer of 1995 through the spring of 1997. See Robert Jackall, *Wild Cowboys: Urban Marauders and the Forces of Order* (Cambridge, MA: Harvard University Press, 1997) for further details.

   Of the 75 police precincts at the time of this research (now 76), the 34th precinct was the largest geographically, extending from 155th Street to the upper tip of Manhattan, river to river. The area, known as Washington Heights, is home to hundreds of thousands of immigrants from the Dominican Republic. Most Dominican immigrants are hard-working, upwardly striving and law-abiding. But some Dominicans choose to live outside the law, either as illegal immigrants or as active participants in a range of criminal activities, often both. These are the focus of 34th precinct squad detectives' work and consequently of this chapter. Beginning in 1985, Washington Heights became the hub of the east-coast drug trade, the principal wholesale and retail distribution point for Columbia-produced cocaine smuggled into John F. Kennedy International Airport.

The New York City Police Department has approximately 39,000 officers, making it by far the largest police department in the world. Along with London's Metropolitan Police, the NYPD is a model for police departments everywhere. As of October 1999, there were approximately 6,900 detectives in the NYPD, about 3,000 of whom were in squads, affiliated precinct robbery units, or transit 'districts' specializing in subway crime whose jurisdictions overlap precincts. The rest were in highly specialized units of one sort or another, such as narcotics, homicide units that assist precinct detectives in murder investigations, crime scene analysis, ballistics, or criminal identification.

2   Squad detectives work a four-two schedule; that is, four days on duty, two days off duty. The first two days of a tour are from 1600 hours until 0000 hours, followed by a 'turnaround' beginning at 0800 hours until 1600 hours for the next two days, followed by a 'swing' of two days off. Their schedule thus moves through a calendar week to compensate for the weekly rhythm of crime, which is typically heavier at the end of weeks and especially on weekends, and sparser in the beginnings of weeks. Detectives 'catch' cases according to schedules constructed by each squad. Typically, a detective catches and is responsible for whatever cases come to the squad during his or her assigned hours, say, from 1600 hours to 2000 hours. Homicides are the exception since each detective in a team catches murders in a sequential 'batting' order.

Crime fell dramatically in New York City from 1994 until 1999. Most notably, the number of homicides decreased precipitously during this period. In the early 1990s, there were regularly over 2,000 homicides each year in New York City, with 100+ each year in the 34th precinct alone. In 1998, there were about 600 murders citywide, and only about a dozen in the two precincts that now cover the territory of the old 34th precinct. This sharp decline in the most serious crime was unquestionably due in part to aggressive police seizure of guns through stop-and-frisk tactics. The new police aggressiveness, initiated in January 1994 with a change in mayors, made New York City temporarily inhospitable to crime. The drop in homicides necessitated a refocusing of squad detectives' attention on the investigation of lesser offences. Some detectives, in squads and in special units, continue to pursue 'cold cases' since murder cases are never closed until an arrest has been made or an exceptional clearance is taken. But, in late 1999, murders in New York City began to rise once again. Police officials attributed the homicide increase to a new proliferation of firearms on the streets, itself a result of decreased police aggressiveness prompted by vehement political protests against aggressive police tactics. The most important protests were spurred by the tragic police shooting of an unarmed African immigrant. Four officers mistakenly thought he was brandishing a gun. However self-serving, police officials' explanations for the sudden increase in murders is plausible. For a start, the more that guns are carried on the street, the more likely are the constant conflicts about honour among street players likely to flare into fatal encounters.

3 Of the 6,900 detectives in the New York City Police Department in October 1999, 655 were second-grade detectives, and only 168 first-grade; all the rest were third-grade. While case clearance is an important criterion for promotion to second grade, 'hooks', as described in the text, are also crucial. Some of the best detectives in the department languish their whole careers in third-grade status because they lack such hooks. The intricacies of achieving 'grade' are always important topics of conversation and, of course, of resentment for those left behind. In 1999, third-grade detectives made a base salary of $45,000 a year, not counting overtime pay; second-grade detectives made $55,000; and first-grade detectives $60,000.

4 The stratification of police organizations by talent and especially by hard work resembles that of all large organizations, but particularly that of other large, civil-service municipal bureaucracies. In the author's estimate, based on wide comparative study of and experience in different bureaucracies, including corporations and the academy, about 20% of the employees of most large organizations have retired while still on the job. Moral entrepreneurs' continual focus on certain types of police corruption – bribery in its various forms, racial profiling, perjury, extortion, and especially excessive or unwarranted use of force, all inexcusable crimes but all committed by a tiny percentage of officers – causes them to miss the most widespread form of corruption, namely laziness.

13   HOW CHILDREN MANAGE EMOTION IN SCHOOLS

GILLIAN BENDELOW AND
BERRY MAYALL

This chapter considers the emotion work of children at school. This is not a fashionable topic among educationalists or among sociologists, at any rate in the UK. Education policy currently emphasizes the child as object of the education system, and, in Durkheimian tradition, regards education as adult work aimed at socializing children towards adequate citizenship. The future of children as adults is prioritized over their present. In this scenario, children's work, their own opinions about education, their experiences of the school day, their activity in managing their bodies and minds are rarely considered. By contrast, we start from the sociology of childhood and understand children as agents who interact with the structures that largely condition their daily lives, and as workers at school.

Western mainstream sociology has continued to the present day with uncritical reliance on the concept of *socialization,* in which children are essentially the objects of adult work to turn them into adults fit to join society and, theoretically, to render them fit objects or subjects of sociology. Though functionalism has been largely eschewed by sociologists, there is a continued reliance upon it in relation to children and to childhood. Indeed, over the last hundred years, children and childhood have become very largely the province of psychology and psychiatry and charting child development has become a major industry in Western industrialized countries. Children have become identified as problems to be solved, as victims and as threats, as vulnerable and as dangerous. However, in recent years, routes through symbolic interactionism (for example, Denzin, 1977) and through various versions of social constructionism (for example, Ingleby, 1986) have attempted to rethink childhood; developmental psychology itself has focused more than before on interactions between social context and the child (for example, Cole, 1996). Most importantly, a concerted sociological effort has begun to develop more adequate understandings and there is now, after 15 years of analysis, a substantial body of theoretical work which challenges notions of children as incompetent, immature and under-socialized (for example, Prout and James, 1990; Alanen, 1992; Mayall, 1996; Jenks, 1996). These writers emphasize the competence of children, their abilities within relationships, their wish to participate in decision making and their drive towards social life. As part of the work towards shifting our understandings, research studies have begun to take seriously children's own accounts – their knowledge of the social order, their experiences and their opinions on the childhoods they are asked to live.

The pioneering work carried out in the sixteen-country Childhood as a Social Phenomenon programme (1987–92) established the idea of children as a social group, one whose interests were not necessarily coterminous with the adult groups with whom they interact – notably parents and teachers (see for example Qvortrup, 1991, 1994). Indeed children may have interests in common as a group, which differ from and may challenge the interests of adult social groups. Further, as with any other social group, children's daily lives, self-appraisal, expectations and opportunities are structured in tension with social policies. But the tensions and the effects will be specific to them as a social group. For instance, their chances of health and education, their freedom of movement, their opportunities for adequate nutrition and exercise will be affected in specific ways, by comparison with adult groups.

Of specific interest, when we consider children's agency at school, is the ambivalence of adult views on the notion of children as workers. Worldwide, most children work, in the sense that they contribute to the maintenance of the household; many also work for pay. They are active participants in maintaining and constructing the social order. But the so-called *scholarization* of children in industrialized countries, coupled with notions of children as dependent and as developing within home and school, have made children as workers invisible to adults (see Morrow, 1994; Oldman, 1994, for discussions). Currently in England and Wales, developments in education policy are providing interesting points of departure for rethinking the notion of children as workers. For instance, government policy in England and Wales is now requiring that under-fives in nurseries should meet certain nationally devised educational targets, so that they are cognitively equipped to enter the primary school at five. This view challenges the long-held Piagetian notion among pre-school staff that play is children's proper 'work', and that learning through play should be child-centred, or child-led. Since the late 1980s, education policy has instituted a National Curriculum, regular testing, regular inspection of schools, and competition for bright children between schools. In the interests of meeting targets in core topics – literacy, numeracy and science, schools have reduced time for free activity (break time) (Blatchford, 1999) and time spent in sports (SPEEDNET, 1999). Children from the age of five now have more formal school experience in teacher-led lessons and less time for child-led activity, and from their first years in school many children also have homework. These developments are beginning to make it evident to both parents and teachers that children are appropriately to be understood as workers.

However, the notion of school as children's work has not so far extended to implementation of children's rights as workers to decent conditions of work. The same set of education policies implemented from the late 1980s in England and Wales effectively reduced budgets for the maintenance of school buildings and outside space, increased class sizes, abolished nutritional standards for school meals and then abolished the requirement on education

authorities and schools to provide school meals (except for
children). Adequate access to professional health care in the ev
or accident at work has never been implemented for schoolchildr
backs in numbers of school nurses, doctors and other health a
professionals have reduced this access. The vast majority of prima
do not have sole-use rooms for health staff to work in, nor quiet roo
children can rest (Mayall et al., 1996).

The school, therefore, under present policies presents children with a
workplace where increasingly stringent and time-consuming demands are
made on them as workers, but where the working conditions are commonly
stressful and may be harmful to health. The school presents a key organization in children's lives where children's everyday emotional and bodily
lives are constructed by adults. Nevertheless, we argue that children,
rather than being merely passive recipients of such embodied processes
as 'civilization', 'regulation' and 'surveillance', can be better understood as
active participants in the management of both their bodies and their minds
(see Mayall, 1996, 1998). As Scheper-Hughes and Lock (1987) emphasize,
emotions are shaped and given meaning at least in part by social or cultural
forces and thus provide links that bridge mind and body, individual, society
and the body politic, ideas which we hope to show fit closely with what we
know of children's experiences.

Emotions across the public/private divide

As has been argued in previous work (see Bendelow and Williams, 1998)
emotions lie at the juncture of a number of fundamental dualisms in Western
thought such as mind/body, nature/culture, public/private, and provide the
'missing link' between 'personal troubles' and broader 'public issues' of social
structure (Mills, 1959). This link that emotions provide between a number
of traditional divisions and debates within the social sciences, such as the
biological versus the social, micro versus macro, public versus private,
quantitative versus qualitative, also enables us, again, to question dominant
notions of Western rationality; modes of thought which have sought to
exclude children and the elderly, like women past and present, from the
public world of (male) reason.

In order to understand how emotion is a mediating force between social
worlds and the body, Mayall (1998) has suggested two factors that structure
children's participation in child–adult transactions. The first point concerns
adult models of what children are, how childhood should be lived, and how,
since childhood is a relational concept, adults should behave in relation to
children. These understandings differ according to setting and, variously,
structure how homes, schools, health and welfare agencies operate (Alanen,
1994). Most crucially, because of the authority and control adults exercise
over all aspects of children's lives, adult models importantly affect children's
experience, knowledge and identity; they are critical in constructing the

personhood of children (Hockey and James, 1993). The requirement that children be happy can lead adults to protect them from knowledge that might sadden them, such as the death of a relative, or the cruelty people enact towards each other. Girls learn not to develop their muscles, if they are to be socially acceptable; and to restrict their bodily movements within smaller spaces than boys do (Young, 1980). More generally, people, especially in their relationships with their superiors, are required to control and organize their emotions (emotion work) and to use these controls to organize bodily movement in ways approved by their superiors and by more general social legitimation (Hochschild, 1979). Consideration of 'emotion work' provides a way into understanding children's management of their emotions at school.

The second point concerns relationships between adult and child groups and how close their interests are; in other words 'generational proximity', which Mayall defines as:

> a continuum ranging from conflict to harmony in child–adult relations. At one extreme, the generations may be experienced as separate, firm, congealed, and standing face-to-face or in opposition to each other, to the extent that the child feels controlled, excluded or defined as object. At the other extreme, children and adults may be engaged in a joint enterprise, in harmony, with similar goals, and with a mutual emotional reinforcement of their satisfaction with the enterprise and the social relationships embedded in it and strengthened through it. (1998: 138)

Generational proximity concerns how far the separation or intersection of the two groups, children and adults, allows children to participate in constructing the social order, and we are arguing here that intersections of these two sets of factors are critical in structuring children's experience and in conditioning their agency. This is because children, uniquely compared to other social groups, are positioned as a 'minority group', socially, economically and politically dependent on another social group, namely adults. In terms of time and social importance, the two sites, home and school, are children's main social environments in the UK, and the complexity of each arena for children's experience is provided by the precise character of the intersecting factors outlined above. Children's accounts make clear that at home they are valued as persons and that, in general, the home offers more opportunity for closeness, for generational proximity. Essentially, the home is the accepted place where attention to the individual can have priority; it is the first and foremost site of holistic health care and where women's health care work, relating to the physical, emotional and cognitive character of their children – and of their men – is commonly regarded as their central work (Graham, 1984). In this context, therefore, children are likely to experience close attention to their emotions, bodies and minds. At school, clearly, children's experiences reflect a somewhat different set of conditions, and children report sharp social separation between children's and adults' interests as a feature of their experience.

By considering children's own accounts of their experiences of health maintenance and health care at primary school (age 5–11) in England and Wales, we show here how the social order conditions bodily experience. Children describe discomfort as well as pleasure, feelings of alienation as well as of togetherness with other children. Our analysis also includes demonstration of children's own awareness of their own 'emotion work' in relation to adults and peers in the construction of the school order.

The study

We draw here on qualitative data using children's own accounts, collected through case-studies from a larger study which explored the status of children's health in primary schools (CHIPS study) in England and Wales. First, we carried out a postal survey (620 schools responded, or 60% of the one in twenty schools randomly targeted); then we carried out case-studies in six schools, and collected data from children, staff and parents. The case-study schools were chosen to represent the variety among the survey schools and included an infant school (ages 5–7), two junior (7–11) and three all-age primary schools (5–11) scattered throughout the midlands and northern and southern England. This geographical variation is indicated by the adopted pseudonyms of the six schools as follows: Inner city London (*City*), rural Midlands (*Village*), suburban South East (*County*) small Midlands town (*Town*) small Northern ex-mining town (*North*) and rural Northern infant school (*Infant*).

Using a mixture of participant observation, interviews and draw-and-write sessions, we encouraged two year groups of children (aged 6–7 and 10–11) in the case-study schools to explore their perceptions of school as an arena for health maintenance, health care and health promotion. The main areas or topics we discussed with the children were:

- the physical environment of the school
- exercise and play
- school curriculum
- illness and accidents at school

Our suggestion in this chapter is that the data show how emotion work acts as a mediating force between the requirements of the social order of the school and the structuring of children's bodies, minds and experience.

The physical environment of the school

Our data indicate that adult and child social worlds are in tension at school, that the social order of the school is formally fixed and that children have generally little chance to take part in its modification. Indeed, these factors may explain in part why people do not recall their schooldays as subjectively important: they are not experienced as participative.

Children's talk about the buildings and playspace linked the physical with the social and emotional, as in the following discussion between some of the younger boys from North school:

Boy 1: At first it were a bit of a shock 'cos it were so big. And someone told us there were ghosts coming out of the toilets and we believed it, and people with Naf Naf tops on beat you up.

Boy 2: Sean J. beat *me* up.

Boy 1: Mrs A wouldn't stop telling us that the school is in a square and we'd never get lost, but this boy got told off because he said he couldn't find his classroom.

In practical terms, larger classes in finite spaces are currently requiring children to regulate their bodies more closely; both children and teachers reported on cramped working and dining conditions. Awareness of how conditions differ from home is vividly illustrated by this account from an older boy at County school:

The hall's really cramped and we only get 15 minutes to eat our lunch because 100 children have to eat in four sittings in one hour.

Responsibility for the health and safety of children at school is a grey area, with competing claims for the local education authority (especially with respect to the building), the governors and the headteacher. In children's experience, adults provide poor opportunities for child health maintenance in many schools; the buildings themselves, the playgrounds and the toilets are commonly described by them and by teachers as inadequate (Mayall et al., 1996: 17–25). Toilets were a particular source of anxiety and displeasure for children, as these accounts from Town school indicate:

Younger girl: Some people do their poo everywhere: there's four toilets, but sometimes two or three have poo in them.

Older girl: There's no privacy – sometimes they step on the toilet seat and look at the other person.

This boy from North school describes his initial feelings of rejection and isolation, involving fear of physical abuse, in contrast to his experience now:

I felt scared [when first came to school] in case anybody came along and picked me up and threw me against the fence and I just felt so scared . . . I was really shy, so I just went to Class 1 and everybody was so horrible to me – said 'Buzz off would ya' and I just felt lonely.

Interviewer: Is it better now?

Yes, I've got billions of friends.

Feeling accepted as part of a child group is more than a pleasant part of school; it is critical to mediation of the social order. Bullying, of course, is a major worry and has to be defended against as this older girl from North School explains

I don't think I've ever been bullied – if Jessie and Mary call me names, I know they're just playing, and I hold up my fist and they leg it.

As other studies have shown, friends are a crucial aspect of school life and both emotional and bodily security is much more likely through the membership of friendship groups.

Exercise and play

The bodily character of children is a marker of their status, their positioning within childhood (Hockey and James, 1993: Chapter 3), a positioning marked by orderly progress through life at home, to nursery, to infant and junior school. At home, especially in their pre-school years, most children experience parental praise for their embodied beauty, achievements and progress. Home therefore encourages children to feel happy in their bodies, to understand which bodily and emotional achievements and actions are valuable, and to understand how these both link in with and contribute to the social order. The school presents a different set of orientations to children's bodies, for instance crowded noisy playgrounds, access to which may be allocated by adults to discrete times, as these accounts from three of the schools show:

Younger girl: I don't like the bigger ones coming down the ramp, because they can knock you over, and I don't like people pushing me off the steps and stuff and I don't like people who are bigger than me pushing me.

Younger boy: I don't like parts where there is too much noise . . . at playtime there's too much running and shouting.

Interviewer: Where do you like best to be?

Where it's lovely and quiet, on the grass and the path and the adventure playground.

Older boy: We're not allowed to go places where the little ones can, if you want to go on the pitch and play around you're not allowed to run really fast.

The infant (5–7 years) and junior (7–11 years) regimes in some schools during the study period were interesting in this respect, for, apart from break times, infant children were allowed to play at will in the classroom after finishing short pieces of 'academic' work; and some of this play included running about, and devising competitions of physical prowess. It seems likely that the increasingly stringent demands of the National Curriculum in the late 1990s have reduced children's freedom; and, certainly for junior children in this study, physical activity was limited to formal physical exercise sessions.

During class-time, their bodies were controlled in the interests of cognitive achievement: in literacy, numeracy and so on. Children also learn at school that the construction of their bodies in socially approved directions is not just a matter for themselves, but is one component of the formal school remit. School offers the chance to delight in the bodily skills and achievements that school proposes, but also the chance of failure to measure up. City schools engaged the children in specifically health-related activity (cf. Kirk and Tinning, 1994), as this older girl reports:

He makes us run all around the playground . . . down the road. [At first] I nearly fainted . . . it's really hard. But it's worth it . . . He tells us about healthy diet, and about too much fat in the body, and not having a healthy heart . . . When I first started in this class I used to be really chubby.

For this class, health promotion included a valued practical activity, but in most cases, although sports feature as a welcome break to classroom learning, essentially children learn that the social order values their cognitive over their physical abilities. They are required to subdue their bodies to 'school' agendas.

School curriculum

Adults, whether teachers or non-teachers, behave in ways that suggest their close identification with the formal remit of the school. Essentially, here the cognitive is distinguished from, and takes precedence over, the emotional and physical.

Older girl: School's better now, because you do harder work, and I like doing maths and writing and being the eldest so people can't bully you.

Younger girl: I don't think others would say this but I think working's the best, 'cos I think well, we only started school a minute ago when it's nearly hometime. Because I look at my work and I don't think about the time.

Whilst teachers at the outset of their careers may want to mother 'their' children (cf. Burgess and Carter, 1992), their work remit demands they maintain physical and emotional distance from the children and treat them equally and even-handedly (King, 1989). The demands of the formal agenda and of the social order lead to tension between these demands and teachers' concern for individual children.

Younger boy: I liked school much more [in reception class] – the teachers looked after you then.

Older boy: School was much better when I was younger, it was easier work, play all the time and you got more stories.

Some children too may initially hope for replication of a mother's complex set of functions – 'Some of them do tend to call me Mum', said one teacher.

In other words, the division of labour for the care of children favours the separation of the cognitive, as priority, from the emotional and the bodily, although both children and teachers may overstep these boundaries on occasion.

Older boy: Sometimes I get things wrong and the teacher gets angry and I get upset.

Younger girl: I've got a nice teacher, she's much kinder than [the last one] because when you're in class, she gives you everything to do, but she doesn't shout as loud.

Although we have focused somewhat on problematic aspects of school, we also note that almost every child finds enjoyment in some experiences. For most children, friendships and companionship are critical to their enjoyment, but most also cite some aspect of the formal curriculum as enjoyable. Sports, drama, music and (for some) maths are the most popular. Notably, these are all areas of learning where children can be active participants, in physical activity, creative engagement, and problem-solving. English, by contrast, is commonly described as dull, repetitive and boring; in other words, children explain, it is activity defined and controlled by adults.

In general, the line between adult and child interests at school is clearly apparent to children. They perceive teachers as those who act to implement the official remit of the school, and are in positions of authority over the children. Teachers themselves emphasize their task of training the children to behave acceptably within the social norms of the school (Hartley, 1987), though these are commonly implicit as well as explicit norms (Waksler, 1991). Staff may think of school as a site of *socialization*, but its teaching relates mainly to the social order of the school and, within this, what constitutes a 'good' school child is not generalizable to life in wider social contexts.

Illness and accidents at school

Amongst others, Freund (1998) has emphasized the relationship between social status, control, emotion work and bodily states, including those that may contribute to health and illness, using the central concept of 'dramaturgical stress'. In other words, the sociocultural situations in which such dramaturgical work takes place are more likely to subordinate those in 'stigmatized' social positions, so that women, minority groups, workers in lower class service occupations and, of course, children are likely to be particularly vulnerable. The onset of illness at school provided specific and dramatic instances in which to consider how children manage emotion and how adults control their emotional and bodily well-being.

We note that whilst the UK national health service provides visiting doctors and nurses to schools, their visits are patchy and generally insufficient in terms of child illness and accident. In practice, on an everyday level, the primary school presents children with a complex lay health care system, which, though it varies between schools, is essentially based on the add-on character of women's work: both teachers and non-teachers add caring to their paid remit. In seeking physical help and sympathy from adults, therefore, children take chances, dependent on adult busy-ness, mood and diagnosis. In turn, children must manage their bodies, through emotional control; they may have to wait for help, or do without it and carry on. In this study, children's accounts of recent illness episodes showed the commonest symptoms were headache, stomach ache and feeling sick. These symptoms would probably be alleviated by time-out from work in a quiet place, lying down and resting – facilities which most schools do not have. Some children reported a caring adult response, but others said that teachers did not listen or respond, or were suspicious of their sickness bid (cf. Prout, 1986), or suggested the child carried on 'till we see how you go'. Our quantitative data show that children's overall assessment was of dissatisfaction in 24% of cases, with staff behaviour as a principal reason. Satisfaction was commonly linked to the arrival of a parent (almost always the mother) to take over. And some children did not seek help at school, but saved up their pains until they got home. The onset of illness provides a clear case where children's ability to manage their body – to respond to its signals – is structured by the interlocking forces outlined earlier. Sharp separation between adult and child groups, in terms of their interests, and the adult view of how childhood should be lived at school, backed by the formal remit of school, constitute a firm framework within which sickness bids may be questioned. For instance, an older girl from Town school commented:

Some teachers say, 'You're acting like a baby – go away!' When it turns out to be serious, they say something different.

Children point to a sometimes unmet need for emotional as well as physical care when they feel ill or have an accident, as in these two accounts from older children in different schools:

Girl: They never take you seriously, they just say 'go and sit in the corner' and things like that and if you've hurt yourself it's not very comforting.

Boy: For a cut knee, I just got given a paper towel. That was it really!

It is not only teachers who respond dismissively. Children reported that dinner ladies and playground supervisors also responded in this way and children have to accept that they may get an unsympathetic rebuff when they ask for help in case of sickness or accident. Sickness bids by those employed to work in an organization may commonly meet with some suspicion by those in authority, who may interpret these as attempts to avoid the formal remit of the organization. But we suggest that children's moral status in the organization is particularly low, in part because according to common psychological understandings, they lack a responsible and mature approach to social life. Children also note that, given their subordination to adult agendas, they do sometimes resort to tactics to get what they want, and these tactics strengthen adult prejudice. Further, our data also show that children recognized that adults in schools suffer from overload; as this boy from Village school observed: 'teachers can't be bothered, they hear too much of the same thing and they're tired'. It seems that age is important here as younger children reported more satisfactory outcomes and their accounts show that staff were more likely to adopt caring roles.

Thus the social order of the school serves to structure the emotional response of staff to children's bodily distress; and the children have to learn to control and manage their bodies through emotion work. Under these circumstances, support from other children is important, as this child relates:

I feel like I could tell my friends (about feeling ill), but sometimes I feel like I can't tell the teacher. It depends what kind of mood's she's in, and sometimes I feel I can't tell her at all.

Emotion work at school thus comprises both teaching one's body to conform to the social norms and providing sympathetic care for other children. The appropriate emotions in face of illness or accident may be stoicism and toughness about one's own condition, coupled with ready sympathy for the conditions of other children.

Discussion

This chapter has focused on the role of emotions in children's own ability to participate in the construction and reconstruction of the social order of the primary school. Children literally learn to manage their bodies at school through emotional control, often in contrast to their more active and inclusive embodied emotion work in constructing the social order of the home. On the other hand, school encourages high valuation of bodily skills in specified times and places, but most of the time asks children to subordinate bodies to minds.

At school in England and Wales, children are required to subordinate their bodies to the formal regime; they have to ask permission to go to the lavatory, can exercise or drink only at adult-specified times and places. Whilst children may be in tune with their bodily needs, they may not be able to satisfy them, for adult agendas and authority prevent this (cf. Freund, 1982). However, as noted above, children gave high praise to the opportunities they did have for bodily exercise, and particularly high praise to those teachers who themselves valued exercise and jointly participated in it with the children. Five-year-olds pointed forcibly to adult controls over their bodily management; by contrast, notably, by the age of nine children had carried out the emotion work necessary to accept these controls (and sometimes circumnavigate them). The price some of them pay is boredom.

At school, compared to home, there is greater emphasis on children's time future, for school is preparation for adult life, a point children themselves understand. At school, adult time-interests structure the school day, week, term and year; indeed time can be seen as organized in adult interests (Oldman, 1994). For children's sense of well-being, therefore, it is critical that they feel themselves to be engaged in a joint enterprise, or contributors to the adult enterprise, rather than merely subject to it. Thus the proximity of adult to child interests, and the extent to which adults regard child participation as appropriate, will serve to determine how comfortable children feel in their embodied selves.

Child–child friendships are a major source of comfort and reward and the child group is an important site, for not only is children's identity constructed through the social group of children (James, 1993; Prendergast and Forrest, 1998); the solidarity of the group is also constructed *vis-à-vis* the adult groups. For instance, children's recognition of another child's distress, expressed needs for help, feelings of alienation or oppression, or of pleasure in achievement, can constitute ratification of that child's evaluation of her embodied experience. The recognition can also confirm the joint interests of children in an adult-ordered world and perhaps it is especially valuable at school (cf. Christensen, 1993), where adult caring is less reliable than at home. Faced with this powerful, separate adult social group, children put great value on activity and achievement and on child social groups as sources of reward and enjoyment. Although they cannot, in the main, participate in constructing the social order of the school, some of the time they do feel they exercise limited control over both work and play. In this study, it was strikingly clear that when children were allowed to participate with staff in improving the social order, for instance, through joint enterprises to tackle bullying or to draw up information leaflets for newcomers to the school, they responded with great enthusiasm (Mayall et al., 1996: 211–14).

In summary, this particular example of the social order of primary schools shows, through children's qualitative accounts, how central are emotional relationships to children's everyday lives, and how they themselves recognize these themes in various ways. First, children recognize the role of emotions in sustaining a balanced and 'healthy' lifestyle in relation to their embodied being. Secondly, children note the importance of enlisting and sustaining friendships as protection across the public/private divide and the institutional 'order' of school life. Thirdly, children understand that they are subordinated to adults and the role of 'emotion work' in the negotiation of these hierarchical relationships. Furthermore, these examples of children's own accounts challenge prevailing conceptualizations of children as emotionally 'incomplete' or 'immature' by comparison with adults.

Acknowledgements

The Children's Health in Primary Schools study (1993–5) was funded by the Economic and Social Research Council, grant no. ROOO 23 4476 (see Mayall et al., 1996). The authors of this chapter gratefully acknowledge the contribution to the study of Sandy Barker, Pamela Storey, Marijcke Veltman, the heads of schools who gave us access, all the teachers who took part and, especially, the children, whose enthusiasm for the project was a real joy.

References

Alanen, L. (1992) *Modern Childhood: Exploring the 'Child Question' in Sociology*, Research Report 50, Finland, University of Jyväskyla.

Alanen, L. (1994) 'The family phenomenon: considerations from a children's standpoint'. Paper presented at the seminar Children and Families: Research and Policy, London, 28–30 April.

Bendelow, G. and Williams, S. (eds) (1998) *Emotions in Social Life*. London: Routledge.

Blatchford, P. (1999) 'The state of play in schools', in M. Woodhead (ed.), *Making Sense of Social Development*. London and New York: Routledge, in association with Open University.

Burgess, H. and Carter, B. (1992) '"Bringing out the best in people": teacher training and the "real" teacher', *British Journal of Sociology of Education*, 13 (3): 349–59.

Christensen, P.H. (1993) 'The social construction of help among Danish schoolchildren', *Sociology of Health and Illness*, 15 (4): 488–502.

Cole, M. (1996) *Cultural Psychology*. Cambridge, MA: Harvard University Press.

Denzin, N.K. (1977) *Childhood Socialization*. San Francisco, CA: Jossey Bass.

Freund, P. (1982) *The Civilised Body: Social Domination, Control and Health*. Philadelphia: Temple University Press.

Freund, P. (1988) 'Bringing society into the body: understanding socialized human nature', *Theory and Society*, 17 (6): 839–64.

Graham, H. (1984) *Women, Health and the Family*. Brighton: Harvester Press.

Hartley, D. (1987) 'The time of their lives: bureaucracy and the nursery school', in A. Pollard, (ed.), *Children and their Primary Schools*. London: Falmer Press.

Hochschild, A. (1979) 'Emotion work, feeling rules and social structure', *American Journal of Sociology*, 85 (3): 551–75.

Hockey, J. and James, A. (1993) *Growing Up and Growing Old: Ageing and Dependency in the Life Course*. London: Sage.

Ingleby, D. (1986) 'Development in social context', in M. Richards and P. Light (eds), *Children of Social Worlds*. Cambridge: Polity Press.

James, A. (1993) *Childhood Identities: Social Relationships and the Self in Children's Experiences*. Edinburgh: Edinburgh University Press.

Jenks, C. (1996) *Childhood*. London: Routledge.

King, R.A. (1989) *The Best of Primary Education: A Sociological Study of Junior Middle Schools*. London: Falmer Press.

Kirk, D. and Tinning, R. (1994) 'Embodied self-identity, healthy life-styles and school physical education', *Sociology of Health and Illness*, 16 (5): 600–25.

Mayall, B. (1996) *Children, Health and the Social Order*. Buckingham: Open University Press.

Mayall, B. (1998) 'Children, emotions and daily life at home and school', in G. Bendelow and S. Williams (eds), *Emotions in Social Life*. London: Routledge.

Mayall, B., Bendelow, G., Barker, S., Storey, P. and Veltman, M. (1996) *Children's Health in Primary Schools*. London: Falmer Press.

Morrow, V. (1994) 'Responsible children? Aspects of children's work and employment outside school in contemporary UK', in B. Mayall (ed.), *Children's Childhoods Observed and Experienced*. London: Falmer.

Mills, C.W. (1959) *The Sociological Imagination*. Harmondsworth: Penguin.

Oldman, D. (1994) 'Childhood as a mode of production', in B. Mayall (ed.), *Children's Childhoods Observed and Experienced*. London: Falmer.

Prendergast, S. and Forrest, S. (1998) '"Shorties, low-lifers, hardnuts and kings": boys, emotions and embodiment in school', in G. Bendelow and S. Williams (eds), *Emotions in Social Life*. London: Routledge.

Prout, A. (1986) '"Wet children" and "little actresses": going sick in primary school', *Sociology of Health and Illness*, 8 (2): 111–36.

Prout, A. and James, A. (1990) 'A new paradigm for the sociology of childhood? Provenance, promise and problems', in A. James and A. Prout (eds), *Constructing and Reconstructing Childhood: Contemporary Issues in the Sociology of Childhood*. London: Falmer Press.

Qvortrup, J. (1991) *Childhood as a Social Phenomenon: An Introduction to a Series of National Reports*. Vienna: European Centre.

Qvortrup, J. (1994) 'Childhood matters: an introduction', in J. Qvortrup, M. Bardy, G. Sgritta and H. Wintersberger (eds), *Childhood Matters: Social Theory Practice and Politics*. Aldershot: Avebury Press.

Scheper-Hughes, N. and Lock, M. (1987) 'The mindful body: a prolegomenon to future work in medical anthropology', *Medical Anthropology Quarterly* 1 (1): 6–41.

Shilling, C. (1993) *The Body and Social Theory*. London: Sage.

SPEEDNET (1999) 'Dramatic fall in primary school physical education'. Press release, 19 August, SPEEDNET Sports and Physical Education Network.

Waksler, F.C. (1991) 'Dancing when the music is over: a study of deviance in a kindergarten classroom', in F.C. Waksler (ed.), *Studying the Social Worlds of Children: Sociological Readings*. London: Falmer Press.

Young, I.M. (1980) 'Throwing like a girl: a phenomenology of feminine body comportment, motility and spatiality', *Human Studies*, 3: 137–56.

14 EMOTION AND INJUSTICE IN THE WORKPLACE

KAREN P. HARLOS AND CRAIG C. PINDER

> There are good days, mostly when he [the boss] is not in . . . I think things are picking up, maybe I'm starting to fit in, maybe I was imagining all the bad stuff and I don't have to look for a new job . . . But then the next day is terribly bad and I just scream in my car on the way home. (Brenda, office clerk)

In his classic novel *Great Expectations*, Charles Dickens observed that 'there is nothing so finely perceived and so finely felt, as injustice'. Although Dickens was referring to injustice perceptions among children, we extend his observation to adults in general and employees in particular. The premise of this chapter is that Dickens's observation holds true in workplaces today: employees are keenly sensitive to injustice experiences. Moreover, we argue that a plethora of emotions underlie injustice perceptions in people's work lives. Indeed, emotions can cause, result from, and/or reflect the simultaneous experience of injustice in work settings.

For example, a supervisor's angry outburst can both simultaneously *reflect* the supervisor's state of perceived injustice and *cause* an angry or fearful response from the subordinate employee toward whom the outburst is directed. An envious impulse by a worker who has been overlooked for a promotion may trigger contempt, anger or even joy by the co-worker who receives the promotion. In these examples, at least two actors are involved. However, injustice can also trigger sequences of emotions within single actors. Thus, an employee who expresses uncontrolled anger after being denied credit for an accomplishment may, as a result of his public displays of pique, experience embarrassment or shame for his or her lack of apparent control.

In this chapter, we explore the relationship between perceived injustice and emotions in work settings. We recognize that issues of injustice are inherently perceptual and thus subjective. Consequently, the adjective 'perceived' is sometimes omitted in relation to injustice to enhance readability. Along with its intractable subjectivity, injustice encompasses our beliefs about what is right and wrong. Broadly defined, injustice involves a violation of a moral contract for goods, services, opportunities or treatment (Fine, 1983). The accounts described here represent employees' perceptions of moral contract violations within employment relationships, especially violations concerning interpersonal treatment at work. As one participant said, his mistreatment 'was just plain wrong, it never should have happened'. Our chapter focuses on intersections between employees' senses of being wronged and the emotions associated with these perceptions.

The inductive study on which this chapter is based takes its place in an emerging organizational research tradition that is concerned with *in*justice at work (see for example Andersson and Pearson, 1999; Cropanzano and Randall, 1993) and its intersection with emotions (for example, Weiss and Cropanzano, 1996; Weiss et al., 1999). The analyses reported here extend from both Fineman's (1993) observation that 'one would expect social activity in organizations to produce as well as reflect emotions' (p. 14) and Pinder's (1998) admonition that 'future theory building and research that seeks to include emotionality . . . should begin with a tolerant stance that will admit emotions to appear in any and all places in causal sequences' (p. 116). Accordingly, we frame our findings by highlighting emotions as causes, accompaniments and consequences of injustice experiences. We begin by clarifying our terms and theoretical perspective before describing our methods. We then summarize two of four injustice patterns that emerged as key features in analyses of emotions. Finally, we discuss our findings in relation to existing research and briefly outline directions that future empirical research might take into the recursive relationships between injustice experiences, their underlying emotionality and other organizational behaviours.

Clarifying our terms and theoretical perspective

Forms of emotion in organizational settings vary widely – from joy to jealousy – as do their functions from adaptive, life-affirming responses (such as fear leading to *flight or fight* reactions) to maladaptive, life-opposing responses (such as anger leading to workplace violence). In addition, there are a variety of perspectives from which to theorize about emotions. We draw on a portion of this literature to clarify the terms and theoretical perspective that underlie our analyses of the emotions related to injustice (for more complete reviews see Ashforth and Humphrey, 1995; Lazarus and Lazarus, 1994; Pinder, 1998).

Focus on emotions

The general domain of affective phenomena includes *emotions*, *moods* and *dispositions* (see Oatley and Jenkins, 1996). *Emotions* refer to states that last a limited amount of time, ranging from a few minutes to a few hours, with one or more causes or identifiable targets (Oatley and Jenkins, 1996). By contrast, *moods* can last for hours, days or even weeks, often with poorly defined beginning and end points. Moods often have no apparent explanations: although we may know that we are really irritable, we might not know why. Whereas moods sustain or resist change, emotions instigate change (see Frijda, 1993). Lastly, *dispositions* describe aspects of personality that are stable and enduring and that predispose us to emotional responses that are consistent with our affective orientation (cf. Warr et al., 1983). For example, some people's positive disposition toward life (seeing life through rose-coloured glasses) starkly contrasts with others' negative outlook.

Our data revealed that, within contexts of organizational injustice, emotions were much more commonly related to injustice experiences than either moods or dispositions. In particular, we discovered that whether injustices occurred the day, month or year(s) before the research interview, their emotional intensities were easily recalled and their emotional arousal during interviews was focused on specific individuals, decisions, processes and systems. As a result, we refer only to emotions, although we hope that future studies may shed light on the roles of moods and dispositions in injustice contexts.

Theoretical perspective

Of the three ontological and epistemological approaches to studying emotions – classical, prototype and social constructionist (see Pinder, 1998) – the most subjective approach conceives of emotions as 'socially-constituted syndromes (transitory social roles) which include an individual's appraisal of the situation and which are interpreted as passions, rather than as actions' (Averill, 1982: 6). Known as the *social constructionist approach*, it acknowledges both biological and environmental factors as predominant influences on human nature: 'there is so much that is learned, "social", interpretive, culturally specific, in the meaning and production of emotions, that strictly biological, in-the-body, explanations soon lose their potency' (Fineman, 1996: 10). As well, 'no single response or set of responses, is a necessary or sufficient condition for the attribution of emotion' (Averill, 1982: 7). This approach posits that emotional responses are learned from experiences (both personal and vicarious) and that emotional expressions vary between and within persons, across cultures and times. For social constructionists, the number of emotions is infinite as a result of the countless social and life events that can interact and then be interpreted by those experiencing and witnessing them. The data and analyses reported in this chapter most closely fit the social constructionist approach, drawing on employees' reports of injustice without requiring definitions of concomitant emotions in terms of necessary and sufficient conditions. More detail on the specific methods used to gather data and to seek connections between injustices and emotional experiences will be reported on pp. 262–4. First, however, we summarize the two injustice patterns that were key elements in analyses of emotions.

Patterns of organizational injustice

From the larger empirical study on which this chapter is based (Harlos, 1998), an empirically grounded taxonomy of organizational injustice was developed. The taxonomy reflects four emergent patterns of injustice experiences that participants identified as unfair: *interactional*, *distributive*, *procedural* and *systemic*. We see these patterns of organizational injustice as conceptually distinct, socially constructed, dynamic patterns that may change over time and across cultures (see Rich, 1992). In fact, a study is currently underway to examine whether employees in New Zealand experience these or other patterns of injustice within their employment relationships. The construction of this taxonomy and its validation are summarized in Harlos and Pinder (1999).

Interactional injustice

In our analyses of emotion and injustice, *interactional injustice* emerged as the predominant pattern. We define interactional injustice as *mistreatment that occurs in the course of workplace relations between employees and one or two authority figures with whom a reporting relationship exists* (see Table 14.1). It occurs in some work relationships involving asymmetrical hierarchical positions and unequal power relations. Many different types of mistreatment were reported, such as yelling until employees cried, repeatedly slapping (privately and publicly) a participant's buttocks, telephoning in the middle of the night to gather information about other employees, and continually criticizing but rarely praising staff. These events often occurred over several months and were reported by participants as significant sources of frustration, fear, depression and stress. This pattern of injustice reflects, but is not limited to, individual discrimination, including racial, religious, sexual and personal harassment (that is, bullying and coercion). Although related to the concept of interactional justice (that is, fairness of interpersonal treatment experienced during organizational procedures; Bies and Moag, 1986), interactional injustice focuses instead on instances of *un*fairness that stem from work relationships, *separate from procedural or distributive concerns*. Thus, unlike justice-based conceptualizations, our research indicates that interactional *in*justice is a unique and substantive source of injustice perceptions. Accordingly, we consider incivility at work (Andersson and Pearson, 1999) as an example of interactional injustice.

We identified eight behavioural dimensions of interactional injustice that collectively reflect substantive behaviours by bosses which participants saw as unjust. Table 14.1 defines and describes *intimidation*, *abandonment*, *inconsistency*, *degradation*, *criticism*, *inaccessibility*, *surveillance* and *manipulation*, with fuller definitions provided for the two dimensions most relevant to our present analyses. Dimensions were frequently interwoven throughout participants' descriptions of their relations with bosses. Thus, our data indicated that the eight dimensions of interactional injustice are conceptually distinct but empirically correlated (see also Harlos and Pinder, 1999).

Table 14.1 *Dimensions of interactional injustice (adapted from Harlos and Pinder, 1999)*

Definition: Perceived interpersonal mistreatment by a hierarchical superior or authority figure

Dimensions directly related to anger

  Intimidation: Use of physical, verbal and/or emotional means to instil fear and induce control in employees

    Key acts: threatens (directly or indirectly) employees with dismissal, discipline and/or violence; yells at staff; throws property

  Degradation: Communicating (verbally and non-verbally) in a disrespectful, hurtful manner

    Key acts: publicly shames or humiliates employees; displays impatience with and/or judgement about inquiries; personally and/or professionally attacks employees; gossips about or disparages other employees

Other dimensions

  Criticism: Frequently finding fault with employees' performance, ideas, personal qualities, and neglecting positive performance

  Abandonment: Neither inquiring about nor responding to employees' physical, cognitive, social or emotional work needs

  Inconsistency: Arbitrarily changing direction, focus or standards for individual performance; poorly communicating changes to employees

  Inaccessibility: Restricting physical and/or emotional availability; discouraging contact with employees

  Surveillance: Closely monitoring and directing employees, providing them with minimal autonomy or authority

  Manipulation: Managing employees' skills, values, hopes and emotions for desired personal or work-related outcomes

---

Systemic injustice

A second pattern of injustice linked to emotions was *systemic injustice*, which we define as *perceptions of unfairness involving the larger organizational context within which work relationships are enacted (that is, interactional), and where allocation decisions are made (that is, distributive) and/or implemented (that is, procedural)*. We conceive of this pattern as the obverse of systemic justice described elsewhere (cf. Sheppard et al., 1992), reflecting *widespread* mistreatment by authority figures yielding pervasive but diffuse perceptions of unfairness from the organizational context.

The two remaining patterns – procedural and distributive injustices – parallel their justice-based counterparts (see Sheppard et al., 1992). Although these injustice patterns reflected some emotionality (for example, anger and envy at not getting a promotion believed to be deserved), they did not reveal the emotional richness and complexity of interactional and systemic injustices. As a result, procedural and distributive injustices figure less prominently in the analyses described here.

Data collection and analysis procedures

In the preface to the first edition of this volume, Arlie Hochschild (1993: xii) observed that 'emotion is a topic which requires subtlety of grasp, [so] we should refrain from counting things before we know precisely what they are'. Her statement suggests not only that emotions are highly complex and remain poorly understood, but also that qualitative methods are still appropriate in studying emotions in organizations given what remains unknown.

Participants and settings

Several populations whose members were likely to have experienced organizational injustice were targeted for recruitment during the winter of 1996 and the spring of 1997. Participation was generally restricted to people who had experienced injustice themselves. As well, participants had to have had access to at least one voice system (for example, open door policy, grievance procedure) in the organization in which their injustice experience had occurred. The aggregate sample was neither intended to be randomly selected nor expected to be representative of any one organization, group or population.

Thirty-two participants from managerial/professional and clerical/line positions, each representing different organizations, described 33 cases of injustice in research interviews. The sample comprised 19 women and 13 men ranging in age from 23 to 71 with an average age of approximately 37 years, although at the time of the injustice their average age was 33 years and 7 months. Their experiences of unfair treatment had occurred from 24 years previously to current situations to which they returned following the interview.

The organizations in which the injustices occurred ranged in size from two employees to more than 5,000 employees. Fourteen organizations had between 1 and 100 employees, 10 organizations had from 101 to 500 employees while at least six organizations employed over 500 employees. Five organizations were based in the public sector, while the remaining 28 organizations were private sector and six of these were non-profit organizations. Twelve industries were represented, including construction, forestry, manufacturing, finance, accommodation and government, education, business and health/social services. Seven organizations were unionized and of participants' positions described therein, three were unionized.

Research approach

Semi-structured, open-ended interviews took place at mutually negotiated times and locations. Interviews allowed large amounts of detailed data to be gathered quickly and gave participants the option to maintain organizational anonymity. Indeed, because of the sensitive nature of the topic, many chose to use organizational pseudonyms. Interviews ranged from 45 to 180 minutes (averaging 90 minutes) and focused on the injustice complaint through a retrospective critical incident technique ('tell me what happened'). In addition, questions about work environments were asked (for example, 'describe what it was like to work there'). As principal researcher, Karen conducted all interviews. She was attentive to participants' emotional states: several expressed a range of deep feelings during interviews – anger, sadness, outrage, grief, shame and hate. Because of the emotionally charged nature of the research topic, the number of interviews conducted in a given day was kept to a minimum, field notes were kept, and personal support and professional debriefing was routinely sought. As well, all interviews were tape-recorded and fully transcribed.

We used grounded theorizing (Glaser and Strauss, 1967) to inductively analyse data from the 33 interview cases. This method is well suited to the study of processual experiences and of organizational issues (see for example, Martin and Turner, 1986), particularly emotions in organizations (Hochschild, 1993). Fourteen hundred pages of transcripts resulted from verbatim transcriptions. These were stored in computer files and printed out for ongoing review. The analytic process involved searching for attendant emotions among the behavioural and cognitive content. We did not identify types or patterns of emotions a priori. However, interview questions asking participants to describe an injustice situation and its effects prompted us to examine the role of emotions in three temporal stages: emotions as causes of injustice, emotions that accompany injustice and emotions as consequences of injustice experiences. Despite indistinct boundaries between stages and emotional content, we were able to derive conceptually distinct patterns from our questions and from participants' responses reflecting the 'before, during and after' of injustice experiences. Our analyses revealed some conceptual overlap among emotions across temporal stages. That is, the same emotion could both accompany and be a consequence of injustice experiences. Not requiring emotions to be uniquely associated with injustice stages is consistent with a naturalistic, social constructionist approach.

We also recognized that recalling injustice events involved retrospective sense-making (Weick, 1995) as participants looked backward to interpret their injustice experiences. For classical or prototype emotion researchers, there may be concerns about the accuracy of recall. However, some research suggests that accuracy is increased when influential stimuli are salient and plausible causes of responses they produce (Nisbett and Wilson, 1977). In our study, recall accuracy may have been enhanced by the strong salience and plausibility associated with such an emotionally charged topic. Regardless, our social constructionist approach focused on current perceptions of injustice, their meaning(s), emotional content and the questions they raise rather than on the actuality of past experiences.

Emotions of researching sensitive topics

We believe it valuable to acknowledge methodological aspects of researching such an emotionally charged, sensitive topic. With its focus on a deeply personal experience that intrudes into the private sphere, including attention to deviance (such as sabotage), the topic can certainly be considered *sensitive* (see Lee and Renzetti, 1993). As noted earlier, many deeply felt emotional states were verbally reported and behaviourally displayed across interviews: anger, fear, dread, sadness, outrage, grief, shame and hate. In one interview, for example, when Joe was considering whether the benefits outweighed the costs of staying with an abusive boss, he responded with sudden tears, saying 'no, on balance it was not worth it . . . I tell people that it was worth it, but it wasn't'. This emotional display was especially poignant because of Joe's notable composure and restrained demeanour during the interview.

Experiencing intense emotions was not restricted to participants, however. On many occasions during and after interviews, Karen also experienced feelings of outrage, sadness and despair. It was tempting, at times, to volunteer unsolicited advice about what participants should do. On other occasions, it was hard for Karen to not respond to requests for advice or to not restrain participants' intense emotional displays, whether to make others feel better, or herself. In short, examining sensitive topics demands of the researcher a keen attention to his or her own emotional states and a willingness to permit emotional reactions among both researchers and participants during the research process. We consider implications for future research into emotionally charged topics in the final section of this chapter.

Emotions as causes of injustice

In this section, we report results concerning the role of particular emotions, especially anger, as major *causes* of many injustice experiences.

Anger and interactional injustice

Anger was a significant source of injustice perceptions. In particular, bosses' anger directed at subordinates was a predominant emotion beneath two dimensions of interactional injustice: *intimidation* and *degradation*. Catriona, an office manager for a large union, described her boss's anger underlying the *intimidation* dimension during one of many outbursts: 'He stood up and reached across his desk as if to hit me and he got really red in the face and said "are you calling me a liar?"' Many bosses routinely yelled at employees to intimidate them, whether during staff meetings or private, one-on-one meetings. Most bosses, however, were not concerned if others heard. For example, Ashley, a project coordinator for a hospital, said that her boss who often yelled at employees 'wasn't hiding it for when we were alone in the office. He didn't care who was within hearing distance.' Joe was general manager in a property development company. He too was yelled at, but behind closed doors. However, 'everybody knew it was happening – the walls aren't that thick'. Another case involved Joanne, a youth counsellor in a private, non-profit organization, whose boss often degraded employees: 'she would get very angry and call one of my fellow staff members a fucking bitch over the telephone'.

Whether reflecting *intimidation* or *degradation*, bosses' angry outbursts were usually unpredictable and intense. As a result, many participants reported feeling afraid, ashamed, hurt and confused. Brenda, an office clerk for a small construction company, was told during her hiring interview that the owner/boss 'vents' his anger and was asked if she could handle it:

> I didn't think that would be a problem, but I just had no idea what he was like – he goes off, I think he's unbalanced. They don't stop him, he's brutally rude, he behaves like a five year old and he thinks he's great. Nobody puts boundaries on him, he just runs.

On her second day on the job, Brenda had not yet been trained to transfer telephone calls. At one point she asked her boss for help with an incoming call:

> He flipped around and with fire coming out of his eyes, he said 'didn't Jean show you how to transfer telephone calls yet?' He took me so off guard. I must have seemed like I was three years old answering him . . . but he'd already dismissed me. He didn't care for my response so I just tried not to cry.

This was the first of many such incidents. The worst for Brenda was his reaction to a mix-up about paperwork that the boss had picked up from the office on the weekend. He had telephoned her on Monday, saying 'you screwed everything up, you fucked it up for me', even though others could have moved the papers. In describing his reaction, Brenda said, 'you'd think I'd ran over his kids or something'. The dispute escalated as Brenda's tears turned to anger.

> I was lippy and he got mad at that too and then he lost it. I thought I was going to get fired. I felt like a little girl who has done something bad and gets sent to her room by her dad. . . . He hung up on me and then I cried.

When the boss returned to the office, he refused to make eye contact with Brenda and repeatedly slammed doors in her face in their small office. Together, these examples illustrate how organizational injustice can both produce and reflect emotions.

Emotionally barren workplaces and systemic injustice

Goleman (1995) has observed that 'a life without passion would be a dull wasteland of neutrality, cut off and isolated from the richness of life itself'

(p. 56). For some participants in our research, it was not the profusion of emotions such as anger but the relative *lack of emotionality* from individuals and the organizational system that contributed to perceptions of injustice. For example, Jennifer was distressed by her boss's impersonal style, who often kept her door closed and made no effort to relate to her. A records analyst for a professional association of educators, Jennifer said: 'when I was a supervisor, I tried to find a common link so you can chat about dogs or Mozart. But she [the boss] wanted the relationship completely about work.' Emotionally barren work relationships were also reflected by bosses' aloof manner, harsh voice tones and unsmiling countenances, illustrating the interactional injustice dimension that we term *inaccessibility* (see Table 14.1).

Cultures of injustice   In some cases, such emotional inaccessibility was endemic throughout participants' entire organizations rather than just restricted to the interpersonal styles of one or two bosses. Faith, a technical writer in a software development company, described the lack of emotionality in her workplace:

> I say good morning to the two fellows on either side of my cubicle and if I didn't, they wouldn't say good morning to me. If I am there first, they don't say good morning when they come in. I did an experiment one day – I didn't say good morning to anybody to see if anybody would speak to me. And a whole day went by and no one spoke to me at all.

She longed for some measure of emotional connection with co-workers or superiors, what she called 'the little things that make you feel like a human being'. This systemic-level emotional barrenness is captured by the concept of *cultures of injustice* (Harlos, 1999). It is a nomothetic conceptualization of organizational culture that reflects shared meanings (cf. Schein, 1992) of what it is like to work within unjust employment relationships. Thus, it comprises common elements within and across organizations, much as we use the terms *service cultures* or *research cultures* when describing certain workplaces. Of the six dimensions that capture the common elements of injustice cultures, five reflect low (if not lack of) emotionality: low supportiveness, low team orientation, tight control, high outcome orientation and low tolerance of conflict. Together, these dimensions and their properties depict cultures of injustice as emotionally barren workplaces marked by intense control, suppressed conflict, a valuing of job relations over human relations, and an emphasis on production through competitive individualism.

Cultures of injustice seem both to influence and to be influenced by injustice perceptions. In other words, working in emotionally barren environments for some participants exacerbated existing senses of injustice. Not getting a promotion, for example, seemed more unfair when routinely being ignored by co-workers. For others, though, the lack of emotionality in organizational cultures helped to create injustice perceptions. Specifically, the emotional barrenness of work settings represented mistreatment and misery from systemic injustice.

Emotions that accompany injustice experiences

The pervasiveness of fear

Not surprisingly, the predominant emotion that participants experienced in the face of powerful others' anger was fear. For example, Gwen, an employment counsellor, described her fear of her perfectionistic yet inconsistent boss:

> I was frightened to death because it seemed like I couldn't do anything right. I was getting paranoid about it. I would go to a co-worker and say, 'can you check this for me, make sure it's all right?' and they'd say, 'For God's sake, calm down.'

However, the *pervasiveness* of fear was unexpected and remarkable; it commonly defied boundaries of time or place. For some, aversive associations remained so strong that they could not bear to see the corporate logo or walk past the company building, even several years after having quit. For Joanne, after years of mistreatment at work, a work-related car accident meant that she had to move several hundreds of miles away for rehabilitation. Despite the physical distance and an absence from work of 1½ years, Joanne was *still* afraid to tell her rehabilitation team of the chaos and stress from her abusive boss. In fact, during the research interview Joanne's voice repeatedly dropped to a near-whisper as she became increasingly afraid from defying her boss by informing others about what she had been repeatedly been ordered to keep secret, namely the mistreatment she had suffered. For Joanne and several others, their fear was so intense that portions of their tapes were rendered inaudible. Joanne's sense of vulnerability resulted not only from challenging her boss's domination but also from a fundamental fear that others would not believe 'how bad it was. They'll say "you're just being a baby because you didn't get along with your supervisor".'

The rainbow of accompanying emotions

Along with deep-seated fear, a wide variety of emotions accompanied the ongoing experience of injustice: anger, rage, desire for revenge, shame, dread, guilt, hopelessness and cynicism. Rahim was a contract administrator supplying corporate materials to business customers. His perceptions of mistreatment derived from feeling left out of decision making by his boss, with whom he did not get along but who related well with Rahim's co-worker. In addition, Rahim found his boss's style 'very confusing . . . outwardly he would say something and inwardly he was meaning something else'. This inconsistency led him to mistrust both him and the organization. Fear and cynicism prevented Rahim from voicing his discontent (see Pinder and Harlos, 1999, for a discussion of silence as a response to injustice). Even during his exit interview, Rahim refused to acknowledge his boss's mistreatment:

> The employee relations manager said to me 'if I were you, I would say like this
> guy is a jerk'. But I couldn't say that because I felt suspicious of them – why are
> they asking this? . . . I wasn't going to be forthright with them because I felt they
> were not being forthright with me.

In another case, Karl felt bitter when the first construction project for
which he was responsible failed, in large part because of inadequate resources
and lack of organizational support. His bitterness stemmed from his
bosses' failure to take any responsibility for the project failure. A new boss
he had after the project failure made his displeasure at having to supervise
Karl well known:

> He would make remarks that were very unprofessional and very rude. I was a
> structural engineer by training, and he would say 'I wouldn't go into any building
> you would design.' And he wasn't joking. That hurt me badly.

For many participants, the type and intensity of emotions they experienced
were unusual for them. For Karl, the stress was extreme. As the project fell
apart, he became increasingly irritable: 'I wasn't friendly any more. I was
very, very short tempered, even with family members.' Similarly, Ashley
described:

> It got to the point where I dreaded going to work. Sunday night I would start to
> get very anxious and that had not been typical of me at all because I had really
> liked working there . . . I hated going to work.

Their unfamiliarity with both the range and depth of emotions accompanying
injustice experiences added to their distress and uncertainty about how to
respond.

Karl's case and others illustrate the tendency for boundaries surrounding
injustice-induced emotions to be indistinct, spilling into employees' lives
outside work. Joe, who had endured interactional injustice for two years,
said:

> My wife could see it at home. I was depressed all the time. I was doing my MBA
> part time and my marks slipped. Instead of doing assignments ahead of time I was
> handing them in three weeks late.

As this excerpt suggests, others often noticed and were sometimes affected
by participants' emotional distress. For Joanne and her husband, who worked
for the same abusive boss, the emotional strain they both suffered led to
marital separation. She said,

> I call myself emotionally dead because I can't express emotions and feel them
> because any time I did they would get stepped on. Right now, I need that
> [emotional] wall up to keep myself safe and not be abused again.

Additionally, boundaries between emotional and physical aspects of individuals' functioning were sometimes inseparable. Gwen reported:

> I was getting really tired, very tight, tense, irritable. I was getting a lot of headaches and tightness in my stomach from feeling confused and not understanding what was going on. . . . I wasn't sleeping very well and I didn't want to go to work.

Next, we report a number of cases to illustrate the emotional consequences of injustice experiences.

Emotions as consequences of injustice

In this section, we highlight key emotional consequences of injustice perceptions drawn from participants' descriptions of the longer-term effects of their injustice experiences. For example, chronic feelings of fear and hopelessness ('no matter what I do they're not going to praise me, so what's the point?') reduced some participants' sense of self-efficacy (Bandura, 1982) such that they no longer felt confident of performance levels that met either their own personal or professional standards. Joe said: 'my ability to be strong in myself was gone'. Similarly, Faith's muddled thinking and flustered speech from injustice-induced nervousness meant that she made more mistakes as her overall performance deteriorated. Consequently, she said: 'My self-confidence is eroding to the extent that I'm losing respect for what I do know, for the skills that I do have.'

One interesting result related emotional impact to the recency of injustice experiences. For those whose experience of injustice occurred within the year preceding the research interview, their beliefs about long-term emotional consequences were mixed. Although some believed that they were not emotionally harmed, others reported deep-seated doubts about future employability and their emotional and physical health. However, among those whose experiences of injustice occurred more than one year before the interview, the overall emotional impact was aversive yet transformative: naive, unassertive employees became more wise and forthright about their work-related needs. Although they still believed that their mistreatment was wrong, several participants acknowledged that their experiences 'toughened' them up emotionally, made them more self-protective and more willing to advocate on their own behalf if they ever felt mistreated in the future (see also Harlos and Pinder, 1999)

Extreme emotional consequences

In several extreme cases, participants did not win their battle for survival: the intensity and range of emotions from their injustice experiences depleted them to the point of breakdown. Vera was an environmental health officer in her early sixties who experienced what she regarded as harassment on the basis of gender, exacerbated by her Asian ethnicity and age. She had unsatisfactory work relationships with several bosses whom she believed undermined her, directed her to do work beyond the organization's mandate, and were sexually inappropriate. Despite 'being a strong person inside', she felt over time that she could not cope and she seriously considered suicide as a means to end her distress. She ended up 'breaking down' and requiring medical leave, which she had been on for six years prior to the interview.

Three others also reported breakdowns, some physical, but all emotional. Eva was a clerk in a hospital whose mistreatment triggered childhood sexual abuse memories with the end result that 'I broke down completely – I mean, you could have come up to me and said your name is Shirley Jones and I would have believed you.' Eva was unable to continue working, but after seeking professional help while on sick leave, she was able to return to part-time work.

Similarly, Joe's breakdown combined cognitive and emotional elements:

> I was losing it . . . I couldn't make a decision, I couldn't think straight . . . the thought of talking to Norm [his boss] scared the hell out of me. I thought I'd break out crying. I'd seen other people cry – with women it happened frequently, and a couple of times with guys. . . . I was just a bunch of emotions.

The intensity and duration of injustice-induced feelings immobilized Joe. For instance, when he heard about a new, interesting job in a different organization, he felt 'emotionally incapable' of even applying, despite wanting to end his employment relationship.

The role of emotions in staying within unjust employment relationships

Paradoxically, emotions acted as both a strong signal warning some away from injustice and as a strong siren pulling others in (see discussion of ambivalence, Chapter 11, this volume). That is, emotions sometimes influenced participants' decisions to *stay* in employment situations that they recognized as unjust. Specifically, for some victims of injustice, dramatic emotional swings were an attractive if puzzling feature of workplace injustice: 'it was weird because it was the best of times and it was the worst of times'. Others believed themselves immune to the detrimental effects of negative emotions.

Emotional swings Unjust employment relationships incorporated a sense of emotional engagement and excitement that was difficult for some participants to resist. Victor, a sales agent who was not paid for over eight months of full-time work, reported:

> I ran everything, which was absolutely exciting and I didn't get paid anything at all . . . I was having an absolute blast. I have never had that much fun working or

been as enthused in something before, which is why I allowed much more [injustice] than anyone else would.

The intensity of the positive emotions made Victor 'fanatically enthusiastic' for a revolutionary environmental product, blinding him to the dangers of working with what he called sociopathic stock promoters. As he said, 'I was so absolutely dedicated to it. I really believed in it – I just didn't know it was impossible.' His extreme emotions, in part, 'made it hard to walk away'.

Intense, positive emotions, combined with ever-present chaos and uncertainty, created almost addictive emotional swings: 'when it worked, it was an absolute high. It was like "*I* got people to do this".' Underlying these swings were elements of financial risk and emotional turbulence that some found to be compelling features of unfair workplaces. Victor, for example, endured eight months without pay in part because 'I wanted the stock options. I knew this was going to be enormous if it worked.' In another case, Joe's boss was emotionally intense and capricious:

> He can be very charismatic. He can be very good at building people up, but he can be just as effective at breaking people apart. He's not a miserable son of a bitch all the time – he can be a really nice guy, really fun and enjoyable to be around, especially when he's excited about something. He's emotionally attached . . . he built it from nothing to a six hundred million dollar company. He goes up and down with every up and down of the company.

These emotional shifts, in turn, were core motivators for Joe, creating their own swings for him: 'in order for me to achieve what he wanted, I needed to be emotionally bought in. So if it didn't work it would create an emotional hurt, certainly a sense of guilt.' However, the long-term effects were not good. As he said, 'I really bought into his philosophy. But as far as I rose, I went down a long way too.'

Perceived emotional immunity   Several participants stayed, at least in part, because they underestimated the emotional impact of chronic injustices. As Joe said,

> I thought I could take it, I really thought I could take his shit. I thought that for years. But it's not until you start being ground down, until I had the breakdown that I realized, 'no, you're wrong, you can't take this' – it gets to you.

Paradoxically, some believed that childhood abuse both prepared them for and protected them from the emotional impact of workplace injustice. For example, Eva knew that her supervisor had a widespread reputation for 'savaging' staff. However, she was unable to quit because 'I was so used to taking shit from people as part of my abusive background. I could get along with anyone . . . but there were all the little things you say to delude yourself. I should have just run, just run.'

Whether because of pride, stubbornness or a false confidence that they could control or manage their emotional reactions, several participants reported that their emotional defences slowly but relentlessly eroded over time. For example, Ashley described her mistreatment:

> It was similar to the military where they grind you down to nothing and then build you back up. But we didn't get to the part where he built us back up - we just got to the part where he beat us down and we had nothing left.

Like several others, she endured mistreatment based on a false belief that it would stop and that she would not be negatively affected.

Discussion and conclusions

In this chapter we explore connections between emotion and workplace injustice, examining relationships between emotions and organizations through employees' senses of being wronged by interactions with bosses (that is, interactional injustice) and by organizational systems (that is systemic injustice). In so doing, we add to knowledge of neglected aspects of emotion, namely social and cultural dimensions (Domagalski, 1999). Specifically, we have shown that emotions precede, accompany and are a consequence of injustice experiences. Table 14.2 summarizes the central emotions that underlie these phases of injustice experiences. Our analyses demonstrate, among other findings, that: (1) bosses' emotional displays of anger and widespread lack of emotion throughout organizations can cause injustice perceptions among employees; (2) employees' felt and displayed emotions reflect ongoing states of injustice and; (3) the long-term affective

Table 14.2 *Summary of predominant emotions as causes, accompaniments and consequences of injustice*

Antecedent emotions	Accompanying emotions	Consequent emotions
Anger (individual level)	Fear	Fear
Lack of emotionality (organizational-level)	Irritation	Anger
	Rage	Hopelessness
	Anger	Sadness
	Desire for revenge	Excitement
	Shame	Decreased emotionality (including emotional collapse, breakdown)
	Embarrassment	
	Dread	
	Guilt	
	Hopelessness	
	Cynicism	

consequences of injustice experiences appear dualistic in nature: they can be both negative and positive.

Displayed versus felt emotions

The emotions underlying injustice experiences can be understood using the widely applied distinction between *displayed* (that is, expressed or active) versus *felt* (that is, experienced or passive) emotions, the latter reflecting the primary focus of emotionality research (see Arvey et al., 1998). As causes, most participants' emotional states were felt rather than displayed and were in response to bosses' displayed anger or the lack of emotionality of the organizational context. As accompaniments, participants' emotions were displayed and to a lesser degree felt, reflecting irritability and anger, for example, along with passive feelings of depression, guilt and hopelessness (see Table 14.2). Together, these more quiescent emotional reactions suggested varying degrees of emotional disengagement, defined as emotional withdrawal from work roles (Kahn, 1993). Emotional withdrawal from family roles also characterized the emotionality that accompanied some participants' injustice experiences. Nevertheless, the predominant emotionality involved here was of a displayed or expressed nature. Consequent emotions, in contrast, were primarily felt with even more intensely experienced states of withdrawal, sometimes to the point of breakdown and collapse.

The predominance of anger and fear

Our data suggest that two emotions are notable for their intensities and prevalence throughout employees' injustice experiences: anger and fear.

Anger Our results indicate that anger can be a major cause, an accompaniment and a consequence of workplace injustice, supporting earlier reports of anger as significant emotional reactions to workplace injustice (see for example Skarlicki and Folger, 1997). The predominance of anger in contexts of injustice may not be surprising considering its prominent role in social relationships (see Oatley and Jenkins, 1996). Indeed, the close association between frustration and aggression (including angry verbal outbursts as commonly reported in our study) has been understood for decades (see Berkowitz, 1993). Of particular interest are angry outbursts that are directed at people who may not be the actual causes of frustration. These instances of *displaced aggression* abound in organizations; in part because of their proximity, innocent parties – usually those who have little or no capacity to resist – can get caught in the crossfire when others aggress against their source(s) of frustration (cf. Janis, 1971; Maier, 1973).

Our data included many cases where superiors' power advantage over subordinates facilitated their perpetration of injustices. In fact, cases of interactional injustice from our study consisted *exclusively* of unjust treatment between employees at different hierarchical levels, with the aggressor or perpetrator occupying positions of greater power. This hierarchical pattern emerged naturally and inductively. Our data yielded no evidence relating gender to the incidence of interactional injustice. That is, both genders reportedly mistreated subordinates: eleven of 16 interview cases of interactional injustice involved male bosses as perpetrators while five involved female bosses. Yet closer inspection shows that anger underlying outbursts, yelling and intimidation associated with interactional injustice were predominantly expressed by male bosses. Female bosses, in contrast, tended to make use of interactional injustice dimensions that did not feature anger as an emotional component (such as *manipulation, inaccessibility, criticism*), although some male bosses displayed these as well as anger-based dimensions. These embedded power inequalities and gender patterns, combined with the tendency to displace aggression, may make mistreatment the norm rather than exception and, even more distressingly, may make injustice inevitable in some workplaces.

Identifying and preventing workplace injustice is problematic, in part because of its underlying morality. This may be especially true in cases involving anger and interactional injustice. By definition, these situations involve bosses' beliefs about right and wrong ways to treat staff that interact with employees' beliefs about right and wrong ways to be treated. Thus, one boss's authoritarian style may be appropriate and effective to some (including the boss) but a disabling violation to others. As well, morality becomes salient for some only when they become recipients: 'it was only when I started getting treated the same way he treated a lot of people that I began to realize how unfair it was'. Additionally, organizations differ in their interpretations of legal and moral obligations to provide workplaces free from discrimination and harassment. Together, these issues of morality and obligations make for contested interpretations of what injustice is and what should be done about it.

Fear   The emergence of fear as a significant emotion accompanying injustice was not surprising given that fear is widely regarded as the emotion of anticipated danger, signalling risks or threats to our survival and existence (DeBecker, 1997; Oatley and Jenkins, 1996). Several examples provided earlier demonstrate that employees' fear can signal, sometimes strongly, potential threat or harm in employment relationships. Unexpectedly, though, fear defied boundaries of time or place; evidence suggests that it is an emotion with an especially long half-life. Indeed, our findings suggest that when chronic, injustice-induced fear can contribute to stress-related emotional breakdowns with symptoms that are consistent with stages of *burnout* (that is, emotional exhaustion, cynicism and futility; Maslach, 1982).

The boundarylessness of injustice-induced fear may be partially explained by findings reported in the literature on abuse (emotional and physical) in domestic relationships. Dutton and Painter (1993a), for example, report that it is the *intermittency*, rather than predictability, of abuse that predicted *post*-relationship distress. In another study, power differentials as well as the extremity of intermittent mistreatment were key relationship factors that affected women's emotional attachments for abusive partners whom they had left, providing support for traumatic bonding theory (Dutton and Painter, 1993b). Traumatic bonding is a social-psychological explanation for paradoxical dynamics in abusive relationships whereby women and children not only stay, risking further abuse, but also show strong emotional ties to the abuser. Studies suggest that unequal power relationship and alternate abusive and positive treatment interact to create a bond between abuser and victim, similar to bonds between captor and hostage (Painter and Dutton, 1985), that are based, in part, on mutual emotional dependencies (DeYoung and Lowry, 1992).

In our study, emotional attachments and traumatic bonding theory would explain why some employees stayed in employment relationships that they recognized as unjust. Moreover, the important role of emotional dependencies in traumatic bonding, as well as financial dependencies, may help explain difficulties reported by male employees in leaving unjust employment relationships. Further studies might explore whether employees who experience intermittent injustice from bosses find it harder to quit and have greater distress after quitting than those experiencing mistreatment (predictable or intermittent) from co-workers.

Implications for future research

When studying sensitive topics, the emotional impact on researchers is probably common although rarely acknowledged. Its impact may result from compassion for or empathy with participants. However, compassion may clash with norms of objectivity (read lack of emotionality) that are sacrosanct in traditional social research. Indeed, Frost (1999) argues that organizational researchers

> tend to see organizations and their members with little other than a dispassionate eye and a training that inclines us toward abstractions that do not include consideration of the dignity and humanity of those in our lens. Our hearts, our compassion, are not engaged. . . . As a result, we miss some pretty fundamental and important aspects of organizational life . . . and our theories and practices probably distort more than they illuminate what they purport to explain. (p. 128)

Our chapter suggests that the nature of some phenomena and the close methods needed for their study override norms of objectivity that many organizational researchers are taught. Future studies of emotions at work would benefit by endorsing Frost's call for compassion when collecting data and developing theory.

The domain of workplace injustice is broad, encompassing mistreatment arising from hierarchical relationships, formal procedures, decisional outcomes and even organizational systems. Within these patterns of injustice, emotions can be subtle and dynamic but they are nevertheless identifiable. Our findings add to previous knowledge by showing that contexts of workplace injustice can both elicit and be elicited by specific emotions. However, our data could not yield insights into the delicate and fluid interrelationships among the emotions of injustice, especially accompanying emotions. Further studies are needed to refine our knowledge of interactions between different types and intensities of emotions, their associations with different patterns of injustice, and the boundary conditions of these complex relationships. We hope that our results, combined with recent theoretical models (see for example Andersson and Pearson; 1999; Weiss and Cropanzano, 1996) will foster further empirical investigations of the recursive interplay between injustice and emotion in work settings.

Acknowledgements

This research is based on the doctoral dissertation research of the first author under the supervision of the second author. It was supported, in part, by separate grants to both authors from the Social Sciences and Humanities Research Council of Canada and a grant to the second author from the Centre for Labour and Management Studies of the University of British Columbia. The authors are grateful to Professors Elvi Whittaker and David McPhillips for their contributions to this research and to Ronald Cohen for comments on the dissertation itself.

References

Andersson, L.M. and Pearson, C.M. (1999) 'Tit for tat? The spiraling effect of incivility in the workplace', *Academy of Management Review*, 24: 452–71.
Arvey, R.D., Renz, G.L. and Watson, T.W. (1998) 'Emotionality and job performance: implications for personnel selection', in G. Ferris (ed.), *Research in Personnel and Human Resource Management*, Vol. 16. Greenwich, CT: JAI Press. pp. 103–47.
Ashforth, B. and Humphrey, R. (1995) 'Emotion in the workplace – a reappraisal', *Human Relations*, 48: 97–125.
Averill, J. (1982) *Anger and Aggression: An Essay on Emotion*. New York: Springer-Verlag.
Bandura, A. (1982) 'Self-efficacy in human agency', *American Psychologist*, 37: 122–47.
Berkowitz, L. (1993) *Aggression: Its causes, Consequences, and Control*. NY: Harper and Row.
Bies, R. and Moag, J. (1986) 'Interactional justice: communication criteria of fairness', in R.J. Lewicki, B.H. Sheppard and M. Bazerman (eds), *Research on Negotiation in Organizations*, Vol. 1. Greenwich, CT: JAI Press. pp. 43–55.
Cropanzano, R. and Randall, M. (1993) 'Injustice and work behavior: a historical review', in R. Cropanzano (ed.), *Justice in the Workplace*. Hillsdale, NJ: Erlbaum. pp. 3–20.
DeBecker, G. (1997) *The Gift of Fear*. Boston: Little, Brown.
DeYoung, M. and Lowry, J. (1992) 'Traumatic bonding: clinical implications in incest', *Child Welfare*, 71: 165–75.

Domagalski, T.A. (1999) 'Emotion in organizations', *Human Relations*, 52: 833–52.

Dutton, D. and Painter, S. (1993a) 'The battered woman syndrome: effects of severity and intermittency of abuse', *American Journal of Orthopsychiatry*, 63: 614–22.

Dutton, D. and Painter, S. (1993b) 'Emotional attachments in abusive relationships: a test of traumatic bonding theory', *Violence & Victims*, 8: 105–20.

Fine, M. (1983) 'The social context and a sense of injustice. The option to challenge', *Representative Research in Social Psychology*, 13: 15–33.

Fineman, S. (ed.) (1993) *Emotion in Organizations*. London: Sage.

Fineman, S. (1996) 'Emotion and organizing', in S. Clegg, C. Hardy and W. Nord (eds), *Handbook of Organization Studies*. London: Sage Publications. pp. 543–64.

Frijda, N.H. (1993) 'Moods, emotion episodes, and emotions', in M. Lewis and J.M. Haviland (eds), *Handbook of Emotions*. New York: Guilford. pp. 381–403.

Frost, P.J. (1999) 'Why compassion counts!', *Journal of Management Inquiry*, 8: 127–33.

Glaser, W. and Strauss, A. (1967) *The Discovery of Grounded Theory: Strategies of Qualitative Research*. London: Wiedenfeld and Nicolson.

Goleman, D. (1995) *Emotional Intelligence*. NY: Bantam Books.

Harlos, K.P. (1998) 'Organizational injustice and its resistance using voice and silence'. Unpublished doctoral dissertation, University of British Columbia, Vancouver, BC.

Harlos, K.P. (1999) 'Cultures of injustice: dimensions and organizational correlates of unjust employment relationships'. Best Paper Proceedings, Third Australian Industrial and Organizational Psychology Conference, pp. 111–19. Brisbane.

Harlos, K.P. and Pinder, C.C. (1999) 'Patterns of organizational injustice: a taxonomy of what employees regard as unjust', *Advances in Qualitative Organizational Research*, Vol. 2. Greenwich, CT: JAI Press. pp. 97–125.

Hochschild, A. (1993) 'Preface', in S. Fineman (ed.), *Emotion in Organizations*. London: Sage.

Janis, I.L. (1971) *Stress and Frustration*. NY: Harcourt Brace Jovanovich.

Kahn, W. (1993) 'Caring for the caregivers: patterns of organizational caregiving', *Administrative Science Quarterly*, 38: 539–63.

Lazarus, R.S. and Lazarus, B.N. (1994) *Passion and Reason*. NY: Oxford University Press.

Lee, R. and Renzetti, C. (1993) 'The problems of researching sensitive topics', in C. Renzetti and C. Lee (eds), *Researching Sensitive Topics*. Newbury Park, CA: Sage.

Maier, N.R.F. (1973) *Psychology in Industrial Organizations*, 4th edn. Boston: Houghton Mifflin.

Martin, P.Y. and Turner, B.A. (1986) 'Grounded theory and organizational research', *Journal of Applied Behavioral Science*, 22 (2): 141–57.

Maslach, C. (1982) *Burnout: The Cost of Caring*. Engelwood Cliffs, NJ: Prentice Hall.

Nisbett, R. and Wilson, T. (1977) 'Telling more than we can know: verbal reports on mental processes', *Psychological Review*, 84: 231–59.

Oatley, K. and Jenkins, J.M. (1996) *Understanding Emotions*. Cambridge, MA: Blackwell Publishers.

Painter, S. and Dutton, D. (1985) 'Patterns of emotional bonding in battered women: traumatic bonding', *International Journal of Women's Studies*, 8: 363–75.

Pinder, C.C. (1998) *Work Motivation in Organizational Behavior*. Upper Saddle River, NJ: Prentice Hall.

Pinder, C.C. and Harlos, K.P. (1999) 'Listening to the unspoken: silence as organizational behavior'. Unpublished manuscript, University of Victoria, Victoria, BC, Canada.

Rich, P. (1992) 'The organizational taxonomy: definitions and design', *Academy of Management Review*, 17: 758–81.

Schein, E.H. (1992) *Organizational Culture and Leadership*. San Francisco: Jossey Bass.

Sheppard, B.H., Lewicki, R.J. and Minton, J.W. (1992) *Organizational Justice: The Search for Fairness in the Workplace.* Toronto: Lexington Books.

Skarlicki, D. and Folger, R. (1997) 'Retaliation for perceived unfair treatment: examining the roles of procedural and interactional justice', *Journal of Applied Psychology*, 82: 434–43.

Warr, P., Barter, J. and Brownridge, G. (1983) 'On the independence of positive and negative affect', *Journal of Personality and Social Psychology*, 44: 644–51.

Weick, K. (1995) *Sensemaking in Organizations.* Thousand Oaks, CA: Sage.

Weiss, H.M. and Cropanzano, R. (1996) 'Affective events theory: a theoretical discussion of the structure, causes, and consequences of affective experiences at work', in B.M. Staw and L.L. Cummings (eds), *Research in Organizational Behavior*, Vol. 18. Greenwich, CT: JAI Press. pp. 1–74.

Weiss, H. M., Suckow, K. and Cropanzano, R. (1999) 'Effects of justice on discrete emotions', *Journal of Applied Psychology.* 84: 786–794.

PART 4
EPILOGUE

---

15   CONCLUDING REFLECTIONS
STEPHEN FINEMAN

The latest, glossily produced, introductory textbooks on organizational behaviour reveal something of the status of emotion-as-taught to students of organizations. Fincham and Rhodes's *Principles of Organizational Behaviour* (1999), for example, makes no mention of emotion. Shermerhorn et al.'s *Organizational Behavior* (2000) offers a paragraph on 'emotional conflict' (under 'Types of Conflict') and a half page on 'emotional adjustment traits' – namely Type A and Type B personality orientations. Greenberg and Baron, in *Behavior in Organizations* (2000), have discovered emotional intelligence, along with 'emotional exhaustion' and 'emotional stability'. All these references are massively overshadowed by the entries on job satisfaction – some 28 pages in total.

We learn little or nothing from these texts about the emotional complexity of life in organizations, of emotion work, or of the emotional naivety of rationalistic formulations. They are silent about the corporatized manipulation of emotion and its value premises, and about the structural, cultural and gender contexts of emotion. Indeed, we learn little about the topics discussed in this book. To all intents and purposes, organizations are emotionally arid, save their different job satisfactions, attitudes and stress. We still have to look elsewhere for emotion insights – to less-mainstream introductions on organizational behaviour (for example, Gabriel et al., 2000; Fineman and Gabriel, 1996), to critical, specialist, texts in organizational studies, or to novelists and journalists.

Not surprisingly, perhaps, there is an inherent conservatism and incrementalism in textbooks – reproducing, in a slightly different package, what came before. The cognitive/behavioural legacy is a tough one to shift. There is also, of course, a danger that emotions become another 'topic' to add to the contents list of the textbook, rather than incorporated into the warp and weft of organizational processes and theory. Either way, the new student of organizations or management is likely to be exposed to an emotionally sanitized picture of the world of work. This, I expect (and hope) will change as professional and popular interest in emotion and emotion research continues its rapid growth.

Paradigm found?

Emotion has emotional appeal to those who take it on board. My impression is that it engages students of organizations in ways that are qualitatively different from other research endeavours, especially those that have been steeped in the rationalistic tradition. There is often a sense of relief and excitement at being able to articulate that which seems so crucial, something they 'know' to be true, but that is obscured by decades of reductionism, objectivism and quantification. Such enthusiasm is a promising basis for constructing a passionate theory of organizations.

Yet that is where the problems begin. As we become keener to grasp that which is hard to grasp, the limitations of our social sciences become all too clear. Do we thrust emotion into the old, paradigmatic pots, or do we break the moulds? And if we step out, who will listen to us and with what credibility? In this book, the authors have shown that it is quite possible to stretch and adapt established approaches, especially ones that are drawn from qualitative social inquiry and interpretive/political perspectives, to illuminate and theorize on emotion. And they have done so in a remarkable range of settings and situations. Reluctant researchers should take heart.

But the aspirant mould-breaker can still be left wanting – or excited by the possibilities. Are there different ways of knowing and conveying emotion and subjectivity? How might we unify our theoretical framings of people, organizations, thinking, feeling and emotion? Should not holism be our goal, spurred by interdisciplinary conversations? A fully contextualized and critical account of emotion requires sociology and psychology to rub shoulders with biology, anthropology, history, organizational behaviour and management studies. We have much to learn from one another. And there are new data-streams to assist us – such as from virtual imagery, collaborative inquiries, organizational interventions, cross-cultural interpretations, non-verbal representations, and from traditionally silent (or silenced) voices of minority groups.

Emotionalizing organization exposes many traditional organizational and management processes to possible new interpretations and understandings – such as in decision making, layoffs, business ethics, organizational control, creativity, change, leadership, strategy, conflict, learning, motivation, work meanings, power and communication. How do feelings and emotions inform and shape these processes? Where do presentation rules apply and why? How do they emotionally connect with one another? What is the power, or shaping-force, of emotions on different cultural or economic structures?

Finally, we might turn our attention to the more dramatic organizational events – like economic collapse, environmental pollution, take-overs, persistent failure or the massive expansion of a new technological form (such as e-commerce). What does an emotion lens reveal in these circumstances? There is much work to be done.

References

Fincham, R. and Rhodes, P. (1999) *Principles of Organizational Behaviour*. Oxford: Oxford University Press.
Fineman, S. and Gabriel, Y. (1996) *Experiencing Organizations*. London: Sage.
Gabriel, Y., Fineman, S. and Sims, D. (2000) *Organizing and Organizations*, 2nd edn. London: Sage.
Greenberg, J. and Baron, R.A. (2000) *Behavior in Organizations*. New Jersey: Prentice Hall.
Shermerhorn, J.R., Hunt, J.G. and Osborn, R.N. (2000) *Organizational Behavior*. New York: Wiley.

AUTHOR INDEX

SUBJECT INDEX